1998 EDITION

CLEP®

OFFICIAL STUDY GUIDE

 College Level Examination Program The College Board

Contents

VI. Interpreting Your Scores

VII. Examination Guides

General Examinations

Subject Examinations

Composition and Literature

Foreign Languages

History and Social Sciences

CONTENTS

Appendices

Introduction

This guide to the College-Level Examination Program (CLEP) exams has been written mainly for adults who are making plans to enroll in college. If you've been out of school for a while and haven't taken a college-level test recently, it's important that you read through all the chapters of this guide.

The study guide contains information of interest to others as well. College-bound high-school students, military personnel, professionals seeking certification, and persons of all ages who have learned or wish to learn college-level material outside the college classroom will find the guide helpful as they strive to accomplish their goals.

CLEP is based on the premise that some individuals enrolling in college have already learned part of what is taught in college courses through noncredit adult courses, job training, independent reading and study, and advanced high–school courses. Often, their job and life experiences have enhanced and reinforced their learning. CLEP provides these individuals with the opportunity to demonstrate their college-level learning by taking exams that assess the knowledge and skills taught in college courses.

The first few sections of this study guide explain how CLEP can help you earn credit for the college-level learning you have acquired and provide suggestions for preparing for the exams. The guides to the individual exams include test descriptions, sample questions, and tips for preparing to take the exams.

If you still have general questions about continuing or adult education after reading this handbook, the following associations can provide advice and information:

American Council on Education
1 DuPont Circle, N.W.
Washington, D.C. 20036
(202) 939-9475

American Association for Adult and Continuing Education
Suite 300
1200 19th Street N.W.
Washington, D.C. 20036
(202) 429-5131

I. The College-Level Examination Program

How the Program Works

CLEP exams are administered at more than 1,200 colleges and universities nationwide, and approximately 2,800 institutions award college credit to those who do well on them. The 34 exams allow people who have acquired knowledge outside the usual educational settings to show that they have learned college-level material so that they can bypass certain college courses.

The CLEP exams cover material that is taught in introductory-level courses at many colleges and universities. Faculties at individual colleges review the exams to ensure that they cover the important material currently taught in their courses. Colleges differ in the CLEP exams for which they award credit; some colleges accept only two or three of the exams while others accept all of them.

Although CLEP is sponsored by the College Board and the exams are scored by Educational Testing Service (ETS), neither of these organizations can award college credit. Only accredited colleges may grant credit toward a degree. When you take a CLEP exam, you may request that a copy of your score report be sent to the college you are attending or planning to attend. After evaluating your scores, the college will decide whether or not to award you credit for a certain course or courses, or to exempt you from them.

If the college gives you credit, it will record the number of credits on your permanent record, thereby indicating that you have completed work equivalent to a course in that subject. If the college decides to grant exemption without giving you credit for a course, you will be permitted to omit a course that would normally be required of you and to take a course of your choice instead.

The General Examinations

Each of the five General Examinations covers material taught in courses that most students take as requirements during their first two years of college. Most colleges require all their students to take three or six semester hours (or the equivalent) in each of the five areas. They may grant credit in the area in which a satisfactory test score is earned rather than for a specific course. General Examinations are available in the following areas: English

Composition (with or without Essay), Humanities, College Mathematics, Natural Sciences, and Social Sciences and History.

The Subject Examinations

Each Subject Examination includes material usually covered in an undergraduate course with a similar title. On the basis of a satisfactory test score, each institution grants credit equal to the amount it gives to students who successfully complete that course. 29 Subject Examinations in several curriculum areas are offered (see pages iv-v for a list).

What the Examinations Are Like

The exams consist of multiple-choice questions to be answered within a 90-minute time limit. There are two versions of the General Examination in English Composition: One is made up entirely of multiple-choice questions; the other has a 45-minute multiple-choice section and a 45-minute essay section. (Additional information about the length, timing, and content of each CLEP exam is given in the exam guides in Chapter 7.)

Optional 90-minute free-response sections are available for the four Subject Examinations in Composition and Literature. These sections are required by some colleges in addition to the 90-minute multiple-choice test. The optional sections are not graded at Educational Testing Service (ETS); rather, they are sent to the college designated by the candidate and graded there by faculty. Before registering for a CLEP exam, find out whether the college that is to receive your score requires the optional free-response section.

Where to Take the Examinations

CLEP exams are administered throughout the year at more than 1,200 test centers in the United States and can be arranged for candidates outside the U.S. on request. Arrangements for foreign administrations take between six weeks and four months, depending on the site. Contact CLEP, P.O. Box 6600, Princeton, NJ 08541-6600 for further information about special administrations.

In Appendix C you will find a list of institutions that award credit for satisfactory scores on CLEP exams. Some colleges administer CLEP exams only to their own students. If your college does not administer the exams, contact the test center in your area for information about its testing schedule.

After you have been tested, your answer sheet will be sent to ETS for scoring. Once the answer sheet is received at ETS, it is scored within 48 hours. Because of mailing considerations and certain unavoidable delays, however, you can expect to receive your score report in about two weeks.

Your score report is mailed to you and to the recipient you designate. CLEP scores are kept on file at ETS for 20 years. During this period, for a small fee, you may have your transcript sent to another college or to anyone else you specify. (Your scores will never be sent to anyone without your approval.)

Active military personnel may take CLEP exams without charge through the Defense Activity for Non-Traditional Education Support (DANTES) program. At military installations, information about CLEP may be obtained from the Education Officer.

II. Approaching a College about CLEP

The following sections provide a step-by-step approach to learning about the CLEP policy at a particular college or university. The person or office that can best assist students desiring CLEP credit may have a different title at each institution, but the following guidelines will lead you to information about CLEP at any institution.

Adults returning to college often benefit from special assistance when they approach a college. Opportunities for adults to return to formal learning in the classroom are now widespread, and colleges and universities have worked hard to make this a smooth process for older students. Many colleges have established special offices that are staffed with trained professionals who understand the kinds of problems facing adults returning to college. If you think you might benefit from such assistance, be sure to find out whether these services are available at your college.

How to Apply for College Credit

Step 1. *Obtain the general information catalog and a copy of the CLEP policy from the colleges you are considering. If you have not yet applied for admission, ask for an admission application form, too.*

Information about admission and CLEP policies can be obtained by writing or visiting college admissions offices. Tell the admissions officer that you are a prospective student and that you are interested in applying for admission and CLEP credit. Ask for a copy of the publication in which the college's complete CLEP policy is explained. Also get the name and the telephone number of the person to contact in case you have further questions about CLEP.

At this stage, you may wish to obtain information from external degree colleges. Many adults find that such colleges suit their needs exceptionally well. External degrees are discussed later in this chapter.

Step 2. *If you have not already been admitted to the college you are considering, look at its admission requirements for undergraduate students to see whether you can qualify.*

Virtually all public community colleges and a number of four-year state colleges have "open admission" policies for in-state students. This usually means that they admit anyone who has graduated from high school or has earned a high-school equivalency diploma (GED).

If you think you do not meet the admission requirements, contact the admission office for an interview with a counselor. Colleges do sometimes make exceptions, particularly for adult applicants. State why you want the interview and ask what documents you should bring with you or send in advance. (These materials may include a high-school transcript, transcript of previous college work, or completed application for admission.) Make an extra effort to have all the information requested in time for the interview.

During the interview, relax and be yourself. Be prepared to state honestly why you think you are ready and able to do college work. If you have already taken CLEP exams and scored high enough to earn credit, you have shown that you are able to do college work. Mention this achievement to the admissions counselor because it may increase your chances of being accepted. If you have not taken a CLEP exam, you can still improve your chances of being accepted by describing how your job training or independent study has helped prepare you for college-level work. Tell the counselor what you have learned from your work and personal experiences.

Step 3. *Evaluate the college's CLEP policy.*

Typically, a college lists all its academic policies, including CLEP policies, in its general catalog. You will probably find the CLEP policy statement under a heading such as Credit-by-Examination, Advanced Standing, Advanced Placement, or External Degree Program. These sections can usually be found in the front of the catalog.

Many colleges publish their credit-by-examination policy in a separate brochure, which is distributed through the campus testing office, counseling center, admissions office, or registrar's office. If you find a very general policy statement in the college catalog, seek clarification from one of these offices.

Review the material in the section of this chapter entitled "Questions to Ask about a College's CLEP Policy." Use these guidelines to evaluate the college's CLEP policy. If you have not yet taken a CLEP exam, this evaluation will help you decide which exams to take. Because individual colleges have different CLEP policies, a review of several policies may help you decide which college to attend.

Step 4. *If you have not yet applied for admission, do so early.*

Most colleges expect you to apply for admission several months before you enroll, and it is essential that you meet the published application deadlines. It takes time to process your application for admission. If you have yet to take a CLEP exam, you may want to take one or more CLEP exams while you are waiting for your application to be processed. Be sure to check the college's CLEP policy beforehand so that you are taking exams your college will accept for credit. You should also find out from the college when to submit your CLEP scores.

Complete all forms and include all documents requested with your application(s) for admission. Normally, an admission decision cannot be reached until all documents have been submitted and evaluated. Unless told to do so, do not send your CLEP scores until you have been officially admitted.

Step 5. *Arrange to take CLEP exam(s) or to submit your CLEP score(s).*

You may want to wait to take your CLEP exams until you know definitely which college you will be attending. Then you can make sure you are taking exams your college will accept for credit. You will also be able to request that your scores be sent to the college, free of charge, when you take the exams.

If you have already taken a CLEP exam but did not have a copy of your score report sent to your college, you may have an official transcript sent at any time for a small fee by filling out the Transcript Request Form that was sent to you with your score report. If you do not have the form, send the following information to CLEP Transcript Service, P.O. Box 6600, Princeton, New Jersey 08541-6600: your name (as it appeared on your answer sheet), social security number, birth date, the name of the test and test center, and the test date. Also include a check or money order made payable to CLEP for $15 (this fee is subject to change).

Your CLEP scores will be evaluated, probably by someone in the admissions office, and sent to the registrar's office to be posted on your permanent record once you are enrolled. Procedures vary from college to college, but the process usually begins in the admissions office.

Step 6. *Ask to receive a written notice of the credit you receive for your CLEP score(s).*

A written notice may save you problems later, when you submit your degree plan or file for graduation. In the event that there is a question about whether or not you earned CLEP credit, you will have an official record of what credit was awarded. You may also need this verification of course credit if you go for academic counseling before the credit is posted on your permanent record.

Step 7. *Before you register for courses, seek academic counseling.*

A discussion with your academic adviser can prevent you from taking unnecessary courses and can tell you specifically what your CLEP credit will mean to you. This step may be accomplished at the time you enroll. Most colleges have orientation sessions for new students prior to each enrollment period. During orientation, students are usually assigned an academic adviser who then gives them individual help in developing long-range plans and a course schedule for the next semester. In conjunction with this counseling, you may be asked to take some additional tests so that you can be placed at the proper course level.

External Degree Programs

If you have acquired a considerable amount of college-level knowledge through job experience, reading, or noncredit courses, if you have accumulated college credits at a variety of colleges over a period of years, or if you prefer studying on your own rather than in a classroom setting, you may want to investigate the possibility of enrolling in an external degree program. Connecticut, New Jersey, and New York offer external degree programs that allow you to earn a degree by passing exams (including CLEP), transferring credit from other colleges, and demonstrating in other ways that you have satisfied certain educational requirements. No classroom attendance is required, and the programs are open to out-of-state candidates as well as residents. Thomas Edison State College in New Jersey and Charter Oak State College in Connecticut are fully accredited independent state colleges; the New York program is part of the state university system and is also fully accredited. If you are interested in exploring an external degree, you may contact:

Charter Oak State College
66 Cedar Street
Newington, CT 06111-2646
(203) 666-4595

Regents College
7 Columbia Circle
Albany, New York 12203-5159
(518) 464-8500

Thomas Edison State College
101 West State Street
Trenton, New Jersey 08608-1176
(609) 984-1150

Many other colleges also have external degree or weekend programs. While they often require that a number of courses be taken on campus, the external degree programs tend to be more flexible in transferring credit, granting credit-by-examination, and allowing independent study than other traditional programs. When applying to a college, you may wish to ask whether it offers these kinds of programs.

Questions to Ask about a College's CLEP Policy

Before taking CLEP exams for the purpose of earning college credit, try to find the answers to these questions:

1. *Which CLEP exams are accepted by this college?*

    A college may accept some CLEP exams for credit and not others — possibly not the one you are considering. For this reason, it is important that you know the specific CLEP exams for which you can receive credit.

2. *Does the college require the optional free-response (essay) section for Subject Examinations in Composition and Literature as well as the multiple-choice portion of the CLEP exam you are considering? Will you be required to pass a departmental test such as an essay, laboratory, or oral exam in addition to the CLEP multiple-choice exam?*

    Knowing the answers to these questions ahead of time will permit you to schedule the optional free-response or departmental exam when you register to take your CLEP exam.

3. *Is credit granted for specific courses at the college? If so, which ones?*

    You are likely to find that credit is granted for specific courses and that the course titles are designated in the college's CLEP policy. It is not necessary, however, that credit be granted for a specific course for you to benefit from your CLEP credit. For instance, at many liberal arts colleges, all students must take certain types of courses; these courses may be labeled the core curriculum, general education requirements, distribution requirements, or liberal arts requirements. The requirements are often expressed in terms of credit hours. For example, all students may be required to take at least six hours of humanities, six hours of English, three hours of mathematics, six hours of natural science, and six hours of social science, with no particular courses in these disciplines specified. In these instances, CLEP credit may be given as "6 hrs. English Credit" or "3 hrs. Math Credit" without specifying for which English or mathematics courses credit has been awarded. To avoid possible disappointment, you should know before taking a CLEP exam what type of credit you can receive or whether you will be exempted from a required course but receive no credit.

4. *How much credit is granted for each exam you are considering, and does the college place a limit on the total amount of CLEP credit you can earn toward your degree?*

Not all colleges that grant CLEP credit award the same amount for individual tests. Furthermore, some colleges place a limit on the total amount of credit you can earn through CLEP or other exams. Other colleges may grant you exemption but no credit toward your degree. Knowing several colleges' policies concerning these issues may help you decide which college to attend. If you think you are capable of passing a number of CLEP exams, you may want to attend a college that will allow you to earn credit for all or most of them. For example, the state external degree programs grant credit for most CLEP exams.

5. *What is the required score for earning CLEP credit for each exam you are considering?*

Most colleges publish the required scores or percentile ranks for earning CLEP credit in their general catalog or in a brochure. The required score may vary from exam to exam, so find out the required score for each exam you are considering.

6. *What is the college's policy regarding prior course work in the subject in which you are considering taking a CLEP exam?*

Some colleges will not grant credit for a CLEP exam if the student has already attempted a college-level course closely aligned with that exam.

For example, if you successfully completed English 101 or a comparable course on another campus, you will probably not be permitted to also receive CLEP credit in that subject. Some colleges will not permit you to earn CLEP credit for a course that you failed.

7. *Does the college make additional stipulations before credit will be granted?*

It is common practice for colleges to award CLEP credit only to their enrolled students. There are other stipulations, however, that vary from college to college. For example, does the college require you to formally apply for or accept CLEP credit by completing and signing a form? Or does the college require you to "validate" your CLEP score by successfully completing a more advanced course in the subject? Getting answers to these and other questions will help to smooth the process of earning college credit through CLEP.

The preceding questions and the discussions that follow them indicate some of the ways in which CLEP policies can vary from college to college. Find out as much as possible about the CLEP policies at the colleges you are interested in so that you can choose a college with a policy that is compatible with your educational goals. Once you have selected the college you will attend, you can find out which CLEP exams your college recognizes and its requirements for earning CLEP credit.

III. Deciding Which Examinations to Take

If You're Taking the Examinations for College Credit or Career Advancement . . .

Most people who take CLEP exams want to earn credit for college courses. Others take the exams to qualify for job promotions or for professional certification or licensing. Whatever the reason, it is vital to most candidates that they be well prepared for the exams so that they can advance as rapidly as possible toward their educational or career goals.

Those who have limited knowledge in the subjects covered by the exams they are considering are advised to enroll in the college courses in which that material is taught. Those who are uncertain about whether or not they know enough to do well on a particular CLEP exam will find the following guidelines helpful.

There is no way to predict whether you will pass a particular CLEP exam, but answering the questions that follow should give you some indication.

1. *Test Descriptions*

   Read the description of the exam provided in this handbook. Are you familiar with most of the topics and terminology in the outline?

2. *Textbooks*

   Examine textbooks and other resource materials used in comparable college courses. Study the textbook used for this course at your college. Are you familiar with most of the topics and terminology used in college textbooks on this subject?

3. *Sample Questions*

   The sample questions are intended to be representative of the content and difficulty of the questions on the exam. Although they do not appear on the actual exam, the proportion of the sample questions you can answer correctly should be a rough estimate of the proportion of questions you will be able to answer correctly on the exam.

Following the instructions and suggestions in Chapter 5, answer as many of the sample questions for the exam as you can. Check your answers against the correct answers in Appendix A. Did you answer more than half the questions correctly?

Because of variations in course content at different institutions, and because questions on CLEP exams vary in difficulty — with most being of moderate difficulty — the average student who passes a course in a subject can usually answer correctly about half the questions on the corresponding CLEP exam. Most colleges set their passing scores near this level, but some set them higher. If your college has set its required score above the level required by most colleges, you may need to answer a larger proportion of questions on the exam correctly.

4. *Previous Study*

Have you taken noncredit courses in this subject offered by an adult school or a private school, through correspondence, or in connection with your job? Did you do exceptionally well in this subject in high school, or did you take an honors course in this subject?

5. *Experience*

Have you learned or used the knowledge or skills included in this exam in your job or life experience? For example, if you lived in a Spanish-speaking country and spoke the language for a year or more, you might consider taking the College Spanish exam. Or, if you have worked at a job in which you used accounting and finance skills, Introductory Accounting would be a likely exam for you to take. Or, if you have read a considerable amount of literature and attended many art exhibits, concerts, and plays, you might expect to do well on the General Examination in Humanities.

6. *Other Exams*

Have you done well on other standardized tests in subjects related to the one you want to take? For example, did you score well above average on a portion of a college entrance exam covering similar skills, or did you obtain an exceptionally high score on a high school equivalency test or a licensing exam in this subject? Although such tests do not cover exactly the same material as the CLEP exams and may be easier, persons who do well on these tests often do well on CLEP exams, too.

7. *Advice*

Has a college counselor, professor, or some other professional person familiar with your ability advised you to take a CLEP exam?

If you answered yes to several of the above questions, you probably have a good chance of passing the CLEP exam you are considering. It is unlikely that you would have acquired sufficient background from experience alone. Learning gained through reading and study is essential, and you will probably find some additional study helpful before taking a CLEP exam. Information on how to review for CLEP exams can be found in Chapter 4 and in the examination guides in Chapter 7.

If You're Taking the Examinations to Prepare for College . . .

Many people entering college, particularly adults returning to college after several years away from formal education, are uncertain about their ability to compete with other college students. You may wonder whether you have sufficient background for college study, and if you've been away from formal study for some time, you may wonder whether you have forgotten how to study, how to take tests, and how to write papers. You may wish to improve your test-taking and study skills prior to enrolling in courses.

One way to assess your ability to perform at the college level and to improve your test-taking and study skills at the same time is to prepare for and take one or more CLEP exams. You need not be enrolled in a college to take a CLEP exam. You may have your scores sent only to yourself and later request that a transcript be sent to a college if you then decide to apply for credit. By reviewing the exam descriptions and sample questions in this handbook, you may find one or several subject areas in which you think you have substantial knowledge. Select one exam, or more if you like, and carefully read at least one college textbook on the subject(s) you have chosen. For some exams, it may be necessary to study more than one textbook to cover the entire scope of material covered by the exam. By doing this, you will get a better idea of how much you know of what is usually taught in a college-level course in that subject. Study as much material as you can, until you think you have a good grasp of the subject matter. Then take the exam at a college in your area. It may be two to three weeks before you receive your score report, and you may wish to begin reviewing for another exam in the meantime.

To find out whether you are eligible for credit based on your CLEP score, you must compare your score with the one required by the college you plan to attend. If you are not yet sure which college you will attend, or whether you will enroll in college at all, you should begin to follow the steps outlined in Chapter 2. It is best that you do this before taking a CLEP exam, but if you are taking the exam only for the experience and to familiarize yourself with college-level material and requirements, you might take the exam before you approach a college. Even if the college you decide to attend does not accept the exam you took, the experience of taking such an exam will give you more confidence about pursuing your college-level studies.

You will find information about how to interpret your scores in *What Your CLEP Score Means*, a pamphlet you will receive with your score report. Many colleges follow the recommendations of the American Council on Education (ACE) for setting their required scores, so you can use this information as a guide in determining how well you did. The ACE recommendations are included in the pamphlet.

If you do not do well enough on the exam to earn college credit, don't be discouraged. The fact that you did not get credit for your score means that you should probably enroll in a college course to learn the material. However, if your score was close to the required score, or if you feel you could do better on a second try or after some additional study, you may retake the test after six months. Do not take it sooner or your score will not be reported and your fee will be forfeited.

If you do earn the score required to earn credit, you will have demonstrated that you already have some college-level knowledge. You will also have a better idea of whether you should take additional CLEP exams.

IV. Preparing to Take CLEP Examinations

Having made the decision to take one or more CLEP exams, most people then want to know how to prepare for them — how much, how long, when, and how should they go about it? The precise answers to these questions vary greatly from individual to individual. However, most candidates find that some type of test preparation is helpful.

Most people who take CLEP exams do so to show that they have already learned the key material taught in a college course. Many of them need only a quick review to assure themselves that they have not forgotten what they once studied, and to fill in some of the gaps in their knowledge of the subject. Others feel that they need a thorough review and spend several weeks studying for an exam. Some people take a CLEP exam as a kind of "final exam" for independent study of a subject. This last group requires significantly more study than those who only need to review, and they may need some guidance from professors of the subjects they are studying.

The key to how you prepare for CLEP exams often lies in locating those skills and areas of prior learning in which you are strong and deciding where to focus your energies. Some people may know a great deal about a certain subject area but may not test well. These individuals would probably be just as concerned about strengthening their test-taking skills as they would about studying for a specific test. Many mental and physical skills are used in preparing for a test. It is important not only to review or study for the exams but to make certain that you are alert, relatively free of anxiety, and aware of how to approach standardized tests. Suggestions on developing test-taking skills and preparing psychologically and physically for a test are given in this chapter. The following section suggests ways of assessing your knowledge of the content of an exam and then reviewing and studying the material.

Using the Examination Guides

In Chapter 7, you will find a guide for each CLEP exam. Each exam guide includes an outline of the knowledge and skills covered by the test, sample questions similar to those that appear on the exam, and tips for preparing to take the exam.

You may also choose to contact a college in your area that offers a course comparable to the CLEP exam you want to take. If possible, use the textbook required for that course to help you prepare. To get this information, check the college's catalog for a list of courses offered. Then call the admission office, explain what subject you're interested in, and ask who in that academic department you can contact for specific information on textbooks and other study resources to use. Be sure that the college you're interested in gives credit for the CLEP exam for which you're preparing.

Begin by carefully reading the test description and outline of knowledge and skills required for the exam in the exam guide. As you read through the topics listed, ask yourself how much you know about each one. Also note the terms, names, and symbols that are mentioned, and ask yourself whether you are familiar with them. This will give you a quick overview of how much you know about the subject. If you are familiar with nearly all the material, you will probably need a minimum of review; however, if less than half of it is familiar, you will probably require substantial study to do well on the exam.

If, after reviewing the test description provided in the exam guide, you find that you need extensive review, delay answering the sample questions until you have done some reading in the subject. If you complete them before reviewing the material, you will probably look for the answers as you study, and they will not be a good assessment of your ability at a later date. Do not refer to the sample questions as you prepare for the exam. None of the sample questions appear on the CLEP exam, so concentrating on them without broader study of the subject won't help you.

If you think you are familiar with most of the test material, try to answer the sample questions. (You may use a copy of the sample answer sheet in Appendix B or the answer spaces provided next to each sample question.) Use the test-taking strategies described in Chapter 5.

Check your answers against the answer key in Appendix A. If you could answer nearly all the questions correctly, you probably do not need to study the subject extensively. If you got about half the questions correct, you ought to review at least one textbook or find other reference material on the subject. If you could answer fewer than half the questions correctly, you will probably benefit from more extensive reading in the subject and thorough study of one or more textbooks.

Assessing Your Readiness
for a CLEP Examination

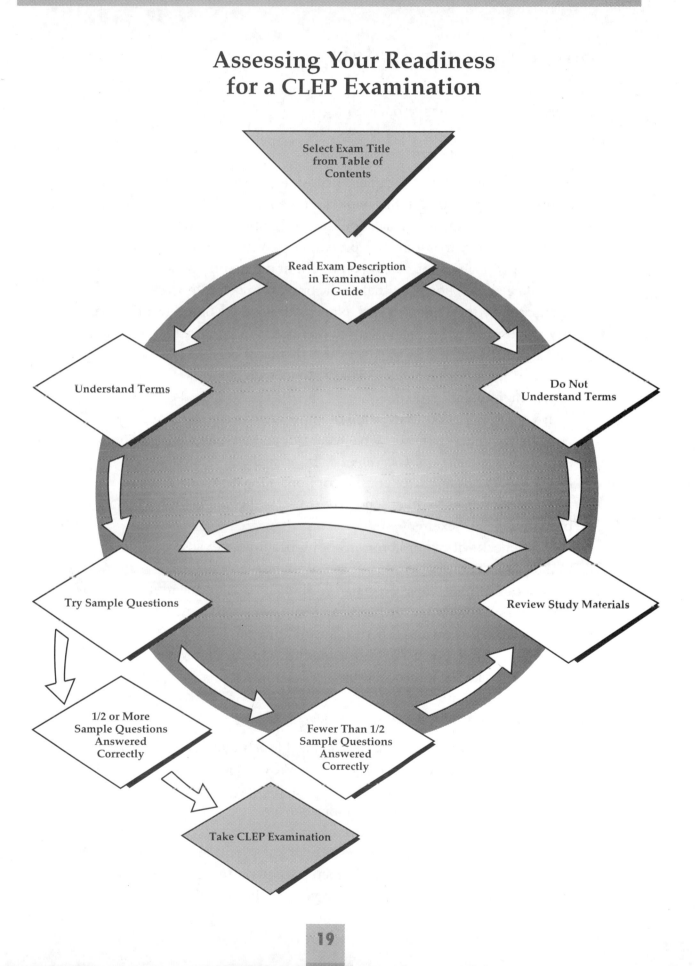

Suggestions for Studying

The following suggestions have been gathered from people who have prepared for CLEP exams or other college-level tests.

1. *Define your goals and locate study materials.*

   First, determine your study goals. Set aside a block of time to review the exam guides provided in this book, and then decide which exam(s) you will take. Using the guidelines for knowledge and skills required, locate suitable resource materials. If a preparation course is offered by an adult school or college in your area, you might find it helpful to enroll. (You should be aware, however, that such courses are not authorized or sponsored by the College Board. Neither the College Board nor ETS has any responsibility for the content of these courses; nor are they responsible for books on preparing for CLEP exams that have been published by other organizations.) If you know others who have taken CLEP exams, ask them how they prepared.

   If you have a good foundation of knowledge in a particular subject but need to brush up on one or two specific areas, you may wish to refer to an encyclopedia. *American Encyclopedia*, *Encyclopedia Britannica*, and *World Book Encyclopedia* are three possible options. Encyclopedias can also provide references to other scholarly works that could be of help as you prepare for CLEP exams.

   Also check with your librarian about locating other study aids relevant to the exams you plan to take. These supplementary materials may include videotapes from *National Geographic*, *Nova*, and other education-oriented companies; audio language tapes; and computer software. And don't forget that what you do with your leisure time can be very educational, whether it's watching a PBS series, reading a financial newsletter, attending a play, or viewing a film.

2. *Find a good place to study.*

   To determine what kind of place you need for studying, ask yourself questions such as, Do I need a quiet place? Does the telephone distract me? Do objects I see in this place remind me of things I should do? Is it too warm? Is it well lit? Am I too comfortable here? Do I have space to spread out my materials? You may find the library more conducive to studying than your home. If you decide to study at home, you might prevent interruptions by other household members by putting a sign on the door of your study room to indicate when you will be available.

3. *Schedule time to study.*

To help you determine where studying best fits into your schedule, try this exercise: Make a list of your daily activities (for example, sleeping, working, and eating) and estimate how many hours a day you spend on each activity. Now, rate all the activities on your list in order of their importance and evaluate your use of time. Often people are astonished at how an average day appears from this perspective. They may discover that they were unaware how large portions of time are spent, or they learn their time can be scheduled in alternative ways. For example, they can remove the least important activities from their day and devote that time to studying or another important activity.

4. *Establish a study routine and a set of goals.*

To study effectively, you should establish specific goals and a schedule for accomplishing them. Some people find it helpful to write out a weekly schedule and cross out each study period when it is completed. Others maintain their concentration better by writing down the time when they expect to complete a study task. Most people find short periods of intense study more productive than long stretches of time. For example, they may follow a regular schedule of several 20- or 30-minute study periods with short breaks between them. Some people like to allow themselves rewards as they complete each study goal. It is not essential that you accomplish every goal exactly within your schedule; the point is to be committed to your task.

5. *Learn how to take an active role in studying.*

If you have not done much studying for some time, you may find it difficult to concentrate at first. Try a method of studying, such as the one outlined below, that will help you concentrate on and remember what you read.

a. First, read the chapter summary and the introduction. Then you will know what to look for in your reading.

b. Next, convert the section or paragraph headlines into questions. For example, if you are reading a section entitled "The Causes of the American Revolution," ask yourself, "What were the causes of the American Revolution?" Compose the answer as you read the paragraph. Reading and answering questions aloud will help you understand and remember the material.

c. Take notes on key ideas or concepts as you read. Writing will also help you fix concepts more firmly in your mind. Underlining key ideas or writing notes in your book can be helpful and will be useful for review. Underline only important points. If you underline more than a third of each paragraph, you are probably underlining too much.

d. If there are questions or problems at the end of a chapter, answer or solve them on paper as if you were asked to do them for homework. Mathematics textbooks (and some other books) sometimes include answers to some or all of the exercises. If you have such a book, write your answers before looking at the ones given. When problem-solving is involved, work enough problems to master the required methods and concepts. If you have difficulty with problems, review any sample problems or explanations in the chapter.

e. To retain knowledge, most people have to review the material periodically. If you are preparing for an exam over an extended period of time, review key concepts and notes each week or so. Do not wait for weeks to review the material or you will need to relearn much of it.

Psychological and Physical Preparation

Most people feel at least some nervousness before taking a test. Adults who are returning to college may not have taken a test in many years, or they may have had little experience with standardized tests. Some younger students, as well, are uncomfortable with testing situations. People who received their education in countries outside the United States may find that many tests given in this country are quite different from the ones they are accustomed to taking.

Not only might candidates find the types of tests and questions unfamiliar, but other aspects of the testing environment may be strange as well. The physical and mental stress that results from meeting this new experience can hinder a candidate's ability to demonstrate his or her true degree of knowledge in the subject area being tested. For this reason, it is important to go to the test center well prepared, both mentally and physically, for taking the test. You may find the following suggestions helpful.

1. Familiarize yourself as much as possible with the test and the test situation before the day of the exam. It will be helpful for you to know ahead of time:

    a. How much time will be allowed for the test and whether there are timed subsections. (This information is included in the examination guides in Chapter 7.)

    b. What types of questions and directions appear on the exam. (See the examination guides.)

    c. How your test score will be computed. (See Chapter 6 for a brief explanation.)

    d. Whether you will record your answers on an answer sheet or on a microcomputer.

    e. How to complete the answer sheet. (See suggestion 4d, below; a sample answer sheet is provided in Appendix B.)

    f. How a microcomputer looks and operates, if you will be using one. (Simple instructions will be given on the day of the test, and you will be given ample time to use the computer in answering practice questions before you begin the actual test.)

    g. In which building and room the exam will be administered. If you don't know where the building is, get directions ahead of time.

    h. The time of the test administration. You might wish to confirm this information a day or two before the exam and find out what time the building and room will be open so that you can plan to arrive early.

    i. Where to park your car or, if you will be taking public transportation, which bus or train to take and the location of the nearest stop.

    j. Whether smoking will be permitted during testing.

    k. Whether there will be a break between exams (if you will be taking more than one on the same day), and whether there is a place nearby where you can get something to eat or drink.

2. Be relaxed and alert while you are taking the exam:

    a. Get a good night's sleep. Last minute cramming, particularly late the night before, is usually counterproductive.

    b. Eat normally. It is usually not wise to skip breakfast or lunch on the day you take the exam or to eat a big meal just before testing.

    c. Avoid tranquilizers and stimulants. If you follow the other directions in this book, you won't need artificial aids. It's better to be a little tense than to be drowsy, but stimulants such as coffee and cola can make you nervous and interfere with your concentration.

   d. Don't drink a lot of liquids before taking the exam. Leaving to use the rest room during testing will disturb your concentration and reduce the time you have to complete the exam.

   e. If you are inclined to be nervous or tense, learn some relaxation exercises and use them to prepare for the exam.

3. Arrive for testing early and prepared. Be sure to:

   a. Arrive early enough so that you can find a parking place, locate the test center, and get settled comfortably before testing begins. Allow some extra time in case you are delayed unexpectedly.

   b. Take the following with you:

   - Your completed Admission Form, which will have been validated in advance by the test administrator. You will need to refer to this form to record on your answer sheet the code number of the college to which you want your scores sent.

   - Personal identification that includes your photograph and signature. You will be asked to show such identification to be admitted.

   - A check or money order for $43 payable to CLEP, if you did not pay for the exam when you registered.

   - Two or more soft-lead (No. 2) pencils with good erasers.

   - An unprogrammed hand calculator if you wish to use one for the Calculus with Elementary Functions, College Algebra, College Mathematics, Introductory Accounting, or General Chemistry exams. Check with the test center in advance for any change in this policy. All calculator memories must be cleared of programs and data, and no peripheral devices such as magnetic cards or tapes will be allowed. Candidates are not permitted to share calculators or other supplies.

   - A watch so that you can time your progress.

   - Your glasses if you need them for reading or seeing the chalkboard or wall clock.

   c. Leave all books, papers, and notes outside the test center. You will not be permitted to use your own scratch paper, but there will be adequate space for notes and calculations on the pages of your test book.

d. Be able to adjust to an uncomfortable temperature in the testing room. Wear layers of clothing that can be removed if the room is too hot but that will keep you warm if it is too cold.

4. When you enter the test room:

   a. Although you will be assigned to a seat, the test center administrator can usually accommodate special needs. For example, if you are left-handed, ask to be assigned a seat with a left-handed writing board, if possible. Be sure to communicate your needs *before* testing begins.

   b. Read directions carefully and listen to all instructions given by the test administrator. If you don't understand the directions, ask for help before test timing begins. If you must ask a question after testing has begun, raise your hand and a proctor will assist you. The proctor can answer certain kinds of questions but cannot help you with the exam.

   c. Know your rights as a test taker. You can expect to be given the full working time allowed for taking the exam and a reasonably quiet and comfortable place in which to work. If a poor test situation is preventing you from doing your best, ask if the situation can be remedied. If bad test conditions cannot be remedied, ask the person in charge to report the problem in the Irregularity Report that will be sent to ETS with the answer sheets. You may also wish to immediately write a letter to CLEP, P.O. Box 6601, Princeton, NJ 08541-6601. Describe the exact circumstances as completely as you can. Be sure to include the name of the test center, the test date, and the name(s) of the exam(s) you took. ETS will investigate the problem to make sure it does not happen again, and, if the problem is serious enough, may arrange for you to retake the exam without charge.

   d. If you will be using an answer sheet as opposed to a microcomputer, complete it correctly. CLEP answer sheets are scored by an electronic optical scanner that reads the marks you make on your answer sheet. Therefore, it is important that all the marks you put on your answer sheet are dark enough, that you put them in the right places, and that you erase completely all marks you do not want the scanner to read. Use a soft-lead (No. 2) pencil when completing your answer sheet.

   A sample CLEP answer sheet is shown in Appendix B. The second and third page have been completed for a fictional candidate, Nancy B. Baker. Familiarize yourself with this completed sample answer sheet before taking your exam so that you are able to complete your answer sheet properly during testing. Filling out your answer sheet incorrectly or incompletely will delay your score report.

If you will be entering your answers on a microcomputer, complete instructions will be provided on the day of testing. You will be given ample time to practice answering sample questions on the microcomputer before you begin the actual exam.

Arrangements for Students with Disabilities

If you have a learning or physical disability that would prevent you from taking a CLEP exam under standard conditions, you may request special accommodations and arrangements to take it on either a regularly scheduled test date or at a specially scheduled administration. For details, please contact the CLEP test administrator at the college where you plan to take the exam.

V. Taking the Examinations

A person may know a great deal about the subject being tested but not be able to demonstrate it on the exam. Knowing how to approach an exam is an important part of the testing process. While a command of test-taking skills cannot substitute for knowledge of the subject matter, it can be a significant factor in successful testing.

Test-taking skills enable a person to use all available information to earn a score that truly reflects her or his ability. There are different strategies for approaching different kinds of exam questions. For example, free-response questions require a very different approach than do multiple-choice questions. Other factors, such as how the exam will be graded, may also influence your approach to the exam and your use of test time. Thus, your preparation for an exam should include finding out all you can about the exam so that you can use the most effective test-taking strategies.

Before taking an exam, you should know approximately how many questions are on the test, how much time you will be allowed, how the test will be scored or graded, whether there is a penalty for wrong answers, what types of questions and directions are on the test, and how you will be required to record your answers. All this information for CLEP exams is discussed in the preceding pages or in the individual examination guides in Chapter 7. The following sections summarize some of the strategies that you may use in taking multiple-choice and free-response exams.

Taking Multiple-Choice Exams

1. Listen carefully to the instructions given by the test administrator and read carefully all directions in the test book before you begin to answer the questions.

2. Note the time that the test administrator starts timing the test. As you proceed, make sure that you are not working too slowly. You should have answered at least half the questions in a section when half the time for that section has passed. If you have not reached that point in the section, speed up your pace on the remaining questions.

3. Before answering a question, read the entire question, including all the answer choices. Don't think that because the first or second answer choice looks good to you, it isn't necessary to read the remaining options. Instructions usually tell you to select the "best" answer. Sometimes one answer choice is partially correct but another option is better; therefore, it is usually a good idea to read all the answers before you choose one.

4. Read and consider every question. Questions that look complicated at first glance may not actually be so difficult once you have read them carefully.

5. Do not puzzle too long over any one question. If you don't know the answer after you've considered it briefly, go on to the next question. Mark that question in your test book and go back to it later, if you have time.

6. Make sure you record your response on the answer sheet or microcomputer screen beside the same number as the number of the question in the test book. If you skip a question, be sure you also skip a space on the answer sheet or microcomputer screen. If you have not answered all the questions in a section when you are told to go on to the next section, be sure to skip the spaces for those questions on your answer sheet. If you discover that you have been marking your answers in the wrong spaces, tell the test supervisor. The test supervisor will note this in the Irregularity Report that will be returned to ETS with the answer sheets, and your answer sheet will be hand-scored.

7. Certain foreign language and mathematics tests have only four answer options to choose from, "A" through "D," even though the answer sheet has five lettered answer spaces for each question. Be careful not to mark answers you intend as "D" in the "E" spaces; "E" answers will not be counted toward your score.

8. Don't hesitate to write notes or to do your calculations in your test book. The test books will not be used again, nor will anything you write in the test book affect your score. Be sure to record all of your answers in the correct space on the answer sheet. Do not, however, make any unnecessary marks on your answer sheet, and be sure you erase all stray marks completely.

9. In trying to determine the correct answer, you may find it helpful to cross out those options that you know are incorrect, and to make marks next to those you think might be correct. If you decide to skip the question and come back to it later, you will save yourself the time of reconsidering all the options.

10. Watch for the following key words in test questions:

all	generally	never	perhaps
always	however	none	rarely
but	may	not	seldom
except	must	often	sometimes
every	necessary	only	usually

When a question or answer option contains words such as "always," "every," "only," "never," and "none," there can be no exceptions to the answer you choose. Use of words such as "often," "rarely," "sometimes," and "generally" indicates that there may be some exceptions to the answer.

11. Do not guess wildly or randomly fill in answers to questions you do not have time to read, because there is a penalty for incorrect answers on CLEP exams. (An explanation of the procedures used for scoring CLEP exams is given in Chapter 6.) It is improbable that mere guessing will improve your score significantly; it may even lower your score, and it does take time. If, however, you are not sure of the correct answer but have some knowledge of the question and are able to eliminate one or more of the answer choices as wrong, your chance of getting the right answer is improved and, on the average, it will be to your benefit to answer such a question.

12. Do not waste your time looking for clues to right answers based on flaws in question wording or patterns in correct answers. Professionals at the College Board and ETS put a great deal of effort into developing valid, reliable, and fair exams. CLEP test development committees are composed of college faculty who are experts in the subject covered by the exam and are appointed by the College Board to write test questions and to scrutinize each question that is included on a CLEP exam. Committee members make every effort to ensure that the questions are not ambiguous, that they have only one correct answer, and that they cover college-level topics. These committees do not intentionally include "trick"

questions. If you think a question is flawed, ask the test administrator to report it, or write immediately to College Board Test Development, P.O. Box 6656, Princeton, NJ 08541-6656. Include the name of the exam and test center, the exam date, and the number of the exam question. All such inquiries are investigated by the ETS test development staff.

Taking Essay Exams

If your college requires the optional essay portion of any of the four CLEP Subject Examinations in Composition and Literature or the General Examination in English Composition with Essay, you should do some additional preparation for your CLEP exam. Taking an essay or a problem-solving test is very different from taking a multiple-choice test, so you will need to use some other strategies.

The essay written as part of the General Examination in English Composition is graded by English professors from a variety of colleges and universities. A process called holistic scoring is used to rate your writing ability. This process is explained in the examination guide for the General Examination in English Composition in Chapter 7. The handbook also includes graded sample essays and essay questions.

The optional essay portions of the Subject Examinations in Composition and Literature, on the other hand, are graded by the faculty of the college you designate as a score recipient. Guidelines and criteria for grading essays are not specified by the College Board or ETS. You may find it helpful, therefore, to talk with someone at your college to find out what criteria will be used to determine whether you will get credit. Ask how much emphasis will be placed on your writing ability and your ability to organize your thoughts as opposed to your knowledge of the subject matter. Find out how much weight will be given to your multiple-choice test score in comparison with your free-response grade in determining whether you will get credit. This will give you an idea of where you should expend the greatest effort in preparing for and taking the exam.

Here are some strategies you will find useful in taking any essay exam:

1. Before you begin to write, read all the questions carefully and take a few minutes to jot down some ideas you might include in each answer.

2. If you are given a choice of questions to answer, choose the questions that you think you can answer most clearly and knowledgeably.

3. Determine in what order you will answer the questions. Answer those you find the easiest first so that any extra time can be spent on the more difficult questions.

4. When you know which questions you will answer and in what order, determine how much testing time remains and estimate how many minutes you will devote to each question. Unless suggested times are given for the questions or one question appears to require more or less time than the others, allot an equal amount of time to each question.

5. Before answering each question, indicate the number of the question as it is given in the test book. You need not copy the entire question from the question sheet, but it will be helpful to you and to the person grading your test if you indicate briefly the topic you are addressing — particularly if you are not answering the questions in the order in which they appear on the exam.

6. Before answering each question, read it again carefully to make sure you are interpreting it correctly. Underline key words, such as those listed below, that often appear in free-response questions. Be sure you know the exact meaning of these words before taking the exam.

analyze	demonstrate	enumerate	list
apply	derive	explain	outline
assess	describe	generalize	prove
compare	determine	illustrate	rank
contrast	discuss	interpret	show
define	distinguish	justify	summarize

If a question asks you to "outline," "define," or "summarize," do not write a detailed explanation; if a question asks you to "analyze," "explain," "illustrate," "interpret," or "show," you must do more than briefly describe the topic.

VI. Interpreting Your Scores

College score requirements for awarding credit vary from institution to institution. The College Board, however, recommends that colleges refer to the standards set by the American Council on Education (ACE). All ACE recommendations are the result of careful and periodic review by evaluation teams made up of faculty who are subject-matter experts and technical experts in testing and measurement. To determine whether you are eligible for credit for your CLEP scores, you should refer to the policy of the college you will be attending. The policy will state either the score or the percentile that is required to earn credit at that institution. Many colleges award credit at the score levels recommended by ACE. Many others use the 50th percentile. Some require scores that are higher or lower than these.

The pamphlet *What Your CLEP Score Means*, which you will receive with your score report, gives detailed information about interpreting your scores. A copy of the pamphlet is in Appendix D. A brief explanation appears below.

How CLEP Scores Are Computed

Your score report will show the total score for each CLEP exam you take. For the General Examinations, total scores fall between 200 and 800, and for the Subject Examinations between 20 and 80. For Subject Examinations, percentile ranks for scaled scores will be shown on the score report. For foreign language exams, subscores are reported.

When your scores are computed, you receive one point for each correct answer. A percentage of the number of your incorrect answers is subtracted from this total to discourage random guessing. As a penalty for guessing, one-fourth of a point is subtracted for each five-choice question you answer incorrectly; one-third of a point is deducted for each incorrect answer to a four-choice question. There is no deduction for a question you do not answer. The resulting figure, called the formula score, is converted to a scaled score between 200 and 800 or between 20 and 80. The more questions you answer correctly, the more points you will earn toward a higher scaled score. This conversion makes scores earned on different forms and editions of the same CLEP examination comparable to one another.

How Essays Are Graded

The College Board arranges for college English professors to grade the essays written for the General Examination in English Composition. These carefully selected college faculty consultants represent the current curriculums being taught at two- and four-year institutions nationwide. The faculty consultants receive extensive training and thoroughly review the College Board scoring policies and procedures before grading the essays. Each essay is read and graded by two professors, the sum of the two grades is combined with the multiple-choice score, and the result is reported as a scaled score between 200 and 800. CLEP does not report separate scores for the multiple-choice and essay sections of the General Examination in English Composition because a 45-minute test is not considered extensive enough to assess reliably a candidate's writing skills for college credit. Although the format of the two sections is very different, both measure skills required for expository writing. Knowledge of formal grammar is necessary for the multiple-choice section, but the emphasis in the free-response section is on writing skills rather than grammar.

Optional essays for CLEP Composition and Literature Subject Examinations are evaluated and graded by the colleges that require them, rather than by ETS or the College Board. If you take an optional essay, it will be sent with a copy of your score report (which includes only the results of your multiple-choice test) to the institution you designate on your answer sheet.

You may opt not to have your score sent to a college until after you have seen it. In this case, your essay can still be sent to the college of your choice as long as you request a transcript within 90 days after you take the exam. Copies of essays are not held by ETS beyond 90 days or after they have been sent to an institution.

VII. Examination Guides

English Composition

Description of the Examination

The General Examination in English Composition measures the skills required in most first-year college composition courses. It measures the writing skills needed for college assignments and, in particular, for writing that explains, interprets, analyzes, presents, or supports a point of view. The exam does not cover some topics included in first-year college writing courses, such as research skills or literary analysis, nor does it require knowledge of grammatical terms as such. However, the student will need to apply the principles and conventions expected of academic written discourse.

Two versions of the exam are offered. One version (known as the all-multiple-choice version) contains approximately 100 multiple-choice questions to be answered in two separately timed 45-minute sections. The other version (known as the version with Essay) has a 45-minute multiple-choice section with approximately 55 questions and another section with one essay question to be responded to in 45 minutes.

The essay is evaluated by college teachers of writing who meet at a central location to do the scoring. Each essay is read and assigned a rating by two scorers; the sum of the two ratings is weighted and then combined with the candidate's multiple-choice score. The resulting combined score is reported as a scaled score between 200 and 800. Separate scores are not reported for the multiple-choice and essay sections.

College policies differ with regard to their acceptance of the two versions of the English Composition exam. Some grant credit only for the version with Essay; others grant credit only for the all-multiple-choice version; still others grant credit for either of the two versions. Many colleges grant six semester hours (or the equivalent) of credit toward satisfying a liberal arts or distribution requirement in English; others grant six hours of course credit for a specific first-year composition or English course that emphasizes expository writing.

Candidates who are taking the exam to gain credit at a particular college should call or write to the admissions office or the counseling and testing office at that college. They should ask the following:

- Is credit given for the all-multiple-choice version of the CLEP General Examination, or for the version with Essay, or for the CLEP Subject Examination in Freshman College Composition?

- How much credit is given and for which requirements or courses?

- What is the minimum score required to receive credit?

On the day of the exam, candidates should check the title on the cover of the test book to make sure they are taking the appropriate exam.

Knowledge and Skills Required

The multiple-choice questions of the exam measure students' writing skills both at the sentence level and within the context of passages. The current General Examination in English Composition does, in fact, reflect a greater emphasis on revising work in progress than did previous forms of the test. The exam is designed so that average students who have completed the general education requirement in English composition can usually answer about half of the multiple-choice questions correctly.

Skills at the Sentence Level

The exam measures the candidate's awareness of a variety of logical, structural, and grammatical relationships within sentences (these skills are tested by approximately 55 percent of the all-multiple-choice version and 30 percent of the multiple-choice questions in the version with Essay). Questions test recognition of acceptable usage relating to:

Sentence boundaries

Economy and clarity of expression

Concord/Agreement: subject-verb; verb tense; pronoun reference, shift, number

Active/passive voice

Diction and idiom

Syntax: parallelism, coordination, subordination, dangling modifiers

Sentence variety

Several kinds of question formats throughout the test are intended to measure these sentence-level skills:

1. *Identifying Sentence Errors* — This type of question appears in Section I of both versions and in Section II of the all-multiple-choice version. It requires the candidate to identify wording that violates the standard conventions of written discourse. Samples of this question type are on pages 42-44 of this guide.

2. *Improving Sentences* — This type of question appears only in Section I of both versions. It requires the candidate to choose the phrase, clause, or sentence that best conveys the intended meaning of a sentence. Samples of this question type are on pages 45-48 of this guide.

3. *Restructuring Sentences* — This type of question appears only in Section II of the all-multiple-choice version. The candidate is given a sentence to reword in order to change emphasis or improve clarity. He or she must then choose from five options the phrase that will likely appear in the new sentence. See pages 53-57 for sample questions.

Skills in Context

Questions in approximately 45 percent of the all-multiple-choice version and 20 percent of the version with Essay measure recognition of the following in the context of works in progress or of published prose.

Main idea, thesis

Organization of ideas in the paragraph or essay

Relevance of evidence, sufficiency of detail, levels of specificity

Audience and purpose (effect on style, tone, language, or argument)

Logic of argument (inductive, deductive reasoning)

Coherence within and between paragraphs

Rhetorical emphasis, effect

Sustaining tense or point of view

Sentence joining, sentence variety

The following kinds of questions measure writing skills in context:

Revising Work in Progress – This type of question appears in Section I of both versions and in Section II of the all-multiple-choice version. The candidate identifies ways to improve an early draft of an essay. See pages 48-52 for sample questions.

Analyzing Writing — Two prose passages written in very different modes appear only in Section II of the all-multiple-choice version. The candidate answers questions about each passage and about the strategies used by the author of each passage. See pages 58-62 for sample questions.

The Essay

This section comprises 50 percent of the version with Essay. The student is expected to present a point of view in response to a topic and to support it with a logical argument and appropriate evidence. See pages 62-66 for sample topics and actual responses.

Scoring the Essays

Shortly after each administration of the CLEP General Examination in English Composition with Essay, college English teachers from throughout the United States assemble to score the essays. Each essay is scored independently by two different readers, and the two scores are then combined. This score is weighted approximately equally with the score from the multiple-choice section, then combined with it to yield the reported score for the test.

The writing assignment varies from one administration to the next, so even though the majority of readers are experienced, they must be trained at each scoring session to calibrate their standards for a new topic. Those responsible for this training are other college teachers: the chief reader, the assistant chief reader, and several table leaders. At the beginning and throughout the scoring session these individuals work to familiarize the readers with the qualities of preselected benchmark papers that represent the 7 points on the scoring scale. The leaders also perform both random and formal quality control checks to ensure reliable scoring, and they adjudicate divergent scores.

CLEP essays are evaluated holistically. Because holistic scoring relies on the total impression that a paper creates, the readers must put aside whatever analytical criteria they use in judging their students' papers. These readers, realizing that the essays are *first drafts* written in 45 minutes, expect to find flaws. However, minor errors and oversights should not detract from a high estimation of an essay that otherwise represents effective writing. Scorers who read holistically are therefore encouraged to keep in mind the constraints placed on the writers in terms of the timing and the topic provided. They also are encouraged to read supportively: that is, to look for what the writer has done well, rather than what the writer has done poorly.

With practice, those who score holistically for CLEP internalize standards for the various score points. Nevertheless, readers must always compare the essays they are scoring with the benchmark papers written for a particular assignment.

The following is a generic description of the characteristics of essays at the various score points:

High range (Scores of 7-8) — Papers in this range are notable for their *high degree of competence and control.* An 8 paper demonstrates more consistent control than a 7. It usually is well organized and clearly focused, contains varied and appropriate detail, uses effective language and varied syntax, and demonstrates a mastery of grammar and mechanics.

Middle range (Scores of 4-6) — Papers earning a score of 5 demonstrate *adequate competence.* While they are generally organized and without serious grammatical errors, the treatment of the topic may be superficial and the language and syntax unremarkable. The 6 papers demonstrate more control and more detail than 5 papers. The 4 papers, which usually contain somewhat more frequent lapses than 5 papers, still manage to develop the topic in a somewhat competent manner.

Low range (Scores of 2-3) — Papers in this range demonstrate *clear deficiencies.* They often fail to focus on the topic; they are thinly developed; diction is immature and awkward; and errors abound in grammar, mechanics, and syntax. The paper earning a score of 2 either fails to develop the topic or contains such an accumulation of errors that meaning is seriously obscured.

Examples of actual essays can be found on pages 63-65.

Sample Questions

The 49 sample questions that follow are similar to questions on the all-multiple-choice version of the General Examination in English Composition; however, they do not appear on the actual test.

Before attempting to answer the sample questions, read all the information about the English Composition exam on the preceding pages. Additional suggestions for preparing for CLEP exams are provided in Chapter 4.

Even if you are taking the version with Essay, you will find it helpful to attempt the sample multiple-choice questions for both sections. The correct answers are given in Appendix A.

Sample essay questions and sample essays follow the multiple-choice questions.

SECTION I
(These are samples of questions that appear in Section I of both the all-multiple-choice version and the version with Essay.)

Identifying Sentence Errors

Directions: The following sentences test your knowledge of grammar, usage, diction (choice of words), and idiom. Note that some sentences are correct, and no sentence contains more than one error.

You will find that the error, if there is one, is underlined and lettered. Assume that elements of the sentence that are not underlined are correct and cannot be changed. In choosing answers, follow the requirements of standard written English.

If there is an error, select the one underlined part that must be changed to make the sentence correct and fill in the corresponding oval on your answer sheet.

If there is no error, select answer (E).

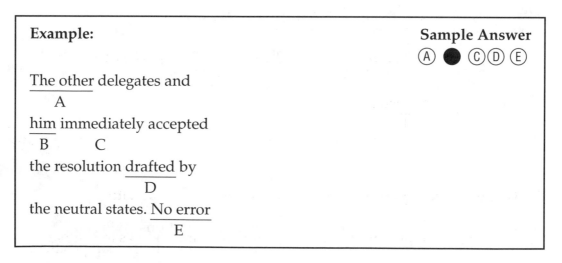

1. Hydroelectric dams work <u>on a simple</u> principle: <u>the greater the</u>
                   A   B

   distance that the water has <u>to fall</u>, the more the power that
                            C

   <u>was generated</u>. <u>No error</u>
       D   E

   Ⓐ Ⓑ Ⓒ Ⓓ Ⓔ

2. Alexis <u>has discovered</u> that she can express her creativity more freely
            A

   <u>through</u> her <u>sketches</u> <u>and not</u> in her photography. <u>No error</u>
     B   C   D   E

   Ⓐ Ⓑ Ⓒ Ⓓ Ⓔ

3. Ms. Marco found that it was easier for her <u>teaching</u> children
                                     A

   arithmetic <u>once</u> <u>they became</u> <u>familiar with</u> the idea of a set. <u>No error</u>
           B   C   D   E

   Ⓐ Ⓑ Ⓒ Ⓓ Ⓔ

4. Many readers <u>still think</u> of Sinclair Lewis, whose strength
                 A

   <u>was supposedly</u> his <u>ability to tell</u> a story, <u>as one of</u> America's best
        B   C   D

   social critics. <u>No error</u>
          E

   Ⓐ Ⓑ Ⓒ Ⓓ Ⓔ

5. <u>Although</u> a lottery may seem a <u>relatively</u> easy way for a state
      A   B

   <u>to increase</u> revenues, <u>they</u> may encourage some individuals to gamble
       C   D

   excessively. <u>No error</u>
          E

   Ⓐ Ⓑ Ⓒ Ⓓ Ⓔ

6. Even when using a calculator, you must have a basic understanding
         A   B

   of mathematics if one expects to solve complex problems correctly.
                    C   D

   No error
     E

   (A) (B) (C) (D) (E)

7. Although science offers the hope of preventing serious genetic
                                  A

   diseases, there is difficult ethical questions raised by the possibility
           B   C   D

   of altering human heredity. No error
                         E

   (A) (B) (C) (D) (E)

8. If they would have known how capricious the winds on Lake
         A   B

   Winasteke were, the boys would have sailed in the larger of their two
                                       C   D

   boats. No error
         E

   (A) (B) (C) (D) (E)

9. Even the careful listener could scarcely tell liberal from conservative
                               A   B

   among the speakers, for the issue had become a highly emotional
                                             C

   one. No error
    D   E

   (A) (B) (C) (D) (E)

10. To learn more about Hispanic culture, we invited a lecturer who had
         A   B

    spoken frequently with regard to the life of early settlers in Santa Fe.
                      C   D

    No error
      E

    (A) (B) (C) (D) (E)

Improving Sentences

Directions: The following sentences test correctness and effectiveness of expression. In choosing answers, follow the requirements of standard written English: that is, pay attention to grammar, diction (choice of words), sentence construction, and punctuation.

In each of the following sentences, part of the sentence or the entire sentence is underlined. Beneath each sentence you will find five versions of the underlined part. Choice A repeats the original; the other four are different.

Choose the answer that best expresses the meaning of the original sentence. If you think the original is better than any of the alternatives, choose it; otherwise choose one of the others. Your choice should produce the most effective sentence — one that is clear and precise, without awkwardness or ambiguity.

Example: **Sample Answer**

Ⓐ ● Ⓒ Ⓓ Ⓔ

Laura Ingalls Wilder published her first book <u>and she was sixty-five years old then.</u>

(A) and she was sixty-five years old then
(B) when she was sixty-five
(C) being age sixty-five years old
(D) upon the reaching of sixty-five years
(E) at the time when she was sixty-five

---

11. Because the eleven women functioned as a <u>team is why they had a successful season.</u>

(A) team is why they had a successful season
(B) team, they had a success this season
(C) team, they had a successful season
(D) team, success was theirs this season
(E) team is why their season was a success

Ⓐ Ⓑ Ⓒ Ⓓ Ⓔ

12. In 1827 *Freedom's Journal* was the first Black American newspaper in the United States, it was published in New York City.

   (A) In 1827 *Freedom's Journal* was the first Black American newspaper in the United States, it was published in New York City.
   (B) In 1827 the first Black American newspaper in the United States, *Freedom's Journal*, was published in New York City.
   (C) In New York City in 1827 *Freedom's Journal*, the first Black American newspaper in the United States, was published there.
   (D) With publication in New York City in 1827, it was the first Black American newspaper in the United States, *Freedom's Journal*.
   (E) The first Black American newspaper published in the United States was when there was *Freedom's Journal* in New York City in 1827.

   Ⓐ Ⓑ Ⓒ Ⓓ Ⓔ

13. Astronomers have developed extremely sophisticated instruments which is helpful for measuring the properties of objects in space.

   (A) instruments, which is helpful for measuring the properties of objects in space
   (B) instruments to help measure the properties of objects in space
   (C) instruments, which are helpful for measurement of space objects' properties
   (D) instruments helpful to measure the properties of objects in space
   (E) instruments, a help for measuring the properties of objects in space

   Ⓐ Ⓑ Ⓒ Ⓓ Ⓔ

14. Foreign correspondents are like birds of passage, resting for a few weeks, then flying off again to a new place.

   (A) then flying off again
   (B) after which again they fly off
   (C) then they fly off again
   (D) when once again they fly off
   (E) but soon they are flying off again

   Ⓐ Ⓑ Ⓒ Ⓓ Ⓔ

15. Reducing individual taxes while eliminating as much waste as possible <u>are traditional methods for increasing</u> a nation's economy.

   (A) are traditional methods for increasing
   (B) is a traditional method for increasing
   (C) is a traditional method of stimulating
   (D) traditionally are methods for increasing
   (E) are traditional methods of stimulating

16. Arguably the most distinctive regional cuisine in the United States, <u>the South is noted for such specialties as</u> Brunswick stew and hush puppies.

   (A) the South is noted for such specialties as
   (B) the South has such specialties of note as
   (C) the South includes among its noteworthy specialties
   (D) southern cooking includes such noteworthy specialties as
   (E) southern cooking is including such specialties of note as

   Ⓐ Ⓑ Ⓒ Ⓓ Ⓔ

17. After the Civil Rights Act of 1964, most inequalities in public accommodations were essentially eliminated, <u>but less progress was made in school desegregation.</u>

   (A) but less progress was made in school desegregation
   (B) with school desegregation being the lesser of the two in terms of
       progress
   (C) school desegregation having lesser progress
   (D) for lesser progress was to be seen in school desegregation
   (E) and school desegregation showed less progress

   Ⓐ Ⓑ Ⓒ Ⓓ Ⓔ

18. Home computers themselves are becoming less expensive, but software, printers, and Internet access <u>cause the total financial cost to rise up greatly</u>.

   (A) cause the total financial cost to rise up greatly
   (B) greatly increase the total cost
   (C) highly inflate the cost totals
   (D) drive up the expense totally
   (E) totally add to the expense

   Ⓐ Ⓑ Ⓒ Ⓓ Ⓔ

19. Today's fashion designers must consider both how much a fabric costs and <u>its wearability</u>.

   (A) its wearability
   (B) is it going to wear well
   (C) if it has wearability
   (D) how well it wears
   (E) the fabric's ability to wear well

   Ⓐ Ⓑ Ⓒ Ⓓ Ⓔ

Revising Work in Progress

Directions: Each of the following selections is an early draft of a student essay in which the sentences have been numbered for easy reference. Some parts of the selections need to be changed.

Read each selection and then answer the questions that follow. Some questions are about particular sentences or parts of sentences and ask you to improve sentence structure and diction (word choice). In making these decisions, follow the conventions of standard written English. Other questions refer to the entire essay or parts of the essay and ask you to consider organization, development, and effectiveness of language in relation to purpose and audience. After you choose each answer, fill in the corresponding oval on your answer sheet.

Questions 20-24 are based on the following draft of a student essay.

(1) *I used to be convinced that people didn't actually win radio contests; I thought that the excited winners I heard were only actors. (2) Sure, people could win T-shirts. (3) They couldn't win anything of real value.*

(4) *I've always loved sports. (5) Unlike my friends, who fall asleep to "Top 40 Radio," I listen to "Sports Night with Dave Sims." (6) His show is hardly usual fare for a young woman. (7) One night I heard Dave Sims announce a sports trivia contest with cash prizes of two thousand dollars. (8) I jump at the chance to combine my talk-show knowledge with everything my father had taught me about sports. (9) I sent in my self-addressed stamped envelope. (10) I forgot about the whole matter. (11) Then the questionnaire appeared in my mailbox ten days later. (12) Its arrival gave me a rude surprise. (13) Instead of sitting down and whipping through it, I trudged to libraries and spent hours digging for answers to such obscure questions as "Which NHL goalie holds the record for most career shutouts?"*

(14) *Finally, after days of double-checking answers, I mailed off my answer sheet, certain I would hear no more about the matter. (15) Certain, until two weeks later, I ripped open the envelope with the NBC peacock and read "Congratulations . . ." (16) I was a winner, a winner of more than a T-shirt.*

20. Which of the following is the best way to revise the underlined portions of sentences 2 and 3 (reproduced below) so that the two sentences are combined into one?

    Sure, people could win <u>T-shirts. They couldn't win</u> anything of real value.

    (A) T-shirts, and they couldn't win
    (B) T-shirts, but they couldn't win
    (C) T-shirts, but not being able to win
    (D) T-shirts, so they do not win
    (E) T-shirts, while there was no winning

    Ⓐ Ⓑ Ⓒ Ⓓ Ⓔ

21. Which of the following sentences, if added after sentence 3, would best link the first paragraph with the rest of the essay?

    (A) I have held this opinion about contests for a long time.
    (B) The prizes offered did not inspire me to enter the contests.
    (C) However, I recently changed my opinion about these contests.
    (D) Usually the questions on these contests are really easy to answer.
    (E) Sometimes my friends try to convince me to enter such contests.

    Ⓐ Ⓑ Ⓒ Ⓓ Ⓔ

22. In the context of the second paragraph, which of the following is the best version of the underlined portion of sentence 8 (reproduced below)?

    I jump at the chance to combine my talk-show knowledge with everything my father had taught me about sports.

    (A) (As it is now)
    (B) I jumped at the chance to combine
    (C) Having jumped at the chance to combine
    (D) Jumping at the chance and combining
    (E) Jumping at the chance by combining

23. Which of the following is the best way to revise and combine sentences 9 and 10 (reproduced below)?

    I sent in my self-addressed stamped envelope. I forgot about the whole matter.

    (A) Having sent in my self-addressed stamped envelope, the whole matter was forgotten.
    (B) After sending in my self-addressed stamped envelope, the matter was wholly forgotten.
    (C) After my self-addressed stamped envelope was sent in, it was then that I forgot the whole matter.
    (D) After sending in my self-addressed stamped envelope, I forgot about the whole matter.
    (E) Forgetting about the whole matter after sending in my self-addressed stamped envelope.

24. All of the following strategies are used by the writer of the passage EXCEPT

    (A) selecting specific examples
    (B) telling a story to develop a point
    (C) criticizing those whose opinions differ from hers
    (D) building suspense with references to the passage of time
    (E) disproving the assumption stated in the first sentence of the passage

    Ⓐ Ⓑ Ⓒ Ⓓ Ⓔ

Questions 25-29 are based on the following early draft of a letter to the editor of a local newspaper.

(1) *Our community needs more parks and play areas.* (2) *Living in a world where concrete surrounds us, it is important that we create places that are green and natural so that children can run and play.*

(3) *It is possible to do much with little expense to the city.* (4) *An abandoned lot can become a big patch of green grass ideal for running games.* (5) *And buying expensive playground equipment and strange pieces of modern art for children to climb on is unnecessary.* (6) *Children will climb on anything if one lets them.* (7) *A large concrete pipe or an old truck with its wheels and doors removed makes an imaginative plaything.* (8) *Simply remove any part that may be breakable or unsafe, then paint the equipment with bright colors.* (9) *Bury the truck or pipe a foot or two deep so that it is stable.* (10) *Great opportunities for fun!* (11) *Children can play for hours, crawling through a secret tunnel or navigating to a distant planet.* (12) *Neighborhood committees could contribute other discards.*

(13) *We should do these things because children need oases in this concrete desert we live in.* (14) *This may take time, but if people get together and contribute both ideas and labor, much can be completed successfully.*

25. Which of the following is the best way to revise the underlined portion of sentence 2 (reproduced below)?

    Living in a world where concrete surrounds us, it is important that we create places that are green and natural so that children can run and play.

    (A) Living in a world where concrete surrounds us, the important thing is to
    (B) We live in a world where concrete surrounds us, it is important that we
    (C) Being surrounded by a world of concrete, it is important to
    (D) Surrounding us with a world of concrete, we need to
    (E) Surrounded by a world of concrete, we need to

    (A) (B) (C) (D) (E)

26. Which of the following would best replace "And" at the beginning of sentence 5?

   (A) Furthermore,
   (B) Instead,
   (C) Despite this,
   (D) Nevertheless,
   (E) Excepting this,   Ⓐ Ⓑ Ⓒ Ⓓ Ⓔ

27. The writer of the passage could best improve sentence 12 by

   (A) acknowledging drawbacks to suggestions
   (B) providing specific examples
   (C) including personal opinions
   (D) discussing other community problems
   (E) defining the idea of a neighborhood   Ⓐ Ⓑ Ⓒ Ⓓ Ⓔ

28. In context, the best phrase to replace *do these things* in sentence 13 is

   (A) accomplish our intentions
   (B) help these children
   (C) consider other options
   (D) build these play areas
   (E) have new ideas   Ⓐ Ⓑ Ⓒ Ⓓ Ⓔ

29. Which is the best version of the underlined portion of sentence 14 (reproduced below)?

   This may take time, but if people get together and contribute both ideas and labor, much can be completed successfully.

   (A) (as it is now)
   (B) and if people get together and they contribute
   (C) but if people will get together and they will also contribute
   (D) but if people get together and they would have contributed
   (E) however, if people get together, also contributing

   Ⓐ Ⓑ Ⓒ Ⓓ Ⓔ

SECTION II

(The following types of questions appear only in the all-multiple-choice version, not in the version with Essay. Section II of the all-multiple-choice version also includes more of the "Identifying Sentence Errors" and "Revising Work in Progress" questions described previously.)

Restructuring Sentences

Directions: Effective revision requires choosing among the many options available to a writer. The following questions test your ability to use these options effectively.

Revise each of the sentences below according to the directions that follow it. Some directions require you to change only part of the original sentence; others require you to change the entire sentence. You may need to omit or add certain words in constructing an acceptable revision, but you should keep the meaning of your revised sentence as close to the meaning of the original sentence as the directions permit. Your new sentence should follow the conventions of standard written English and should be clear and concise.

Look through answer choices A-E under each question for the exact word or phrase that is included in your revised sentence and fill in the corresponding space on your answer sheet. If you have thought of a revision that does not include any of the words or phrases listed, try to revise the sentence again so that it does include the wording in one of the answer choices.

You may make notes in your test book, but be sure to mark your answers on the separate answer sheet.

Examples:

I.   **Sentence:** Owing to her political skill, Ms. French had many supporters.

     Directions: Begin with <u>Many people supported</u>.

     (A) so
     (B) while
     (C) although
     (D) because
     (E) and

Sample Answer

Ⓐ Ⓑ Ⓒ ● Ⓔ

Your rephrased sentence will probably read: "Many people supported Ms. French because she was politically skillful." This new sentence contains the correct answer: (D), "because." None of the other choices will fit into an effective, grammatically correct sentence that retains the original meaning.

_____

II. **Sentence:** Coming to the city as a young man, he found a job as a newspaper reporter.

     Directions: Change <u>Coming</u> to <u>He came</u>.

     (A) and so he found
     (B) and found
     (C) and there he had found
     (D) and then finding
     (E) and had found

Sample Answer

Ⓐ ● Ⓒ Ⓓ Ⓔ

Your rephrased sentence will probably read: "He came to the city as a young man and found a job as a newspaper reporter." This new sentence contains the correct answer: (B), "and found."

30. Should Antarctica's average temperature ever rise ten degrees, the oceans of the world would drown out all low-lying coastal regions.

Begin with If Antarctica's average temperature rises.

(A) should drown
(B) will drown
(C) will have drowned
(D) will result in the drowning
(E) drowning would be

Ⓐ Ⓑ Ⓒ Ⓓ Ⓔ

31. Ms. Perry claimed that, because of special promotions by the airline industry, air travel has become "as American as apple pie."

Change that, because to that special.

(A) industry, making
(B) industry, which has made
(C) industry had made
(D) industry have made
(E) industry, and they have made

Ⓐ Ⓑ Ⓒ Ⓓ Ⓔ

32. Luther Burbank's development of an edible pitless plum was accomplished by crossing a pitless plum tree many times with standard varieties of plum trees.

Begin with Luther Burbank.

(A) by many crossings
(B) frequent crossings
(C) by repeatedly crossing
(D) plum was crossed many times
(E) it was by repeated crossings

Ⓐ Ⓑ Ⓒ Ⓓ Ⓔ

33. Most people who run in marathons have little expectation of being among the first to finish.

Begin with Few people.

(A) lack expectation
(B) expect to be
(C) expect their being
(D) have no expectation
(E) have much to expect

Ⓐ Ⓑ Ⓒ Ⓓ Ⓔ

34. The new ideas that influenced several American painters were brought to the United States in the 1940's by artists who left Europe during the war.

Begin with The artists.

(A) and brought
(B) ideas have been brought
(C) war have brought
(D) thus bringing
(E) war brought

Ⓐ Ⓑ Ⓒ Ⓓ Ⓔ

35. Posters, buttons, and balloons were considered by many volunteers to be the most effective vote-getting devices.

Change were considered to considered.

(A) balloons in the light of
(B) balloons would be
(C) balloons that
(D) balloons the
(E) balloons being the most

Ⓐ Ⓑ Ⓒ Ⓓ Ⓔ

36. "My production of *Hamlet* will have only a shadow of the Ghost on stage, with a recorded tape and no actor," the director announced.

    Begin with The director announced that.

    (A) my *Hamlet* will have
    (B) her production of *Hamlet* had
    (C) her production of *Hamlet* would have
    (D) her production of *Hamlet* was
    (E) *Hamlet* were to have   Ⓐ Ⓑ Ⓒ Ⓓ Ⓔ

37. Madeline's seemingly innocuous announcement caused considerable consternation among her students.

    Change caused to but it caused.

    (A) announcement, and it seemed
    (B) announcement seemed
    (C) announcement which seemed
    (D) announcement, seemingly
    (E) announcement, despite seeming   Ⓐ Ⓑ Ⓒ Ⓓ Ⓔ

38. When we consider how technology encroaches on our daily life, we can understand why many works of modern art are strident and fragmented.

    Change we can understand to explains.

    Your new sentence will begin with which of the following?

    (A) Technology encroaching
    (B) On account of technology's encroaching
    (C) The fact of technology's encroachment
    (D) Due to the encroachment of technology
    (E) The encroachment of technology   Ⓐ Ⓑ Ⓒ Ⓓ Ⓔ

Analyzing Writing

Directions: Each of the following passages consists of numbered sentences. Because the passages are part of longer writing samples, they do not necessarily constitute a complete discussion of the issues presented.

Read each passage carefully and answer the questions that follow it. The questions test your awareness of a writer's purpose and of characteristics of prose that are important to good writing.

Questions 39-44 refer to the following paragraph.

(1) In Lovedu society, the individual was held to be inviolate. (2) The exercise of force of any kind, except in dealing with the very young infant, was never approved. (3) Even the courts of law refrained from executing their decisions, on the principle that to do so would be to coerce, and coercion should be avoided. (4) The parties involved in a case were expected to work out matters between them, aiming at a conciliatory solution and implementing the court decision through mutual agreement. (5) The culprit, if there was one, was left to pay restitution at his or her own pace. (6) Preferably, disputes were settled before they came to the point where they had to be submitted for a court decision. (7) If an individual wronged another, either deliberately or accidentally, it was the usual practice to send a conciliator to express regret and to offer a goat as a gesture of reconciliation. (8) This procedure was urged first of all, as the preferred solution, even when disagreements were brought to court. (9) Explicit condemnation was avoided as violating the individual, and as not leading to rehabilitation; punishment was seen as bad because it meant vengeful retribution.

39. Which of the following best describes the relationship of sentence 1 to the rest of the paragraph?

    (A) It establishes the organization for the paragraph as a whole.
    (B) It establishes the basis for comparisons later in the paragraph between one kind of society and another.
    (C) It demonstrates the writer's authority on the subject to be discussed in the paragraph.
    (D) It presents the principle on which the behavior described in the rest of the paragraph is based.
    (E) It describes the idea that will be refuted in the rest of the paragraph.

    Ⓐ Ⓑ Ⓒ Ⓓ Ⓔ

40. Which of the following best describes the function of sentence 4?

(A) It indicates the procedure by which the court's decisions were carried out.
(B) It demonstrates the laxness of the court in not executing its own decisions.
(C) It gives an example of what can happen when the courts do not exercise common sense.
(D) It alludes to the disorder that resulted from the court's decision.
(E) It forces the reader to make an independent judgment about the issues in the case.

Ⓐ Ⓑ Ⓒ Ⓓ Ⓔ

41. In sentence 5, the effect of using the expression "if there was one" is to

(A) reveal the writer's uncertainty about the details of the sequence of events
(B) emphasize the court decision mentioned in sentence 4 by referring back to it
(C) reinforce the idea that assigning blame was not always important in the view of justice under discussion
(D) suggest the carelessness inherent in this method of dealing with injustices
(E) prepare the reader for the statement about court decisions in sentence 6

Ⓐ Ⓑ Ⓒ Ⓓ Ⓔ

42. The function of sentence 7 is primarily to

(A) illustrate the ineffectiveness of informal methods of dealing with conflict
(B) present a specific incident that symbolizes the issues discussed in the paragraph
(C) give an example to support the generalization in sentence 5
(D) indicate the method by which the ideal described in sentence 6 would be realized
(E) prepare for the suggestion in sentence 8 that most disputes eventually ended up in court

Ⓐ Ⓑ Ⓒ Ⓓ Ⓔ

43. Which treatment of sentence 6 is most needed?

 (A) Leave it as it is.
 (B) It should be placed after sentence 7.
 (C) It should be omitted.
 (D) "Preferably" should be changed to "In any event".
 (E) "Preferably, disputes were settled" should be changed to "Disputes were thus settled".

44. The purpose of the paragraph is primarily to

 (A) tell the story of a society that is not well known
 (B) demonstrate the extremes of behavior arising from a specific idea
 (C) describe a particular system of social interactions
 (D) analyze the effects on society of dogmatic ideas
 (E) propose a change in methods of administering justice

Ⓐ Ⓑ Ⓒ Ⓓ Ⓔ

Questions 45-49 refer to the following passage.

(1) Michael Goldman wrote in a poem, "When the Muse comes She doesn't tell you to write;/She says get up for a minute, I've something to show you, stand here." (2) What made me look up at that roadside tree?

(3) The road to Grundy, Virginia, is, as you might expect, a narrow scrawl scribbled all over the most improbably peaked and hunched mountains you ever saw. (4) The few people who live along the road also seem peaked and hunched. (5) But what on earth . . . ? (6) It was hot, sunny summer. (7) The road was just bending off sharply to the right. (8) I hadn't seen a house in miles, and none was in sight. (9) At the apogee of the road's curve grew an enormous oak, a massive bur oak 200 years old, 150 feet high, an oak whose lowest limb was beyond the span of the highest ladder. (10) I looked up; there were clothes spread all over the tree. (11) Red shirts, blue trousers, black pants, little baby smocks — they weren't hung from branches. (12) They were outside, carefully spread, splayed as if to dry, on the outer leaves of the great oak's crown. (13) Were there pillowcases, blankets? (14) I can't remember. (15) There was a gay assortment of cotton underwear, yellow dresses, children's green sweaters, plaid skirts. . . . (16) You know roads. (17) A bend comes and you take it, thoughtlessly, moving on. (18) I looked behind me for another split second, astonished; both sides of the tree's canopy, clear to the top, bore clothes.

45. Which of the following best describes the relationship between the two paragraphs in this passage?

  (A) The second paragraph answers the question at the end of the first.
  (B) The second paragraph offers a concrete illustration of the quotation in the first.
  (C) The second paragraph takes an opposite point of view from the first.
  (D) The second paragraph generalizes about the quotation in the first.
  (E) The second paragraph is an elaborate contradiction of the thesis in the first.

  (A) (B) (C) (D) (E)

46. Which of the following most accurately describes what happens in the second paragraph?

  (A) The speaker has a poetic vision symbolizing cleansing renewal.
  (B) The speaker has a hallucination brought on by the heat.
  (C) The speaker tries to explain how what was seen is possible.
  (D) The speaker sees a tree full of flowers and imagines they are someone's washing.
  (E) The speaker sees a large tree inexplicably covered with clothes spread to dry.

  (A) (B) (C) (D) (E)

47. The descriptive details in sentences 9-15 provide a

  (A) precise visual image
  (B) picture of something unearthly
  (C) representation of a blur of color
  (D) view from a child's perspective
  (E) distorted sense of motion

  (A) (B) (C) (D) (E)

48. Which of the following pairs of words best describes the speaker's reaction to the experience?

  (A) Ecstasy and fear
  (B) Dismay and wonder
  (C) Delight and fear
  (D) Disgust and disbelief
  (E) Wonder and delight

  (A) (B) (C) (D) (E)

49. The main implication of the passage is that

    (A) you never know what you will see on country roads
    (B) people are resourceful in finding ways to rise above domestic tasks
    (C) inspiration or vision is often a matter of chance or caprice
    (D) the poet sees more intensely than other people
    (E) the Muse encourages only the eccentric to write

Sample Essays and Essay Topics

The section that follows includes directions as they appear in the test book, as well as a sample essay topic and three essays that were written in response to the topic. Although the papers written by candidates are actually rated on a scale from 8 to 2, the three essays presented here have been assigned one of only three ratings — high, middle, or low — to illustrate the scoring process in simplified form. Rating these three papers can give you a sense of the general quality of the papers and of the scoring process. You should read the essays and use the criteria described on pages 40-41 to assign a rating (high, middle, or low) to each one. Then compare these ratings with those given at the end of the essays.

    Following the three sample essays are two additional essay topics that may be used to practice writing essays.

Directions: You will have 45 minutes to plan and write an essay on the topic specified. Read the topic carefully. You are expected to spend a few moments considering the topic and organizing your thoughts before you begin writing. *Do not write on a topic other than the one specified. An essay on a topic of your own choice is not acceptable.*

    The essay is intended to give you an opportunity to demonstrate your ability to write effectively. Take care to express your thoughts on the topic clearly and to make them of interest to the reader. Be specific, using supporting examples whenever appropriate. Remember that how well you write is much more important than how much you write.

Sample Topic 1:

In describing the times of the French Revolution, Charles Dickens wrote: "It was the best of times, it was the worst of times." Think about how Dickens' description might apply to today's times. Write an essay in which you use specific examples to explain how today could be described as *both* the best of times and the worst of times.

Essay A

"It was the best of times, it was the worst of times." Charles Dickens wrote this phrase to describe the times of the French revolution. This concept not only applies to historic times, but also to the present.

It is true that we live in both the best and the worst of times even though there might possibly be a small number of people taking sides. People present arguments stating that we are in the best of times, better off than we have ever been. But again, there are those people on the opposite side saying we are not making any progress at all. What these people don't realize is that they are both correct in their opinions. Perhaps we are better off than two-hundred years ago but aren't making any progress to prove that point.

With each new day we discover more things and make more technological advances. These advances include such things as more powerful rockets, better agricultural methods, and cures for diseases once considered terminal. One very important improvement that these advances has caused is the increase in the number of opportunities open to both men and women. You can look all around and see the endless number of things women can and will accomplish in today's society. The advances in our technology have also resulted in better wages for workers, not to mention better jobs, and, also, safety and efficiency in the many commodities of our everyday lives.

The times of today can also be termed the worst of times because of the many problems we face. We have heard so often of a shortage of one thing or another. We seem to be running out of the things that are vital to our existence. A major problem today is unemployment. Technology has introduced us to the robot age; thus, putting many laborers out of work. Many old people who grew up in "the olden days" often remark on the morals of today's young people. Our parents and grandparents believe that children grew up properly when they were young because they had more discipline. This resulted not only in higher personal morals but also closer family bonds.

Today we live in a society where things are more efficient, safer, and much more convenient for our ease and comfort. In this aspect we exist in "the best of times"; but, perhaps, our struggle for improvement has also caused us to suffer the consequences. "It was the best of times, it was the worst of times."

Essay B

The media and other attitude-shapers would have us believe that disaster is at our doorstep, the youth of this country have little faith that they will reach middle age, and millions of people all over the world are sick and starving. The general social mood today is one of pessimism, and yet is this really the worst of times? As Dickens so wisely observed, hope and despair can co-exist: the close of the twentieth century, just like the close of the eighteenth century, can as easily be called "the best of times" as "the worst of times."

Clearly, the future of the U.S. looks bleak in comparison to its prosperous past. Most Americans lack faith in the very institutions that once formed the backbone of the nation: the family, the public school and government. While our tax dollars are funnelled into preparations for the most gruesome and permanent destruction ever conceived, millions of the world's people are suffering for lack of food and medicine. Moreso than in any other period in history, the disrepancy between the standards of living of the rich and poor are staggering, and each day the gap grows wider. The impending doom of nuclear war, and the more immediate threat of poverty and starvation for millions all over the world in order to fuel the vision of destruction, create an impression that this is the worst of all possible worlds.

However, the prospects for curing today's social ills are bright indeed, and the outcome of our collective nightmare may well be a united world dedicated to the health of the planet. In the breakdown of our institutions lies a change for a new order, and the types of organizations that replace the old in our lifetimes are likely to bring humanity to a greater achievement of our social values than have ever before been realized. The very technology that is currently being used for spoiling the rich and planning world disaster could just as easily serve all the world's people, to meet the basic human needs of health, food, and shelter for all. Our era is one of revolution and immense progress in science and technology: this is a promise that if used wisely and with humanity, technology may help to bring about "the best of times."

The creative solution to today's world-wide problems lies not just in technology, but in the shared responsibility for the future of our race and our planet. To make these "the best of times," it is our challenge to reverse the trends that threaten to destroy us. Increased participation by people united with this one purpose, all over the world, is a positive trend. The "best of times" are those in which all mankind sees the world as one, and every person becomes an active world citizen: creating "the best of times" is the greatest challenge of all times.

Essay C

Revolution means change and it can be in the best of time when it brings out the changes it needs.

In order to make a country great, the government must look to the social and economic upliftment of the people. Many people nowadays need jobs in order to get the necessary things in their life. If there will be a decrease in the percentage of unemployment, less problems will arise.

It is the best of time when everyone has a job, the elderly are taken care of, there is equal opportunity for every one, desegregation in school, no long lines in the social services, no big companies are closed and people are well-secured in their jobs.

Today could be the worst of time if many people could not have jobs. If the situation is like this, many people will have great problems. It is like in the French revolution when many people revolted against the government because they were discontented. They were discontented because they saw that only the upper class or the elite had the nice things in life.

Ratings by Evaluators:

Essay A — middle rating
Essay B — high rating
Essay C — low rating

Sample Topic 2:

The school board has proposed to alleviate a serious budget problem for next year by eliminating certain extracurricular activities. The board has proposed eliminating the marching band and football trips outside the immediate vicinity. Next year, in the event of continued tight budgets, the board will eliminate student newspapers and courses in drama, music, and art.

As a thoughtful and concerned citizen, write an essay setting forth your ideas on this subject. You may either support these budget cuts or oppose them. Draw upon your own educational experiences or those of your children, if you wish to do so. You need not know the details of school finance. For purposes of your essay you may invent some statistics and situations related to the school system that are appropriate to your argument.

Sample Topic 3:

Some people feel that studying "traditional" subjects such as history, sciences, and literature does not have much importance today. They believe that education should be directed toward a career and that the most significant studies in college are those that will help one earn a living in today's society. As examples, they point to accounting courses, secretarial studies, electronics courses, and data processing courses.

Write an essay in which you support or refute this argument for career-oriented education. Be sure to give reasons for your opinion and to support those reasons with specific examples from your reading or experience.

Study Resources

To become aware of the processes and the principles involved in presenting your ideas logically and expressing them clearly and effectively, you should practice writing. Ideally, you should try writing on a variety of subjects and issues, starting with those you know best and care about most. Ask someone you know and respect to respond to what you write and to help you discover which parts of your writing communicate effectively and which parts need revision to make the meaning clear. You should also try to read the works of published writers in a wide range of subjects, paying particular attention to the ways in which they use language to express their meaning.

Visit your local college bookstore to determine which textbooks, handbooks, and guides are used by the college for English composition courses. You would do well to consult two or three books because they vary in content, approach, and emphasis. When selecting a book, check the table of contents against the "Knowledge and Skills Required" section on pages 38-40. The Internet is another resource you could explore.

Humanities

Description of the Examination

The General Examination in Humanities tests general knowledge of literature, art, and music. It is broad in its coverage, with questions on all periods from classical to contemporary and in many different fields: poetry, prose, philosophy, history of art, music, dance, and theater. The exam requires candidates to demonstrate their understanding of the humanities through recollection of specific information, comprehension and application of concepts, and analysis and interpretation of various works of art.

Because the exam is very broad in its coverage, it is unlikely that any one person will be equally proficient in all the fields it covers. The exam is 90 minutes long and includes approximately 150 multiple-choice questions to be answered in two separately timed 45-minute sections.

For candidates with satisfactory scores on the Humanities exam, colleges may grant up to six semester hours (or the equivalent) of credit toward fulfillment of a distribution requirement. Some may grant credit for a particular course that matches the exam in content.

Knowledge and Skills Required

Questions on the test require candidates to demonstrate one or more of the following abilities.

- Knowledge of factual information such as names, works, etc. (about 50 percent of the exam)

- Recognition of techniques such as rhyme scheme, medium, and matters of style, and ability to identify them as characteristic of certain writers, artists, schools, or periods (about 30 percent of the exam)

- Understanding and interpretation of literary passages and art works (provided in reproductions) that most candidates probably will not have seen before (about 20 percent of the exam)

The subject matter of the General Examination in Humanities is drawn from the following topics.

Approximate Percent of Examination

Fine Arts (50%)

25%	Visual arts (painting, sculpture, etc.)
15%	Music
5%	Performing arts (film, dance, etc.)
5%	Architecture

Literature (50%)

5-10%	Drama
15-20%	Poetry
10-15%	Fiction
5-10%	Nonfiction
5%	Philosophy

The exam questions, drawn from the entire history of Western art and culture, are fairly evenly divided among the following periods: Classical, Medieval and Renaissance, seventeenth and eighteenth centuries, nineteenth century, and twentieth century. In addition, there are questions that draw on non-Western cultures, such as those of Africa and Asia. Some of the questions cross disciplines and/or chronological periods, and a substantial number test knowledge of terminology, genre, and style.

Sample Questions

The 25 sample questions that follow are similar to questions on the Humanities exam, but they do not appear on the actual exam. Four examples (followed by answers and explanations) are provided first to give you an idea of the types of questions that appear in the Humanities exam.

Before attempting to answer the sample questions, read all the information about the Humanities exam on the preceding pages. Additional suggestions for preparing for CLEP exams are provided in Chapter 4.

Try to answer correctly as many questions as possible. Then compare your answers with the correct answers, given in Appendix A.

EXAMPLE 1

The following lines are from a poem by Elizabeth Barrett Browning that you would not be expected to have read before. In fact, it was chosen because it is not likely to be familiar to you already. The questions that accompany such a passage are designed to examine your ability to analyze and interpret.

> I tell you, hopeless grief is passionless;
> That only men incredulous of despair,
> Half-taught in anguish, through the midnight air
> Beat upward to God's throne in loud access
> Of shrieking and reproach.

In the context of the lines quoted above, "passionless" (line 1) means

(A) reasonable   (B) practical and efficient
    (C) numb and still   (D) uncaring and untouched
        (E) able to find release

Ⓐ Ⓑ Ⓒ Ⓓ Ⓔ

Explanation and Answer

This question concerns the basic point of the passage. It focuses on the word *passionless*, which is central to the meaning of the lines. Normally, one describes grief as a state of extreme emotion; the point Browning makes is that hopeless grief has gone beyond despair. It is without passion; the emotions are frozen. The correct answer, therefore, is (C) *numb and still.*

The hasty reader may choose (A) *reasonable* because of the familiar contrast between reason and emotion (passion), or (B) *practical and efficient* because these descriptions are typical contrasts with the word *passionate.* In both instances, the reader would be somewhat careless; he or she would not be considering the special meaning Browning chose for the word in the context of the lines. Without careful examination, *passionless* might suggest that the person who grieves is simply without emotion, *uncaring and untouched,* and that (D) is then the answer. Or, the reader might assume that, if passionless, a person is (E) *able to find release.* Again, both (D) and (E) miss the central point and are not logical in terms of the rest of the passage.

In this question, you are asked to deal with an idea about grief that is somewhat unusual. If you read inattentively or have a preconception about poetry that leads you to expect all poems to be optimistic or soothing, you may be misled. Answering the question correctly, however, demonstrates your ability to deal with poetic language.

EXAMPLES 2 AND 3

Test questions on passages may also deal with such matters as rhyme scheme, poetic devices, and matters of style. If the style or ideas expressed are particularly distinctive and representative, you may be asked to identify the author. The questions below ask you to apply what you know to two lines of poetry.

>   Nature and Nature's laws lay hid in night;
>   God said, Let Newton be! and all was light.

The lines above were written by

(A) Geoffrey Chaucer   (B) Alexander Pope
(C) William Blake   (D) Robert Frost
(E) Emily Dickinson   Ⓐ Ⓑ Ⓒ Ⓓ Ⓔ

Which of the following describes the lines above?

(A) Blank verse   (B) Free verse   (C) A triolet
(D) A couplet   (E) A quatrain   Ⓐ Ⓑ Ⓒ Ⓓ Ⓔ

Explanation and Answers

The quotation is a typical example of its period, and you should be able to use both form and content in answering the first question. [The correct answer is (B).] For the second question, you must apply your knowledge of poetic forms. [The correct answer is (D).] In the same way, you may be asked to identify the style of a building or a painting or to recognize or interpret its subject matter.

EXAMPLE 4

Another type of test question asks you to relate the content of one work of art to another work of art. In the following question, for example, you are asked about the style and subject of a work by the twentieth-century painter Lois Mailou Jones.

The National Museum of American Art, Smithsonian Institution, Purchase made possible by Mrs. N.H. Green, Dr. R. Harlan, and Francis Musgrave.

The painting above has been influenced most strongly by which of the following?

(A) Japanese prints   (B) Native American blankets

(C) Assyrian sculpture   (D) Gothic gargoyles

(E) African masks

Ⓐ Ⓑ Ⓒ Ⓓ Ⓔ

Explanation and Answer

To answer this question correctly, you must look at the picture carefully, note the principal features of its style, and connect that style to another kind of art. The painting features a mask-like shape in which the elements of the human face are highly abstracted to almost purely geometric forms.

Japanese prints, choice (A), use abstraction but not in the way seen in the face here. Some Japanese prints of the eighteenth century, for example, use bold lines and decorative patterns to create a tension between the representation of space and the use of two-dimensional patterns. Native American blankets, choice (B), such as some from the Pacific Northwest made by the Tlingit people, sometimes feature abstract portrayals of faces. However, these faces are often represented in a two-dimensional manner, again focusing on line rather than on three-dimensional shapes. Assyrian sculpture, choice (C), often uses monumental sculpted figures of human heads with animal bodies, a combination not seen in this mask-like representation. Gothic gargoyles, choice (D), are grotesque, sculpted, animal-like figures that were incorporated in the architecture of Gothic cathedrals. In contrast to the work shown here, they did not depict human figures. African masks, choice (E), the correct choice, are often similar to the mask-like image seen in this painting. Masks from the Dan people of Liberia, for example, frequently emphasize abstraction of human features, as well as symmetry of design and sharpness of carving. African art exerted a strong influence on Cubist art of the early twentieth century. In this work of 1938, an African American artist interprets an African tradition.

Now, try to answer correctly as many of the following questions as possible. Then compare your answers with the correct answers, in Appendix A.

Directions: Each of the questions or incomplete statements below is followed by five suggested answers or completions. Select the one that is best in each case.

1. Often read as a children's classic, it is in reality a scathing indictment of human meanness and greed. In its four books, the Lilliputians are deranged, the Yahoos obscene.

   The passage above discusses

   (A) *Tom Jones*
   (B) *David Copperfield*
   (C) *The Pilgrim's Progress*
   (D) *Gulliver's Travels*
   (E) *Alice in Wonderland*   Ⓐ Ⓑ Ⓒ Ⓓ Ⓔ

2. Which of the following deals with the bigotry an anguished Black family faces when it attempts to move into an all-White suburb?

   (A) O'Neill's *Desire Under the Elms*
   (B) Miller's *Death of a Salesman*
   (C) Baraka's *Dutchman*
   (D) Albee's *Who's Afraid of Virginia Woolf?*
   (E) Hansberry's *A Raisin in the Sun*   Ⓐ Ⓑ Ⓒ Ⓓ Ⓔ

3. Which of the following has as its central theme the idea that wars are mass insanity and that armies are madhouses?

   (A) *Song of Solomon*
   (B) *Portnoy's Complaint*
   (C) *Catch-22*
   (D) *The Invisible Man*
   (E) *The Color Purple*   Ⓐ Ⓑ Ⓒ Ⓓ Ⓔ

4. Which of the following is often a symbol of new life arising from death?

   (A) A gorgon
   (B) The minotaur
   (C) A unicorn
   (D) A griffin
   (E) The phoenix   Ⓐ Ⓑ Ⓒ Ⓓ Ⓔ

5. The lute is most similar to the modern

   (A) guitar
   (B) piano
   (C) violin
   (D) accordion
   (E) flute   Ⓐ Ⓑ Ⓒ Ⓓ Ⓔ

6. The troubadours of the Middle Ages are best described as

   (A) poet-musicians
   (B) moralistic orators
   (C) free-lance illustrators
   (D) character actors
   (E) religious philosophers   Ⓐ Ⓑ Ⓒ Ⓓ Ⓔ

Questions 7-9 refer to illustrations (A) through (E).

(A)

(B)

(C)

(D)

(E)

The Metropolitan Museum of Art, gift of Thomas F. Ryan, 1910.

7. Which is a bas-relief? Ⓐ Ⓑ Ⓒ Ⓓ Ⓔ

8. Which is by Rodin? Ⓐ Ⓑ Ⓒ Ⓓ Ⓔ

9. Which is Mayan? Ⓐ Ⓑ Ⓒ Ⓓ Ⓔ

Questions 10-12 refer to the following lines.

(A) "Where the bee sucks there suck I:
   In a cowslip's bell I lie . . ."

(B) "Exult O shores, and ring O bells!
   But I with mournful tread,
   Walk the deck my Captain lies,
   Fallen cold and dead."

(C) "Ring out, wild bells, to the wild sky."

(D) "Oh, what a noble mind is here o'erthrown!
   . . . I now see that noble and most sovereign reason,
   Like sweet bells jangled, out of tune and harsh, . . . "

(E) "Oh, the bells, bells, bells!
   What a tale their terror tells
      Of Despair!
   . . . Yet the ear, it fully knows.
      By the twanging,
      And the clanging, . . .
      In the jangling,
      And the wrangling . . ."

10. Which excerpt contains several
    examples of onomatopoeia?   Ⓐ Ⓑ Ⓒ Ⓓ Ⓔ

11. Which is from *Hamlet*?   Ⓐ Ⓑ Ⓒ Ⓓ Ⓔ

12. Which alludes to Abraham Lincoln's death?   Ⓐ Ⓑ Ⓒ Ⓓ Ⓔ

Questions 13-15 refer to the following.

13. The work pictured above is

   (A) a fresco
   (B) a stabile
   (C) a woodcut
   (D) an illumination
   (E) an etching   Ⓐ Ⓑ Ⓒ Ⓓ Ⓔ

14. The theme of the work is the

   (A) sacrifice of Isaac
   (B) expulsion from Eden
   (C) reincarnation of Vishnu
   (D) creation of Adam
   (E) flight of Icarus   Ⓐ Ⓑ Ⓒ Ⓓ Ⓔ

15. The work is located in the

   (A) Alhambra
   (B) Sistine Chapel
   (C) Parthenon
   (D) palace at Versailles
   (E) Cathedral of Notre Dame   Ⓐ Ⓑ Ⓒ Ⓓ Ⓔ

Questions 16-17 refer to the following descriptions of the stage settings of plays.

(A) The exterior of a two-story corner building on a street in New Orleans which is named Elysian Fields and runs between the L & N tracks and the river

(B) The living room of Mr. Vandergelder's house, over his hay, feed, and provision store in Yonkers, fifteen miles north of New York City

(C) In, and immediately outside of, the Cabot farmhouse in New England, in the year 1850

(D) The stage of a theater; daytime

(E) A room that is still called the nursery. . . . It is May, the cherry trees are in blossom, but in the orchard it is cold, with a morning frost.

16. Which is for a play by Tennessee Williams? Ⓐ Ⓑ Ⓒ Ⓓ Ⓔ

17. Which is for a play by Anton Chekhov? Ⓐ Ⓑ Ⓒ Ⓓ Ⓔ

Questions 18-20 refer to the following groups of people.

(A) George Balanchine, Agnes de Mille, Martha Graham

(B) John Cage, Aaron Copland, Paul Hindemith

(C) Spike Lee, Robert Altman, Federico Fellini

(D) Allen Ginsberg, Gwendolyn Brooks, Sylvia Plath

(E) I. M. Pei, Philip Johnson, Frank Lloyd Wright

18. Which is a group of architects? Ⓐ Ⓑ Ⓒ Ⓓ Ⓔ

19. Which is a group of choreographers? Ⓐ Ⓑ Ⓒ Ⓓ Ⓔ

20. Which is a group of twentieth-century poets? Ⓐ Ⓑ Ⓒ Ⓓ Ⓔ

21. He believed that tragedy effects the proper purgation of those emotions of pity and fear that it has aroused.

    The author and concept referred to in the sentence above are

    (A) Plato..*hubris* (B) Leibniz..monad
      (C) Aristotle..catharsis (D) Locke..*tabula rasa*
        (E) Kant..the categorical imperative

    Ⓐ Ⓑ Ⓒ Ⓓ Ⓔ

22. Which of the following composers was Picasso's closest musical contemporary?

    (A) Monteverdi (B) Josquin des Prez (C) Chopin
      (D) Stravinsky (E) Beethoven

    Ⓐ Ⓑ Ⓒ Ⓓ Ⓔ

23. Which of the following satirizes the eighteenth-century doctrine "whatever is, is right" in this "best of all possible worlds"?

    (A) Brontë's *Wuthering Heights*
    (B) Voltaire's *Candide*
    (C) Defoe's *Moll Flanders*
    (D) Hugo's *Les Misérables*
    (E) Hawthorne's *The Scarlet Letter*

    Ⓐ Ⓑ Ⓒ Ⓓ Ⓔ

24. Haiku is a form of Japanese

    (A) drama (B) poetry (C) pottery
      (D) sculpture (E) architecture

    Ⓐ Ⓑ Ⓒ Ⓓ Ⓔ

25. The terms "pas de deux," "plié," "tendu," and "glissade" are primarily associated with

    (A) ballet (B) string quartets (C) painting
      (D) theater (E) opera

    Ⓐ Ⓑ Ⓒ Ⓓ Ⓔ

Study Resources

To do well on the Humanities exam, you should know something about each of the forms of literature and fine arts from the various periods and cultures listed earlier, in the paragraph following the examination percentages. No single book covers all these areas, so it will be necessary for you to refer to college textbooks, supplementary reading, and references for introductory courses in literature and fine arts at the college level. You can find these books in most college bookstores.

In addition to reading, a lively interest in the arts — going to museums and concerts, attending plays, seeing motion pictures, watching public television programs such as "Great Performances" and "Masterpiece Theatre," and listening to radio stations that play classical music and feature discussions of the arts — constitutes excellent preparation. The Internet is another resource you could explore.

Additional suggestions for preparing for CLEP exams are provided in Chapter 4.

College Mathematics

Description of the Examination

The CLEP College Mathematics exam was developed to cover material generally taught in a college course for non-mathematics majors and majors in other fields not requiring a knowledge of advanced mathematics. Nearly half of the exam requires the candidate to solve routine straightforward problems; the remainder involves solving nonroutine problems in which candidates must demonstrate their understanding of concepts. The exam includes questions on logic and sets, the real number system, functions and their graphs, probability and statistics, and topics from algebra. Familiarity with certain symbolism and notation as illustrated by the sample questions is assumed. The exam places little emphasis on arithmetic calculations, and it does not contain any questions that require the use of a calculator. However, the use of a scientific calculator (non-graphing, non-programmable) is permitted during the exam.

The exam contains approximately 65 multiple-choice questions to be answered in two separately timed 45-minute sections.

Some colleges grant credit for, or exemption from, a specific required mathematics course that covers material similar to that contained in this exam; others may grant up to six semester hours (or the equivalent) of general credit toward fulfillment of a liberal arts or distribution requirement in mathematics.

Knowledge and Skills Required

Within the subject-matter content described, questions on the exam require candidates to demonstrate the following abilities in the approximate proportions indicated.

- Solving routine, straightforward problems (about 50 percent of the exam)

- Solving nonroutine problems requiring an understanding of concepts and the application of skills and concepts (about 50 percent of the exam)

The subject matter of the College Mathematics exam is drawn from the following topics.

	Approximate Percent of Examination
10%	Sets
	Union and intersection
	Subsets
	Venn diagrams
	Cartesian product
10%	Logic
	Truth tables
	Conjunctions, disjunctions, implications, and negations
	Conditional statements
	Necessary and sufficient conditions
	Converse, inverse, and contrapositive
	Hypotheses, conclusions, and counterexamples
20%	Real Number System
	Prime and composite numbers
	Odd and even numbers
	Factors and divisibility
	Rational and irrational numbers
	Absolute value and order
	Binary number system
20%	Functions and Their Graphs
	Domain and range
	Linear, polynomial, and composite functions
25%	Probability and Statistics
	Counting problems, including permutations and combinations
	Computation of probabilities of simple and compound events
	Simple conditional probability
	The mean and median
15%	Additional Algebra Topics
	Complex numbers
	Logarithms and exponentials
	Applications

Sample Questions

The following questions are provided to give an indication of the types of items that appear on the College Mathematics exam. CLEP exams are designed so that average students who have completed distribution requirements in this area can usually answer about half the questions correctly.

Before attempting to answer the sample questions, read all the information about the College Mathematics exam on the preceding pages. Additional suggestions for preparing for CLEP exams are provided in Chapter 4.

Try to answer correctly as many questions as possible. Then compare your answers with the correct answers, given in Appendix A.

Directions: For each of the following problems, choose the best answer for each question.

Notes:

(1) Unless otherwise specified, the domain of any function f is assumed to be the set of all real numbers x for which $f(x)$ is a real number.

(2) i will be used to denote $\sqrt{-1}$.

(3) Figures that accompany the following problems are intended to provide information useful in solving the problems. They are drawn as accurately as possible EXCEPT when it is stated in a specific problem that its figure is not drawn to scale. All figures lie in a plane unless otherwise indicated.

1. If $R = \{x : x > 0\}$ and $S = \{x : x < 3\}$, what is the number of integers in $R \cap S$?

   (A) None (B) Two (C) Three (D) Four   Ⓐ Ⓑ Ⓒ Ⓓ

2. Which of the following is an irrational number?

   (A) $\sqrt{36}$ (B) $\sqrt{14}$ (C) $\dfrac{2}{\sqrt{9}}$ (D) $\sqrt[3]{-8}$ Ⓐ Ⓑ Ⓒ Ⓓ

3. What is the remainder when $x^3 + 5x^2 - 6x + 10$ is divided by $x + 3$?

   (A) 7 (B) 10 (C) 46 (D) 64   Ⓐ Ⓑ Ⓒ Ⓓ

4. If $g(x) = x^3 - 1$, then $g(-2) =$

   (A) 5 (B) -3 (C) -7 (D) -9 Ⓐ Ⓑ Ⓒ Ⓓ

5. Which of the following is a Venn diagram of $A \cap (B \cup C)$?

Ⓐ Ⓑ Ⓒ Ⓓ

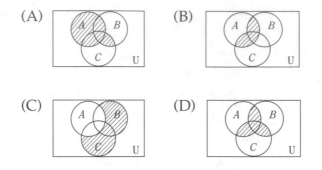

(A)   (B)

(C)   (D)

6. A student asserted that $n^2 \geqq n$ for all real numbers. Of the following, which is a value of n that provides a counterexample to the student's claim?

(A) $-\dfrac{1}{2}$ (B) 0   (C) $\dfrac{1}{2}$ (D) 2

Ⓐ Ⓑ Ⓒ Ⓓ

7. If m is an odd integer, which of the following is an even integer?

(A) $2m - 1$ (B) $2m + 1$ (C) $m^2 - m$ (D) $m^2 + m + 1$

Ⓐ Ⓑ Ⓒ Ⓓ

8. If $f(x) = 4x^2 + 5$ and $g(x) = 2^x$, then $f(g(-1)) =$

(A) $\dfrac{1}{2}$ (B) 6   (C) 9   (D) 21

Ⓐ Ⓑ Ⓒ Ⓓ

9. If x and y are nonzero integers, which of the following is necessarily an integer?

(A) $x + \dfrac{y}{x}$ (B) $\dfrac{x + y^2}{x}$

(C) $\dfrac{x^2 + xy}{x}$ (D) $\dfrac{x^2 + y^2}{x}$

Ⓐ Ⓑ Ⓒ Ⓓ

10. A drawer contains exactly 5 red, 4 blue, and 3 green pencils. If two pencils are selected at random one after the other without replacing the first, what is the probability that the first one is red and the second one is green?

(A) $\dfrac{5}{44}$ (B) $\dfrac{5}{48}$ (C) $\dfrac{91}{132}$ (D) $\dfrac{2}{3}$

Ⓐ Ⓑ Ⓒ Ⓓ

11. If f is a linear function such that $f(-1) = 3$, and $f(5) = 15$, then $f(2) =$

   (A) 6   (B) 8   (C) 9   (D) 12   Ⓐ Ⓑ Ⓒ Ⓓ

12. If $i = \sqrt{-1}$, then $i + i^2 + i^3 + i^4 =$

   (A) $-i$ (B) i (C) -1 (D) 0   Ⓐ Ⓑ Ⓒ Ⓓ

13. A fair coin is tossed and a fair die is rolled. What is the probability that the coin will fall heads up and the top face of the die will show 3 or 5?

   (A) $\dfrac{1}{12}$ (B) $\dfrac{1}{6}$ (C) $\dfrac{1}{3}$ (D) $\dfrac{5}{6}$ Ⓐ Ⓑ Ⓒ Ⓓ

14. The difference between the mean and the median of the numbers 27, 27, 29, 32, and 35 is

   (A) 0   (B) 1   (C) 3   (D) 8   Ⓐ Ⓑ Ⓒ Ⓓ

15. In base two, the next whole number greater than 10101 is

   (A) 101011   (B) 10110   (C) 10111   (D) 10102   Ⓐ Ⓑ Ⓒ Ⓓ

16. If $\log_b x = 6$ and $\log_b y = 2$, then $\log_b \left(\dfrac{x^2}{y} \right) =$

   (A) 4   (B) 8   (C) 10   (D) 18   Ⓐ Ⓑ Ⓒ Ⓓ

17. A poetry club has 18 members consisting of 8 men and 10 women. How many different slates of a three member steering committee can be formed for the club if there must be at least one man and one woman on the steering committee?

   (A) 640   (B) 720   (C) 1,280   (D) 4,896   Ⓐ Ⓑ Ⓒ Ⓓ

18. One root of $x^2 + x + 1 = 0$ is

   (A) $-\dfrac{1}{2}$ (B) $\dfrac{i\sqrt{3}}{2}$

   (C) $\dfrac{1}{2} - \dfrac{i\sqrt{3}}{2}$ (D) $-\dfrac{1}{2} + \dfrac{i\sqrt{3}}{2}$ Ⓐ Ⓑ Ⓒ Ⓓ

19. "If not S, then not R" is logically equivalent to which of the following?

    (A) If S, then R.
    (B) If R, then S.
    (C) If not R, then not S.
    (D) If not R, then S.

    Ⓐ Ⓑ Ⓒ Ⓓ

20. If $8^x = 15$ and $8^y = 25$, then $8^{(2x + y)} =$

    (A) 55   (B) 80   (C) 250   (D) 5,625

    Ⓐ Ⓑ Ⓒ Ⓓ

Study Resources

To prepare for the College Mathematics exam, students should read and study a variety of introductory college level mathematics textbooks. Elementary algebra textbooks cover many of the topics on the Mathematics exam. Students should visit their local college bookstore to determine which textbooks are used by the college for mathematics courses. When selecting a textbook, students should check the table of contents against the "Knowledge and Skills Required" section on pages 81-82.

Additional suggestions for preparing for CLEP exams are provided in Chapter 4.

Natural Sciences

Description of the Examination

The CLEP General Examination in Natural Sciences covers a wide range of topics frequently taught in introductory courses surveying both biological and physical sciences at the freshman or sophomore level. Such courses generally satisfy distribution or general education requirements. The Natural Sciences exam is not intended for those specializing in science; it is intended to test the understanding of scientific concepts that an adult with a liberal arts education should have. The exam does not stress the retention of factual details; rather, it emphasizes the knowledge and application of the basic principles and concepts of science, the comprehension of scientific information, and the understanding of issues of science in contemporary society.

The primary objective of the exam is to give candidates the opportunity to demonstrate a level of knowledge and understanding expected of college students meeting a distribution or general education requirement in the natural sciences. Colleges may grant up to six semester hours (or the equivalent) of credit toward fulfillment of such a requirement, for satisfactory scores on the exam. Some may grant specific course credit, on the basis of the total score for a two-semester survey course covering both biological and physical sciences.

The test contains 120 multiple-choice questions to be answered in two separately timed 45-minute sections, one covering biological science, the other physical science.

Knowledge and Skills Required

Questions on the exam require candidates to demonstrate one or more of the following abilities.

- Knowledge of fundamental facts, concepts, and principles (about 40 percent of the exam).

- Interpretation and comprehension of information (about 20 percent of the exam), presented in the form of graphs, diagrams, tables, equations, or verbal passages.

- Qualitative and quantitative application of scientific principles (about 40 percent of the exam), including applications based on material presented in the form of graphs, diagrams, tables, equations, or verbal passages. More emphasis is given to qualitative than quantitative applications.

The subject matter of the General Examination in Natural Sciences is drawn from the following topics.

Approximate Percent of Examination

Biological Science (50%)

10%	Origin and evolution of life, classification of organisms
10%	Cell organization, cell division, chemical nature of the gene, bioenergetics, biosynthesis
20%	Structure, function, and development in organisms; patterns of heredity
10%	Concepts of population biology with emphasis on ecology

Physical Science (50%)

7%	Atomic and nuclear structure and properties, elementary particles, nuclear reactions
10%	Chemical elements, compounds and reactions; molecular structure and bonding
12%	Heat, thermodynamics, and states of matter; classical mechanics; relativity
4%	Electricity and magnetism, waves, light and sound
7%	The universe: galaxies, stars, the solar system
10%	The Earth: atmosphere, hydrosphere, structure, properties, surface features, geological processes, history

The exam includes some questions that are interdisciplinary and cannot be classified in one of the above categories. Some of the questions on the exam cover topics that overlap with those listed above, drawing on areas such as history and philosophy of science, scientific methods, science applications and technology, and the relationship of science to contemporary problems of society, such as environmental pollution and depletion of energy supply. Some questions on the exam are laboratory oriented.

Sample Questions

The following questions are provided to give an indication of the types of items that appear on the General Examination in Natural Sciences.

Before attempting to answer the sample questions, read all the information about the Natural Sciences exam on the preceding pages. Additional suggestions for preparing for CLEP exams are provided in Chapter 4.

Try to answer correctly as many questions as possible. Then compare your answers with the correct answers, given in Appendix A.

Directions: Each group of questions below consists of five lettered choices followed by a list of numbered phrases or sentences. For each numbered phrase or sentence select the one choice that is most closely related to it. Each choice may be used once, more than once, or not at all in each group.

Questions 1-2

    (A) Cell wall
    (B) Cell membrane
    (C) Nucleus
    (D) Mitochondrion
    (E) Ribosome

1. The chief site of energy production in the cell   Ⓐ Ⓑ Ⓒ Ⓓ Ⓔ

2. The site of protein synthesis in the cell   Ⓐ Ⓑ Ⓒ Ⓓ Ⓔ

Questions 3-5

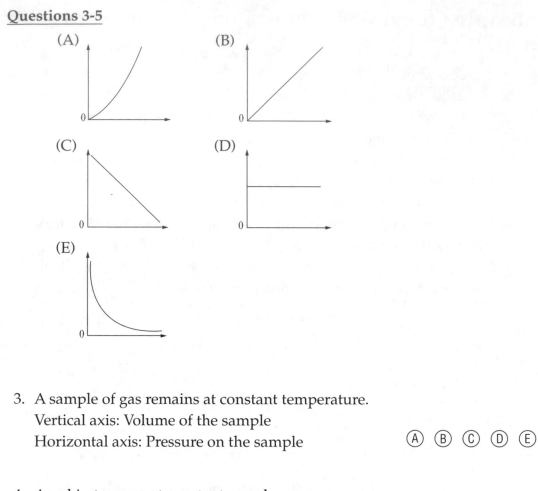

3. A sample of gas remains at constant temperature.
   Vertical axis: Volume of the sample
   Horizontal axis: Pressure on the sample   Ⓐ Ⓑ Ⓒ Ⓓ Ⓔ

4. An object moves at constant speed.
   Vertical axis: Distance traveled since time t = 0
   Horizontal axis: Time   Ⓐ Ⓑ Ⓒ Ⓓ Ⓔ

5. A constant unbalanced force acts on an object.
   Vertical axis: Acceleration of the object
   Horizontal axis: Time   Ⓐ Ⓑ Ⓒ Ⓓ Ⓔ

Directions: Each of the questions or incomplete statements below is followed by five suggested answers or completions. Select the one that is best in each case.

6. As a direct result of photosynthesis, energy is stored in molecules of which of the following?

   (A) RNA   (B) DNA   (C) glucose
   (D) H_2O (E) CO_2 Ⓐ Ⓑ Ⓒ Ⓓ Ⓔ

7. A person whose gallbladder has been removed has a decreased ability to store bile and therefore to digest

(A) fats   (B) starches   (C) sugars
(D) proteins   (E) vitamins

Ⓐ Ⓑ Ⓒ Ⓓ Ⓔ

Questions 8-9

In fruit flies, "straight wings" (S) is dominant over "curly wings" (s), and gray body color (G) is dominant over black body color (g). A straight-winged female with gray body color was mated with a straight-winged male with black body color and the following ratios of offspring resulted. The experiment was conducted at 25°C.

Ratio	Phenotype
3/8	straight-winged; gray body color
3/8	straight-winged; black body color
1/8	curly-winged; gray body color
1/8	curly-winged; black body color

8. The data above suggest that the genotype of the male parent is

(A) SsGg   (B) SSGg   (C) ssgg
(D) Ssgg   (E) ssGg

Ⓐ Ⓑ Ⓒ Ⓓ Ⓔ

9. The data above suggest that the genotype of the offspring with curly wings and black body color is

(A) SsGg   (B) SSGg   (C) ssgg
(D) Ssgg   (E) ssGg

Ⓐ Ⓑ Ⓒ Ⓓ Ⓔ

10. The classification characteristics that define the genus of an animal or a plant are usually more general than those defining

(A) a class   (B) an order   (C) a species
(D) a family   (E) a phylum

Ⓐ Ⓑ Ⓒ Ⓓ Ⓔ

11. Which of the following adaptations is more likely to be found in the leaves of desert plants than in those of plants that grow in moist regions?

(A) Stomata mostly on upper leaf surface
(B) A thin, transparent cuticle
(C) A smooth leaf surface free of hairs
(D) A thickened epidermis and cuticle
(E) A loosely packed mesophyll layer   Ⓐ Ⓑ Ⓒ Ⓓ Ⓔ

12. In embryonic origin, nerve cells are most similar to

(A) epidermal cells
(B) bone cells
(C) red blood cells
(D) liver cells
(E) reproductive cells   Ⓐ Ⓑ Ⓒ Ⓓ Ⓔ

13. Which of the following best completes the statement below?

"Among multicellular animals, the insects exhibit the greatest diversity of life-forms; therefore _____."

(A) the total number of insect species is limited
(B) the presence of wings on an insect is probably an evolutionary error
(C) insects probably occupy the greatest number of niches
(D) insect control by human beings is simplified
(E) any genetic mutation in fruit flies is likely to escape detection   Ⓐ Ⓑ Ⓒ Ⓓ Ⓔ

14. A father will transmit the genes of his Y chromosome to

(A) one-half of his sons only
(B) one-half of his daughters only
(C) all of his sons only
(D) all of his daughters only
(E) none of his sons   Ⓐ Ⓑ Ⓒ Ⓓ Ⓔ

15. A theory fails to meet the criteria of scientific methodology if

   (A) it is unpopular
   (B) it contradicts other theories
   (C) it has not been conclusively proved
   (D) it has not been stated in mathematical terms
   (E) no experiments can be designed to test it

   (A) (B) (C) (D) (E)

16. Dark lines in the Sun's spectrum are explained as resulting from

   (A) emission of radiation of certain frequencies from the Sun's
       atmosphere
   (B) absorption of energy by atoms in the outer layers of the Sun
   (C) radiation of ultraviolet light from sunspots
   (D) continuous radiation from the corona
   (E) x-rays emanating from the Sun's atmosphere

   (A) (B) (C) (D) (E)

17. Which of the following best describes the principal way in which the
    Earth's atmosphere is heated?

   (A) Heat flows from the center of the Earth and is conducted through the
       ground to the air.
   (B) The atmosphere absorbs short-wave radiation from the Sun as the
       Sun's rays pass through it.
   (C) The Earth absorbs short-wave radiation from the Sun and reradiates
       long-wave radiation which is absorbed by the atmosphere.
   (D) The air absorbs short-wave radiation from the Sun after it has been
       reflected by the clouds.
   (E) Warm air rises and cold air sinks and, as it sinks, it is warmed
       by compression.

   (A) (B) (C) (D) (E)

18. Which of the following natural resources is NOT a fossil fuel?

    (A) Uranium   (B) Natural gas   (C) Petroleum
        (D) Anthracite   (E) Bituminous coal   Ⓐ Ⓑ Ⓒ Ⓓ Ⓔ

19. The half-life of $^{14}_{6}C$ is 5,600 years. Which of the following statements about a 10-gram sample of $^{14}_{6}C$ is correct?

    (A) The radioactive decay of the sample will be complete after 5,600 years.
    (B) The $^{14}_{6}C$ sample will start radioactive decay after 5,600 years.
    (C) A time of 5,600 years has been required to produce this sample of $^{14}_{6}C$ in nature.
    (D) After 5,600 years the sample will contain only 5 grams of $^{14}_{6}C$.
    (E) After 11,200 years the sample will not contain any $^{14}_{6}C$.

                                                    Ⓐ Ⓑ Ⓒ Ⓓ Ⓔ

20. Of the following planets that are visible with the naked eye (Venus, Mars, Jupiter, Saturn), only Venus has an orbit smaller than that of Earth. This means that Venus

    (A) is seen only in the morning or the evening sky
    (B) can be seen in the sky near midnight more often than at other times
    (C) can rarely be seen at all
    (D) has an orbit that is more elliptical than that of the Earth
    (E) has a longer year than the Earth

                                                    Ⓐ Ⓑ Ⓒ Ⓓ Ⓔ

21. An unsorted mixture of clay, boulders, sand, and silt would most likely be deposited from which of the following?

    (A) Glacial ice   (B) Subsurface water
        (C) Streams   (D) Waves   (E) Wind   Ⓐ Ⓑ Ⓒ Ⓓ Ⓔ

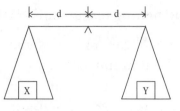

22. The balance shown above is in equilibrium at the Earth's surface and the two arms have the same length d. Thus the two objects, X and Y (not necessarily drawn to scale), must have identical

(A) densities   (B) masses   (C) shapes
(D) specific gravities   (E) volumes

Ⓐ Ⓑ Ⓒ Ⓓ Ⓔ

Questions 23-25

$$CuO + H_2 \longrightarrow Cu + H_2O$$

The drawing below depicts an apparatus for reducing copper(II) oxide to the metal by the reaction above.

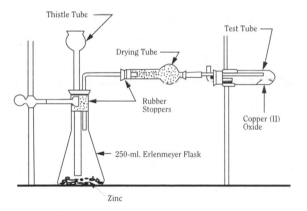

23. In order to produce a stream of hydrogen gas for this reaction, one should add which of the following through the thistle tube?

(A) Water
(B) Dilute hydrochloric acid
(C) Dilute copper (II) sulfate solution
(D) Hydrogen peroxide
(E) Dilute ammonia solution

Ⓐ Ⓑ Ⓒ Ⓓ Ⓔ

24. After the production of hydrogen gas starts, withdrawing the thistle tube would result in which of the following?

   (A) Moisture would collect in the flask.
   (B) The evolution of hydrogen gas would stop.
   (C) Much hydrogen gas would escape without coming in contact with the copper oxide.
   (D) Air would enter the flask faster than hydrogen gas would be evolved.
   (E) The rate of production of hydrogen gas would increase.

25. Which of the following would most likely increase the effectiveness of the hydrogen gas reducing the copper(II) oxide?

   (A) Heating the test tube
   (B) Cooling the test tube
   (C) Putting the test tube under reduced pressure
   (D) Filling the test tube with dilute HCl solution
   (E) Filling the test tube with dilute NaOH solution

   Ⓐ Ⓑ Ⓒ Ⓓ Ⓔ

Study Resources

Visit a local college bookstore to determine which textbooks are used by the college for natural science courses. To prepare for the Natural Sciences exam, students are advised to study from more than one textbook to cover all the subject matter, selecting at least one biological science and one physical science textbook. When choosing a textbook, students should check the table of contents against the "Knowledge and Skills Required" section on pages 87-88.

   If students maintain an interest in scientific issues, read science articles in newspapers and magazines, watch public television programs such as "Nova," or work in fields that require a knowledge of certain areas of science such as nursing and laboratory work, they will probably be knowledgeable about many of the topics included on the Natural Sciences exam. The Internet is another resource students could explore.

   Additional suggestions for preparing for CLEP exams are provided in Chapter 4.

Social Sciences and History

Description of the Examination

The General Examination in Social Sciences and History covers a wide range of topics from the social science and history areas. While the exam is based on no specific course, its content is drawn from introductory college courses that cover United States history, Western Civilization, World Civilization, government/political science, economics, sociology, anthropology, psychology, and geography.

The primary objective of the exam is to give candidates the opportunity to demonstrate that they possess the level of knowledge and understanding expected of college students meeting a distribution or general education requirement in the social science/history area. Many colleges award three or six semester hours (or the equivalent) for a satisfactory CLEP score reflecting the required level of knowledge and understanding. Some may grant specific course credit for a survey course that discusses social science and history topics and that closely matches the exam.

This exam, however, is not intended for use in granting course credit for specific social science or history courses. The CLEP Subject Examinations in Introductory Microeconomics, Introductory Macroeconomics, Introductory Sociology, American History I and II, Western Civilization I and II, and American Government cover more completely the material taught in these courses.

The Social Sciences and History exam includes approximately 125 multiple-choice questions to be answered in two separately timed 45-minute sections.

Knowledge and Skills Required

Questions on the exam require candidates to demonstrate one or more of the following abilities.

- Familiarity with terminology, facts, conventions, methodology, concepts, principles, generalizations, and theories

- Ability to understand, interpret, and analyze graphic, pictorial, or written material

- Ability to apply abstractions to particulars, and to apply hypotheses, concepts, theories, or principles to given data

The content of the Social Science and History exam is drawn from the following topics.

Approximate Percent of Examination

History (40%)

17%   United States history

Requires a general understanding of historical issues associated with the following periods in United States history: colonial, revolutionary, late eighteenth and early nineteenth centuries, Civil War and Reconstruction, and late nineteenth and twentieth centuries

15%   Western Civilization

Requires familiarity with three broad historical periods: ancient, medieval, and modern

8%   World Civilization

Requires general knowledge of important historical topics in six broad chronological periods:

Prehistory

Ancient history to 500 B.C.E.

500 B.C.E. to 500 C.E.

500 C.E. to 1500 C.E.

1500 C.E. to 1900 C.E.

The twentieth century in Africa, Asia, Europe, and Latin America

Social Sciences (60%)

13%   Government/Political Science, including topics such as

Methods

Constitutional government

Voting and political behavior

International relations

Comparative government

→ *Approximate Percent of Examination*

11% Sociology, including topics such as

    Methods

    Demography

    Ecology

    Social stratification

    Deviance

    Social organization

    Interaction

    Social change

10% Economics, with emphasis on topics such as

    Opportunity cost

    Comparative advantage

    Competitive markets

    Monetary and fiscal policy

    International trade

    Measurement concepts

10% Psychology, including topics such as

    Aggression

    Socialization

    Conformity

    Methodology

    Group formation

    Performance

10% Geography, including topics such as

    Weather and climate

    Cultural geography

    Ecology

6%   Anthropology, including topics such as

Cultural anthropology

Physical anthropology

Demography

Family

Methods

Sample Questions

The following questions are provided to give an indication of the types of items that appear on the General Examination in Social Sciences and History. CLEP exams are designed so that average students who have completed distribution requirements in this area can usually answer about half the questions correctly.

Before attempting to answer the sample questions, read all the information about the Social Science and History exam on the preceding pages. Additional suggestions for preparing for CLEP exams are provided in Chapter 4.

Try to answer correctly as many questions as possible. Then compare your answers with the correct answers given in Appendix A.

Directions: Each of the questions or incomplete statements below is followed by five suggested answers or completions. Select the one that is best in each case.

1. Prior to the campaign of 1828, most candidates for President of the United States were nominated by

   (A) state legislatures
   (B) the electoral college
   (C) national party conventions
   (D) state primary elections
   (E) party leaders in Congress   Ⓐ Ⓑ Ⓒ Ⓓ Ⓔ

2. Which of the following best describes the impact of Spanish colonization on the Indians of Central and South America in the sixteenth and early seventeenth centuries?

(A) Their economic well-being was improved by the wealth they produced at the direction of the Spanish rulers.

(B) The Indians maintained a separate society and culture that coexisted with that of the Spanish colonial system.

(C) Their high level of artistic and scientific development put them at the top of the colonial class system.

(D) Their system of religious beliefs and practices was unaffected.

(E) Their populations decreased dramatically as a result of contact with the Spanish.

Ⓐ Ⓑ Ⓒ Ⓓ Ⓔ

3. An individual who believes that "government is best which governs not at all" favors

(A) anarchy   (B) tyranny   (C) monarchy
  (D) oligarchy   (E) democracy

Ⓐ Ⓑ Ⓒ Ⓓ Ⓔ

4. Which of the following statements concerning the process of socialization is true?

(A) In the upbringing of a child, the agencies of socialization tend to function together harmoniously.

(B) In a modern society, the individual is subjected to many diverse socializing influences.

(C) In a traditional society, socializing influences are likely to be in conflict.

(D) In a traditional society, there are no socializing agencies.

(E) In modern society, the media has little impact on the socialization of children.

Ⓐ Ⓑ Ⓒ Ⓓ Ⓔ

CONFIDENCE IN AMERICAN INSTITUTIONS, 1973-1986
(Percentage saying "a great deal or quite a lot")

ORGANIZATION	1973	1977	1981	1986
Military	NA*	57%	50%	63%
Church-organized religion	66%	64%	64%	57%
U.S. Supreme Court	44%	46%	46%	53%
Public Schools	58%	54%	42%	49%
Congress	42%	40%	29%	41%
Organized labor	30%	39%	28%	29%
Big Business 28%	26%	33%	20%	

*Not asked   The Gallup Poll News Service

5. Which of the following can be inferred about American public opinion from the table above?

(A) In the 1980's public schools functioned to the satisfaction of American citizens.

(B) Big business generally enjoys more confidence than organized labor.

(C) Confidence in the military has remained constant over time.

(D) During the Reagan presidency, esteem for the Supreme Court increased.

(E) Support for Congress depends on the popularity of individual members of Congress.

Ⓐ Ⓑ Ⓒ Ⓓ Ⓔ

6. Which of the following statements about the concept of charisma is correct?

(A) It is possible only in the absence of legitimate authority.

(B) It involves a basically political appeal.

(C) It rests on devotion of followers to the exceptional qualities of an individual.

(D) It is an inherited personality trait.

(E) It is a prerequisite for high office in traditional societies.

Ⓐ Ⓑ Ⓒ Ⓓ

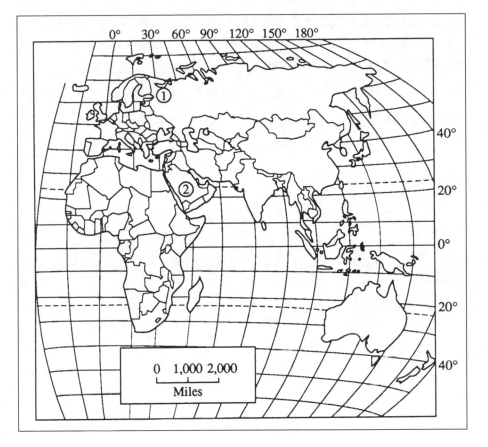

7. A traveler going from Nation 1 to Nation 2, shown on the map above, would experience a climatic change from

   (A) humid cold to desert
   (B) humid subtropical to Mediterranean
   (C) desert to tropical rain forest
   (D) tropical wet and humid to Mediterranean
   (E) Mediterranean to humid cold

   (A) (B) (C) (D) (E)

8. In most cultures where a belief in ancestral spirits exists, these beings are generally seen as

   (A) being primarily malevolent
   (B) being responsible for natural disasters
   (C) having no authority over the living
   (D) being beyond the spiritual reach of the living
   (E) retaining an active membership in the society

   (A) (B) (C) (D) (E)

9. "To industry and frugality I owe the early easiness of my circumstances and the acquisition of my fortune with all that knowledge that has enabled me to be a useful citizen."

The statement above is most characteristic of which of the following?

(A) Franklin   (B) Emerson   (C) Thoreau
  (D) Vanderbilt   (E) Jefferson

Ⓐ Ⓑ Ⓒ Ⓓ Ⓔ

10. One of the fundamental changes taking place in the twentieth century is the gradual

(A) decline in nationalistic feelings among peoples of the Eastern
        Hemisphere
(B) decline in the economic self-sufficiency of individuals
(C) decline in world trade
(D) decrease in the pressure of world population on economic resources
(E) decrease in services, as opposed to manufacturing, in developed
        nations

Ⓐ Ⓑ Ⓒ Ⓓ Ⓔ

11. A person who lived in the 1790's in the United States and who believed in a strong central government, broad construction of the Constitution, and funding of the public debt would most probably have been

(A) a socialist   (B) an anti-Federalist   (C) a Federalist
    (D) a believer in monarchy   (E) a Jeffersonian Republican

Ⓐ Ⓑ Ⓒ Ⓓ Ⓔ

12. Among the several social science methods of research, the one used for conducting public opinion polls can best be described as

(A) laboratory experimentation
(B) participant observation
(C) field experimentation
(D) survey research
(E) computer simulation

Ⓐ Ⓑ Ⓒ Ⓓ Ⓔ

13. Which of the following policies is likely to result in the greatest reduction in aggregate demand?

   (A) A $5 billion increase in personal income taxes
   (B) A $5 billion decrease in government transfer payments
   (C) A $5 billion decrease in government purchases of goods and services
   (D) A $5 billion decrease in government purchases accompanied by a
       $5 billion increase in personal income taxes
   (E) A $5 billion decrease in government purchases accompanied by a
       $5 billion decrease in personal income taxes

   Ⓐ Ⓑ Ⓒ Ⓓ Ⓔ

14. Which of the following statements about the control group in a well-designed experiment is correct?

   (A) It differs from the experimental group in the way in which subjects
       are sampled.
   (B) It is like the experimental group except for differences in exposure to
       the dependent variable.
   (C) It is like the experimental group and receives the same experimental
       treatment.
   (D) It is like the experimental group except for differences in exposure to
       the independent variable.
   (E) It must contain the same number of individuals as the experimental
       group.

   Ⓐ Ⓑ Ⓒ Ⓓ Ⓔ

15. The area of the African continent is approximately

   (A) half the area of Western Europe
   (B) the same as the area of the United States east of the Mississippi River
   (C) three times the area of the continental United States
   (D) two times the area of California
   (E) four times the area of South America

   Ⓐ Ⓑ Ⓒ Ⓓ Ⓔ

16. Chinese culture and influence were most significant in shaping the institutions of which of the following countries?

    (A) Bangladesh, Burma, and Pakistan
    (B) India, Japan, and Korea
    (C) Indonesia, the Philippines, and Thailand
    (D) Japan, Korea, and Vietnam
    (E) Korea, Nepal, and the Philippines

    (A) (B) (C) (D) (E)

17. The most immediate consequence of abolitionism in the United States in the 1830's and 1840's was

    (A) widespread support for the abolition of slavery
    (B) intensified resentment toward the movement by slaveholders
    (C) better treatment of freed African Americans in the North
    (D) greater sympathy for popular sovereignty
    (E) increased interest in African colonization

    (A) (B) (C) (D) (E)

18. "We know so little about how to live in this life that there is no point in worrying about what may happen to us after death. First let us learn to live in the right way with other people and then let whatever happens next take care of itself."

    The above quotation best expresses the philosophy of

    (A) Jesus
    (B) Muhammad
    (C) Confucius
    (D) Marx
    (E) Aquinas

    (A) (B) (C) (D) (E)

19. Major political revolutions in the twentieth century have most often occurred in countries with

    (A) comparatively low unemployment
    (B) high levels of industrialization
    (C) small industrial and large agricultural sectors
    (D) representative governments
    (E) small populations

    (A) (B) (C) (D) (E)

20. The tendency for an individual's rank on one status dimension to be positively correlated with his or her rank on other status dimensions is known as

   (A) structural balance
   (B) rank ordering
   (C) status polarization
   (D) status congruence
   (E) status stability   Ⓐ Ⓑ Ⓒ Ⓓ Ⓔ

21. To reduce inflationary pressure in the economy, the Federal Reserve would most likely

   (A) sell government securities on the open market
   (B) reduce margin requirements
   (C) lower legal reserve requirements
   (D) decrease the discount rate
   (E) encourage member banks to increase their loans

       Ⓐ Ⓑ Ⓒ Ⓓ Ⓔ

22. Participant satisfaction will increase in those groups that

   (A) have competing subgroups in interaction
   (B) are low in cohesion among group members
   (C) identify clear goals and supportive roles
   (D) have incompatible directions
   (E) fail to coordinate member interaction   Ⓐ Ⓑ Ⓒ Ⓓ Ⓔ

23. The construction of the Panama Canal shortened the sailing time between New York and

   (A) London
   (B) Port-au-Prince
   (C) Rio de Janeiro
   (D) New Orleans
   (E) San Francisco   Ⓐ Ⓑ Ⓒ Ⓓ Ⓔ

24. Of the following, which is the earliest human innovation?

(A) Development of complex urban societies
(B) Extensive use of written language
(C) Use and control of fire
(D) Domestication of animals
(E) Dependence on agriculture for the major source of food

Ⓐ Ⓑ Ⓒ Ⓓ Ⓔ

25. Which of the following prompted African Americans to move to cities in the North during the first quarter of the twentieth century?

   I. The impact of the boll weevil plague
  II. The availability of industrial opportunities in the North
 III. The impact of segregation legislation in the South

(A) II only   (B) I and II only   (C) I and III only
  (D) II and III only   (E) I, II, and III

Ⓐ Ⓑ Ⓒ Ⓓ Ⓔ

26. Abolition of the transatlantic slave trade was difficult to achieve in the early 1800's because

(A) the British were strongly in favor of slavery
(B) slave labor was needed in Europe
(C) the profits from slavery were high
(D) most countries in Europe had extensive African colonies
(E) slavery was widespread in all parts of the New World

Ⓐ Ⓑ Ⓒ Ⓓ Ⓔ

27. Public opinion polls in the United States commonly make use of

(A) sampling theory
(B) population trends
(C) intelligence tests
(D) clinical interviews
(E) Rorschach tests

28. A population that is aging necessarily has

(A) more people over 40 than under 40
(B) more males than females
(C) a decreasing death rate
(D) an increasing mean age
(E) an increasing birthrate

Ⓐ Ⓑ Ⓒ Ⓓ Ⓔ

UNITED STATES MARKET FOR APPLES

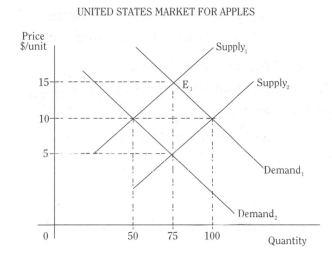

29. The United States market for apples is in equilibrium at E, where 75 units are sold for $15 each. If consumers' per capita disposable income decreases, the equilibrium price and quantity of apples sold will be which of the following?

	PRICE	QUANTITY
(A)	$15	75
(B)	$10	50
(C)	$10	100
(D)	$ 5	75
(E)	$ 5	100

Ⓐ Ⓑ Ⓒ Ⓓ Ⓔ

30. In psychology, the biosocial approach seeks to explain behavior in terms of

(A) environmental influences
(B) genetic factors
(C) unconscious motivations
(D) an integration of cultural and biological factors
(E) genetic drifts within population groups

Ⓐ Ⓑ Ⓒ Ⓓ Ⓔ

31. In the late twentieth century Islamic fundamentalism had the least influence in which of the following countries?

    (A) Algeria
    (B) China
    (C) Egypt
    (D) India
    (E) Indonesia   Ⓐ Ⓑ Ⓒ Ⓓ Ⓔ

32. In which of the following types of societies do women typically have as much power as men?

    (A) Hunting-gathering
    (B) Pastoral
    (C) Horticultural
    (D) Agricultural
    (E) Industrial   Ⓐ Ⓑ Ⓒ Ⓓ Ⓔ

33. Which of the following is true of the First Amendment to the United States Constitution?

    (A) It established presidential control over the budget.
    (B) It created the Supreme Court.
    (C) It declared all people to be equal.
    (D) It outlined the basic pattern of church-state relations.
    (E) It guaranteed citizens the right to bear arms.
                            Ⓐ Ⓑ Ⓒ Ⓓ Ⓔ

34. The Peloponnesian Wars were primarily the result of

    (A) Athenian imperialism
    (B) Spartan militarism
    (C) the invasion of Greece by Hammurabi's army
    (D) the conquests of Alexander the Great
    (E) the spread of Athenian democracy
                            Ⓐ Ⓑ Ⓒ Ⓓ Ⓔ

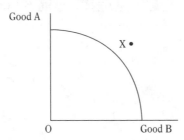

35. In the production-possibility curve for a closed economy illustrated above, X indicates a point at which

    (A) intended saving is greater than investment
    (B) the economy cannot achieve its existing productive potential
    (C) the factors of production are not fully employed
    (D) the production level cannot be maintained in the long run
    (E) income is unequally distributed to the factors of production

    Ⓐ Ⓑ Ⓒ Ⓓ Ⓔ

36. Which of the following philosophers asserted that all human beings possess the natural rights of life, liberty, and property?

    (A) Thomas Hobbes   (B) John Locke   (C) Thomas Aquinas
        (D) Karl Marx   (E) Socrates

    Ⓐ Ⓑ Ⓒ Ⓓ Ⓔ

37. Which of the following is NOT compatible with the traditional conception of bureaucracy?

    (A) Salaried remuneration
    (B) Recruitment of personnel by examination
    (C) A hierarchical structure
    (D) A decentralization of authority
    (E) A formal allocation of obligation and duties

    Ⓐ Ⓑ Ⓒ Ⓓ Ⓔ

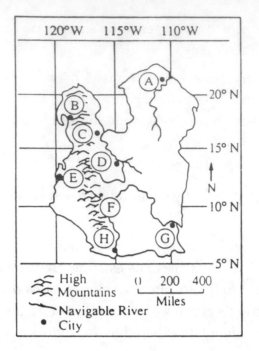

38. According to the map above, which of the following land formations would most likely be found near city A?

(A) A plateau
(B) A volcano
(C) A delta
(D) A peninsula
(E) A mountain

Ⓐ Ⓑ Ⓒ Ⓓ Ⓔ

39. On the basis of empirical evidence gathered during the Second World War, which of the following was most successful in motivating United States soldiers to perform well under overseas combat conditions?

(A) Emphasizing to them that the civilian population is dependent on them
(B) Developing their dedication to dominant political and ethical values
(C) Instilling in the soldiers loyalty to national leaders
(D) Developing in the soldiers a satisfactory self-image of their individual abilities
(E) Emphasizing positive relationships among members of small combat units

Ⓐ Ⓑ Ⓒ Ⓓ Ⓔ

40. Of the following, which first opened up lines of trade with East Africa and the upper Niger Valley?

    (A) Portuguese navigators sailing around Africa on their way to India
    (B) English merchants seeking slaves for the American colonies
    (C) Arab traders extending their trade routes to include both the Persian Gulf and northern Africa
    (D) Spanish nobles seeking sources of gold in Africa
    (E) French explorers crossing the Mediterranean and penetrating through the Sahara

    Ⓐ Ⓑ Ⓒ Ⓓ Ⓔ

Study Resources

To prepare for the Social Sciences and History exam, you should consult several introductory college level textbooks because there are none that cover all the major topics on the exam. Visit your local college bookstore to determine which textbooks are used by the college for History, Sociology, Western Civilization, and other related courses. When selecting a textbook, check the table of contents against the "Knowledge and Skills Required" section on pages 97-100.

   The materials suggested for preparing for other CLEP exams may also be helpful. Study resources for the Subject Examinations in American Government, History of the United States I and II, Principles of Macroeconomics and Principles of Microeconomics, Introductory Sociology, and Western Civilization I and II are particularly relevant, and can be found in the Study Resources section for these exams. The Internet is another resource you could explore.

American Literature

Description of the Examination

The Subject Examination in American Literature covers the material that is usually taught in a two-semester survey course (or the equivalent) at the college level. It deals with prose and poetry written in the United States from colonial times to the present. It is primarily a test of knowledge about literary works — their content, backgrounds, and authors — but also requires familiarity with the terminology used by literary critics and historians. The exam emphasizes fiction and poetry, and deals to a lesser degree with the essay, drama, and autobiography.

In both coverage and approach, the exam resembles the chronologically organized survey of American literature offered by many colleges. It assumes that the candidate has read widely and developed an appreciation of American literature, knows the basic literary periods, and has a sense of the historical development of American literature.

The test contains approximately 100 multiple-choice questions to be answered in two separately timed 45-minute sections.

There is also an optional essay section that can be taken in addition to the multiple-choice test. *Contact the school where you would like to receive credit for your CLEP exam to see if they require the optional essay section for this exam.* The essay section is graded by the institution that requests it.

Knowledge and Skills Required

Questions on the test require candidates to demonstrate one or more of the following abilities.

- Knowledge of the content of particular literary works — their characters, plots, settings, themes, etc. (about 50-60 percent of the exam)

- Ability to understand and interpret short poems or excerpts from long poems and prose works presented in the test book (about 25-35 percent of the exam)

- Knowledge of the historical and social settings of specific works, their authors, and their relations to other literary works and to literary traditions (about 10 percent of the exam)

115

- Understanding of the critical theories of American writers, and of critical terms, verse forms, and literary devices (about 5 percent of the exam)

The American Literature exam requires a knowledge and understanding of the works and writers of the following periods. The column at the left indicates the percentage of questions devoted to each of the five periods.

	Approximate Percent of Examination
10-15%	Colonial and Early National (1620-1830)
25%	Romantic (1830-1870)
25%	Realistic and Early Naturalistic (1870-1910)
25%	Modern (1910-1945)
10-15%	Contemporary (1945-present)

Sample Questions

The 23 sample questions that follow are similar to questions on the American Literature exam, but they do not actually appear on it.

Before attempting to answer the sample questions, read all of the information about the American Literature exam on the preceding pages. Additional suggestions for preparing for CLEP exams are provided in Chapter 4.

Try to answer correctly as many questions as possible. Then compare your answers with the correct answers, given in Appendix A.

Directions: Each of the questions or incomplete statements below is followed by five suggested answers or completions. Select the one that is best in each case.

1. Which of the following first recognized Walt Whitman as the great poet of the democratic spirit of America?

(A) Nathaniel Hawthorne   (B) Ralph Waldo Emerson
    (C) Herman Melville   (D) Edgar Allan Poe
        (E) Henry David Thoreau

Ⓐ Ⓑ Ⓒ Ⓓ Ⓔ

2. The "unpardonable sin" committed by Ethan Brand is

   (A) allowing one's intellectual curiosity to violate the privacy of others
   (B) any mortal transgression not followed by repentance
   (C) the attempt to improve upon God's handiwork
   (D) loss of faith in God
   (E) ambition deteriorating into a lust for power

   Ⓐ Ⓑ Ⓒ Ⓓ Ⓔ

Questions 3-4

    Thou ill-formed offspring of my feeble brain,
    Who after birth didst by my side remain,
    Till snatched from thence by friends, less wise than true,
    Who thee abroad, exposed to public view,
(5) Made thee in rags, halting to th' press to trudge
    Where errors were not lessened (all may judge).
    At thy return my blushing was not small,
    My rambling brat (in print) should mother call,
    I cast thee by as one unfit for light,
    Thy visage was so irksome in my sight . . . .

3. In line 1, "offspring" most probably refers to the author's

   (A) philosophy   (B) book of poems
      (C) unwanted child   (D) despair
        (E) intelligence

   Ⓐ Ⓡ Ⓒ Ⓓ Ⓔ

4. "My rambling brat" (line 8) is an example of

   (A) epigram
   (B) alliteration
   (C) simile
   (D) personification
   (E) hyperbole

   Ⓐ Ⓑ Ⓒ Ⓓ Ⓔ

5. In his *Autobiography,* Benjamin Franklin claims that success can best be achieved by

  (A) hard work and moral self-improvement
  (B) religious study and ascetic denial of worldly goods
  (C) study of the classics and of several languages
  (D) extensive investment of capital and strict attention to business
  (E) inducing scholars to participate in business ventures

6. Characters with the last names of Sutpen, Compson, and Sartoris figure prominently in the fiction of

  (A) Eudora Welty   (B) Flannery O'Connor
    (C) Thomas Wolfe   (D) William Faulkner
      (E) Ernest Hemingway

Ⓐ Ⓑ Ⓒ Ⓓ Ⓔ

Questions 7-8

The mass of men lead lives of quiet desperation.

To be a philosopher is not merely to have subtle thoughts, nor even to found a school, but so to love wisdom as to live according to its dictates a life of simplicity, independence, magnanimity, and trust.

(5) I had three pieces of limestone on my desk, but I was terrified to find that they required to be dusted daily, when the furniture of my mind was all undusted still, and I threw them out the window in disgust.

7. The sentences above are taken from the opening pages of

  (A) *The House of the Seven Gables,* Hawthorne
  (B) *Nature,* Emerson
  (C) *Bartleby the Scrivener,* Melville
  (D) *Democratic Vistas,* Whitman
  (E) *Walden,* Thoreau

Ⓐ Ⓑ Ⓒ Ⓓ Ⓔ

8. The phrase "the furniture of my mind was all undusted still" (lines 6-7) can best be paraphrased by which of the following?

(A) I had become morose and antisocial.
(B) I had not examined my ideas and beliefs.
(C) I needed a change of scene.
(D) I was intellectually and emotionally exhausted.
(E) I had become so lazy that I could not work.

Ⓐ Ⓑ Ⓒ Ⓓ Ⓔ

9. Which of the following poets derived the title, the plan, and much of the symbolism of one of his or her major poems from Jessie Weston's *From Ritual to Romance?*

(A) Wallace Stevens   (B) T. S. Eliot
  (C) Robert Frost   (D) Marianne Moore
    (E) Langston Hughes

Ⓐ Ⓑ Ⓒ Ⓓ Ⓔ

10. Of which of the following works did Ernest Hemingway say, "It's the best book we've had. All American writing comes from that"?

(A) *The Last of the Mohicans*
(B) *Moby-Dick*
(C) *The Scarlet Letter*
(D) *Walden*
(E) *Adventures of Huckleberry Finn*

Ⓐ Ⓑ Ⓒ Ⓓ Ⓔ

11. Which of the following writers was particularly important in the development of the short story as a literary form?

(A) James Fenimore Cooper   (B) Harriet Beecher Stowe
  (C) Frederick Douglass   (D) Edgar Allan Poe
    (E) Edith Wharton

Ⓐ Ⓑ Ⓒ Ⓓ Ⓔ

Make me, O Lord, thy Spining Wheele compleate,
Thy Holy Worde my Distaff make for mee.
Make mine Affections thy Swift Flyers neate
And make my Soule thy holy Spoole to bee.
(5) My Conversation make to be thy Reele
And reele the yarn thereon spun of thy Wheele.

12. The passage above is notable chiefly for

(A) irony of statement   (B) pathetic fallacy
   (C) a literary conceit   (D) a paradox
      (E) a simile

13. The last part of Richard Wright's *Native Son* is about

(A) the main character's trial
(B) the wedding of two characters
(C) the main character's journey to a new home
(D) a resolution of the racial conflicts in the book
(E) the main character's later years

Ⓐ Ⓑ Ⓒ Ⓓ Ⓔ

14. Henry James and William Dean Howells are commonly described by literary critics as

(A) transcendentalists   (B) symbolists
   (C) realists   (D) romantics   (E) naturalists

Ⓐ Ⓑ Ⓒ Ⓓ Ⓔ

15. All of the following were written by Toni Morrison EXCEPT

(A) *Song of Solomon*   (B) *Tar Baby*
   (C) *The Bluest Eye*   (D) *Sula*
      (E) *The Color Purple*

Ⓐ Ⓑ Ⓒ Ⓓ Ⓔ

Questions 16-17

Tree at my window, window tree,
My sash is lowered when night comes on;
But let there never be curtain drawn
Between you and me.

(5) Vague dream-head lifted out of the ground,
And thing next most diffuse to cloud,
Not all your light tongues talking aloud
Could be profound.

But, tree, I have seen you taken and tossed,
(10) And if you have seen me when I slept,
You have seen me when I was taken and swept
And all but lost.

That day she put our heads together,
Fate had her imagination about her,
(15) Your head so much concerned with outer,
Mine with inner, weather.

16. The "light tongues" (line 7) are a metaphorical reference to the tree's

    (A) frivolous thoughts   (B) inquisitiveness   (C) large branches
    (D) imagination   (E) leaves

    Ⓐ Ⓑ Ⓒ Ⓓ Ⓔ

17. When the tree is "taken and tossed" (line 9), the speaker sees the tree as an image of

    (A) the ruthlessness of nature
    (B) his own troubled mind
    (C) the uncertainty of Fate herself
    (D) a lack of seriousness in nature
    (E) shaken but unbowed human will

    Ⓐ Ⓑ Ⓒ Ⓓ Ⓔ

18. All of the following are images from the poems of Emily Dickinson EXCEPT a

   (A) fly in a still room making an "uncertain stumbling buzz"
   (B) "narrow fellow in the grass" who moves quickly
   (C) rain-filled red wheelbarrow "beside the white chickens"
   (D) "certain slant of light" seen during the winter
   (E) saddened person who "never lost as much but twice"

   Ⓐ Ⓑ Ⓒ Ⓓ Ⓔ

Questions 19-20

Let me tell you about the very rich. They are different from you and me. They possess and enjoy early, and it does something to them, makes them soft where we are hard, and cynical where we are trustful, in a way that, unless you were born rich, it is very difficult to understand. They
(5) think, deep in their hearts, that they are better than we are because we had to discover the compensations and refuges of life for ourselves. Even when they enter deep into our world or sink below us, they still think that they are better than we are. They are different.

19. In the passage, which of the following best describes the speaker's attitude toward the very rich?

   (A) He finds their cynicism alarming and unwarranted.
   (B) He believes that, because of their advantages and experience, the rich know more than others do.
   (C) He is envious of their moral superiority.
   (D) He thinks that he understands their psychology even though he has not shared their advantages.
   (E) He finds them so different from the rest of society as to be unknowable.

   Ⓐ Ⓑ Ⓒ Ⓓ Ⓔ

20. The passage was written by

    (A) F. Scott Fitzgerald   (B) Willa Cather   (C) John Steinbeck
    (D) Sinclair Lewis   (E) Theodore Dreiser

    Ⓐ Ⓑ Ⓒ Ⓓ Ⓔ

21. At the end of Kate Chopin's *The Awakening*, the heroine does which of the following?

    (A) Travels to a new home.
    (B) Walks into the sea.
    (C) Makes a speech.
    (D) Has a child.
    (E) Marries for the second time.

    Ⓐ Ⓑ Ⓒ Ⓓ Ⓔ

22. John Steinbeck's *The Grapes of Wrath* depicts

    (A) the plight of dispossessed farmers who migrate to California
    (B) prison conditions in turn-of-the-century America
    (C) a wounded soldier who tries in vain to escape the effects of war
    (D) racial problems in a small farming town in Oklahoma
    (E) a drifter and his friend who dream hopelessly of better lives

    Ⓐ Ⓑ Ⓒ Ⓓ Ⓔ

23. All of the following were first published in the 1850's EXCEPT

    (A) Thoreau's *Walden*
    (B) Emerson's *Nature*
    (C) Whitman's *Leaves of Grass*
    (D) Melville's *Moby-Dick*
    (E) Hawthorne's *The Scarlet Letter*

    Ⓐ Ⓑ Ⓒ Ⓓ Ⓔ

Optional Essay Section

If your college requires that the optional essay section be taken in addition to the multiple-choice exam, you should review the following information.

The optional essay section of the American Literature exam draws from the same general content as does the multiple-choice test. Its purpose is to test the candidate's ability to write about American literature in an informed and organized manner. While good writing skills and knowledge of grammar will enhance the candidate's ability to respond to the questions, the optional section is not intended to be a test of these abilities.

Candidates are required to answer two of three essay questions within a 90-minute period. The first question, which is required, asks candidates to apply to American authors a critical generalization stated in the test book. They must support their statements with examples from the works of a list of American authors. For the second essay, candidates may choose to discuss either a prose passage or a poem printed in the test book. Instructions for each selection indicate what should be included in the discussion, and some thought-provoking comments and questions are provided as guides in organizing the essay.

For additional information, read the sections on "Taking Essay Tests," in Chapter 5, and "How Essays Are Graded," in Chapter 6.

Study Resources

To prepare for the American Literature exam, you should read critically the contents of at least one anthology, which you can find in most college bookstores. Most textbook anthologies contain a representative sample of readings as well as discussions of historical background, literary styles and devices characteristic of various authors and periods, and other material relevant to the test. The anthologies do vary somewhat in their content, approach, and emphasis; you are advised to consult more than one or to consult some specialized books on major authors, periods, and literary forms and terminology. You should also read some of the major novels that are mentioned or excerpted in the anthologies, such as Nathaniel Hawthorne's *The Scarlet Letter*, Mark Twain's *Adventures of Huckleberry Finn*, and Kate Chopin's *The Awakening*. Other novelists whose major works you should be familiar with include Melville, Crane, Wharton, Cather, Fitzgerald, Hemingway, Faulkner, Ellison, and Wright. You can probably obtain an extensive reading list of American literature from a college English department, library, or bookstore.

Additional suggestions for preparing for CLEP exams are given in Chapter 4.

Analyzing and Interpreting Literature

Description of the Examination

The Subject Examination in Analyzing and Interpreting Literature covers material that is usually taught in a general two-semester undergraduate course in literature. Although the exam does not require familiarity with specific works, it does assume that the student has read widely and perceptively in poetry, drama, fiction, and nonfiction. The questions are based on passages supplied in the test. These passages have been selected so that no previous experience with them is required to answer the questions. The passages are taken primarily from American and British literature.

The exam includes approximately 90 multiple-choice questions to be answered in two separately timed 45-minute sections.

There is also an optional essay section that can be taken in addition to the multiple-choice exam. The essay section is graded by the institution that requests it. Contact the school where you would like to receive credit for your CLEP exam to see if they require the optional essay section for this exam.

Knowledge and Skills Required

Questions on the Analyzing and Interpreting Literature exam require candidates to demonstrate the following abilities.

- Ability to read prose, poetry, and drama with understanding

- Ability to analyze the elements of a literary passage and to respond to nuances of meaning, tone, imagery, and style

- Ability to interpret metaphors, to recognize rhetorical and stylistic devices, to perceive relationships between parts and wholes, and to grasp a speaker's or author's attitudes

- Knowledge of the means by which literary effects are achieved

- Familiarity with the basic terminology used to discuss literary texts

The exam emphasizes comprehension, interpretation, and analysis of literary works. Only a minimum of specific factual knowledge is required; however, a broad knowledge of literature gained through reading widely is assumed, as is a familiarity with basic literary terminology. The following outline indicates the relative emphasis given to the various types of literature and the periods from which the passages are taken.

	Approximate Percent of Examination
35-45%	Poetry
35-45%	Prose (fiction and nonfiction)
15-25%	Drama
50-65%	British literature
30-45%	American literature
5-15%	Works in translation
3-7%	Classical and pre-Renaissance
20-30%	Renaissance and 17th century
35-45%	18th and 19th centuries
25-35%	20th century

Sample Questions

The 38 sample questions that follow are similar to questions on the Analyzing and Interpreting Literature exam, but they do not actually appear on it.

Before attempting to answer the sample questions, read all the information about the Analyzing and Interpreting Literature exam on the preceding pages. Additional suggestions for preparing for CLEP exams are provided in Chapter 4.

Try to answer correctly as many questions as possible. Then compare your answers with the correct answers, given in Appendix A.

Directions: The following samples consist of selections from literary works and questions on their content, form, and style. After reading a selection, choose the best answer to each question.

Questions 1-5

The Child at Winter Sunset

The child at winter sunset,
Holding her breath in adoration of the peacock's tail
That spread its red — ah, higher and higher —
Wept suddenly. "It's going!"

(5)   The great fan folded;
Shortened; and at last no longer fought the cold, the dark.
And she on the lawn, comfortless by her father,
Shivered, shivered. "It's gone!"

"Yes, this time. But wait,
(10) Darling. There will be other nights — some of them even better."
"Oh, no. It died." He laughed. But she did not.
It was her first glory.

Laid away now in its terrible
Lead coffin, it was the first brightness she had ever
(15) Mourned. "Oh, no, it's dead." And he her father
Mourned too, for more to come.

"Child at Winter Sunset," from *Collected and New Poems, 1924-1963*, by Mark Van Doren.
Copyright © 1963 by Mark Van Doren. Reprinted by permission of Hill & Wang, a division
of Farrar, Straus & Giroux, Inc.

1. At the end of the poem, the father's attitude toward his daughter's crying
   is best characterized as

   (A) patronizing and selfish
   (B) patient but stern
   (C) sympathetic and understanding
   (D) condescending and detached
   (E) good-humored but naïve   Ⓐ Ⓑ Ⓒ Ⓓ Ⓔ

2. Which of the following lines most clearly presents the difference in perspective between the father and the daughter?

(A) "And she on the lawn, comfortless by her father," (line 7)
(B) " 'Darling. There will be other nights — some of them even better.' " (line 10)
(C) " 'Oh, no. It died.' He laughed. But she did not." (line 11)
(D) "It was her first glory." (line 12)
(E) "And he her father / Mourned too, for more to come." (lines 15-16)

Ⓐ Ⓑ Ⓒ Ⓓ Ⓔ

3. The image of the lead coffin (line 14) functions to

(A) diminish and caricature the child's sorrow at the sunset
(B) confirm the significance of the child's feelings of loss
(C) indicate that the sunset symbolizes the child's own death
(D) suggest that the father is now mourning his dead child
(E) represent the specter of death hovering over the father

Ⓐ Ⓑ Ⓒ Ⓓ Ⓔ

4. The last two lines of the poem suggest that the father

(A) laments his own losses, both past and future
(B) fears that he will ultimately lose his daughter
(C) has come to mourn the sunset in the same way that his daughter does
(D) dreads his own inevitable death
(E) realizes that his child faces future sorrows that he cannot prevent

Ⓐ Ⓑ Ⓒ Ⓓ Ⓔ

5. The central subject of the poem is

(A) the indifference of fathers to the sensibilities of their daughters
(B) facing one's own death
(C) dealing with loss and sorrow
(D) the cruelty of time and the seasons
(E) the difficulty parents have in understanding their children

Ⓐ Ⓑ Ⓒ Ⓓ Ⓔ

Questions 6-13

"A clear fire, a clean hearth, and the rigor of the game." This was the celebrated wish of old Sarah Battle (now with God) who, next to her devotions, loved a good game at whist. She was none of your lukewarm gamesters, your half-and-half players, who have no objection to take a

(5)   hand, if you want one to make up a rubber; who affirm that they have no pleasure in winning; that they like to win one game, and lose another; that they can while away an hour very agreeably at a card table, but are indifferent whether they play or no; and will desire an adversary, who has slipt a wrong card, to take it up and play another.

(10)   These insufferable triflers are the curse of a table. One of these flies will spoil a whole pot. Of such it may be said, that they do not play at cards, but only play at playing at them.

Sarah Battle was none of that breed. She detested them, as I do, from her heart and soul; and would not, save upon a striking emergency,

(15)   willingly seat herself at the same table with them. She loved a thorough-paced partner, a determined enemy. She took, and gave, no concessions. She hated favors. She never made a revoke, nor ever passed it over in her adversary without exacting the utmost forfeiture. She fought a good fight: cut and thrust. She held not her sword (her cards) "like a dancer."

(20)   She sat bolt upright; and neither showed you her cards, nor desired to see yours. All people have their blind side — their superstitions; and I have heard her declare, under the rose,* that Hearts was her favourite suit.

---

*under the rose: *sub rosa*, in confidence

6. The phrase "now with God" (line 2) reveals that Sarah Battle

    (A) was a religious person
    (B) had an unexpected religious experience
    (C) placed devotion to God ahead of whist
    (D) has decided to give up cards
    (E) is no longer alive

    Ⓐ Ⓑ Ⓒ Ⓓ Ⓔ

7. In line 2, "next to" is best paraphrased as

   (A) second only to
   (B) besides
   (C) before
   (D) in addition to
   (E) even more than   Ⓐ Ⓑ Ⓒ Ⓓ Ⓔ

8. To Sarah Battle, the most significant characteristic of the triflers described in lines 3-12 is their

   (A) amiable sociability
   (B) generosity toward their opponents
   (C) nonchalant attitude toward whist
   (D) ability to keep the game in perspective
   (E) inability to play whist well   Ⓐ Ⓑ Ⓒ Ⓓ Ⓔ

9. It can be inferred from the description of Sarah Battle's behavior at the whist table that she

   (A) would respect a superior opponent
   (B) had an ironic sense of humor
   (C) would do anything to win
   (D) did not really enjoy playing whist
   (E) enjoyed being catered to in whist   Ⓐ Ⓑ Ⓒ Ⓓ Ⓔ

10. The most apparent metaphor in this character sketch is drawn from

    (A) nature
    (B) religion
    (C) finance
    (D) swordplay
    (E) gamesmanship   Ⓐ Ⓑ Ⓒ Ⓓ Ⓔ

11. The attitude of the narrator toward Sarah Battle is chiefly one of

    (A) sarcastic anger
    (B) affectionate respect
    (C) tolerant understanding
    (D) arrogant condescension
    (E) fearful regard   Ⓐ Ⓑ Ⓒ Ⓓ Ⓔ

12. The passage suggests all of the following about the narrator EXCEPT that the narrator

    (A) has a sense of humor
    (B) has spent time in Sarah Battle's presence
    (C) is an excellent whist player
    (D) scorns casual whist players
    (E) sees Sarah Battle's weakness

    Ⓐ Ⓑ Ⓒ Ⓓ Ⓔ

13. Which of the following best summarizes the structure of the passage?

    (A) The first paragraph concentrates on Sarah Battle's serious side; the second, on her fun-loving side.
    (B) The first paragraph defines Sarah Battle by what she is not; the second, by what she is.
    (C) The passage interprets, in turn, what Sarah Battle would regard as "A clear fire, a clean hearth, and the rigor of the game" (line 1).
    (D) The passage moves from a discussion of the refinements of whist to an explanation of what makes Sarah Battle like the game.
    (E) The first paragraph describes Sarah Battle as a gambler; the second, as a soldier of reform.

    Ⓐ Ⓑ Ⓒ Ⓓ Ⓔ

Questions 14-19

> How many thousand of my poorest subjects
> Are at this hour asleep! O sleep, O gentle sleep,
> Nature's soft nurse, how have I frightened thee
> That thou no more wilt weigh my eyelids down
> (5)   And steep my senses in forgetfulness?
> Why rather, sleep, liest thou in smoky cribs,
> Upon uneasy pallets stretching thee
> And hushed with buzzing night-flies to thy slumber,
> Than in the perfumed chambers of the great,
> (10)   Under the canopies of costly state,
> And lulled with sound of sweetest melody?
> O thou dull god, why liest thou with the vile
> In loathsome beds, and leavest the kingly couch
> A watch-case or a common 'larum bell?
> (15)   Wilt thou upon the high and giddy mast
> Seal up the ship-boy's eyes, and rock his brains
> In cradle of the rude imperious surge
> And in the visitation of the winds,
> Who take the ruffian billows by the top,
> (20)   Curling their monstrous heads and hanging them
> With deafening clamor in the slippery clouds,
> That, with the hurly, death itself awakes?
> Canst thou, O partial sleep, give thy repose
> To the wet sea-son in a hour so rude,
> (25)   And in the calmest and most stillest night,
> With all appliances and means to boot,
> Deny it to a king? Then happy low, lie down!
> Uneasy lies the head that wears a crown.

14. The dramatic situation suggested by the speech is that of a king

    (A) cast down from high estate
    (B) concerned about the poverty of his subjects
    (C) setting forth on a dangerous journey
    (D) fearful of death
    (E) restless with cares   Ⓐ Ⓑ Ⓒ Ⓓ Ⓔ

15. The point of the anecdote in lines 15-22 is that

    (A) death is an inevitable extension of sleep
    (B) common folk are accustomed to danger even though the king is not
    (C) fear is best overcome by sleep
    (D) evil inevitably overtakes the weak
    (E) sleep comes to common folk even in perilous circumstances

    Ⓐ Ⓑ Ⓒ Ⓓ Ⓔ

16. In the context of the passage, "partial" (line 23) means

    (A) biased
    (B) unsatisfying
    (C) half-waking
    (D) two-faced
    (E) favorite

    Ⓐ Ⓑ Ⓒ Ⓓ Ⓔ

17. In line 27, "low" refers to

    (A) "my poorest subjects" (line 1)
    (B) "sweetest melody" (line 11)
    (C) "rude imperious surge" (line 17)
    (D) "O partial sleep" (line 23)
    (E) "a king" (line 27)

    Ⓐ Ⓑ Ⓒ Ⓓ Ⓔ

18. The speaker's tone in addressing sleep changes from

    (A) confident to insecure
    (B) bitter to victorious
    (C) pleading to reproachful
    (D) outraged to sarcastic
    (E) angry to bewildered

    Ⓐ Ⓑ Ⓒ Ⓓ Ⓔ

19. With minor variations, the passage is written in

    (A) elegy form
    (B) blank verse
    (C) free verse
    (D) heroic couplets
    (E) the form of an ode

    Ⓐ Ⓑ Ⓒ Ⓓ Ⓔ

Questions 20-23

In My Craft or Sullen Art

In my craft or sullen art
Exercised in the still night
When only the moon rages
And the lovers lie abed
(5)   With all their griefs in their arms,
I labour by singing light
Not for ambition or bread
Or the strut and trade of charms
On the ivory stages
(10)   But for the common wages
Of their most secret heart.

Not for the proud man apart
From the raging moon I write
On these spindrift* pages
(15)   Nor for the towering dead
With their nightingales and psalms
But for the lovers, their arms
Round the griefs of the ages.
Who pay no praise or wages
(20)   Nor heed my craft or art.

*spindrift: wind-blown sea spray

20. The negative constructions "Not . . . But" (lines 7 and 10) and "Not . . . Nor . . . But" (lines 12, 15, and 17) are a feature of the structure of the poem that emphasizes a contrast between the

    (A) typical human motivations and the motivation of the speaker
    (B) attitudes of the speaker toward himself and toward the lovers
    (C) lovers embracing their own griefs and embracing the griefs of the ages
    (D) attitude of the speaker toward the lovers and their attitude toward the speaker
    (E) common craft of writing light verse and the sublime art of writing poetry

    (A) (B) (C) (D) (E)

21. Which of the following is the antecedent of "their" (line 11)?

    (A) "lovers" (line 4)
    (B) "griefs" (line 5)
    (C) "strut and trade of charms" (line 8)
    (D) "ivory stages" (line 9)
    (E) "wages" (line 10)

    (A) (B) (C) (D) (E)

22. The phrase "the towering dead / With their nightingales and psalms" (lines 15-16) alludes to the

    (A) oppressive weight of time and eternity
    (B) poet's physical and spiritual future
    (C) voices of nature and the supernatural
    (D) artificiality and futility of human institutions
    (E) great poets and poetry of the past

    (A) (B) (C) (D) (E)

23. How does the speaker feel about the response of the lovers to his efforts?

    (A) The speaker wishes to get vengeance by revealing the secrets of the lovers.
    (B) The speaker will stop writing out of resentment for their indifference.
    (C) The speaker will seek a new audience and relegate the lovers to the position of the proud man.
    (D) The speaker will continue to write for the lovers regardless of their response.
    (E) The speaker really writes only for himself and does not desire an audience.

    (A) (B) (C) (D) (E)

Questions 24-28

All towns should be made capable of purification by fire, or of decay, within each half century. Otherwise, they become the hereditary haunts of vermin and noisomeness, besides standing apart from the possibility of such improvements as are constantly introduced into the rest of

(5) man's contrivances and accommodations. It is beautiful, no doubt, and exceedingly satisfactory to some of our natural instincts, to imagine our far posterity dwelling under the same rooftree as ourselves. Still, when people insist on building indestructible houses, they incur, or their children do, a misfortune analogous to that of the Sibyl, when she

(10) obtained the grievous boon of immortality. So, we may build almost immortal habitations, it is true; but we cannot keep them from growing old, musty, unwholesome, dreary, full of death scents, ghosts, and murder stains; in short, such habitations as one sees everywhere in Italy, be they hovels or palaces.

24. The first sentence of the passage serves primarily to

   (A) state a fact
   (B) express a generally accepted opinion
   (C) startle by its unorthodoxy
   (D) say the opposite of what the speaker means
   (E) present an unwarranted conclusion   Ⓐ Ⓑ Ⓒ Ⓓ Ⓔ

25. What misfortune of the Sibyl is implied in lines 7-10?

   (A) She lived in an indestructible house.
   (B) She remained young forever.
   (C) She did not get what she asked for.
   (D) Her children lived in old houses.
   (E) She could not die but continued to age.   Ⓐ Ⓑ Ⓒ Ⓓ Ⓔ

26. The speaker objects to "almost immortal habitations" (lines 10-11) because they

    (A) start as palaces and end as hovels
    (B) are full of memories, gloom, and violence
    (C) are unhealthy for growing children
    (D) satisfy natural inclinations
    (E) are structurally unsound   Ⓐ Ⓑ Ⓒ Ⓓ Ⓔ

27. The speaker apparently regards changes brought about by modernization with

    (A) approval
    (B) indifference
    (C) resentment
    (D) hesitancy
    (E) bewilderment   Ⓐ Ⓑ Ⓒ Ⓓ Ⓔ

28. The speaker's attitude toward houses in Italy is best described as one of

    (A) envy
    (B) aversion
    (C) ambivalence
    (D) enthusiasm
    (E) defensiveness   Ⓐ Ⓑ Ⓒ Ⓓ Ⓔ

Questions 29-33

Behind Me — dips Eternity —
Before Me — Immortality —
Myself — the Term between —
Death but the Drift of Eastern Gray,
(5)   Dissolving into Dawn away,
Before the West begin —

'Tis Kingdoms — afterward — they say —
In perfect — pauseless Monarchy —
Whose Prince — is Son of None —
(10) Himself — His Dateless Dynasty —
Himself — Himself diversify —
In Duplicate divine —

'Tis Miracle before Me — then —
'Tis Miracle Behind — between
(15) A Crescent in the Sea —
With Midnight to the North of Her —
And Midnight to the South of Her —
and Maelstrom — in the Sky —

Reprinted by permission of the publishers and the Trustees of Amherst College from *The Poems of Emily Dickinson,* edited by Thomas H. Johnson, Cambridge, Mass.: The Belknap Press of Harvard University Press, copyright 1951, © 1955, 1979, 1983 by the President and Fellows of Harvard College.

29. The first stanza reveals the speaker's

(A) vision of life in heaven
(B) certainty of the truth of Christian doctrine
(C) view of her location in the span of time
(D) fear at facing a new day
(E) longing for death   Ⓐ Ⓑ Ⓒ Ⓓ Ⓔ

30. In which of the following sentences does the word "but" function grammatically in the same way as in line 4?

    (A) She likes him but for his table manners.
    (B) He spoke softly but carried a big stick.
    (C) She never comes but she stays for dinner.
    (D) His strictness was but an expression of his love.
    (E) But I would never intentionally undermine your efforts.

    Ⓐ Ⓑ Ⓒ Ⓓ Ⓔ

31. The imagery in lines 4-5 suggests that death is

    (A) a beginning
    (B) oblivion
    (C) an eclipse
    (D) release
    (E) a journey

    Ⓐ Ⓑ Ⓒ Ⓓ Ⓔ

32. Lines 16-18 suggest that the speaker sees life as

    (A) promising
    (B) fulfilling
    (C) corruptive
    (D) empty
    (E) terrifying

    Ⓐ Ⓑ Ⓒ Ⓓ Ⓔ

33. All of the following techniques are used in the poem EXCEPT

    (A) alliteration
    (B) off-rhyme
    (C) onomatopoeia
    (D) syntactic repetition
    (E) metaphor

    Ⓐ Ⓑ Ⓒ Ⓓ Ⓔ

Questions 34-38

Besides the neutral expression that she wore when she was alone, Mrs. Freeman had two others, forward and reverse, that she used for all her human dealings. Her forward expression was steady and driving like the advance of a heavy truck. Her eyes never swerved to left or right but
(5) turned as the story turned as if they followed a yellow line down the center of it. She seldom used the other expression because it was not often necessary for her to retract a statement, but when she did, her face came to a complete stop, there was an almost imperceptible movement of her black eyes, during which they seemed to be receding, and then
(10) the observer would see that Mrs. Freeman, though she might stand there as real as several grain sacks thrown on top of each other, was no longer there in spirit. As for getting any thing across to her when this was the case, Mrs. Hopewell had given it up. She might talk her head off. Mrs. Freeman could never be brought to admit herself wrong on
(15) any point. She would stand there and if she could be brought to say something, it was something like, "Well, I wouldn't of said it was and I wouldn't of said it wasn't," or letting her gaze range over the top shelf where there was an assortment of dusty bottles, she might remark, "I see you ain't ate many of them figs you put up last summer."

34. The metaphor suggested by "forward and reverse" in the opening sentence is also suggested by all of the following words EXCEPT

   (A) "advance" (line 4)
   (B) "swerved" (line 4)
   (C) "turned" (line 5)
   (D) "retract" (line 7)
   (E) "stop" (line 8)   Ⓐ Ⓑ Ⓒ Ⓓ Ⓔ

35. What quality of Mrs. Freeman's character does the controlling image of the passage suggest?

   (A) Her forbearance
   (B) Her insecurity
   (C) Her rigidity
   (D) Her proper manners
   (E) Her sense of irony   Ⓐ Ⓑ Ⓒ Ⓓ Ⓔ

36. That Mrs. Freeman "might stand there as real as several grain sacks thrown on top of each other" (lines 10-11) suggests that she is all of the following EXCEPT

   (A) plain and down-to-earth
   (B) undecided in her opinions
   (C) clearly visible
   (D) part of the country scene
   (E) closed and contributing nothing at present

   Ⓐ Ⓑ Ⓒ Ⓓ Ⓔ

37. The kind of remark Mrs. Freeman makes in lines 16-17 is called

   (A) a cliché
   (B) an allusion
   (C) a non sequitur
   (D) a circular argument
   (E) a metaphoric statement

   Ⓐ Ⓑ Ⓒ Ⓓ Ⓔ

38. Mrs. Freeman's remarks are best described as

   (A) self-protective
   (B) self-censuring
   (C) self-analytical
   (D) aggressive
   (E) contemptuous

   Ⓐ Ⓑ Ⓒ Ⓓ Ⓔ

Optional Free-Response Section

The optional free-response section of the Analyzing and Interpreting Literature examination requires candidates to demonstrate their ability to write well-organized critical essays. Candidates are asked to write two essays within a 90-minute time period. In the first essay, they are asked to discuss a poem printed in the test book; in the second essay, they must apply a general literary statement to a work of recognized literary merit that they have read. The following is an example of the kind of question a candidate might be asked to address in the second essay:

> The settings in works of literature — particular houses, cities, localities; particular institutions; particular periods of time — often have great influence on the development of a central character. Choose a novel, short story, or play of recognized literary merit that you have read. Briefly describe its setting. Then discuss in detail how the setting affects and, in turn, reveals the character of the protagonist.

In responding to the questions, candidates are expected to avoid vague generalities, irrelevant philosophizing, and unnecessary plot summaries. They should pay particular attention to the quality of their writing (organization, sentence structure, diction, clarity, the relevance of their illustrations to the questions asked, and the critical perceptiveness of their answers).

For additional information, read the sections on "Taking Essay Exams," in Chapter 5, and "How Essays Are Graded," in Chapter 6.

Study Resources

The most relevant preparation for the Analyzing and Interpreting Literature exam is attentive and reflective reading of the various literary genres of poetry, drama, and prose. There are several ways to prepare for the exam:

1. Read a variety of poetry, drama, fiction, and nonfiction.
2. Read critical analyses of various literary works.
3. Write your own analysis and interpretation of the works you read.
4. Discuss with others the meaning of the literature you read.

Textbooks used in college courses in analysis and interpretation of literature contain a sampling of literary works in a variety of genres. They also contain material that can help you to comprehend the sense and intent of literary works and to recognize the devices used by writers to convey that sense and intent. To prepare for the exam, you should study the contents of at least one college textbook, which you can find in most college bookstores. You would do well to consult two or three texts because they do vary somewhat in content, approach, and emphasis. For example, Perrine's book is a basic introduction to reading literature; Edgar Roberts emphasizes literary analysis; books by Sylvan Barnet and Perrine include glossaries of literary terms.

Additional suggestions for preparing for CLEP exams are given in Chapter 4.

English Literature

Description of the Examination

The Subject Examination in English Literature covers the material that is usually taught in a two-semester course (or the equivalent) at the college level. The test is primarily concerned with major authors and literary works, but it also includes questions on some minor writers. Candidates are expected to be acquainted with common literary themes, common literary terms, such as metaphor and personification, and basic literary forms, such as the sonnet and ballad.

In both coverage and approach, the exam resembles the historically organized survey of English literature offered by many colleges that deals with literature from Beowulf to the present. It assumes that the candidate has read widely and developed an appreciation of English literature, knows the basic literary periods, has a sense of the historical development of English literature, and is able to identify the author of a representative quotation or to recognize the period in which an excerpt was written.

The exam consists of approximately 105 multiple-choice questions to be answered in two separately timed 45-minute sections.

There is also an optional essay section that can be taken in addition to the multiple-choice test. The essay section is graded by the institution that requests it. Contact the school where you would like to receive credit for your CLEP exam to see if they require the optional essay section for this exam.

Knowledge and Skills Required

The English Literature exam requires the following knowledge and abilities. The percentages at the left show the relative emphasis given to knowledge and ability, but most questions draw on both.

Approximate Percent of Examination

45%   Knowledge of information related to:

    Literary background

    Identification of authors

    Metrical patterns

    Literary references

55%   Ability to:

    Analyze the elements of form in a literary passage

    Perceive meanings

    Identify tone and mood

    Follow patterns of imagery

    Identify characteristics of style

Sample Questions

The 26 sample questions that follow are similar to questions on the English Literature exam, but they do not actually appear on it.

Before attempting to answer the sample questions, read all the information about the English Literature exam on the preceding page and above. Additional suggestions for preparing for CLEP exams are provided in Chapter 4.

Try to answer correctly as many questions as possible. Then compare your answers with the correct answers, given in Appendix A.

Directions: Each of the questions or incomplete statements on the following pages is followed by five suggested answers or completions. Select the one that is best in each case.

In a pungent critique of humanity addressed to the mature imagination, the author comments on human nature by examining the life of the Lilliputians, Yahoos, and Houyhnhnms.

1. The book described above is

(A) *The Way of All Flesh*
(B) *Through the Looking Glass*
(C) *Gulliver's Travels*
(D) *The Pilgrim's Progress*
(E) *Robinson Crusoe*

Ⓐ Ⓑ Ⓒ Ⓓ Ⓔ

One of the great triumphs of the play is Shakespeare's addition of the character of the Fool, who attempts to comfort his old master and is distressed and puzzled by his madness, but who also ironically emphasizes the folly and the tragedy of the old man.

2. The play referred to above is

(A) *Macbeth*   (B) *Julius Caesar*   (C) *King Lear*
(D) *Othello*   (E) *Hamlet*

Ⓐ Ⓑ Ⓒ Ⓓ Ⓔ

Questions 3-4

> For I have learned
> To look on nature, not as in the hour
> Of thoughtless youth; but hearing oftentimes
> The still, sad music of humanity,
> Nor harsh nor grating, though of ample power
> To chasten and subdue. And I have felt
> A presence that disturbs me with the joy
> Of elevated thoughts; a sense sublime
> Of something far more deeply interfused,
> Whose dwelling is the light of setting suns,
> And the round ocean and the living air,
> And the blue sky, and in the mind of man.

3. The lines above are written in

(A) heroic couplets   (B) terza rima   (C) ballad meter
(D) blank verse   (E) iambic tetrameter

Ⓐ Ⓑ Ⓒ Ⓓ Ⓔ

4. The language and ideas in these lines are most characteristic of which of the following literary periods?

   (A) Medieval   (B) Restoration   (C) Augustan
     (D) Romantic   (E) Early twentieth century   Ⓐ Ⓑ Ⓒ Ⓓ Ⓔ

---

5. Samuel Richardson, Henry Fielding, and Tobias Smollett are best known as eighteenth-century

   (A) novelists   (B) dramatists   (C) essayists
     (D) poets   (E) critics   Ⓐ Ⓑ Ⓒ Ⓓ Ⓔ

The business of a poet is to examine, not the individual, but the species; to remark general properties and large appearances. He does not number the streaks of the tulip, or describe the different shades in the verdure of the forest. He is to exhibit in his portraits of nature such prominent and striking features, as recall the original to every mind; and must neglect the minuter discriminations.

6. Which of the following statements most agrees with the paragraph above?

   (A) Poetry is the spontaneous overflow of powerful feelings.
   (B) Poetry is the precious lifeblood of a master spirit.
   (C) Poetry is the just representation of general nature.
   (D) Poetry should not mean but be.
   (E) Poets are the unacknowledged legislators of the world.

   Ⓐ Ⓑ Ⓒ Ⓓ Ⓔ

7. An anonymous narrative poem focusing on the climax of a particularly dramatic event and employing frequent repetition, conventional figures of speech, and sometimes a refrain — altered and transmitted orally in a musical setting — is called a

   (A) popular ballad   (B) pastoral elegy
     (C) courtly lyric   (D) villanelle
       (E) chivalric romance   Ⓐ Ⓑ Ⓒ Ⓓ Ⓔ

Questions 8-10

> They, looking back, all the eastern side beheld
> Of Paradise, so late their happy seat,
> Waved over by that flaming brand, the gate
> With dreadful faces thronged and fiery arms.
> (5)   Some natural tears they dropped, but wiped them soon;
> The world was all before them, where to choose
> Their place of rest, and Providence their guide:
> They hand in hand, with wandering steps and slow
> Through Eden took their solitary way.

8. These lines were written by

    (A) John Donne   (B) Edmund Spenser   (C) Christopher Marlowe
    (D) William Shakespeare   (E) John Milton

    Ⓐ Ⓑ Ⓒ Ⓓ Ⓔ

9. In line 2, "late" is best interpreted to mean

    (A) recently   (B) tardily   (C) unfortunately
    (D) long   (E) soon

    Ⓐ Ⓑ Ⓒ Ⓓ Ⓔ

10. The people referred to as "they" in the passage were probably experiencing all the following emotions EXCEPT

    (A) awe   (B) anticipation   (C) suspicion
    (D) regret   (E) sorrow

    Ⓐ Ⓑ Ⓒ Ⓓ Ⓔ

> Whan that Aprill with his shoures soote
> The droghte of March hath perced to the roote

11. The lines above were written by

    (A) Geoffrey Chaucer   (B) William Shakespeare
    (C) Alexander Pope   (D) William Wordsworth
    (E) Robert Browning

    Ⓐ Ⓑ Ⓒ Ⓓ Ⓔ

12. Alfred Tennyson's "Ulysses" and T. S. Eliot's "The Love Song of J. Alfred Prufrock" are both

   (A) pastoral elegies
   (B) literary ballads
   (C) mock epics
   (D) dramatic monologues
   (E) irregular odes

   (A) (B) (C) (D) (E)

Questions 13-14

> Our two souls therefore, which are one,
>   Though I must go, endure not yet
> A breach, but an expansion,
>   Like gold to airy thinness beat.

13. The passage contains an example of

   (A) an epic simile
   (B) a metaphysical conceit
   (C) an epic catalog
   (D) an alexandrine
   (E) sprung rhythm

   (A) (B) (C) (D) (E)

14. The passage is from a poem by

   (A) Alexander Pope
   (B) Robert Herrick
   (C) Samuel Taylor Coleridge
   (D) Samuel Johnson
   (E) John Donne

   (A) (B) (C) (D) (E)

Questions 15-17

> . . . He's here in double trust:
> First, as I am his kinsman and his subject,
> Strong both against the deed; then, as his host,
> Who should against his murtherer shut the door,
> (5) Not bear the knife myself. Besides, this Duncan
> Hath borne his faculties so meek, hath been
> So clear in his great office, that his virtues
> Will plead like angels, trumpet-tongu'd, against
> The deep damnation of his taking-off;
> (10) And pity, like a naked new-born babe,
> Striding the blast, or heaven's cherubin, hors'd
> Upon the sightless couriers of the air,
> Shall blow the horrid deed in every eye,
> That tears shall drown the wind.

15. The speaker of these lines might best be described as a

    (A) coward
    (B) man badly treated by Duncan
    (C) man seeking revenge
    (D) man concerned only with his own safety
    (E) man troubled by moral law   Ⓐ Ⓑ Ⓒ Ⓓ Ⓔ

16. The "horrid deed" (line 13) is compared metaphorically to

    (A) a cinder or speck irritating the eye
    (B) a naked newborn babe
    (C) an assassination
    (D) the wind
    (E) the consequences of the murder of Duncan   Ⓐ Ⓑ Ⓒ Ⓓ Ⓔ

17. These lines are spoken by

    (A) Hamlet   (B) Cassius   (C) Macbeth
    (D) Iago   (E) Richard III   Ⓐ Ⓑ Ⓒ Ⓓ Ⓔ

18. Which of the following is the first line of a poem by John Keats?

    (A) "What dire offence from amorous causes springs"
    (B) "They flee from me that sometime did me seek"
    (C) "Thou still unravished bride of quietness"
    (D) "I weep for Adonais — he is dead"
    (E) "Not, I'll not, carrion comfort, Despair, not feast on thee"

Ⓐ Ⓑ Ⓒ Ⓓ Ⓔ

Questions 19-20

> O threats of Hell and Hopes of Paradise!
> One thing at least is certain — *This* life flies;
>   One thing is certain and the rest is Lies:
> The Flower that once has blown for ever dies.

19. In the fourth line, "blown" means

    (A) blown up   (B) blown away   (C) bloomed
    (D) died   (E) been planted

Ⓐ Ⓑ Ⓒ Ⓓ Ⓔ

20. Which of the following is the best summary of the four lines?

    (A) Do not ignore the serious aspects of life; earnest dedication is
        necessary for success.
    (B) Do not rely on a theoretical afterlife; you can be sure only that the
        present moment will pass.
    (C) Life is like a flower with roots in both good and evil.
    (D) Religious belief is essential to a happy life.
    (E) The only safe course in life is to ignore outside events and cultivate
        one's own garden.

Ⓐ Ⓑ Ⓒ Ⓓ Ⓔ

21. Which of the following was written earliest?

    (A) *The Waste Land*
    (B) *The Rime of the Ancient Mariner*
    (C) *Songs of Innocence*
    (D) *The Faerie Queene*
    (E) *The Rape of the Lock*

    Ⓐ Ⓑ Ⓒ Ⓓ Ⓔ

Questions 22-23

She was alone and still, gazing out to sea; and when she felt his presence and the worship of his eyes turned to him in quiet suffrance of his gaze, without shame or wantonness. Long, long she suffered his gaze and then quietly withdrew her eyes from his and bent them towards the stream, gently stirring the water with her foot hither and thither. The first faint noise of gently moving water broke the silence, low and faint and whispering, faint as the bells of sleep; hither and thither, hither and thither: and a faint flame trembled on her cheek.

—Heavenly God! cried Stephen's soul, in an outburst of profane joy.

22. The passage above appears in which of the following novels?

    (A) *Victory*
    (B) *A Portrait of the Artist as a Young Man*
    (C) *Tess of the D'Urbervilles*
    (D) *The Egoist*
    (E) *Sons and Lovers*

    Ⓐ Ⓑ Ⓒ Ⓓ Ⓔ

23. The passage presents an example of what its author would have termed

    (A) synecdoche
    (B) pathetic fallacy
    (C) stream of consciousness
    (D) an eclogue
    (E) an epiphany

    Ⓐ Ⓑ Ⓒ Ⓓ Ⓔ

Questions 24-25 are based on an excerpt from Henry Fielding's *Joseph Andrews.*

> Now, the rake Hesperus has called for his breeches, and having well rubbed his drowsy eyes, prepared to dress himself for all night; by whose example his brother rakes on earth likewise leave those beds in which they slept away the day. Now Thetis, the good housewife, began
> (5) to put on the pot, in order to regale the good man Phoebus after his daily labours were over. In vulgar language, it was the evening when Joseph attended his lady's orders.

24. Which of the following describes Hesperus (line 1), Thetis (line 4), and Phoebus (line 5) in the passage above?

    (A) They are references to Greek mythology.
    (B) They are references to fellow authors.
    (C) They are references to Biblical heroes.
    (D) They refer to figures from English folklore.
    (E) They are characters in the novel.

    Ⓐ Ⓑ Ⓒ Ⓓ Ⓔ

25. In line 6, "vulgar language" means

    (A) commonly spoken language
    (B) elevated and archaic language
    (C) ungrammatical language
    (D) language laden with sexual puns
    (E) language characterized by obsolete and dialectal terms

    Ⓐ Ⓑ Ⓒ Ⓓ Ⓔ

---

26. The "Age of Johnson" in English literature was dominated by which of the following styles?

    (A) Romanticism
    (B) Neoclassicism
    (C) Expressionism
    (D) Naturalism
    (E) Abstractionism

    Ⓐ Ⓑ Ⓒ Ⓓ Ⓔ

Optional Essay Section

If your college requires that the optional essay section be taken in addition to the multiple-choice exam, you may wish to review the following information.

The optional essay section of the English Literature exam requires the candidate to write two essays. The first essay should be a well-organized critical essay on an excerpt from a literary work provided in the test book. For the second essay, candidates must discuss one of two given general statements, drawing from their reading for pertinent examples and supportive evidence.

For additional information, read the sections on "Taking Essay Tests," in Chapter 5, and "How Essays Are Graded," in Chapter 6.

Study Resources

To prepare for the English Literature exam, you should read critically the contents of at least one anthology, many of which are used as textbooks in English literature courses at the college level. Visit your local college bookstore to determine which anthologies and textbooks are used by the college for English Literature courses.

Most textbook anthologies contain a representative sample of readings as well as discussions of historical background, literary styles and devices characteristic of various authors and periods, and other material relevant to the test. The anthologies do vary somewhat in content, approach, and emphasis, and you are therefore advised to consult more than one anthology or some specialized books on major authors, periods, and literary forms and terminology. When selecting a more specialized book, check the table of contents against the "Knowledge and Skills Required" section on pages 143-144. You should also read some of the major novels that are mentioned or excerpted in the anthologies. You can probably obtain an extensive reading list of English literature from a college English department, library, or bookstore. The Internet is another resource you could explore.

Additional suggestions for preparing for CLEP examinations are provided in Chapter 4.

Freshman College Composition

Description of the Examination

The Subject Examination in Freshman College Composition measures the skills required in most first-year English courses. It addresses elements of language and grammar; various types of writing, both formal and informal; and limited analysis and interpretation of short passages of prose and poetry. The exam assumes that the candidate knows the fundamental principles of rhetoric and can apply the principles of standard written English. In addition, the exam requires familiarity with research papers and reference skills.

The exam has approximately 100 multiple-choice questions to be answered in two separately timed 45-minute sections.

There is also an optional essay section that can be taken in addition to the multiple-choice test. The essay section is graded by the institution that requests it. Contact the school where you would like to receive credit for your CLEP exam to see if they require the optional essay section for this exam.

Knowledge and Skills Required

The multiple-choice questions of the exam measure students' writing skills both at the sentence level and within the context of passages. Elements of language, grammar, different styles of writing, and limited literary analysis of short prose and poetry selections are tested. The exam is designed so that average students who have completed the first-year English requirement in composition can usually answer about half of the multiple-choice questions correctly.

1. *Ability to Recognize and Use Standard Written English* — The exam measures the candidate's awareness of a variety of logical, structural, and grammatical relationships within sentences. These skills are tested by approximately 20 percent of the multiple-choice questions in the exam. Questions test recognition of acceptable usage relating to:

Syntax: parallelism, coordination, subordination, dangling modifiers
Sentence boundaries (comma-splice, run-ons, sentence fragments)
Recognition of correct sentences

Sentence variety

Concord/Agreement: subject-verb, verb tense, pronoun reference, shift, number

Correct idiom

Active/passive voice

Logical comparison

Test of punctuation

Several kinds of question formats throughout the exam are intended to measure the above skills:

- *Identifying Sentence Errors* — This type of question appears in Section I of the exam. It requires the candidate to identify wording that violates the standard conventions of written discourse. Samples of this question type are on pages 158-160 in this guide.

- *Improving Sentences* — This type of question appears only in Section I of the exam. It requires the candidate to choose the version of a phrase, clause, or sentence that best conveys the intended meaning of a sentence. Samples of this question type are on pages 160-163 in this guide.

2. ***Ability to Recognize Logical Development*** — Questions in approximately 65 percent of the exam measure recognition of the following in the context of works in progress (student drafts) or of published prose.

Organization

Evaluation of evidence

Awareness of audience, tone, and purpose

Level of detail

Consistency of topic focus (sustaining coherence between paragraphs)

Sentence variety

Paragraph coherence

Main idea, thesis

Rhetorical effects and emphasis

Use of language

Evaluation of author's authority and appeal

Evaluation of reasoning

Shift in point of view

The following kinds of multiple-choice questions measure writing skills in context.

- *Revising Work in Progress* — This type of question appears in Section I of the exam. The candidate identifies ways to improve an early draft of an essay. See pages 163-168 for sample questions.

- *Analyzing Writing* — Two prose passages written in very different modes and a poetry selection appear in Section II of the exam. The candidate answers questions about each passage and poem and about the strategies used by the author of each selection. See pages 170-174 for sample questions.

- *Analyzing and Evaluating Writers' Choices* — This type of question appears in Section II of the exam. The candidate answers questions about tone, attitude, ambiguity, and clarity within short prompts. See pages 174-176 for sample questions.

3. *Ability to Use Resource Materials* — Approximately 15 percent of the questions in Section I of the exam test the candidate's familiarity with the following basic reference skills, which are tested both in context and in individual questions.

Evaluating sources

Integrating resource material into the research paper

Manuscript format and documentation

Reference skills

Use of reference books

See pages 168-169 for sample questions.

Sample Questions

The 50 sample questions that follow are similar to questions on the Freshman College Composition exam, but they do not appear on the actual test.

Before attempting to answer the sample questions, read all the information about the Freshman College Composition exam on the preceding pages. Additional suggestions for preparing for CLEP exams are provided in Chapter 4.

Try to answer correctly as many questions as possible. Then compare your answers with the correct answers, given in Appendix A.

SECTION I

IDENTIFYING SENTENCE ERRORS

Directions: The following sentences test your knowledge of grammar, usage, diction (choice of words), and idiom. Note that some sentences are correct, and no sentence contains more than one error.

You will find that the error, if there is one, is underlined and lettered. Assume that elements of the sentence that are not underlined are correct and cannot be changed. In choosing answers, follow the requirements of standard written English.

If there is an error, select the one underlined part that must be changed to make the sentence correct and fill in the corresponding oval on your answer sheet.

If there is no error, fill in answer oval E.

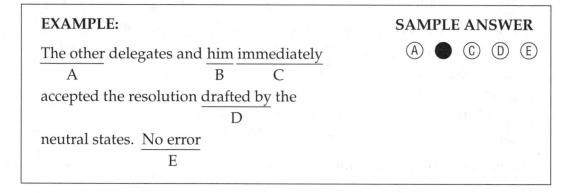

1. Hydroelectric dams work <u>on a simple</u> principle: <u>the greater the</u>
                           A   B
   distance that the water has <u>to fall</u>, the more the power that
                               C
   <u>was generated.</u> <u>No error</u>
        D   E

   Ⓐ Ⓑ Ⓒ Ⓓ Ⓔ

2. Alexis <u>has discovered</u> that she can express her creativity more freely
          A
   <u>through</u> her <u>sketches</u> <u>and not in</u> her photography. <u>No error</u>
      B   C   D   E

   Ⓐ Ⓑ Ⓒ Ⓓ Ⓔ

3. To learn <u>more</u> about Hispanic culture, we invited a <u>lecturer who</u> had
       A   B

   spoken frequently <u>with regard to</u> <u>the life of</u> early settlers in Santa Fe.
                         C   D

   <u>No error</u>
      E

   Ⓐ Ⓑ Ⓒ Ⓓ Ⓔ

4. Many readers <u>still think</u> of Sinclair Lewis, whose strength
                   A

   <u>was allegedly</u> his <u>ability to tell</u> a story, <u>as one of</u> America's best
      B   C   D

   social critics. <u>No error</u>
                 E

   Ⓐ Ⓑ Ⓒ Ⓓ Ⓔ

5. <u>Although</u> a lottery may seem a <u>relatively easy</u> way for a state
     A   B

   <u>to increase revenues,</u> <u>they</u> may encourage some individuals to gamble
        C   D

   excessively. <u>No error</u>
             E

   Ⓐ Ⓑ Ⓒ Ⓓ Ⓔ

6. Even when <u>using</u> a calculator, you must have a basic <u>understanding of</u>
           A   B

   mathematics if <u>one expects</u> to solve complex problems <u>correctly</u>.
                 C   D

   <u>No error</u>
      E

   Ⓐ Ⓑ Ⓒ Ⓓ Ⓔ

7. Gwendolyn Brooks is <u>widely known</u> and highly praised for her <u>poetry,</u>
                         A   B

   fewer people <u>realize that</u> she has <u>also</u> published a novel. <u>No error</u>
              C   D   E

   Ⓐ Ⓑ Ⓒ Ⓓ Ⓔ

8. Although science offers the hope <u>of preventing</u> serious genetic
A

diseases, <u>there is</u> difficult ethical questions <u>raised by</u> the <u>possibility of</u>
B   C   D

altering human heredity. <u>No error</u>
E

Ⓐ Ⓑ Ⓒ Ⓓ Ⓔ

9. If they <u>would have</u> known how capricious the winds on Lake
A

Winasteke <u>are</u>, the boys would have sailed in the <u>larger</u> of <u>their</u> two
B   C D

boats. <u>No error</u>
E

Ⓐ Ⓑ Ⓒ Ⓓ Ⓔ

10. Faulkner <u>had published</u> <u>only</u> a few novels when critics <u>seriously began</u>
A   B   C

to compare his work to <u>Hemingway.</u> <u>No error</u>
D   E

Ⓐ Ⓑ Ⓒ Ⓓ Ⓔ

IMPROVING SENTENCES

Directions: The following sentences test correctness and effectiveness of expression. In choosing answers, follow the requirements of standard written English: that is, pay attention to grammar, diction (choice of words), sentence construction, and punctuation.

In each of the following sentences, part of the sentence or the entire sentence is underlined. Beneath each sentence you will find five versions of the underlined part. Choice A repeats the original; the other four are different.

Choose the answer that best expresses the meaning of the original sentence. If you think the original is better than any of the alternatives, choose it; otherwise choose one of the others. Your choice should produce the most effective sentence — one that is clear and precise, without awkwardness or ambiguity.

Example   **Sample Answer**

Ⓐ ● Ⓒ Ⓓ Ⓔ

Laura Ingalls Wilder published her first book <u>and she was sixty-five</u> <u>years old then</u>.

    (A)   and she was sixty-five years old then
    (B)   when she was sixty-five
    (C)   being age sixty-five years old
    (D)   upon the reaching of sixty-five years
    (E)   at the time when she was sixty-five

11. <u>In 1827 *Freedom's Journal* was the first Black American newspaper</u> <u>in the United States, it was published in New York City.</u>

    (A) In 1827 *Freedom's Journal* was the first Black American newspaper in the United States, it was published in New York City.
    (B) In 1827 the first Black American newspaper in the United States, *Freedom's Journal*, was published in New York City.
    (C) In New York City in 1827 *Freedom's Journal*, the first Black American newspaper in the United States, was published there.
    (D) With publication in New York City in 1827, it was the first Black American newspaper in the United States, *Freedom's Journal*.
    (E) The first Black American newspaper published in the United States was when there was *Freedom's Journal* in New York City in 1827.

Ⓐ Ⓑ Ⓒ Ⓓ Ⓔ

12. Astronomers have developed extremely sophisticated <u>instruments,</u> <u>which is helpful for measuring the properties of objects in space.</u>

    (A) instruments, which is helpful for measuring the properties of objects in space
    (B) instruments to help measure the properties of objects in space
    (C) instruments, which are helpful for measurement of space objects' properties
    (D) instruments helpful to measure the properties of objects in space
    (E) instruments, a help for measuring the properties of objects in space

Ⓐ Ⓑ Ⓒ Ⓓ Ⓔ

13. Foreign correspondents are like birds of passage, resting for a few weeks, then flying off again to a new place.

    (A) then flying off again
    (B) after which again they fly off
    (C) then they fly off again
    (D) when once again they fly off
    (E) but soon they are flying off again

    Ⓐ Ⓑ Ⓒ Ⓓ Ⓔ

14. Reducing individual taxes while eliminating as much waste as possible are traditional methods for increasing a nation's economy.

    (A) are traditional methods for increasing
    (B) is a traditional method for increasing
    (C) is a traditional method of stimulating
    (D) traditionally are methods for increasing
    (E) are traditional methods of stimulating

    Ⓐ Ⓑ Ⓒ Ⓓ Ⓔ

15. Arguably the most distinctive regional cuisine in the United States, the South is noted for such specialties as Brunswick stew and hush puppies.

    (A) the South is noted for such specialties as
    (B) the South has such specialties of note as
    (C) the South includes among its noteworthy specialties
    (D) southern cooking includes such noteworthy specialties as
    (E) southern cooking is including such specialties of note as

    Ⓐ Ⓑ Ⓒ Ⓓ Ⓔ

16. Today's fashion designers must consider both how much a fabric costs and its wearability.

    (A) its wearability
    (B) is it going to wear well
    (C) if it has wearability
    (D) how well it wears
    (E) the fabric's ability to wear well

    Ⓐ Ⓑ Ⓒ Ⓓ Ⓔ

17. Because the eleven women functioned as a <u>team is why they had a successful season</u>.

    (A) team is why they had a successful season
    (B) team, they had a success this season
    (C) team, they had a successful season
    (D) team, success was theirs this season
    (E) team is why their season was a success

Ⓐ Ⓑ Ⓒ Ⓓ Ⓔ

18. Home computers themselves are becoming less expensive, but software, printers, and Internet access <u>cause the total financial cost to rise up greatly</u>.

    (A) cause the total financial cost to rise up greatly
    (B) greatly increase the total cost
    (C) highly inflate the cost totals
    (D) drive up the expense
    (E) totally add to the expense

Ⓐ Ⓑ Ⓒ Ⓓ Ⓔ

REVISING WORK IN PROGRESS

Directions: Each of the following selections is an early draft of a student essay in which the sentences have been numbered for easy reference. Some parts of the selections need to be changed.

Read each selection and then answer the questions that follow. Some questions are about particular sentences or parts of sentences and ask you to improve sentence structure and diction (word choice). In making these decisions, follow the conventions of standard written English. Other questions refer to the entire essay or parts of the essay and ask you to consider organization, development, and effectiveness of language in relation to purpose and audience. After you choose each answer, fill in the corresponding oval on your answer sheet.

Questions 19-23 are based on the following draft of a student essay.

(1) *I used to be convinced that people didn't actually win radio contests; I thought that the excited winners I heard were only actors.* (2) *Sure, people could win T-shirts.* (3) *They couldn't win anything of real value.*

(4) *I've always loved sports.* (5) *Unlike my friends, who fall asleep to "Top 40 Radio," I listen to "Sports Night with Dave Sims."* (6) *His show is hardly usual fare for a young woman.* (7) *One night I heard Dave Sims announce a sports trivia contest with cash prizes of two thousand dollars.* (8) *I jump at the chance to combine my talk-show knowledge with everything my parents had taught me about sports.* (9) *I sent in my self-addressed stamped envelope.* (10) *I forgot about the whole matter.* (11) *Then the questionnaire appeared in my mailbox ten days later.* (12) *Its arrival gave me a rude surprise.* (13) *Instead of sitting down and whipping through it, I trudged to libraries and spent hours digging for answers to such obscure questions as "Which National Hockey League goalie holds the record for most career shutouts?"*

(14) *Finally, after days of double-checking answers, I mailed off my answer sheet, certain I would hear no more about the matter.* (15) *Certain, until two weeks later, I ripped open the envelope with the NBC peacock and read "Congratulations…"* (16) *I was a winner, a winner of more than a T-shirt.*

19. Which of the following is the best way to revise the underlined portions of sentences 2 and 3 (reproduced below) so that the two sentences are combined into one?

    Sure, people could win T-shirts. They couldn't win anything of real value.

    (A) T-shirts, and they couldn't win
    (B) T-shirts, but they couldn't win
    (C) T-shirts, but not being able to win
    (D) T-shirts, so they do win
    (E) T-shirts, while there was no winning

    Ⓐ Ⓑ Ⓒ Ⓓ Ⓔ

20. Which of the following sentences, if added after sentence 3, would best link the first paragraph with the rest of the essay?

    (A) I have held this opinion about contests for a long time.
    (B) The prizes offered did not inspire me to enter the contests.
    (C) However, I recently changed my opinion about these contests.
    (D) Usually the questions on these contests are really easy to answer.
    (E) Sometimes my friends try to convince me to enter such contests.

21. In the context of the second paragraph, which of the following is the best version of the underlined portion of sentence 8 (reproduced below)?

    I jump at the chance to combine my talk-show knowledge with everything my parents had taught me about sports.

    (A) (As it is now)
    (B) I jumped at the chance to combine
    (C) Having jumped at the chance to combine
    (D) Jumping at the chance and combining
    (E) Jumping at the chance by combining

    Ⓐ Ⓑ Ⓒ Ⓓ Ⓔ

22. Which of the following is the best way to revise and combine sentences 9 and 10 (reproduced below)?

    I sent in my self-addressed stamped envelope. I forgot about the whole matter.

    (A) Having sent in my self-addressed stamped envelope, the whole matter was forgotten.
    (B) After sending in my self-addressed stamped envelope, the matter was wholly forgotten.
    (C) After my self-addressed stamped envelope was sent in, it was then that I forgot the whole matter.
    (D) After sending in my self-addressed stamped envelope, I forgot about the whole matter.
    (E) Forgetting about the whole matter after sending in my self-addressed stamped envelope.

    Ⓐ Ⓑ Ⓒ Ⓓ Ⓔ

23. All of the following strategies are used by the writer of the passage EXCEPT

   (A) selecting specific examples
   (B) telling a story to develop a point
   (C) criticizing those whose opinions differ from hers
   (D) building suspense with references to the passage of time
   (E) disproving the assumption stated in the first sentence of the passage

Questions 24-28 are based on the following early draft of a letter to the editor of a local newspaper.

(1) *Our community needs more parks and play areas.* (2) *Living in a world where concrete surrounds us, it is important that we create places that are green and natural so that children can run and play.*

(3) *It is possible to do much with little expense to the city.* (4) *An abandoned lot can become a big patch of green grass ideal for running games.* (5) *And buying expensive playground equipment and strange pieces of modern art for children to climb on is unnecessary.* (6) *Children will climb on anything if one lets them.* (7) *A large concrete pipe or an old truck with its wheels and doors removed makes an imaginative plaything.* (8) *Simply remove any part that may be breakable or unsafe, then paint the equipment with bright colors.* (9) *Bury the truck or pipe a foot or two deep so that it is stable.* (10) *Great opportunities for fun!* (11) *Children can play for hours, crawling through a secret tunnel or navigating to a distant planet.* (12) *Neighborhood committees could contribute other discards.*

(13) *We should do these things because children need oases in this concrete desert we live in.* (14) *This may take time, but if people get together and contribute both ideas and labor, much can be completed successfully.*

24. Which of the following is the best way to revise the underlined portion of sentence 2 (reproduced below)?

Living in a world where concrete surrounds us, it is important that we create places that are green and natural so that children can run and play.

(A) Living in a world where concrete surrounds us, the important thing is to
(B) We live in a world where concrete surrounds us, it is important that we
(C) Being surrounded by a world of concrete, it is important to
(D) Surrounding us with a world of concrete, we need to
(E) Surrounded by a world of concrete, we need to

Ⓐ Ⓑ Ⓒ Ⓓ Ⓔ

25. Which of the following would best replace "*And*" at the beginning of sentence 5?

(A) Furthermore,
(B) Instead,
(C) Despite this,
(D) Nevertheless,
(E) Excepting this,

Ⓐ Ⓑ Ⓒ Ⓓ Ⓔ

26. The writer of the passage could best improve sentence 12 by

(A) acknowledging drawbacks to suggestions
(B) providing specific examples
(C) including personal opinions
(D) discussing other community problems
(E) defining the idea of a neighborhood

Ⓐ Ⓑ Ⓒ Ⓓ Ⓔ

27. In context, the best phrase to replace *"do these things"* in sentence 13 is

   (A) accomplish our intentions
   (B) help these children
   (C) consider other options
   (D) build these play areas
   (E) have new ideas

   Ⓐ Ⓑ Ⓒ Ⓓ Ⓔ

28. Which is the best version of the underlined portion of sentence 14 (reproduced below)?

   This may take time, but if people get together and contribute both ideas and labor, much can be completed successfully.

   (A) (as it is now)
   (B) and if people get together and they contribute
   (C) but if people will get together and they will also contribute
   (D) but if people get together and they would have contributed
   (E) however, if people get together, also contributing

   Ⓐ Ⓑ Ⓒ Ⓓ Ⓔ

RECOGNIZING AND APPLYING WRITING SKILLS

Directions: For each question below, choose the best answer and fill in the corresponding oval on the answer sheet.

29. In a student's research paper, the place at which a footnote is introduced should be marked with an Arabic numeral that is

   (A) elevated slightly above the line
   (B) followed by a quotation mark
   (C) enclosed in brackets
   (D) followed by a period
   (E) preceded by a slash and followed by a period

   Ⓐ Ⓑ Ⓒ Ⓓ Ⓔ

30. The best way to find current data for a library research paper on long-term health care facilities is to

    (A) consult a medical textbook
    (B) look in indexes to journals and periodicals
    (C) go through recent issues of newspapers and magazines
    (D) locate the section of the library containing science books
    (E) check in a recent almanac

    Ⓐ Ⓑ Ⓒ Ⓓ Ⓔ

31. Siegfried Sassoon, "The Old Huntsman," *The Revised College Omnibus*, ed. James D. McCallum (New York: Harcourt, Brace and Company, 1939), p. 87.

    The footnote given above shows that

    (A) the author of *The Revised College Omnibus* is James D. McCallum
    (B) *The Revised College Omnibus* is a periodical
    (C) "The Old Huntsman" is technically termed a subtitle
    (D) "The Old Huntsman" is the name of a book
    (E) Siegfried Sassoon wrote a work that appears in *The Revised College Omnibus*

    Ⓐ Ⓑ Ⓒ Ⓓ Ⓔ

32. When you consult a glossary in a book, you can expect to find

    (A) a list of other books the author has written
    (B) a biographical sketch of the author
    (C) a description of characters who appear in the book
    (D) a list of the books the author consulted
    (E) definitions of technical or unfamiliar words in the book

    Ⓐ Ⓑ Ⓒ Ⓓ Ⓔ

SECTION II

ANALYZING WRITING

Directions: Each of the following passages consists of numbered sentences. Because the passages are part of longer writing samples, they do not necessarily constitute a complete discussion of the issues presented.

Read each passage carefully and answer the questions that follow it. The questions test your awareness of a writer's purpose and of characteristics of prose that are important to good writing.

Questions 33-36 refer to the following passage.

(1) The place called the Great Plains spreads southward from the upper Saskatchewan River down to the Rio Grande — a high country, a big country of vast reaches, tremendous streams, and stories of death on the ridges, derring-do in the valleys, and the sweetness and heartbreak of springtime on the prairies.

(2) Half of this geographical area was the old Nebraska Territory that lay like a golden hackberry leaf in the sun, a giant curling, tilted leaf. (3) The veins of it were the long streams rising out near the mountains and flowing eastward to the Big Muddy, the wild Missouri. (4) The largest that cut through the center of the Plains was the broad, flat-watered Platte, usually pleasant and easygoing as an October day, and below it the Republican, deceptively limpid but roaring into sudden gullywashers that flooded all the wide valley and could sweep away even the most powerful of the wilderness herds.

33. The language, style, and subject of this passage suggest that it can best be classified as

    (A) a narrative episode
    (B) an expository statement
    (C) a descriptive piece
    (D) an exclamatory tribute
    (E) a rational argument

    Ⓐ Ⓑ Ⓒ Ⓓ Ⓔ

34. The effect of the second paragraph depends most heavily on the use of

    (A) irony
    (B) understatement
    (C) reasoned argument
    (D) metaphor and simile
    (E) dramatic exaggeration

    Ⓐ Ⓑ Ⓒ Ⓓ Ⓔ

35. As used in the last sentence, "limpid," most nearly means

    (A) calm
    (B) cool
    (C) troublesome
    (D) destructive
    (E) beautiful

    Ⓐ Ⓑ Ⓒ Ⓓ Ⓔ

36. In the second paragraph, the image of the leaf suggests the

    (A) barrenness of the dry land
    (B) topography of the territory
    (C) rich forest of the river valleys
    (D) changes caused by the seasons
    (E) vigor of life throughout the land

    Ⓐ Ⓑ Ⓒ Ⓓ Ⓔ

Questions 37-41 refer to the following passage.

(1) Michael Goldman wrote in a poem, "When the Muse comes She doesn't tell you to write;/She says get up for a minute, I've something to show you, stand here." (2) What made me look up at that roadside tree?

(3) The road to Grundy, Virginia, is, as you might expect, a narrow scrawl scribbled all over the most improbably peaked and hunched mountains you ever saw. (4) The few people who live along the road also seem peaked and hunched. (5) But what on earth...? (6) It was hot, sunny summer. (7) The road was just bending off sharply to the right. (8) I hadn't seen a house in miles, and none was in sight. (9) At the apogee of the road's curve grew an enormous oak, a massive bur oak 200 years old, 150 feet high, an oak whose lowest limb was beyond the span of the highest ladder. (10) I looked up; there were clothes spread all over the tree. (11) Red shirts, blue trousers, black

pants, little baby smocks — they weren't hung from branches. (12) They were outside, carefully spread, splayed as if to dry, on the outer leaves of the great oak's crown. (13) Were there pillowcases, blankets? (14) I can't remember. (15) There was a gay assortment of cotton underwear, yellow dresses, children's green sweaters, plaid skirts.... (16) You know roads. (17) A bend comes and you take it, thoughtlessly, moving on. (18) I looked behind me for another split second, astonished; both sides of the tree's canopy, clear to the top, bore clothes.

37. Which of the following best describes the relationship between the two paragraphs in this passage?

(A) The second paragraph answers the question at the end of the first.
(B) The second paragraph offers a concrete illustration of the quotation in the first.
(C) The second paragraph takes an opposite point of view from the first.
(D) The second paragraph generalizes about the quotation in the first.
(E) The second paragraph is an elaborate contradiction of the thesis in the first.

Ⓐ Ⓑ Ⓒ Ⓓ Ⓔ

38. Which of the following most accurately describes what happens in the second paragraph?

(A) The speaker has a poetic vision symbolizing cleansing renewal.
(B) The speaker has a hallucination brought on by the heat.
(C) The speaker tries to explain how the phenomenon was accomplished.
(D) The speaker sees a tree full of flowers and imagines they are someone's washing.
(E) The speaker sees a large tree inexplicably covered with clothes spread to dry.

Ⓐ Ⓑ Ⓒ Ⓓ Ⓔ

39. The descriptive details in sentences 9-15 provide a

(A) precise visual image
(B) picture of something unearthly
(C) representation of a blur of color
(D) view from a child's perspective
(E) distorted sense of motion

Ⓐ Ⓑ Ⓒ Ⓓ Ⓔ

40. Which of the following pairs of words best describes the speaker's reaction to the experience?

   (A) Ecstasy and fear
   (B) Dismay and wonder
   (C) Delight and fear
   (D) Disgust and disbelief
   (E) Wonder and delight

   Ⓐ Ⓑ Ⓒ Ⓓ Ⓔ

41. The main implication of the passage is that

   (A) people should be more observant as they travel country roads
   (B) people are resourceful in finding ways to rise above domestic tasks
   (C) inspiration or vision is often a matter of chance or caprice
   (D) the poet sees more intensely than other people
   (E) the Muse encourages only the eccentric to write

   Ⓐ Ⓑ Ⓒ Ⓓ Ⓔ

Questions 42-43 refer to the following poem.

> From the road looking to the hill I saw
> One hollow house hunched in the shoulder.
> Windows blinded in a level sun
> Stared with not random malice,
> Though I had not been in that place.

42. To the speaker, the house is

   (A) foreboding
   (B) quaint
   (C) majestic
   (D) cheerful
   (E) tranquil

   Ⓐ Ⓑ Ⓒ Ⓓ Ⓔ

43. That the house's windows are "blinded in a level sun" indicates that the

    (A) windows in the abandoned house are broken
    (B) setting for the poem is about noontime
    (C) sun is low on the horizon
    (D) speaker feels the warmth of the sun
    (E) word "sun" plays on the word "son"

    Ⓐ Ⓑ Ⓒ Ⓓ Ⓔ

ANALYZING AND EVALUATING WRITERS' CHOICES

Directions: For each question below, choose the best answer and fill in the corresponding oval on the answer sheet.

44. The controversy was a bitter one, but reasonable compromise <u>alleviated</u> some of the ill will.

    Which of the following best captures the meaning of the underlined word above?

    (A) Spared
    (B) Delayed
    (C) Eased
    (D) Made obvious
    (E) Militated against

    Ⓐ Ⓑ Ⓒ Ⓓ Ⓔ

45. Anita <u>pays attention</u> to details.

    Which of the following substitutions for the underlined words presents most emphatically a negative picture of Anita?

    (A) is finicky about
    (B) focuses only on
    (C) handles
    (D) likes to deal with
    (E) is very exact

    Ⓐ Ⓑ Ⓒ Ⓓ Ⓔ

46. He told Henry that his package would arrive tomorrow.

    Which of the following is a correct revision of the ambiguous sentence above?

    (A) That "his" package would arrive tomorrow is what Henry told him.
    (B) He told Henry that it was his package which would arrive tomorrow.
    (C) He said to Henry "that your package will arrive tomorrow."
    (D) "Henry, your package will arrive tomorrow," he said.
    (E) "Henry," he said, "tomorrow will be arriving the package."

    Ⓐ Ⓑ Ⓒ Ⓓ Ⓔ

Questions 47-48 refer to the following excerpts.

(A) When will it all end? The idiocy and the tension, the dying of young people, the destruction of homes, of cities, starvation, exhaustion, disease, children parentless and lost, the endless pounding of the battle line.

(B) Yet let us begin today as though the millennium were tomorrow, and start "Village Improvement Parade" down Main Street, and turn the corner east toward the rising sun to a land of clear picture and young hearts.

(C) Beyond the gate and above the wall, one sees a littered cobbled street, an old gas street lamp, and, beyond that again, the blue expanse of the bay, with Fort Sumter showing on the horizon.

(D) Prohibition of the production and sale of alcoholic drinks was a social experiment that had behind it more than a century of agitation and local legislation.

(E) Still, whatever the plans for repairing the damage wrought on the land, chances are that the genius for destruction will not be daunted by pious vows and mammoth budgets. Free enterprise will prevail.

47. In which excerpt does the speaker's tone convey a profound urgency?

    Ⓐ Ⓑ Ⓒ Ⓓ Ⓔ

48. In which excerpt is the tone sarcastic?

    Ⓐ Ⓑ Ⓒ Ⓓ Ⓔ

Questions 49-50 refer to the following excerpt.

The two speech writers were amused by the contrast between the two speakers. The press-club president had edited her speech heavily, changing the phrases "in a nutshell" to "to summarize" and "a man needing no introduction" to "someone well known to this audience."

(5) The governor, in turn, had delivered a major policy speech without even reviewing the speech writer's text. "That was a bit of a risk," said the first speech writer. "That was bungee jumping!" said the second.

49. The two changes that the press-club president made were in an effort to avoid

(A) irony
(B) cliches
(C) sexist language
(D) metaphor
(E) jargon

Ⓐ Ⓑ Ⓒ Ⓓ Ⓔ

50. The second speech writer makes use of all of the following in the final statement (line 7) EXCEPT

(A) metaphor
(B) exclamatory tone
(C) structure parallel to that of the first speech writer
(D) hyperbole
(E) speculation

Ⓐ Ⓑ Ⓒ Ⓓ Ⓔ

Optional Essay Section

If your college requires that the optional essay section be taken in addition to the multiple-choice exam, you may wish to review the following information.

The optional essay section of the Freshman College Composition exam requires candidates to demonstrate their ability to write clearly and effectively on two essays. Three topics are given in the test book. An essay on the first topic is required, and candidates are advised to spend 35-40 minutes on this essay. For the second essay, candidates choose one of two topics and may spend the remainder of the 90-minute period on this essay. Local faculty assumes essay-grading responsibility. Below are examples of possible essay topics. The topic in which the candidate writes a letter is required.

Sample Topic 1:

Suppose that you injure your shoulder while exercising. You are immediately rushed to a hospital emergency room and wait to be seen by the physician on duty. After your shoulder is X-rayed, the physician on duty reports that you have a separated shoulder; she then instructs a nurse to wrap your arm and place it in a sling. You are told to see your physician for follow-up treatment.

Two weeks later, your doctor examines you and your hospital X-rays and says that your shoulder was not separated but only sprained. You are relieved, yet surprised that your injury had been misdiagnosed.

Eventually, you receive several medical bills, one of which is from a Dr. Robin Smith, a specialist in orthopedic surgery, for "Consultation in the emergency room." The bill is for $80.00. When you call Dr. Smith's office, you learn that Dr. Smith consulted the attending physician about the diagnosis; however, you do not remember ever having met Dr. Smith.

Write the first two paragraphs of a letter to Dr. Smith explaining why you will recommend that your insurance company refuse payment. Refer to an enclosed copy of your doctor's diagnosis. (Spend approximately 35-40 minutes on essay.)

Sample Topic 2:

In describing the times of the French Revolution, Charles Dickens wrote: "It was the best of times, it was the worst of times." Think about how Dickens' description might apply to today's times. Write an essay in which you use specific examples to explain how today could be described as both the best of times and the worst of times.

For additional information, read the sections on "Taking Essay Tests," in Chapter 5, and "How Essays Are Graded," in Chapter 6.

Study Resources

You will find books that are typically used as textbooks or reference books for first-year English composition and rhetoric courses useful in preparing for the Freshman College Composition exam. The books in the first group are valuable primarily as reference books; they include handbooks of grammar and manuals for writing papers and research papers. They offer guidance on the various elements of writing (sentences, paragraphs, essays) as well as examples illustrating acceptable usage, and punctuation. As you attempt to develop and refine your writing skills, it is helpful to consult at least one book of this type.

The books in the second group are aids to improvement in reading comprehension and guides to different kinds of writing. They suggest ways to make your own writing interesting, effective, and suitable to a particular purpose, and they can help heighten your awareness about your writing.

Visit your local college bookstore to determine which textbooks are used by the college for English composition and rhetoric courses. When selecting a textbook, check the table of contents against the "Knowledge and Skills Required" section on pages 155-157.

The suggestions and resources for preparing for the General Examination in English Composition will also be helpful in preparing for the Freshman College Composition exam.

College French — Levels 1 and 2

Description of the Examination

The College Level French Language Examination is designed to measure knowledge and ability equivalent to that of students who have completed two to four semesters of college French language study. The exam focuses on skills typically achieved from the end of the first year through the second year of college study; material taught during both years is incorporated into a single exam.

The exam is 90 minutes long and is administered in two separately timed sections:

- a 30-minute **Listening Section** of approximately 50 questions, presented on a tape;

- a 60-minute **Reading Section** of approximately 80 questions, presented in a test book.

The two sections are weighted so that they contribute equally to the total score. Subscores are reported for the two sections; however, they are computed independently. An individual's total score, therefore, is not necessarily the average of the two subscores.

Most colleges that award credit for the College Level French Language Examination award either two or four semesters of credit, depending on the student's scores on the exam. The subscores are not intended to be used to award credit separately for Listening and Reading, but colleges may require that both scores be above a certain level to ensure that credit is not awarded to a student who is deficient in either of these skills.

Knowledge and Skills Required

Candidates must demonstrate their ability to comprehend written and spoken French by answering various types of questions. The following components of reading and listening skills are tested in the exam.

Approximate Percent of Examination

40%	**Section I: Listening**		
	15%	Part A	Rejoinders (listening comprehension through short oral exchanges)
	25%	Part B	Short and long dialogues/narratives (listening comprehension through longer spoken selections)
60%	**Section II: Reading**		
	10%	Part A	Discrete sentences (vocabulary and structure)
	20%	Part B	Short cloze passages (vocabulary and structure)
	30%	Part C	Reading passages and authentic stimulus materials (reading comprehension)

Sample Questions

The following questions are typical of those that are on the College French Levels 1 and 2 exam. The CLEP French exam is designed so that the average student completing a first or second year French language course can usually answer about half the questions correctly.

Before attempting to answer the sample questions, read all the information about the College French exam above and on the preceding page. Additional suggestions for preparing for CLEP exams are provided in Chapter 4.

Try to answer correctly as many questions as possible. Then compare your answers with the correct answers, given in Appendix A.

Section I: Listening

All italicized material in Section I represents what you would hear on an actual test recording. This material does not appear in the actual test book.

Part A

Directions: In this part of the test, you will hear several short conversations or parts of conversations spoken in French. You will then hear four response choices also spoken in French. After you hear the four response choices, choose the one that most logically continues or completes the conversation and mark your answer on your answer sheet. Neither the conversations nor the choices will be printed in your test book. Now listen to the following example:

Example: **Sample Answer**

You will hear: (A) (B) ● (D)

(Female Voice) *Où est la bibliothèque, s'il vous plaît?*

You will also hear:

(Male Voice)   *(A) A six heures.*
                 (B) Je suis prêt.
                 (C) A côté d'ici.
                 (D) J'irai demain.

The choice that most logically continues the conversation is (C), "A côté d'ici." Therefore, you should choose answer (C).

Now listen to the first conversation.

1. (Male Voice)   *Je viens de commencer à jouer dans un petit orchestre et je me sens un peu perdu.*

   (Female Voice)   *(A) Ça viendra, il faut essayer d'être patient.*
                     (B) J'espère que tu le trouveras bientôt.
                     (C) Moi non plus, je n'ai pas aimé ce concert.
                     (D) De quel instrument joue-t-il?

                                                     (A) (B) (C) (D)

2. (Female Voice A) *J'aimerais bien aller dans le parc avec toi, mais il me faut faire des courses. A quelle heure voudrais-tu y aller?*

   (Female Voice B) *(A) J'ai passé des heures et des heures dans le parc.*
                     (B) J'ai fait toutes mes courses en une demi-heure.
                     (C) Vers trois heures; tu pourrais faire tes commissions avant.
                     (D) Vers la fin de l'après-midi, quand il n'y a plus autant de monde au marché.

                                                     (A) (B) (C) (D)

3. (Male Voice)   *Où as-tu passé tes vacances l'année dernière?*

   (Female Voice)   *(A) Je préfère les vacances d'été.*
                     (B) Je suis allée en Angleterre.
                     (C) J'ai passé l'examen d'entrée.
                     (D) Je veux y aller l'année prochaine.   (A) (B) (C) (D)

4. (Male Voice)   *Tu as perdu ta montre? Est-ce qu'elle était précieuse?*

   (Female Voice)   (A) *Non, tu n'y perdras pas grand chose.*
                    (B) *Non, ces bracelets sont très bon marché.*
                    (C) *Oui, tu peux me la montrer.*
                    (D) *Oui, c'était un cadeau de ma tante.*

                    (A) (B) (C) (D)

5. (Male Voice A)   *Ecoute, Jean-Pierre, il faut que tu conduises très*
                    prudemment ce matin à cause de la pluie.

   (Male Voice B)   (A) *Rassure-toi, papa, je vais faire attention.*
                    (B) *Je te promets, papa, je vais rentrer avant minuit.*
                    (C) *Sa conduite me gêne, moi aussi.*
                    (D) *Dommage qu'on n'ait pas de pluie; tout est si sec.*

                    (A) (B) (C) (D)

Part B

Directions: You will now hear a series of selections, such as dialogues, announcements, news reports, and narratives spoken in French. You will hear each one <u>only once</u>. Therefore, you must listen very carefully. For each selection, you will see printed in your test booklet one or more questions followed by four possible answers. They will not be spoken. Choose the best answer to each question from among the four choices printed and fill in the corresponding oval on the answer sheet. You will have 12 seconds to answer each question. There will be no example for this part. Now listen to the first selection.

(Narrator)   *Sélection numéro 1. Deux personnes se parlent.*

(Male Voice)   *Quel est votre emploi, Madame Robitaille?*
(Female Voice)   *Ingénieur-chimiste, monsieur, chez Cresson.*
(Male Voice)   *Pourquoi voulez-vous changer de compagnie?*
(Female Voice)   *Je préfère ne plus travailler pour une grande entreprise. Je*
                  voudrais avoir plus de responsabilités.

(Narrator)   *Répondez aux questions 6 et 7.*   (24 seconds)

Sélection numéro 1

6. Où se trouve-t-on?

    (A) Dans un bureau de placement.
    (B) Dans un restaurant.
    (C) Dans une boutique de mode.
    (D) Dans une agence de voyage.   Ⓐ Ⓑ Ⓒ Ⓓ

7. Pourquoi la femme veut-elle faire un changement?

    (A) Parce que la qualité des produits a diminué.
    (B) Parce qu'elle voudrait un poste plus intéressant.
    (C) Parce qu'elle a trop de responsabilités.
    (D) Parce qu'elle voudrait gagner plus d'argent.   Ⓐ Ⓑ Ⓒ Ⓓ

(Narrator)   *Sélection numéro 2. Ecoutez un bulletin météo.*

(Male Voice)   *Région parisienne—En matinée, le ciel restera couvert et les pluies seront abondantes. Dans l'après-midi, poussés par un vent d'ouest puis de nord-ouest assez violent, les nuages vont se dégager par moment, laissant passer un peu de soleil, mais il fera plus frais.*

(Narrator)   *Répondez aux questions 8 et 9.*   (24 seconds)

Sélection numéro 2

8. Quand est-ce qu'il va pleuvoir?

    (A) Le matin.
    (B) L'après-midi.
    (C) Le soir.
    (D) Pendant toute la journée.   Ⓐ Ⓑ Ⓒ Ⓓ

9. Comment la température évoluera-t-elle dans l'après-midi?

    (A) Il va faire plus chaud.
    (B) Il va faire plus froid.
    (C) La température va rester constante.
    (D) La température va augmenter, puis baisser.   Ⓐ Ⓑ Ⓒ Ⓓ

(Narrator)   *Sélection numéro 3. Un événement imprévu.*

(Female Voice)   *Et bien voilà, monsieur l'agent. Je faisais tranquillement les vitrines lorsqu'un inconnu s'est approché de moi.*

(Male Voice)   *Bon. Et après, madame, continuez . . .*

(Female Voice)   *Alors l'homme m'a bousculée et puis il s'est sauvé. C'est à ce moment-là que je me suis rendu compte que mon porte-monnaie avait disparu.*

(Male Voice)   *Asseyez-vous là, madame, et signez votre déposition.*

(Narrator)   *Répondez aux questions 10, 11 et 12.*   (36 seconds)

Sélection numéro 3

10. Qui parle?

    (A) Un policier et une femme.
    (B) Un homme et sa femme.
    (C) Un assureur et sa cliente.
    (D) Un étranger et une vendeuse.   Ⓐ Ⓑ Ⓒ Ⓓ

11. Où cette conversation a-t-elle lieu?

    (A) Dans une agence d'assurances.
    (B) Dans un bureau des objets trouvés.
    (C) Dans un commissariat de police.
    (D) Dans un bureau de poste.   Ⓐ Ⓑ Ⓒ Ⓓ

12. De quoi s'agit-il?

    (A) D'un achat.
    (B) D'un vol.
    (C) D'une interview.
    (D) D'un accident.   Ⓐ Ⓑ Ⓒ Ⓓ

(Narrator)   *Sélection numéro 4. Le ministre fait une visite.*

(Female Voice)   *Le ministre de l'Education Nationale, accompagné de son épouse, est arrivé ce matin dans notre ville où il assistera à l'inauguration du nouveau lycée. Il a été accueilli à sa descente d'avion par monsieur le maire ainsi que par un groupe de jeunes élèves qui ont remis à la femme du ministre un beau bouquet de fleurs.*

(Narrator)   *Répondez aux questions 13 et 14.*   (24 seconds)

Sélection numéro 4

13. Avec qui le ministre est-il arrivé?

    (A) Avec le maire.
    (B) Avec ses filles.
    (C) Avec des enfants.
    (D) Avec sa femme.   Ⓐ Ⓑ Ⓒ Ⓓ

14. Pourquoi le ministre est-il venu?

    (A) Pour passer ses vacances.
    (B) Pour un concours d'aviation.
    (C) Pour une exposition de fleurs.
    (D) Pour l'ouverture d'une école.   Ⓐ Ⓑ Ⓒ Ⓓ

Section II: Reading

Part A

Directions: This part consists of a number of incomplete statements, each having four suggested completions. Select the most appropriate completion and fill in the corresponding oval on the answer sheet. There is no example for this part.

15. En Normandie, les pommes mûres sont déjà toutes tombées par -------

    (A) écrit
    (B) terre
    (C) avion
    (D) coeur   Ⓐ Ⓑ Ⓒ Ⓓ

16. Dans les restaurants chics, on n'utilise pas de ------- en papier.

    (A) ceintures
    (B) serrures
    (C) serveuses
    (D) serviettes   Ⓐ Ⓑ Ⓒ Ⓓ

17. Il vaudrait mieux que vous ------- à l'heure.

    (A) rentrez
    (B) finissez
    (C) soyez
    (D) partez   Ⓐ Ⓑ Ⓒ Ⓓ

18. Regarde donc ce chêne là-bas. Celui-là, c'est vraiment un ------- arbre.

    (A) belle
    (B) beau
    (C) bel
    (D) beaux   Ⓐ Ⓑ Ⓒ Ⓓ

Part B

Directions: In each of the following paragraphs, there are numbered blanks indicating that words or phrases have been omitted. For each numbered blank, four possible completions are provided. First read through the entire paragraph. Then, for each numbered blank, choose the completion that is most appropriate given the context of the entire paragraph and fill in the corresponding oval on the answer sheet. There is no example for this part.

Questions 19-25

    Quand j'étais enfant, j'adorais ___(19)___ animaux. Ma passion allait surtout aux chiens: je ne pouvais pas ___(20)___ voir un sans me ___(21)___ pour aller le caresser; je ___(22)___ un tas de livres ___(23)___ parlaient des chiens ou les mettaient en ___(24)___. Malheureusement mes parents ne ___(25)___ pas mon enthousiasme.

19. (A) l'
    (B) d'
    (C) les
    (D) des   Ⓐ Ⓑ Ⓒ Ⓓ

20. (A) en
    (B) y
    (C) lui
    (D) le

    (A) (B) (C) (D)

21. (A) précipitant
    (B) précipitais
    (C) précipité
    (D) précipiter

    (A) (B) (C) (D)

22. (A) dévorais
    (B) mangeais
    (C) dénonçais
    (D) mordais

    (A) (B) (C) (D)

23. (A) que
    (B) qui
    (C) dont
    (D) lesquels

    (A) (B) (C) (D)

24. (A) scène
    (B) chemin
    (C) plateau
    (D) étage

    (A) (B) (C) (D)

25. (A) joignaient
    (B) manquaient
    (C) ravissaient
    (D) partageaient

    (A) (B) (C) (D)

Part C

Directions: Read the following texts carefully. Each text is followed by one or more questions or incomplete statements. Select the answer or completion that is best according to the text and fill in the corresponding oval on the answer sheet. There is no example for this part.

Questions 26-28

> L'été dernier, j'ai revisité la maison de mon enfance. La dernière fois que je l'avais vue, c'était pour l'enterrement de ma mère alors que j'étais encore à l'université à Paris. Pendant les dix ans qui s'étaient écoulés depuis lors, elle n'avait guère changé. Elle était là, éclatante de blancheur, parmi les vignobles qui couvraient les coteaux à perte de vue. Au loin, très loin, on pouvait apercevoir le clocher du village voisin.

26. Quand l'auteur a-t-il perdu sa mère?

    (A) A l'âge de dix ans
    (B) Quand il était adolescent
    (C) Au cours de ses études
    (D) Au début de sa carrière   Ⓐ Ⓑ Ⓒ Ⓓ

27. Où l'auteur a-t-il passé son enfance?

    (A) A la campagne
    (B) A Paris
    (C) Au bord de la mer
    (D) En haute montagne   Ⓐ Ⓑ Ⓒ Ⓓ

28. D'après ce passage, la maison est située dans un pays où l'on fait surtout

    (A) du cidre
    (B) du vin
    (C) du fromage
    (D) des saucisses   Ⓐ Ⓑ Ⓒ Ⓓ

29. Cette annonce vous intéresserait si vous désiriez acheter

   (A) des jouets
   (B) des livres
   (C) des pommes
   (D) des poissons   Ⓐ   Ⓑ   Ⓒ   Ⓓ

Questions 30-33

Les Français sont aujourd'hui conscients que les médias sont des entreprises commerciales, dont la vocation n'est pas de servir toute la population, mais d'accroître leur audience et leurs recettes publicitaires. La qualité de leur contenu et la véracité de l'information qu'ils délivrent ont été progressivement mises en doute.

La mise en oeuvre du nouveau paysage audiovisuel au début des années 80 n'est pas étrangère à cette perte de crédibilité. Libérée d'une partie des contraintes du passé, la télévision ne se donne presque plus de mission éducatrice ou culturelle. Guidée par les résultats des sondages, elle s'efforce de flatter les attentes des Français en faisant couler l'émotion à flots dans les émissions de variétés, les *Reality shows*, et autres programmes populaires.

Les Français ont de plus en plus de doutes à propos de l'influence des médias sur le fonctionnement de la démocratie. Si les enquêtes des médias permettent parfois de faire éclater la vérité, il arrive qu'elles troublent la sérénité nécessaire au fonctionnement de la justice en instruisant les procès devant l'opinion en même temps qu'ils ont lieu devant les juges ou même antérieurement.

30. D'après le texte, les Français savent que le but principal des médias en France est

(A) de renseigner le public
(B) de présenter des nouveautés
(C) de gagner de l'argent
(D) d'influencer l'opinion public   Ⓐ Ⓑ Ⓒ Ⓓ

31. En ce qui concerne les médias, le public devient de plus en plus

(A) favorable
(B) fasciné
(C) silencieux
(D) sceptique   Ⓐ Ⓑ Ⓒ Ⓓ

32. D'après les sondages, la majorité des téléspectateurs aimerait que la télévision

    (A) augmente le nombre d'émissions sentimentales
    (B) multiplie les émissions culturelles
    (C) reprenne son rôle d'autrefois
    (D) limite le nombre d'émissions violentes   Ⓐ Ⓑ Ⓒ Ⓓ

33. D'après le texte, quel est l'effet des médias sur le travail des juges?

    (A) Ils le rendent inutile.
    (B) Ils le facilitent.
    (C) Ils l'accélèrent.
    (D) Ils le compliquent.   Ⓐ Ⓑ Ⓒ Ⓓ

Questions 34-35

ENTRE CIEL ET MER

VOTRE 2 PIECES
289000F*
Cuisine équipée
Terrasse Tennis, Piscine
Accès direct a la mer
ST MANDRIER
entre Bandol et Hyères
credit personnalisé
location assurée

POUR RECEVOIR UNE DOCUMENTATION GRATUITE ECRIRE A
MEDITERRANEE HOLIDAYS 101, avenue du Général-Leclerc,
75014 PARIS · Tél. : (1) 539.22.12
NOM ....
ADRESSE ....
TEL ....
    PNT 13-5

34. Qu'est-ce qu'on offre dans cette annonce?

    (A) Des chambres d'hôtel avec cuisine
    (B) Un voyage pour deux à St. Mandrier
    (C) Des appartements en bord de mer
    (D) Un stage de sports variés   Ⓐ Ⓑ Ⓒ Ⓓ

35. Pourquoi écririez-vous à Méditerranée Holidays?

(A) Pour réserver des chambres

(B) Pour obtenir des renseignements

(C) Pour louer un appartement

(D) Pour vous abonner à un magazine

Ⓐ Ⓑ Ⓒ Ⓓ

Study Resources

Familiarize yourself thoroughly with the contents of at least one introductory French textbook, which you can find in most college bookstores. Besides studying basic vocabulary, you should understand and be able to apply the grammatical principles that make up the language. To improve your reading comprehension, read passages from textbooks, short magazine or newspaper articles, or other printed material of your choice. To improve your listening comprehension, seek opportunities to hear the language spoken by native speakers and to converse with native speakers. French records and tapes are available in many libraries. Take advantage of opportunities to join organizations with French-speaking members, to attend French movies, or to hear French-language radio broadcasts. The Internet is another resource you should explore.

Additional suggestions for preparing for CLEP exams are provided in Chapter 4.

College Level German Language

Description of the Examination

The College Level German Language Examination is designed to measure knowledge and ability equivalent to that of students who have completed two to four semesters of college German language study. The examination focuses on skills typically achieved from the end of the first year through the second year of college study; material taught during both years is incorporated into a single exam.

The exam is 90 minutes long and is administered in two separately timed sections:

- a 30-minute **Listening Section** of approximately 50 questions, presented on a tape;

- a 60-minute **Reading Section** of approximately 80 questions, presented in a test book.

The two sections are weighted so that they contribute equally to the total score. Subscores are reported for the two sections; however, they are computed independently. An individual's total score, therefore, is not necessarily the average of the two subscores.

Most colleges that award credit for the College Level German Language Examination award either two or four semesters of credit, depending on the student's scores on the exam. The subscores are not intended to be used to award credit separately for the Listening and Reading, but colleges may require that both scores be above a certain level to ensure that the credit is not awarded to a student who is deficient in either of these skills.

Knowledge and Skills Required

Questions on the College Level German Language Examination require candidates to demonstrate the abilities listed on the following page.

→ *Approximate Percent of Examination*

40%   **Section I: Listening**

24%   Understanding of spoken language through short stimuli or everyday situations

16%   Ability to understand the language as spoken by native speakers in longer dialogues and narratives

60%   **Section II: Reading**

15%   Vocabulary mastery: meaning of words and idiomatic expressions in the context of printed sentences and situations

20%   Grammatical control: ability to identify usage that is structurally correct and appropriate

25%   Reading comprehension: ability to read and understand texts representative of various styles and levels of difficulty

Sample Questions

The questions that follow are provided to give an indication of the types of items that appear on the College Level German Language Examination. The CLEP German exam is designed so that the average student completing a first or second year German language course can usually answer about half the questions correctly.

Before attempting to answer the sample questions, read all the information about the College German exam on the preceding page and above. Additional suggestions for preparing for CLEP exams are provided in Chapter 4.

Try to answer correctly as many questions as possible. Then compare your answers with the correct answers, given in Appendix A.

Section I: Listening

All italicized material in Section I represents what you would hear on an actual test recording. This material does not appear in an actual test book.

Part A

Directions: In this part of the test you will hear statements or short conversations spoken in German, each followed by a question and four answer choices also spoken in German. The sentences, questions and answer choices you hear will be spoken just once and will <u>not</u> be written in your test booklet. Therefore, you must listen very carefully. Select the best answer and fill in the corresponding oval on the answer sheet. Now listen to this example.

Example:

(N) You will hear: (MAN 1)   *Verzeihung. Welche Linie geht zum Rathaus?*

                (WOMAN)   *Mit welchem Verkehrsmittel will der Mann fahren?*

(N) You will   (MAN 2)   *(A) Mit der Straßenbahn.*   (5 seconds)
    also hear: *(B) Mit dem Flugzeug.*
                             (C) Mit einem Taxi.
                             (D) Mit einem Fahrrad.

The best answer to the question „Mit welchem Verkehrsmittel will der Mann fahren?" is choice (A) „Mit der Straßenbahn." Therefore, you should choose answer (A).

(N) Now let us begin this part with question Number 1.

1.   (MAN)   *Gehen Sie hier durch das Affenhaus, dahinter liegt der Kiosk. Dort können Sie Filme bekommen.*

    (WOMAN)   *Wo befindet sich der Mann?*

    (MAN)   *(A) Im Kino.*   (5 seconds)
                  (B) Beim Arzt.
                  (C) Im Zoo.
                  (D) Im Bahnhof.   Ⓐ Ⓑ Ⓒ Ⓓ

2. (MAN)   *Unsere Deutschlandreise war teuer und anstrengend, aber doch hochinteressant. Ich muß sagen, sie hat sich trotz der hohen Kosten wirklich gelohnt.*

    (WOMAN)   *Wie war die Deutschlandreise?*

    (MAN)   *(A) Preiswert.*   (5 seconds)
               (B) Langweilig.
               (C) Interessant.
               (D) Erholsam.   Ⓐ Ⓑ Ⓒ Ⓓ

3. (MAN 1)   *Du, Jürgen, wie wär's, wenn wir morgen mal am Buxacher Bach angeln gingen?*

    (MAN 2)   *Ach, nee; dort hat noch keiner je etwas gefangen.*

    (WOMAN 1) *Warum hat Jürgen keine Lust, am Buxacher Bach angeln zu gehen?*

    (WOMAN 2) *(A) Er kann nicht schwimmen.*   (5 seconds)
               (B) Die Fische beißen nicht.
               (C) Er ist viel zu müde.
               (D) Das Wetter ist schlecht.   Ⓐ Ⓑ Ⓒ Ⓓ

4. (MAN)   *Frau Schmidt, Ihren Artikel für die heutige Zeitung inde ich sehr interessant. Könnten Sie mir nächste Woche noch einen zweiten zum selben Thema schreiben?*

    (WOMAN)   *Das würde ich gerne tun, aber zeitlich ist das unmöglich. Ich müßte dann ja noch mehr Leute interviewen.*

    (MAN)   *Wer spricht hier wohl?*

    (WOMAN)   *(A) Zwei Journalisten.*   (5 seconds)
               (B) Zwei Schüler.
               (C) Ein Ehepaar.
               (D) Zwei Zeitungsverkäufer.   Ⓐ Ⓑ Ⓒ Ⓓ

5.   (WOMAN 1)   *Entschuldigen Sie, ich suche die Vorlesung von Herrn*
     Professor Gromann.

     (WOMAN 2)   *Oh, da sind Sie hier falsch. Die ist drüben im Hörsaal sieben.*

     (MAN 1)   *Wo sind wohl die beiden?*

     (MAN 2)   (A) *Im Gymnasium.*   (5 seconds)
                (B) *Im Krankenhaus.*
                (C) *Im Sportzentrum.*
                (D) *In der Universität.*   Ⓐ Ⓑ Ⓒ Ⓓ

6.   (MAN)   *Guten Tag. Was kann ich für Sie tun?*

     (WOMAN)   *Ich möchte einen Brief und ein Telegramm aufgeben.*

     (MAN)   *Der Brief kostet 1,70 DM, und für das Telegramm füllen Sie*
                bitte dieses Formular aus.

     (WOMAN)   *Wo findet das Gespräch statt?*

     (MAN)   (A) *In einer Bank.*   (5 seconds)
                (B) *Im Restaurant.*
                (C) *Auf der Post.*
                (D) *An einem Kiosk.*   Ⓐ Ⓑ Ⓒ Ⓓ

Part B

Directions: For each question in this part, you will hear a brief exchange between two people. From the four choices printed in your test booklet, choose the most appropriate remark that the first speaker could make in response to the remark of the second speaker. For example, you will hear an exchange such as this:

(WOMAN)   *Du, Ernst, der Gustav hat schon wieder ein Buch von uns*
           mitgenommen, ohne vorher zu fragen.

(MAN)   *Ich sage ja, der weiß nicht, was sich gehört.*

Now read the four choices in your test booklet.   (12 seconds)

Example:

Sample Answer

Ⓐ Ⓑ ● Ⓓ

(A) Hat er ihn denn wenigstens mitgebracht?

(B) Wir hätten ihn nicht mitnehmen sollen.

(C) Ich hoffe nur, er bringt es wieder.

(D) Von wem hat er es denn gehört?

Of the four choices, C is the most appropriate reply; therefore fill in the corresponding oval on the answer sheet.

Now get ready for the first brief exchange.

7. (MAN) *Mensch, heute abend um 20 Uhr 30 ist doch das Jazzkonzert in der Uni!*

(WOMAN) *Ja, da wollten wir doch hin, — oder ist es schon zu spät?*

(12 seconds)

(A) Nein, da gehe ich nicht hin, das ist mir zu albern.

(B) Karten gibt es nur am Vormittag.

(C) Ja, leider, es ist bereits kurz nach neun.

(D) Ich habe leider um zehn eine Verabredung.

Ⓐ Ⓑ Ⓒ Ⓓ

8. (MAN) *Meine Freundin Anke Peters, Hubertusstraße 5, hat heute Geburtstag. Können Sie dorthin ein Dutzend rote Rosen liefern?*

(WOMAN) *Selbstverständlich! Ist jemand zu Hause?* (12 seconds)

(A) Ja, sie wird heute zwölf.

(B) Ja, bitte, ein Dutzend.

(C) Ja, sie ist einkaufen.

(D) Ja, ab fünf Uhr.

Ⓐ Ⓑ Ⓒ Ⓓ

9. (MAN) *Ist die U-Bahn denn immer noch nicht da? Ich warte schon seit einer halben Stunde.*

(WOMAN) *Da kommt sie gerade.* (12 seconds)

(A) Die Haltestelle ist dort drüben?

(B) Gut, dann kann sie ja wieder zurückfahren.

(C) Na, es ist auch höchste Zeit.

(D) Dann wollen wir zu Fuß gehen.

Ⓐ Ⓑ Ⓒ Ⓓ

10. (WOMAN)   *Diese Pullover haben wir erst gestern reinbekommen. Die Qualität ist hervorragend, und sie sind angenehm leicht und waschecht.*

     (MAN)   *Kratzt das Material?*   (12 seconds)

                 (A) Nur in bar.
                 (B) Bestimmt bei der nächsten Lieferung.
                 (C) Bestimmt nicht.
                 (D) In der Reinigung.   Ⓐ Ⓑ Ⓒ Ⓓ

Part C

Directions: You will now listen to some extended dialogues or monologues. You will hear each <u>only once</u>. After each dialogue or monologue, you will be asked several questions about what you have just heard. These questions are not printed in your test book. From the four printed choices, select the best answer to each question and fill in the corresponding oval on the answer sheet. There is no sample question for this part.

(Narrator)   <u>Selection number one:</u> *You will hear a conversation between two friends.*

(WOMAN)   *Tag Michael, wie geht's dir denn?*

(MAN)   *Viel besser, und in 14 Tagen werde ich schon hier aus dem Krankenhaus entlassen.*

(WOMAN)   *Also sag mal. Wie ist der Unfall eigentlich passiert?*

(MAN)   *Na ja, Inge und ich waren letztes Wochenende im „Big Apple" tanzen. . .*

(WOMAN)   *Du hast doch nicht etwa getrunken??*

(MAN)   *Nein, nein! Außerdem gibt's im „Big Apple" ja gar keinen Alkohol.*

(WOMAN)   *Aber ich habe doch gehört, daß du voll in 'nen Baum geknallt bist.*

(MAN)   *Na ja, ich habe doch meinen Führerschein erst seit acht Wochen, und außerdem war es schrecklich nebelig, und die Straße war naß und . . .*

(WOMAN)   *Also, mit anderen Worten, zu schnell gefahren! Da kannst du nur von Glück reden, daß dir nicht mehr passiert ist.*

11. (WOMAN)   *Wo findet dieses Gespräch wohl statt?*   (12 seconds)

    (A) Im „Big Apple".
    (B) Im Krankenhaus.
    (C) In einem Café.
    (D) Auf der Straße.   Ⓐ Ⓑ Ⓒ Ⓓ

12. (WOMAN)   *Wann darf Michael nach Hause?*   (12 seconds)

    (A) In vier Tagen.
    (B) In zwei Wochen.
    (C) In vier Wochen.
    (D) In vierzig Tagen.   Ⓐ Ⓑ Ⓒ Ⓓ

13. (WOMAN)   *Wie war das Wetter an dem Wochenende, an dem Michael und Inge tanzen gingen?*   (12 seconds)

    (A) Es gab ein Gewitter.
    (B) Es war windig und kalt.
    (C) Es war naß und nebelig.
    (D) Es war eine klare Nacht.   Ⓐ Ⓑ Ⓒ Ⓓ

14. (WOMAN)   *Was waren die Folgen des Unfalls?*   (12 seconds)

    (A) Michael hat seinen Führerschein verloren.
    (B) Inge darf nicht mehr Auto fahren.
    (C) Inge darf keinen Alkohol mehr trinken.
    (D) Michael muß im Hospital liegen.   Ⓐ Ⓑ Ⓒ Ⓓ

15. (WOMAN)   *Was meinte Michaels Bekannte am Ende?*   (12 seconds)

    (A) Michael war betrunken.
    (B) Michael ist ein guter Tänzer.
    (C) Michael ist zu jung.
    (D) Michael ist zu schnell gefahren.   Ⓐ Ⓑ Ⓒ Ⓓ

(Narrator)   <u>Selection number two:</u> In 1992 the following report became public:

(MAN)   *Am Montag, den 7. September, berichtete der Präsident der Bundesanstalt für Arbeit, daß in der ehemaligen DDR immer noch mehr Frauen als Männer arbeitslos seien. Ungefähr jede vierte Frau ist auf der Suche nach einer Stelle. Die Arbeitslosenquote von Frauen ist mit 16,8 Prozent genau doppelt so hoch wie die der Männer. Ein Grund dafür sei, so behauptete der Präsident, die Bevorzugung von Männern auf dem Arbeitsmarkt. Hilfe verspricht man sich durch ein Programm, das junge Frauen bereits in der Ausbildung verstärkt an zukunftsorientierte Gebiete heranführt.*

16. (WOMAN)   *Worüber wird hier gesprochen?*   (12 seconds)

(A) Über Frauen, die in der Ausbildung stehen.
(B) Über Männer, die auf dem Markt arbeiten.
(C) Über Frauen, die Arbeit suchen.
(D) Über Männer, die Programme schreiben.

Ⓐ Ⓑ Ⓒ Ⓓ

17. (WOMAN)   *Welcher Grund wird für den Unterschied in der Arbeitslosenquote zwischen Frauen und Männern angeführt?*   (12 seconds)

(A) Männer werden bevorzugt.
(B) Frauen werden noch ausgebildet.
(C) Frauen haben mehr Beziehungen.
(D) Männer arbeiten doppelt so viel.   Ⓐ Ⓑ Ⓒ Ⓓ

Section II: Reading

Part A

Directions: Each of the sentences in this part has one or more blank spaces indicating that a word or phrase has been omitted. From the four choices select the ONE that when inserted in the sentence fits *grammatically and logically* with the sentence as a whole. Then fill in the corresponding oval on the answer sheet.

Example: **Sample Answer**

                                                Ⓐ Ⓑ ● Ⓓ

Anton las die Zeitung, . . . er den Tisch gedeckt hatte.

(A) ob
(B) während
(C) nachdem
(D) daß

---

18. Meine Eltern lassen dich . . . grüßen.

    (A) kürzlich
    (B) herzlich
    (C) neulich
    (D) gut   Ⓐ Ⓑ Ⓒ Ⓓ

19. Ich kann mir seine Telefonnummer einfach nicht . . .

    (A) erhalten
    (B) halten
    (C) merken
    (D) erinnern   Ⓐ Ⓑ Ⓒ Ⓓ

20. Der Park liegt außerhalb des . . . Stadtzentrums.

    (A) alten
    (B) altem
    (C) alter
    (D) altes   Ⓐ Ⓑ Ⓒ Ⓓ

21. Ich fragte ihn, ob er Lust . . ., mit uns in ein Café zu gehen.

    (A) hat
    (B) hattet
    (C) hatte
    (D) hätte   Ⓐ Ⓑ Ⓒ Ⓓ

22. Ich . . . mir keinen Rat mehr.

    (A) kenne
    (B) weiß
    (C) kann
    (D) muß   Ⓐ Ⓑ Ⓒ Ⓓ

23. Seit Monaten hofft Renate . . . einen Hauptgewinn im Lotto.

    (A) auf
    (B) für
    (C) an
    (D) zu   Ⓐ Ⓑ Ⓒ Ⓓ

24. Der Baum steht . . . dem Haus.

    (A) aus
    (B) zu
    (C) nach
    (D) vor   Ⓐ Ⓑ Ⓒ Ⓓ

25. Heute kommt ein neuer . . . im Fernsehen.

    (A) Schalter
    (B) Krimi
    (C) Rundfunk
    (D) Bildschirm   Ⓐ Ⓑ Ⓒ Ⓓ

26. Rechnen Sie damit, daß . . .?

    (A) bald finden Sie eine Wohnung
    (B) eine Wohnung finden Sie bald
    (C) Sie bald eine Wohnung finden
    (D) Sie finden bald eine Wohnung   Ⓐ Ⓑ Ⓒ Ⓓ

Part B

Directions: The paragraph below contains blank spaces indicating omissions in the text. For some blanks, it is necessary to choose the completion that is most appropriate to the meaning of the paragraph; for other blanks, to choose the one completion that forms a grammatically correct sentence. In each case, indicate your answer by filling in the corresponding oval on the answer sheet. Be sure to read the paragraph completely before answering the questions related to it. There is no sample question for this part.

Questions 27-31

Ich bin schon oft mit dem Flugzeug zwischen Deutschland und den USA hin und her _____(27)_____; aber nächste Woche nehme ich zum erstenmal ein Schiff. In Bremerhaven geht es _____(28)_____, und fünf Tage _____(29)_____ werden wir hoffentlich in New York _____(30)_____. Ich freue mich schon sehr auf diese _____(31)_____.

27. (A) geschwommen
    (B) gelaufen
    (C) genommen
    (D) gereist   Ⓐ Ⓑ Ⓒ Ⓓ

28. (A) vor
    (B) los
    (C) zu
    (D) an   Ⓐ Ⓑ Ⓒ Ⓓ

29. (A) bald
    (B) davor
    (C) erst
    (D) später   Ⓐ Ⓑ Ⓒ Ⓓ

30. (A) hinkommen
    (B) erreichen
    (C) ankommen
    (D) gelangen   Ⓐ Ⓑ Ⓒ Ⓓ

31. (A) Reise
    (B) Luft
    (C) Karte
    (D) Spur

Ⓐ Ⓑ Ⓒ Ⓓ

Part C

Directions: Each of the selections below is followed by one or more incomplete statements or questions based on its content. Briefly examine each selection (advertisement, table, chart, paragraph, or similar material). Then choose the completion or answer that is most appropriate according to the information given and fill in the corresponding oval on your answer sheet. There is no sample question for this part.

```
DEUTSCHE BUNDESPOST
Einzahlungsschein                                    Bitte stark umrandetes
                                                     Feld deutlich ausfüllen

Postsparbuch Nr.                              DM              Pf
                               Guthaben im
| | | | | | |                  Postsparbuch  | | | | | | |

Vor- und Zuname des Sparers                   DM              Pf
                               Einzahlung (+) | | | | | | |

                               Postvermerk    DM              Pf
                               Neues
                               Guthaben       | | | | | | |

                                                     Besonderes

              ⌒
            (    )
              ⌣          ...........................
                         (Unterschrift des Beamten)

| Erledigungskennzahl | × | Art | × | PSpBNr. | × | Betrag | × | Neues Guth. | × | Datum | PZ |

         Bitte dieses Feld nicht beschriften und nicht bestempeln
```

32. Was bedeutet hier „Guthaben"?

    (A) Kapital
    (B) Scheck
    (C) Postleitzahl
    (D) Bankkonto

Ⓐ Ⓑ Ⓒ Ⓓ

Questions 33-36:

Wir sind ein erfolgreiches, mittelständisches Unternehmen mit Fertigungsstätten an zwei Standorten. Unser Hauptsitz ist in Wilhelmshaven. Unsere Produkte genießen den Ruf guter Qualität und unsere Kundenzahl wächst ständig.

Wir suchen zum baldmöglichsten Termin einen/eine

Produktionsleiter/in

für unsere Backwarenabteilung. Sie sollten über Erfahrungen auf dem Gebiet der Lebensmittelindustrie sowie der Qualitätskontrolle verfügen.

Zu Ihren Aufgaben zählen die Leitung und Steuerung der Produktion unter Einhaltung der Qualitätsvorschriften und Erfüllung der Produktionsziele, die Führung des Personals, die Fähigkeit, Produkte zu optimieren und Entwicklung zu betreiben.

Wir bieten Ihnen zuerst einmal viel Arbeit, die aber viel Freude macht. Dann bekommen Sie kreative Mitarbeiter. Gleitzeit, Fortbildung und ein angenehmes Betriebsklima sind selbstverständlich. Sie erhalten ein angemessenes Gehalt, entsprechende Sozialleistungen, eine intensive Einarbeitung und einen modernen Arbeitsplatz.

Wenn Sie sich angesprochen fühlen, rufen Sie Herrn Günter Neumann an – Tel. 04421/75942 – oder senden Sie Ihre Bewerbung mit Lebenslauf, Lichtbild und Zeugniskopien an die Personalabteilung, Wenzel GmbH, 26389 Wilhelmshaven.

33. Was produziert die Firma Wenzel GmbH?

(A) Nahrungsmittel
(B) Haushaltsgeräte
(C) Getränke
(D) Industriewaren

Ⓐ Ⓑ Ⓒ Ⓓ

34. Was bietet die Firma dem neuen Firmenmitglied an?

    (A) Kostenlose Backwaren
    (B) Eine Fertigungsstätte bei Wilhelmshaven
    (C) Gebrauch eines Dienstwagens
    (D) Ein zeitgemäßes Büro   Ⓐ Ⓑ Ⓒ Ⓓ

35. Was sollen die Bewerber an die Firma schicken?

    (A) Einen Gehaltsnachweis
    (B) Ein Resümee
    (C) Eine Arbeitsbescheinigung
    (D) Einen Führerschein   Ⓐ Ⓑ Ⓒ Ⓓ

36. Wie sieht die Lage für das neue Firmenmitglied aus?

    (A) Es wird eine führende Stellung übernehmen.
    (B) Es wird Schichtarbeit leisten.
    (C) Es wird eine Lehrlingsstelle bekommen.
    (D) Es wird Teilzeitbeschäftigung ausüben.   Ⓐ Ⓑ Ⓒ Ⓓ

Questions 37-38:

37. Welchen Vorteil dieses Anrufbeantworters könnten Sie in Anspruch nehmen, wenn Sie auf Reisen sind?

    (A) Preisempfehlungen
    (B) Mithören
    (C) Fernabfrage
    (D) Überweisungen   Ⓐ Ⓑ Ⓒ Ⓓ

38. Wann beginnt das Gerät einen Anruf zu beantworten?

    (A) Nach dem Signalton
    (B) Nach einer Zeitansage
    (C) Nach achtundzwanzig Sekunden
    (D) Nach fünfmaligem Klingeln   Ⓐ Ⓑ Ⓒ Ⓓ

Study Resources

Familiarize yourself thoroughly with the contents of at least one introductory level college German textbook which you can find in most college bookstores. Besides studying basic vocabulary, you should understand and be able to apply the grammatical principles that make up the language. To improve your reading comprehension, read passages from textbooks, short magazine or newspaper articles, and other printed material of your choice. To improve your listening comprehension, seek opportunities to hear the language spoken by native speakers and to converse with native speakers. If you have opportunities to join organizations with German-speaking members, to attend German movies, or to listen to German-language radio broadcasts, take advantage of them. The Internet is another resource you could explore.

Additional suggestions for preparing for CLEP exams are provided in Chapter 4.

College Level Spanish Language

Description of the Examination

The College Level Spanish Language exam is designed to measure knowledge and ability equivalent to that of students who have completed two to four semesters of college Spanish language study. The exam focuses on skills typically achieved from the end of the first year through the second year of college study; material taught during both years is incorporated into a single exam.

The exam is 90 minutes long and is administered in two separately timed sections:

- a 30-minute **Listening Section** of approximately 50 questions, presented on a tape;

- a 60-minute **Reading Section** of approximately 80 questions, presented in a test book.

The two sections are weighted so that they contribute equally to the total score. Subscores are reported for the two sections; however, they are computed independently. An individual's total score, therefore, is not necessarily the average of the two subscores.

Most colleges that award credit for the College Level Spanish Language exam award either two or four semesters of credit, depending on the student's scores on the test. The subscores are not intended to be used to award credit separately for the Listening and Reading, but colleges may require that both scores be above a certain level to ensure that the credit is not awarded to a student who is deficient in either of these skills.

Knowledge and Skills Required

Candidates must demonstrate their ability to comprehend written and spoken Spanish by answering various types of questions. The following components of reading and listening skills are tested in the exam.

Approximate Percent of Examination

40% **Section I: Listening**

    15%   Part A   Rejoinders (oral exchanges)

    25%   Part B   Short and long dialogues, and narratives

60% **Section II: Reading**

    10%   Part A   Vocabulary and structure

    20%   Part B   Short, contextualized cloze passages

    30%   Part C   Reading comprehension (passages and authentic stimulus materials)

Sample Questions

The following questions indicate the types of items that are on the College Level Spanish Language exam. The CLEP Spanish exam is designed so that the average student completing the first or second year of a Spanish language course can usually answer about half the questions correctly.

Before attempting to answer the sample questions, read all the information about the College Spanish exam on the preceding pages. Additional suggestions for preparing for CLEP exams are provided in Chapter 4.

Try to answer correctly as many questions as possible. Then compare your answers with the correct answers, given in Appendix A.

Section I: Listening

Part A

Directions: In this part of the test, you will hear several short conversations or parts of conversations spoken in Spanish. You will then hear four responses, designated (A), (B), (C), and (D). After you hear the four responses, choose the one that most logically continues or completes the conversation and mark your answer sheet. Neither the conversations nor the choices will be printed in your test book. Now listen to the following example.

Example: **Sample Answer**

Ⓐ   Ⓑ   Ⓒ   Ⓓ

You will hear:

    (MA) *Perdone, ¿dónde está la biblioteca?*

You will also hear:

    (WA) (A) A las seis y media.
             (B) Tengo prisa.
             (C) Voy mañana.
             (D) En la calle Mayor.

The choice that most logically continues the conversation is (D), "En la calle Mayor." Therefore, you should choose answer (D).

Now listen to the first conversation.

1. (WA) *¿Cómo está Ud. Señora Gómez?*

    (WB) (A) *Hace frío.*
             (B) *Bastante bien, gracias.*
             (C) *Mañana a las ocho.*
             (D) *Sí, por favor.*   Ⓐ   Ⓑ   Ⓒ   Ⓓ

2. (MA) *¿Cómo vino Julio?*

    (WA) (A) *Yo como con vino.*
             (B) *El vino no está bueno.*
             (C) *Vino en coche.*
             (D) *Vino en Julio.*   Ⓐ   Ⓑ   Ⓒ   Ⓓ

3. (MA) *¿Quién llamó anoche?*

    (WA) (A) *No sé quién va.*
             (B) *Yo llamo después.*
             (C) *Viene esta noche.*
             (D) *Fue mi primo Luis.*   Ⓐ   Ⓑ   Ⓒ   Ⓓ

4. (WA) *¿Qué están poniendo dentro del cajón?*

    (MA) (A) *Está muy bien puesto.*
             (B) *Compraron las estampillas.*
             (C) *Lo están llenando con cartas.*
             (D) *Están trabajando en el sótano.*   Ⓐ   Ⓑ   Ⓒ   Ⓓ

5. (MA) *¿Si sigo esta calle llego a la Avenida Bolívar?*

   (WA) (A) *Bolívar fue el libertador de Venezuela.*
         (B) *Pues sí, es un señor hecho y derecho.*
         (C) *No señor, conduce al Paseo de la República.*
         (D) *Si tu mamá te lo permite, te lo consentiré.*   Ⓐ Ⓑ Ⓒ Ⓓ

Part B

Directions: You will now hear a series of selections, such as dialogues, announcements, news reports, and narratives. You will hear each one only once. Therefore, you must listen very carefully. For each selection, you will see printed in your test booklet one or more questions with four possible answers. They will not be spoken. Choose the best answer to each question from among the four choices printed and fill in the corresponding oval on your answer sheet. You will have 12 seconds to answer each question. There will be no example for this part. Now listen to the first selection.

(N)   *Selección número 1. Hablan una madre y su hijo.*

(WA)   *Vamos, hijo, que ya es hora.*
(MA)   *Un poco más, mamá.*
(WA)   *Sonó el reloj hace cinco minutos.*
(MA)   *Estoy cansado.*
(WA)   *Llegarás tarde si no te apuras.*

(N)   Ahora contesten la pregunta 6.   (12 seconds)

Selección número 1.

6. ¿Qué debe hacer el muchacho?

   (A) Levantarse.
   (B) Esperar cinco minutos.
   (C) Hablar del tiempo.
   (D) Poner el reloj en hora.   Ⓐ Ⓑ Ⓒ Ⓓ

(N)   *Selección número 2. En el aeropuerto.*

(MA)   *Señorita, ¿ya salió el vuelo 45 para Quito?*

(WA)   *Sí señor, acaba de salir.*

(MA)   *¡Qué lástima! ¿Y cuándo es el próximo vuelo? Tengo necesidad de llegar a Quito esta noche.*

(WA)   *Lo siento mucho, señor, pero no hay vuelos a Quito de noche. El próximo sale a las siete de la mañana y llega a Quito a las nueve.*

(N)   Ahora contesten la pregunta 7.   (12 seconds)

Selección número 2.

7. ¿Cuándo llegará el señor a Quito?

   (A) Esa noche.
   (B) Dentro de dos horas.
   (C) Al día siguiente.
   (D) La semana próxima.   Ⓐ Ⓑ Ⓒ Ⓓ

(N)   *Selección número 3. Escuchen esta conversación entre amigos.*

(WA)   *Oye, Ricardo, espéranos. ¿Adónde vas con tanta prisa?*

(MA)   *Me muero de hambre, Ana. Después de un examen tan difícil, voy corriendo para la cafetería. ¿Y tú?*

(WA)   *Pues, yo te acompaño, Ricardo. Quiero tomar un refresco, por lo menos.*

(N)   Ahora contesten las preguntas 8 y 9.   (24 seconds)

Selección número 3.

8. ¿Por qué tiene prisa Ricardo?

   (A) Quiere comer.
   (B) Quiere ir al cine.
   (C) Quiere correr.
   (D) Quiere charlar con Ana.   Ⓐ Ⓑ Ⓒ Ⓓ

9. ¿Qué va a hacer Ana?

    (A) Va a la cafetería también.

    (B) Vuelve a la residencia.

    (C) Come mucho.

    (D) Va a otra clase.   Ⓐ Ⓑ Ⓒ Ⓓ

(N)   *Selección número 4. En el restaurante.*

(MA)   *Buenas tardes, señores.*

(WA)   *Buenas tardes. ¿Nos trae la carta en seguida, por favor? Tenemos mucha prisa.*

(MA)   *Aquí la tienen ustedes. Recomiendo el plato del día hoy.*

(N)   Ahora contesten la pregunta 10.   (12 seconds)

Selección número 4.

10. ¿Con quién habla la mujer?

    (A) Con un invitado.

    (B) Con el cocinero.

    (C) Con su esposo.

    (D) Con el camarero.   Ⓐ Ⓑ Ⓒ Ⓓ

(N)   *Selección número 5. Una opinión sobre Barcelona.*

(WA)   A mi me encanta Barcelona. Es una ciudad muy grande donde encuentras de todo: restaurantes, tiendas, actividades. Si te gusta el arte, tiene buenos y variados museos. Si prefieres la música, Barcelona tiene una orquesta sinfónica excelente y un gran repertorio de ópera. Pero a mí, lo que más me gusta es la arquitectura de la ciudad. Barcelona está situada a orillas del mar Mediterráneo y tiene unas vistas muy bonitas. Lo que no me gusta es la contaminación y lo peor de todo, es el ruido de la ciudad.

(N)   Ahora contesten las preguntas 11, 12, y 13.   (36 seconds)

Selección número 5.

11. La ciudad tiene un hermoso paisaje porque está

    (A) en las montañas.
    (B) cerca del mar.
    (C) a la orilla de un lago.
    (D) en el desierto.   Ⓐ Ⓑ Ⓒ Ⓓ

12. A la narradora, ¿qué es lo que más le gusta de Barcelona?

    (A) Los museos.
    (B) Los restaurantes.
    (C) La orquestra sinfónica.
    (D) Los edificios.   Ⓐ Ⓑ Ⓒ Ⓓ

13. ¿Qué es lo peor de la ciudad?

    (A) La ópera.
    (B) El ruido.
    (C) Las tiendas.
    (D) La playa.   Ⓐ Ⓑ Ⓒ Ⓓ

(N)   *Selección número 6. Escuchen para saber quiénes hablan.*

(MA)   *Señora, Ud. recibió los libros el 18 del pasado mes, y hasta la fecha no hemos recibido su pago.*

(WA)   *Lo sé, pero cuando abrí el paquete, vi que me habían mandado dos libros que no pedí.*

(N)   Ahora contesten la pregunta 14.   (12 seconds)

Selección número 6.

14. ¿Quiénes hablan?

    (A) Un profesor y su alumna.
    (B) Un vendedor y su cliente.
    (C) Un abogado y la acusada.
    (D) Un cartero y su jefe.   Ⓐ Ⓑ Ⓒ Ⓓ

Section II: Reading

Part A

Directions: This part consists of a number of incomplete statements, each having four suggested completions. Select the most appropriate completion and fill in the corresponding oval on the answer sheet.

15. Para cortar la carne necesitas -------

    (A) una cuchara
    (B) un mantel
    (C) una botella
    (D) un cuchillo   Ⓐ Ⓑ Ⓒ Ⓓ

16. Dudo que ------- terminar el capítulo.

    (A) pudo
    (B) puedo
    (C) podía
    (D) pueda   Ⓐ Ⓑ Ⓒ Ⓓ

17. El se enfadó y yo no ------- dije nada.

    (A) se
    (B) le
    (C) lo
    (D) la   Ⓐ Ⓑ Ⓒ Ⓓ

18. Mi padre me mandó devolver el libro a la ------- antes de que se venciera el plazo.

    (A) biblioteca
    (B) revista
    (C) página
    (D) publicidad   Ⓐ Ⓑ Ⓒ Ⓓ

Part B

Directions: In the following paragraph, there are numbered blanks indicating that words or phrases have been omitted. For each numbered blank, four completions are provided. First read through the entire paragraph. Then, for each numbered blank, choose the completion that is most appropriate given the context of the entire paragraph and fill in the corresponding oval on the answer sheet.

Questions 19-25

Si ustedes piensan ir en coche (19) Minneapolis, sería bueno que primero lo (20) a un taller, para una revisión técnica, (21) si van a viajar para las Navidades. Ahora, me parece mejor que (22) una parada por lo menos. Les recomiendo que conduzcan el primer día hasta Wichita. Luego, después de dormir bien, creo que al día siguiente (23) llegar a Minneapolis. En fin, pónganse (24) sobre los días y los horarios. Yo (25) esperaré en la ciudad.

19. (A) bajo
    (B) contra
    (C) dentro
    (D) hasta   Ⓐ Ⓑ Ⓒ Ⓓ

20. (A) lleven
    (B) llevan
    (C) llevaron
    (D) llevarán   Ⓐ Ⓑ Ⓒ Ⓓ

21. (A) difícilmente
    (B) especialmente
    (C) lentamente
    (D) activamente   Ⓐ Ⓑ Ⓒ Ⓓ

22. (A) hagan
    (B) hacen
    (C) harán
    (D) hicieron   Ⓐ Ⓑ Ⓒ Ⓓ

23. (A) pueden
    (B) puedan
    (C) poder
    (D) pudieron   Ⓐ Ⓑ Ⓒ Ⓓ

24. (A) en recuerdo
    (B) en desacuerdo
    (C) de acuerdo
    (D) con acuerdo   Ⓐ Ⓑ Ⓒ Ⓓ

25. (A) los
    (B) les
    (C) nos
    (D) se   Ⓐ Ⓑ Ⓒ Ⓓ

Part C

Directions: Read the following texts carefully. Each text is followed by one or more questions or incomplete statements. Select the answer or completion that is best according to the text and fill in the corresponding oval on the answer sheet.

Questions 26-27

Querida amiga María:

Hace algún tiempo que quería escribirte, pero he estado muy ocupada con mis estudios. Tengo cuatro clases este semestre y apenas tengo tiempo para atender mis asuntos personales. No quiero que pienses que me he olvidado de nuestra amistad. Siempre recuerdo con cariño los buenos momentos que pasamos juntas cuando éramos niñas. Dentro de unos meses, cuando termine mis estudios, espero que podamos reunirnos nuevamente y conversar muchísimo. ¡Tengo tanto que contarte!

Recibe todo el cariño de tu amiga que nunca te olvida,

Emilia.

26. ¿Por qué razón Emilia no le había escrito antes a María?

    (A) Porque estudiaban juntas cuando eran niñas.
    (B) Porque sus estudios no se lo permitían.
    (C) Porque María se había olvidado de su amiga.
    (D) Porque Emilia no tenía ganas de escribirle a nadie.   Ⓐ Ⓑ Ⓒ Ⓓ

220

27. María y Emilia son dos

   (A) estudiantes de la misma universidad
   (B) antiguas y buenas amigas
   (C) invitadas a una fiesta
   (D) famosas escritoras contemporáneas

   Ⓐ Ⓑ Ⓒ Ⓓ

Question 28

¡El libro que usted esperaba!

¡NUEVO!

Gráfico, práctico, útil. Así es este magnífico libro que trae la historia y la evolución de los emblemas nacionales e información básica sobre cada nación del mundo.

También:
•Simbolismo de los colores
•Glosario de términos heráldicos
•Mapas físicos de los continentes.

¡UN LIBRO ÚNICO EN SU CLASE!

Banderas y Escudos del Mundo casa

ENCICLOPEDIA GRÁFICA PRÁCTICA, ÚTIL, ÚNICA EN SU CLASE. • CON LA HISTORIA Y LA EVOLUCIÓN DE LOS EMBLEMAS NACIONALES • INFORMACIÓN BÁSICA SOBRE CADA NACIÓN DEL MUNDO

28. ¿Qué tipo de datos se encontrarán en este libro?

   (A) El origen de las características físicas de los continentes
   (B) Un glosario de palabras extranjeras
   (C) Una descripción de los escudos de armas de varias generaciones
   (D) Una explicación sobre los colores de las banderas

   Ⓐ Ⓑ Ⓒ Ⓓ

Questions 29-33

Benicarló, 24 de agosto. — "Día sin sol, día perdido", parecen pensar los turistas que visitan las playas españolas, a juzgar por su paciente exposición al sol todas las horas en que es posible. Un avispado hotelero, dueño de una serie de apartamentos en la zona de playa que va desde Benicarló a Peñíscola, ha decidido hacer de esta frase su lema. Por ello ha hecho colocar grandes anuncios declarando que está dispuesto a bajar el precio a sus inquilinos por cada día sin sol. Hasta ahora, y como es tradicional en la zona, el sol no le ha hecho perder dinero porque ha lucido a más y mejor. A pesar de todo, el lema no deja de hacer efecto en los turistas que llenan sus apartamentos, tostándose muy a gusto en las playas cercanas.

29. La frase, "Día sin sol, día perdido", sirvió

   (A) para confirmar el pésimo clima de la región
   (B) como lema de la campaña propagandista del hotelero
   (C) para desilusionar a los más fuertes tradicionalistas
   (D) como serio obstáculo a todo plan de
       desarrollo económico   Ⓐ Ⓑ Ⓒ Ⓓ

30. Benicarló y Peñíscola deben ser dos
   (A) turistas
   (B) hoteleros
   (C) pueblos de la costa
   (D) casas de apartamentos   Ⓐ Ⓑ Ⓒ Ⓓ

31. Los turistas frequentan aquella zona de España para

   (A) lucir sus trajes de moda
   (B) alquilar apartamentos en la sierra
   (C) asistir a exposiciones
   (D) aprovechar el sol y la playa   Ⓐ Ⓑ Ⓒ Ⓓ

32. ¿Qué les pasaría a los clientes del hotelero los días sin sol?

   (A) Podrían pintar dentro del hotel.
   (B) Dejarían el apartamento.
   (C) Le pagarían menos al hotelero.
   (D) No le pagarían nada al hotelero.   Ⓐ Ⓑ Ⓒ Ⓓ

33. El dueño de los apartamentos quedó satisfecho con su plan porque

(A) los inquilinos se resignaron a pagar la cuota extraordinaria
(B) el sol salió a lucir como nunca en la zona
(C) a los turistas les gustó pasar todo el tiempo fuera de la zona
(D) habría muchos inquilinos los días sin sol   (A) (B) (C) (D)

Questions 34-35

Con una avanzada tecnología educativa, un cuerpo docente integrado por profesionales en actividad y moderno equipamiento.
Nuestros planes de estudio ofrecen salidas laborales concretas y de gran porvenir.

CARRERAS QUE SE CURSAN: PUBLICIDAD - DIRECCIÓN Y ADMINISTRACIÓN DE EMPRESAS - COMERCIO EXTERIOR - PERIODISMO - DISEÑO GRÁFICO Y PUBLICITARIO - ADMINISTRACIÓN DE SEGUROS - ADMINISTRACIÓN DE SALUD - ADMINISTRACIÓN BANCARIA - GESTIÓN AMBIENTAL - TURISMO - SISTEMAS DE DISTRIBUCIÓN.

UNIVERSIDAD DE CIENCIAS EMPRESARIALES Y SOCIALES

ABIERTA LA INSCRIPCIÓN

CENTROS DE ATENCIÓN
Rivadavia 1376 - Buenos Aires
Horario de atención : de 9 a 20 hs.
Teléfono : 555-0202

34. ¿Que tipo de profesión se puede estudiar en esta universidad?

(A) Cursos de astrofísica
(B) Cursos de medicina
(C) Estudios técnico-profesionales
(D) Estudios del área legal   (A) (B) (C) (D)

35. Un estudiante interesado podrá obtener

(A) información por teléfono
(B) admisión gratuita de inmediato
(C) tecnología avanzada por teléfono
(D) actividad profesional en seguida   (A) (B) (C) (D)

Study Resources

Familiarize yourself thoroughly with the contents of at least one Spanish textbook used in courses during the first two years of college Spanish, which you can find in most college bookstores. Besides studying basic vocabulary, you should understand and be able to apply the grammatical principles that make up the language. To improve your reading comprehension, read passages from textbooks, short magazine or newspaper articles, or other printed material of your choice. To improve your listening comprehension, seek opportunities to hear the language spoken by native speakers and to converse with native speakers.

If you have opportunities to join organizations with Spanish-speaking members, to attend Spanish movies, or to listen to Spanish-language television or radio broadcasts, take advantage of them. The Internet is another resource you should explore.

Additional suggestions for preparing for CLEP exams are provided in Chapter 4.

American Government

Description of the Examination

The Subject Examination in American Government covers material that is usually taught in a one-semester introductory course in American government and politics at the college level. The scope and emphasis of the exam reflect what is most commonly taught in introductory American government courses that emphasize the national government. The exam covers topics such as the institutions and policy processes of the federal government, the federal courts and civil liberties, political parties and pressure groups, political beliefs and behavior, and the content and history of the Constitution.

The exam is 90 minutes long and includes approximately 100 multiple-choice questions to be answered in two separately timed 45-minute sections.

Knowledge and Skills Required

Questions on the exam require candidates to demonstrate one or more of the following abilities.

- Knowledge of American government and politics (about 55-60 percent of the exam)

- Understanding of typical patterns of political processes and behavior (including the components of the behavioral situation of a political actor), and the principles used to explain or justify various governmental structures and procedures (about 30-35 percent of the exam)

- Analysis and interpretation of simple data that are relevant to American government and politics (10-15 percent of the exam)

The subject matter of the American Government exam is drawn from the following topics.

Approximate Percent of Examination

30-35%   Institutions and policy processes: Presidency, Bureaucracy, and Congress

> The major formal and informal institutional arrangements and powers
>
> Structure, policy processes, and outputs
>
> Relationships among these three institutions and links between them and political parties, interest groups, the media, and public opinion

15-20%   Federal courts, civil liberties, and civil rights

> Structure and processes of the judicial system with emphasis on the role and influence of the Supreme Court
>
> The development of civil rights and civil liberties by judicial interpretation
>
> First Amendment freedoms
>
> The rights of the accused
>
> Equal protection and due process

15-20%   Political parties and interest groups

> Political parties (including their function, organization, historical development, and effects on the political process)
>
> Interest groups (including the variety of activities they typically undertake and their effects on the political process)
>
> Elections (including the electoral process)

◄   *Approximate Percent of Examination*

10-15%   Political beliefs and behavior

 Processes by which citizens learn about politics

 Political participation (including voting behavior)

 Public opinion

 Beliefs that citizens hold about their government and its leaders

 Political culture (the variety of factors that predispose citizens to differ from one another in terms of their political perceptions, values, attitudes, and activities)

 The relationships between the general public and its political leaders

15-20%   Constitutional underpinnings of American democracy

 The development of concepts such as:

  Federalism (with attention to intergovernmental relations)

  Separation of powers

  Majority rule

  Minority rights

 Considerations that influenced the formulation and adoption of the Constitution

Sample Questions

The 40 sample questions that follow are similar to questions on the American Government exam, but they do not appear on the actual exam.

Before attempting to answer the sample questions, read all the information above about the American Government exam. Additional suggestions for preparing for CLEP exams are provided in Chapter 4.

Try to answer correctly as many questions as possible. Then compare your answers with the correct answers, given in Appendix A.

Directions: Each of the questions or incomplete statements below is followed by five suggested answers or completions. Select the one that is best in each case.

1. Which of the following statements best reflects the pluralist theory of American politics?

   (A) American politics is dominated by a small elite.
   (B) Public policies emerge from cooperation among elites in business, labor, and government.
   (C) Public policies emerge from compromises reached among competing groups.
   (D) American politics is dominated by cities at the expense of rural areas.
   (E) The American political arena is made up of isolated individuals who have few group affiliations outside the family.

   Ⓐ Ⓑ Ⓒ Ⓓ Ⓔ

2. Which of the following is the most influential source of a citizen's attitudes about politics, political values, and public issues?

   (A) Religious affiliation
   (B) Family
   (C) Formal education
   (D) Party affiliation
   (E) Peers

   Ⓐ Ⓑ Ⓒ Ⓓ Ⓔ

3. A member of the House of Representatives who wanted to increase his or her power and influence in Congress would be best advised to seek appointment to which of the following committees?

   (A) Agriculture
   (B) Ways and Means
   (C) Veteran's Affairs
   (D) Armed Services
   (E) Education and Labor

   Ⓐ Ⓑ Ⓒ Ⓓ Ⓔ

4. Which of the following statements about *Brown v. Board of Education of Topeka* is correct?

   (A) It declared Bible reading in the public schools unconstitutional.
   (B) It established the principle of one person, one vote.
   (C) It required that citizens about to be arrested be read a statement concerning their right to remain silent.
   (D) It declared segregation by race in the public schools unconstitutional.
   (E) It declared segregation by race in places of public accommodation unconstitutional.

   Ⓐ Ⓑ Ⓒ Ⓓ Ⓔ

5. Prior to the Voting Rights Act of 1965, literacy tests were used by some Southern states to

   (A) determine the educational achievement of potential voters
   (B) prevent Black people from exercising their right to vote
   (C) assess the general population's understanding of the Constitution
   (D) hinder the migration of northerners
   (E) defend the practice of segregation

   Ⓐ Ⓑ Ⓒ Ⓓ Ⓔ

6. Presidents often have difficulty getting their legislative programs passed because of the

   (A) contrasting views of elected officials in the national government and elected officials in state and local governments
   (B) conflicts between conservative and liberal wings within each party's congressional delegation
   (C) role the electoral college plays in presidential elections
   (D) bipartisan nature of congressional committees
   (E) uncertain guidelines from the Supreme Court

   Ⓐ Ⓑ Ⓒ Ⓓ Ⓔ

7. Usually, the first political figure perceived by a young child is the

   (A) President of the United States
   (B) House representative from the child's congressional district
   (C) governor of the state in which the child lives
   (D) city council representative from the child's district
   (E) mayor of the city in which the child lives

   Ⓐ Ⓑ Ⓒ Ⓓ Ⓔ

8. Which of the following principles protects a citizen from imprisonment without trial?

   (A) Representative government
   (B) Separation of powers
   (C) Due process
   (D) Checks and balances
   (E) Popular sovereignty

   Ⓐ Ⓑ Ⓒ Ⓓ Ⓔ

9. The fact that many bills passed by Congress are the result of a system of mutual accommodations means that to some extent congressional behavior is often based on

   (A) ideological divisions
   (B) partisan division
   (C) the principle of reciprocity
   (D) deference to state legislatures
   (E) party loyalty

   Ⓐ Ⓑ Ⓒ Ⓓ Ⓔ

10. The President's veto power is accurately described by which of the following statements?

    I. A President sometimes threatens to veto a bill that is under discussion in order to influence congressional decision-making.
    II. A President typically vetoes about a third of the bills passed by Congress.
    III. Congress is usually unable to override a President's veto.

    (A) I only
    (B) III only
    (C) I and III only
    (D) II and III only
    (E) I, II, and III

    Ⓐ Ⓑ Ⓒ Ⓓ Ⓔ

11. All of the following issues were decided at the Constitutional Convention of 1787 EXCEPT

(A) representation in the legislature
(B) voting qualifications of the electorate
(C) method of electing the President
(D) congressional power to override a presidential veto
(E) qualifications for members of the House and Senate

12. Which of the following statements about political action committees (PAC's) is true?

(A) PAC's may give unlimited contributions to the election campaigns of individual candidates.
(B) PAC spending has not kept pace with inflation.
(C) PAC activity is limited to direct contributions to candidates.
(D) Social-issue groups are the source of most PAC dollars.
(E) PAC spending makes up a higher percentage of congressional campaign funds than of presidential campaign funds.

13. The usefulness to the President of having cabinet members as political advisers is undermined by the fact that

(A) the President has little latitude in choosing cabinet members
(B) cabinet members have no political support independent of the President
(C) cabinet members are usually drawn from Congress and retain loyalties to Congress
(D) the loyalties of cabinet members are often divided between loyalty to the President and loyalty to their own executive departments
(E) the cabinet operates as a collective unit and individual members have no access to the President

14. All of the following constitutional rights of the accused have been interpreted to apply to state criminal proceedings EXCEPT the right to

    (A) be represented by counsel
    (B) remain silent during questioning
    (C) be indicted by grand jury
    (D) be informed of the charges pending
    (E) receive a trial by jury in a criminal case

    (A) (B) (C) (D) (E)

15. In the electoral history of the United States, third parties have been effective vehicles of protest when they

    (A) aligned themselves with one of the major parties
    (B) presented innovative programs in Congress
    (C) dramatized issues and positions that were being ignored by the major parties
    (D) chose the President by depriving either of the major parties of an electoral college victory
    (E) supported a political agenda that appealed especially to women

    (A) (B) (C) (D) (E)

16. Which of the following best defines the term "judicial activism"?

    (A) The tendency of judges to hear large numbers of cases on social issues
    (B) The efforts of judges to lobby Congress for funds
    (C) The attempts by judges to influence election outcomes
    (D) The unwillingness of judges to remove themselves from cases in which they have a personal interest
    (E) The tendency of judges to interpret the Constitution according to their own views

    (A) (B) (C) (D) (E)

17. High levels of political participation have been found to be positively associated with which of the following?

    I. A high level of interest in politics
   II. A sense of efficacy
  III. A strong sense of civic duty

(A) III only
(B) I and II only
(C) I and III only
(D) II and III only
(E) I, II, and III

Ⓐ Ⓑ © Ⓓ Ⓔ

18. In the last thirty years, the single most important variable in determining the outcome of an election for a member of the House of Representatives has been

(A) incumbency
(B) personal wealth
(C) previous political office held in the district
(D) membership in the political party of the President
(E) positions on key social issues

Ⓐ Ⓑ © Ⓓ Ⓔ

19. Which of the following best describes the concept of federalism embodied in the United States government?

(A) Powers are constitutionally divided between a central government and its constituent governments, with some powers being shared
(B) All governmental powers are constitutionally given to the central government, which may delegate authority to its constituent elements
(C) Constituent governments join together and form a central government, which exists by approval of the constituent governments
(D) The central government creates constituent governments
(E) Constituent governments are sovereign in all matters except foreign policy, which is reserved to the central government

20. The power of the Rules Committee in the House of Representatives rests on its authority to

(A) choose the chairs of other standing committees and issue rules for the selection of subcommittee chairs
(B) initiate all spending legislation and hold budget hearings
(C) limit the time for debate and determine whether amendments to a bill can be considered
(D) determine the procedures by which nominations by the President will be approved by the House
(E) choose the President if no candidate wins a majority in the electoral college

Ⓐ Ⓑ Ⓒ Ⓓ Ⓔ

21. All of the following are formal or informal sources of presidential power EXCEPT

(A) presidential authority to raise revenue
(B) presidential access to the media
(C) precedents set during previous administrations
(D) public support
(E) the Constitution

Ⓐ Ⓑ Ⓒ Ⓓ Ⓔ

22. A major difference between political parties and interest groups is that interest groups generally do NOT

(A) suggest new legislation that is supportive of their interests
(B) try to influence the outcome of legislation
(C) occupy a place on the ballot
(D) concern themselves with elections
(E) have a national organization

Ⓐ Ⓑ Ⓒ Ⓓ Ⓔ

23. An election is a "realigning" or "critical" election if

(A) one party controls the Congress and the other controls the Presidency
(B) voter turnout is higher than expected
(C) it occurs during a major war
(D) there is a lasting change in party coalitions
(E) the same party controls both Congress and the presidency

Ⓐ Ⓑ Ⓒ Ⓓ Ⓔ

24. Which of the following Supreme Court cases involved the principle of "one person, one vote"?

(A) *Baker* v. *Carr*
(B) *Roe* v. *Wade*
(C) *Mapp* v. *Ohio*
(D) *Korematsu* v. *United States*
(E) *Gideon* v. *Wainwright*

Ⓐ Ⓑ Ⓒ Ⓓ Ⓔ

25. The passage of broad legislation that leaves the making of specific rules to the executive branch is an example of

(A) shared powers
(B) delegated authority
(C) checks and balances
(D) executive agreement
(E) a line item veto

Ⓐ Ⓑ Ⓒ Ⓓ Ⓔ

26. In the United States, the two-party system has had all of the following effects EXCEPT

(A) lessening class and regional loyalties
(B) promoting majority rule
(C) increasing the need for runoff elections
(D) fostering bargaining and compromise between parties prior to general elections
(E) helping voters to organize and interpret political information

Ⓐ Ⓑ Ⓒ Ⓓ Ⓔ

27. The details of legislation are usually worked out in which of the following settings?

(A) A party caucus
(B) The majority leader's office
(C) The floor of the House
(D) Legislative hearings
(E) A subcommittee

Ⓐ Ⓑ Ⓒ Ⓓ Ⓔ

28. A philosophical explanation of the operation of diverse interests in American politics is found in

    (A) the Virginia Plan
    (B) John Calhoun's *A Disquisition on Government*
    (C) *The Federalist*
    (D) the Declaration of Independence
    (E) John Locke's *The Second Treatise of Civil Government*

    Ⓐ Ⓑ Ⓒ Ⓓ Ⓔ

29. Which of the following best describes the jurisdiction that the Constitution gives to the Supreme Court?

    (A) Much original jurisdiction and little appellate jurisdiction
    (B) Much original jurisdiction and no appellate jurisdiction
    (C) Little original jurisdiction and much appellate jurisdiction
    (D) No original jurisdiction and much appellate jurisdiction
    (E) No original jurisdiction and little appellate jurisdiction

    Ⓐ Ⓑ Ⓒ Ⓓ Ⓔ

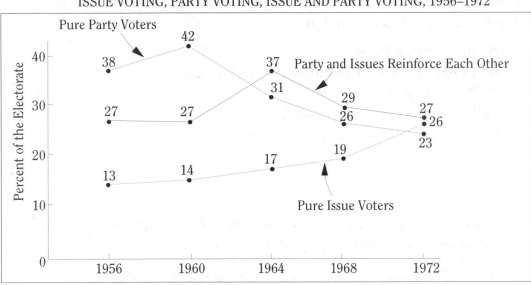

ISSUE VOTING, PARTY VOTING, ISSUE AND PARTY VOTING, 1956–1972

30. According to the information in the chart above, which of the following statements are true?

   I. The proportion of pure issue voters in the electorate increased continuously between 1956 and 1972.

   II. The proportion of pure party voters in the electorate decreased continuously between 1956 and 1972.

   III. The net change in the proportion of the electorate for which party and issues reinforce each other was zero between 1956 and 1972.

   IV. In 1956, compared to the number of pure issue voters, there were about twice as many voters for whom party and issues reinforced each other, and about three times as many pure party voters.

   (A) I and II only
   (B) III and IV only
   (C) I, II, and III only
   (D) I, III, and IV only
   (E) I, II, III, and IV

   Ⓐ Ⓑ Ⓒ Ⓓ Ⓔ

31. Which of the following activities of American labor unions is recognized by law?

    (A) Engaging in strikes
    (B) Denying the public access to a business
    (C) Refusing a subpoena to appear before Congress
    (D) Disobeying a court injunction to return to work
    (E) Requiring members to make political contributions

    Ⓐ Ⓑ Ⓒ Ⓓ Ⓔ

32. Which of the following best describes the relationship between socioeconomic status and participation in politics?

    (A) The lower one's socioeconomic status, the more likely it is that one will run for public office.
    (B) The higher one's socioeconomic status, the greater the probability of active involvement in the political process.
    (C) Adults who are unemployed have a greater personal interest in policy and tend to participate more actively in politics than do employed adults.
    (D) People in the lower middle class are the most likely to participate in politics.
    (E) There is no relationship between socioeconomic status and political participation.

    Ⓐ Ⓑ Ⓒ Ⓓ Ⓔ

STUDENT PARTY IDENTIFICATION BY
PARENT PARTY IDENTIFICATION

Student Party Identification	Parent Party Identification		
	Democrat	Independent	Republican
Democrat	66%	29%	13%
Independent	27%	53%	36%
Republican	7%	18%	51%
Total	100%	100%	100%

M. Kent Jennings and Richard G. Niemi, *The Political Character of Adolescence: The Influence of Families and Schools.*
Copyright © 1974 by Princeton University Press. Reprinted by permission of Princeton University Press.

33. According to the information in the table above, which of the following statements is correct?

    (A) Students who identify themselves as independents are most likely to have parents who are Republicans.
    (B) Of the three groups of parents, the Democrats are the most likely to pass on their party identification to their children.
    (C) Students who identify with the Democratic party are more likely to have parents who are Republicans than parents who are independents.
    (D) The children of Republicans are less likely to identify themselves as independents than are the children of Democrats.
    (E) Parents who are independents are the least likely to have children who share their party identification.

    Ⓐ Ⓑ Ⓒ Ⓓ Ⓔ

34. Which of the following is an example of the institutionalization of the Presidency?

    (A) Creation of the National Security Council
    (B) Creation of the Securities and Exchange Commission
    (C) Impoundment by the President of funds appropriated by Congress
    (D) Invocation of the principle of executive privilege in denying information to Congress
    (E) Use of executive agreements rather than congressionally ratified treaties in the conduct of foreign policy

    Ⓐ Ⓑ Ⓒ Ⓓ Ⓔ

35. All of the following statements correctly describe judicial appointments at the federal level EXCEPT:

(A) The President, rather than Congress, has control over the creation of new federal judicial positions.

(B) Federal judicial appointments are sent for evaluation to the American Bar Association's Committee on the Federal Judiciary.

(C) If a senator is a member of the President's party, tradition may allow the senator to exercise an informal veto over an individual being considered from the senator's state.

(D) Presidents seldom recommend for judicial appointment individuals from the opposition political party.

(E) Federal judgeships are often considered by Presidents as patronage positions.

Ⓐ Ⓑ Ⓒ Ⓓ Ⓔ

36. Which of the following agencies determines the domestic monetary policy of the United States?

(A) The Council of Economic Advisors
(B) The United States Department of the Treasury
(C) The Office of Management and Budget
(D) The Federal Reserve Board
(E) The Export-Import Bank

Ⓐ Ⓑ Ⓒ Ⓓ Ⓔ

37. Under which of the following conditions are interest groups most likely to influence policymaking?

(A) When a problem has been dramatized by television network news
(B) When the President has made a major address on the subject
(C) When the parties in Congress have taken alternative positions on the issue
(D) When presidential candidates have been disagreeing with one another on the subject
(E) When the issue is a highly technical one requiring very detailed legislation

Ⓐ Ⓑ Ⓒ Ⓓ Ⓔ

38. All of the following help to explain the President's difficulty in controlling cabinet-level agencies EXCEPT:

(A) Agencies often have political support from interest groups.
(B) Agency staff often have information and technical expertise that the President and presidential advisers lack.
(C) The President can only fire appointees before they have been confirmed by the Senate.
(D) Civil servants who remain in their jobs through changes of administration develop loyalties to their agencies.
(E) Congress is a competitor for influence over the bureaucracy.

(A) (B) (C) (D) (E)

39. In the Constitution as originally ratified in 1788, the provisions regarding which of the following most closely approximate popular, majoritarian democracy?

(A) Election of members of the House of Representatives
(B) Election of members of the Senate
(C) Election of the President
(D) Ratification of treaties
(E) Confirmation of presidential appointments

(A) (B) (C) (D) (E)

40. The most likely and often the most powerful policy coalition of interests is likely to include a federal agency plus which of the following?

(A) Related agencies in the bureaucracy and a congressional committee chairperson
(B) Congress and the President
(C) An interest group and the President
(D) An interest group and a congressional subcommittee
(E) An interest group and the majority party

(A) (B) (C) (D) (E)

Study Resources

To prepare for the American Government exam, you should read several introductory textbooks used in college courses on this subject. Visit your local college bookstore to determine which textbooks are used by the college for American Government courses. You would do well to consult several textbooks because they vary in content, approach, and emphasis. When selecting a textbook, check the table of contents against the "Knowledge and Skills Required" section on pages 225-227. The Internet is another resource you should explore. Additional reading will enrich your understanding of American politics.

Additional suggestions for preparing for CLEP exams are provided in Chapter 4.

History of the United States I: Early Colonizations to 1877

Description of the Examination

The Subject Examination in History of the United States I: Early Colonizations to 1877 covers material that is usually taught in the first semester of what is often a two-semester course in American history. The exam covers the period of American history from the Spanish and French colonizations to the end of Reconstruction, with the majority of questions on the period of nationhood. In the seventeenth and eighteenth centuries, emphasis is placed on the English colonies.

There are approximately 120 multiple-choice questions on the 90-minute exam, to be answered in two separately timed 45-minute sections.

Knowledge and Skills Required

Questions on the test require candidates to demonstrate one or more of the following abilities.

- Identification and description of historical phenomena (about 45 percent of the exam)

- Analysis and interpretation of historical phenomena (about 40 percent of the exam)

- Comparison and contrast of historical phenomena (about 10 percent of the exam)

The subject matter of the History of the United States I exam is drawn from the following topics.

	Approximate Percent of Examination
35%	Political institutions and behavior and public policy
25%	Social developments
10%	Economic developments
15%	Cultural and intellectual developments
15%	Diplomacy and international relations

About one-third of the questions deal with the period from 1500 to 1789, and about two-thirds are on the period from 1790 to 1877. Among the specific topics tested are the following:

The character of Colonial society

British relations with the Atlantic colonies in North America

The motivations and character of American expansionism

The content of the Constitution and its amendments, and their interpretation by the Supreme Court

The growth of political parties

The changing role of government in American life

The intellectual and political expressions of nationalism

Agrarianism, abolitionism, and other such movements

Long-term demographic trends

The process of economic growth and development

The origins and nature of Black slavery in America

Immigration and the history of racial and ethnic minorities

The causes and impacts of major wars in American history

Major movements and individual figures in the history of American arts and letters

Major movements and individual figures in the history of women and the family

Sample Questions

The following questions are provided to give an indication of the types of items that appear on the History of the United States I exam.

Before attempting to answer the sample questions, read all the information about the History of the United States I exam on the preceding pages. Additional suggestions for preparing for CLEP exams are provided in Chapter 4.

Try to answer correctly as many of the questions as possible. Then compare your answers with the correct answers, given in Appendix A.

Directions: Each of the questions or incomplete statements below is followed by five suggested answers or completions. Select the one that is best in each case.

1. In a sermon given aboard ship on the way to America, John Winthrop told the Puritans that their society would be regarded as "a city upon a hill" and that therefore they should be bonded together by love. But first he explained that there would always be inequalities of wealth and power, that some people would always be in positions of authority while others would be dependent. His statements best illustrate the Puritans'

   (A) reaction to unsuccessful socialist experiments in the Low Countries
   (B) acceptance of the traditional belief that order depended on a system of ranks
   (C) intention to vest political power exclusively in the ministers
   (D) desire to better themselves economically through means that included the institution of slavery
   (E) inability to take clear stands on social issues   Ⓐ Ⓑ Ⓒ Ⓓ Ⓔ

2. The French and Indian War was a pivotal point in America's relationship to Great Britain because it led Great Britain to

   (A) encourage colonial manufactures
   (B) impose revenue taxes on the colonies
   (C) restrict emigration from England
   (D) ignore the colonies
   (E) grant increased colonial self-government   Ⓐ Ⓑ Ⓒ Ⓓ Ⓔ

3. Under the Articles of Confederation, which of the following was true about the national government?

    (A) It had the power to conduct foreign affairs.
    (B) It had the power to regulate commerce.
    (C) It had the power to tax.
    (D) It included a President.
    (E) It included a federal judiciary. Ⓐ Ⓑ Ⓒ Ⓓ Ⓔ

4. Thomas Jefferson opposed some of Alexander Hamilton's programs because Jefferson believed that

    (A) the common bond of a substantial national debt would serve to unify the different states
    (B) the French alliance threatened to spread the violence of the French Revolution to America
    (C) the federal government should encourage manufacturing and industry
    (D) Hamilton's programs were weakening the military strength of the nation
    (E) Hamilton's programs favored wealthy financial interests

    Ⓐ Ⓑ Ⓒ Ⓓ Ⓔ

5. The Louisiana Purchase was significant because it

    (A) eliminated Spain from the North American continent
    (B) gave the United States control of the Mississippi River
    (C) eased tensions between Western settlers and Native Americans
    (D) forced the British to evacuate their posts in the Northwest
    (E) reduced sectional conflict over the slavery issue

    Ⓐ Ⓑ Ⓒ Ⓓ Ⓔ

6. The issue of constitutionality figured most prominently in the consideration of which of the following?

    (A) Tariff of 1789
    (B) First Bank of the United States
    (C) Funding of the national debt
    (D) Assumption of state debts
    (E) Excise tax on whiskey Ⓐ Ⓑ Ⓒ Ⓓ Ⓔ

7. The idea of Manifest Destiny included all of the following EXCEPT the belief that

(A) commerce and industry would decline as the nation expanded its agriculture base
(B) the use of land for settled agriculture was preferable to its use for nomadic hunting
(C) westward expansion was both inevitable and beneficial
(D) God selected America as a chosen land populated by a chosen people
(E) the ultimate extent of the American domain was to be from the tropics to the Arctic

Ⓐ Ⓑ Ⓒ Ⓓ Ⓔ

8. Which of the following represents William Lloyd Garrison's attitude toward slavery?

(A) Immediate emancipation and resettlement in Liberia
(B) Immediate emancipation and resettlement in the Southwest
(C) Immediate emancipation with compensation for owners
(D) Gradual emancipation without compensation for owners
(E) Immediate emancipation without compensation for owners

Ⓐ Ⓑ Ⓒ Ⓓ Ⓔ

9. Which of the following was NOT an element of the Compromise of 1850?

(A) A stronger fugitive slave law
(B) Abolition of the slave trade in Washington, D.C.
(C) Admittance of California as a free state
(D) Organization of the Kansas Territory without slavery
(E) Adjustment of the Texas-New Mexico boundary

Ⓐ Ⓑ Ⓒ Ⓓ Ⓔ

10. At the end of the Civil War, the vast majority of freed slaves found work as

(A) factory workers
(B) railroad employees
(C) independent craftsmen
(D) tenant farmers
(E) domestic servants

Ⓐ Ⓑ Ⓒ Ⓓ Ⓔ

11. Which of the following is a correct statement about the use of slave labor in colonial Virginia?

    (A) It was forced on reluctant White Virginians by profit-minded English merchants and the mercantilist officials of the Crown.
    (B) It was the first case in which Europeans enslaved Black people.
    (C) It fulfilled the original plans of the Virginia Company.
    (D) It first occurred after the invention of Eli Whitney's cotton gin, which greatly stimulated the demand for low-cost labor.
    (E) It spread rapidly in the late seventeenth century, as Black slaves replaced White indentured servants in the tobacco fields.

Questions 12-13 refer to the following statement.

The present king of Great Britain . . . has combined with others to subject us to a jurisdiction foreign to our constitution, and unacknowledged by our laws.

12. The "constitution" referred to in the quotation above from the Declaration of Independence was

    (A) the principles common to all of the colonial charters
    (B) the Articles of Confederation
    (C) a constitution for the colonies written by Sir William Blackstone
    (D) the laws passed concurrently by the several colonial legislatures
    (E) the principles the colonists believed had traditionally regulated English government

    Ⓐ Ⓑ Ⓒ Ⓓ Ⓔ

13. The protest that the king had "combined with others to subject us to a jurisdiction foreign to our constitution" referred to George III's

    (A) alliance with the king of France
    (B) use of Hessian mercenaries
    (C) reliance on his representatives in the colonies
    (D) approval of parliamentary laws impinging on colonial self-government
    (E) intention to place a German prince on the throne of British America

    Ⓐ Ⓑ Ⓒ Ⓓ Ⓔ

14. Which of the following best describes the United States' position in the world economy during the period 1790-1860?

(A) It was the leading producer of finished and manufactured goods for export.

(B) It was a debtor nation that relied heavily on European capital for its economic expansion.

(C) It had an inadequate merchant marine and depended largely on foreign vessels to carry its trade.

(D) It was strengthened by the acquisition of overseas colonies.

(E) It was severely hampered by its reliance on slave labor.

15. All of the following conditions influenced the development of American agriculture during the first half of the nineteenth century EXCEPT

(A) a government policy favoring rapid settlement of the public domain

(B) a widespread interest in conserving soil and natural resources

(C) the trend toward regional economic specialization

(D) the enthusiasm for land speculation

(E) improvements in transportation by water

Questions 16-17 refer to the following cartoon.

16. According to the cartoon, allowing the Southern states to leave the Union would cause

(A) the North to be threatened by internal dissension
(B) the Democratic party to collapse
(C) the Southern states to be dominated by European powers
(D) the Confederacy to expand into Latin America
(E) President Buchanan to be impeached and removed

Ⓐ Ⓑ Ⓒ Ⓓ Ⓔ

17. The best evidence to support the cartoonist's contention that Hickory (Jackson) would have acted to stop secession was Jackson's earlier reaction to the

(A) election of John Quincy Adams to the presidency
(B) Spanish and American Indian border attacks on Florida
(C) South Carolina Nullification Ordinance
(D) requests for annexation of Texas
(E) Maysville Road Bill

Ⓐ Ⓑ Ⓒ Ⓓ Ⓔ

18. Which of the following is a correct statement about farm families in the North between 1820 and 1860?

    (A) They were as isolated as they had been in the late eighteenth century.
    (B) They increasingly used scientific methods to improve crop production.
    (C) They increased markedly in number due to the enactment of the Homestead Act.
    (D) They experienced a steady decline in their standard of living.
    (E) They divided their world into sharply distinct public and private spheres.

19. The establishment of Brook Farm and the Oneida Community in the antebellum United States reflected

    (A) the influence of Social Darwinism on American thinkers
    (B) the continued impact of Calvinist ideas on American thought
    (C) the blossoming of perfectionist aspirations
    (D) attempts to foster racial integration
    (E) the implementation of all-female utopian communities

20. In the pre-Civil War era, the railroad's most important impact on the economy was that it

    (A) created a huge new market for railway equipment
    (B) created the basis for greater cooperation between Southern planters and Northern textile manufacturers
    (C) generated new employment opportunities for unskilled urban workers
    (D) involved the federal government in the financing of a nationwide transportation network
    (E) provided Midwestern farmers accessibility to Eastern urban markets

21. All of the following elements of the Radical Republican program were implemented during Reconstruction EXCEPT

    (A) provision of 40 acres to each freedman
    (B) enactment of the Fourteenth Amendment
    (C) military occupation of the South
    (D) punishment of the Confederate leaders
    (E) restrictions on the power of the President ⒶⒷⒸⒹⒺ

VOLUME OF AMERICAN COLONIES' EXPORTS TO ENGLAND AND IMPORTS FROM ENGLAND (VALUE IN POUNDS STERLING)

Year	New England		New York		Pennsylvania		Virginia and Maryland		Carolina	
	Exports	Imports	Exports	Imports	Exports	Imports	Exports	Imports	Exports	Imports
1743	63,185	172,461	15,067	135,487	9,596	79,340	557,821	328,195	235,136	111,499
1742	53,166	148,899	13,536	167,591	8,527	75,295	427,769	264,186	154,607	127,063
1741	60,052	198,147	21,142	140,430	17,158	91,010	577,109	248,582	236,830	204,770
1740	72,389	171,081	21,498	118,777	15,048	56,751	341,997	281,428	266,560	181,821

22. According to eighteenth-century theories of mercantilism, and in light of England's pattern of trade with America as shown in the chart above, England's most valuable colony or group of colonies was which of the following?

    (A) New England
    (B) New York
    (C) Pennsylvania
    (D) Virginia and Maryland
    (E) Carolina ⒶⒷⒸⒹⒺ

23. By the time of the Revolution, the American colonists had generally come to believe that creation of a republic would solve the problems of monarchical rule because a republic would establish

    (A) a highly centralized government led by a social elite
    (B) a strong chief executive
    (C) a small, limited government responsible to the people
    (D) unlimited male suffrage
    (E) a society in which there were no differences of rank and status

    ⒶⒷⒸⒹⒺ

24. All state constitutions drafted during the American Revolutionary era were significant because they

    (A) were based on the principle of virtual representation
    (B) included clauses that immediately emancipated slaves
    (C) provided for the confiscation and redistribution of the property of wealthy Loyalists
    (D) reinforced the principle of a written frame of government
    (E) introduced the concept of checks and balances

    Ⓐ Ⓑ Ⓒ Ⓓ Ⓔ

25. Deists of the late eighteenth and early nineteenth centuries believed that

    (A) natural laws, set by the Creator, govern the operation of the universe
    (B) prayer has the power to make significant changes in a person's life
    (C) the idea of God is merely the creation of people's minds
    (D) the universe was created by a natural, spontaneous combining of elements
    (E) intuition rather than reason leads people to an awareness of the divine

    Ⓐ Ⓑ Ⓒ Ⓓ Ⓔ

26. Jacksonian banking policies did which of the following?

    (A) Removed banking issues from national politics.
    (B) Stalled the westward movement.
    (C) Ended foreign investment in the United States.
    (D) Abolished state banks.
    (E) Encouraged the expansion of credit and speculation.

    Ⓐ Ⓑ Ⓒ Ⓓ Ⓔ

27. Which of the following had the greatest impact on the institution of slavery in the United States in the first quarter of the nineteenth century?

    (A) Demands of Southern textile manufacturers for cotton
    (B) Introduction of crop rotation and fertilizers
    (C) Use of more stringent techniques for controlling the lives of slaves
    (D) Invention of the cotton gin
    (E) The "three-fifths" compromise

    Ⓐ Ⓑ Ⓒ Ⓓ Ⓔ

28. The presidential election of 1840 is often considered the first "modern" election because

(A) the slavery issue was first raised in this campaign
(B) it was the first election in which women voted
(C) voting patterns were similar to those later established in the 1890's
(D) both parties for the first time widely campaigned among all the eligible voters
(E) a second era of good feeling had just come to a close, marking a new departure in politics

29. The 1848 women's rights convention in Seneca Falls, New York, was a protest against

(A) the use of women workers in textile factories
(B) the abuse of female slaves on Southern plantations
(C) the failure of the Democratic party to endorse a women's suffrage amendment
(D) customs and laws that gave women a status inferior to that of men
(E) state restrictions that prevented women from joining labor unions

30. Abraham Lincoln delayed making any commitment about emancipation of the slaves after his inauguration as President because he

(A) basically had no sympathy with those who wanted to end slavery
(B) was concerned that foreign governments might be critical of a proclamation freeing slaves
(C) did not feel bound by the 1860 Republican party platform
(D) did not feel he had the constitutional right to make such a commitment in regard to slavery in the territories
(E) hoped to keep as many slave states as possible in the Union

Ⓐ Ⓑ Ⓒ Ⓓ Ⓔ

31. Liberty of conscience was defended by Roger Williams on the ground that

    (A) all religions were equal in the eyes of God
    (B) the institutions of political democracy would be jeopardized
        without it
    (C) Puritan ideas about sin and salvation were outmoded
    (D) theological truths would emerge from the clash of ideas
    (E) the state was an improper and ineffectual agency in matters of the
        spirit

    Ⓐ Ⓑ Ⓒ Ⓓ Ⓔ

32. "There is an opinion that parties in free countries are useful checks upon
    the administration of the government and serve to keep alive the spirit
    of liberty. This within certain limits is probably true, and in governments
    of a monarchical cast patriotism may look with indulgence, if not with
    favor, upon the spirit of party. But in those of the popular character, in
    governments purely elective, it is a spirit not to be encouraged."

    Which of the following was most likely to have made these remarks while
    President?

    (A) George Washington
    (B) Thomas Jefferson
    (C) James Madison
    (D) Andrew Jackson
    (E) Abraham Lincoln   Ⓐ Ⓑ Ⓒ Ⓓ Ⓔ

33. The Embargo Act of 1807 had which of the following effects on the United
    States?

    (A) It severely damaged American manufacturing.
    (B) It enriched many cotton plantation owners.
    (C) It severely damaged American shipping.
    (D) It was ruinous to subsistence farmers.
    (E) It had little economic impact.   Ⓐ Ⓑ Ⓒ Ⓓ Ⓔ

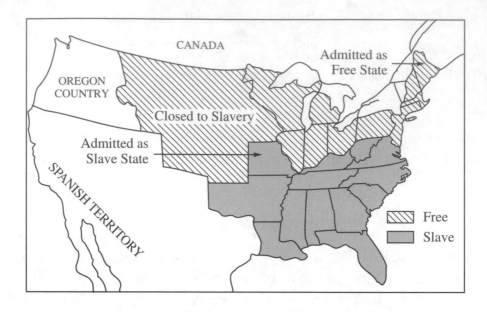

34. The map above shows the United States immediately following the

    (A) passage of the Northwest Ordinance
    (B) negotiation of the Adams-Onis treaty
    (C) passage of the Missouri Compromise
    (D) settlement of the Mexican War
    (E) passage of the Compromise of 1850   Ⓐ Ⓑ Ⓒ Ⓓ Ⓔ

35. Of the following, the most important foreign affairs issue that faced the
    United States between the enunciation of the Monroe Doctrine (1823) and
    the Civil War (1861) was

    (A) securing access to Canadian fisheries
    (B) reopening the British West Indies to direct trade with the United
        States
    (C) securing international recognition
    (D) defining the nation's northern and southern boundaries
    (E) responding to Cuban independence

                                              Ⓐ Ⓑ Ⓒ Ⓓ Ⓔ

36. Henry Clay's "American System" was a plan to

   (A) compromise on the issue of extending slavery to new United States territories
   (B) foster the economic integration of the North, West, and South
   (C) export United States political and economic values to oppressed peoples
   (D) maintain United States noninvolvement in the internal affairs of Europe
   (E) assert the right of states to nullify decisions of the national government

37. The Great Awakening in the American colonies in the mid-eighteenth century had all of the following consequences EXCEPT

   (A) separatism and secession from established churches, due to the democratizing effect of more accessible forms of piety
   (B) the renewed persecution of people for witchcraft, because of the heightened interest in the supernatural
   (C) the growth of institutions of higher learning to fill the need for more ministers to spread the gospel
   (D) a flourishing of the missionary spirit as an outgrowth of more intensive religious devotion
   (E) the lessening of doctrinal rigor and a concomitant appreciation for the more direct experiences of faith

   Ⓐ Ⓑ Ⓒ Ⓓ Ⓔ

Courtesy, Museum of Fine Arts, Boston. Gift of Maxim Karolik for the proposed M. + M. Karolik Collection of American Watercolors, Drawings and Prints.

38. The drawing above has been cited as evidence of the nineteenth-century middle-class view of the

(A) home as a refuge from the world rather than as a productive unit
(B) declining influence of women in the family structure
(C) economic value of children to families
(D) importance of religious education
(E) widening role of women in society

Ⓐ Ⓑ Ⓒ Ⓓ Ⓔ

39. "Upon these considerations, it is the opinion of the court that the act of Congress which prohibited a citizen from holding and owning property of this kind in the territory of the United States north of the line therein mentioned, is not warranted by the Constitution, and is therefore void; and that neither the plaintiff himself, nor any of his family, were made free by being carried into this territory; even if they had been carried there by the owner, who intended to become a permanent resident."

The congressional act referred to in the passage was the

(A) Kansas-Nebraska Act
(B) Missouri Compromise
(C) Northwest Ordinance
(D) Compromise of 1850
(E) Fugitive Slave Act

Ⓐ Ⓑ Ⓒ Ⓓ Ⓔ

40. The 1850's have been called the "American Renaissance" because of the important literary works that appeared in that decade. Included among these works are all of the following EXCEPT

(A) Herman Melville's *Moby-Dick*
(B) Nathaniel Hawthorne's *The Scarlet Letter*
(C) Mark Twain's *Huckleberry Finn*
(D) Walt Whitman's *Leaves of Grass*
(E) Henry David Thoreau's *Walden*

Ⓐ Ⓑ Ⓒ Ⓓ Ⓔ

Study Resources

Students will find it useful to study representative examples of widely used college-level textbooks and readers in History of the United States I and II, which can be found in most college bookstores. Standard comprehensive texts are typically published in two volumes, usually corresponding in coverage to the two CLEP exams (Early Colonizations to 1877, and 1865 to the Present). To prepare for either of the History of the United States exams, read thoroughly the relevant material in one textbook. Because textbooks may differ in content, emphasis, and interpretation, consult a second or third textbook on some of the major topics. New editions of textbooks are usually published every three or four years. If you are purchasing a book, it is recommended that you specify the most recent edition. When selecting a textbook, check the table of contents against the "Knowledge and Skills Required" section on pages 243-244.

Additional detail and differing interpretations can be gained by consulting readers and specialized historical studies. Pay attention to visual materials (pictures, maps, and charts) as you study. The Internet is another resource you could explore.

Additional suggestions for preparing for CLEP exams are provided in Chapter 4.

History of the United States II: 1865 to the Present

Description of the Examination

The Subject Examination in History of the United States II: 1865 to the Present covers material that is usually taught in the second semester of what is often a two-semester course in United States history. The exam covers the period of United States history from the end of the Civil War to the present, with the majority of questions on the twentieth century.

The exam contains approximately 120 questions to be answered in two separately timed 45-minute sections.

Knowledge and Skills Required

Questions on the exam require candidates to demonstrate one or more of the following abilities.

- Identification and description of historical phenomena (about 45 percent of the exam)

- Analysis and interpretation of historical phenomena (about 45 percent of the exam)

- Comparison and contrast of historical phenomena (about 10 percent of the exam)

The subject matter of the History of the United States II exam is drawn from the following topics.

	Approximate Percent of Examination
35%	Political institutions and behavior and public policy
25%	Social developments
10%	Economic developments
15%	Cultural and intellectual developments
15%	Diplomacy and international relations

About one-third of the questions deal with the period from 1865 to 1914, and about two-thirds are on the period from 1915 to the present. The following are among the specific topics tested.

The motivations and character of American expansionism

The content of constitutional amendments and their interpretations by the Supreme Court

The changing nature of agricultural life

The development of American political parties

The emergence of regulatory and welfare-state legislation

The intellectual and political expressions of liberalism, conservatism, and other such movements

Long-term demographic trends

The process of economic growth and development

The changing occupational structure, nature of work, and labor organization

Immigration and the history of racial and ethnic minorities

Urbanization and industrialization

The causes and impacts of major wars in American history

Major movements and individual figures in the history of American arts and letters

Trends in the history of women and the family

Sample Questions

The following 40 questions are provided to give an indication of the types of items that appear on the History of the United States II exam. CLEP exams are designed so that average students completing a course in the subject can usually answer about half the questions correctly.

Before attempting to answer the sample questions, read all the information about the History of the United States II exam on the preceding pages. Additional suggestions for preparing for CLEP exams are provided in Chapter 4.

Try to answer correctly as many questions as possible. Then compare your answers with the correct answers, given in Appendix A.

Directions: Each of the questions or incomplete statements below is followed by five suggested answers or completions. Select the one that is best in each case.

1. *Brown v. Board of Education of Topeka* was a Supreme Court decision that

    (A) was a forerunner of the Kansas-Nebraska Act
    (B) established free public colleges in the United States
    (C) declared racially segregated public schools inherently unequal
    (D) established free public elementary and secondary schools in the
       United States
    (E) provided for federal support of parochial schools

    Ⓐ Ⓑ Ⓒ Ⓓ Ⓔ

2. The American Federation of Labor under the leadership of Samuel Gompers organized

    (A) skilled workers into craft unions in order to achieve economic gains
    (B) all industrial and agricultural workers into "one big union"
    (C) unskilled workers along industrial lines
    (D) women into the Women's Trade Union League
    (E) workers into a fraternal organization to provide unemployment and
       retirement benefits

    Ⓐ Ⓑ Ⓒ Ⓓ Ⓔ

3. In his interpretation of the historical development of the United States, Frederick Jackson Turner focused on the importance of the

    (A) traditions of Western European culture
    (B) role of women in socializing children to become good citizens
    (C) historical consequences of the enslavement of Black people
    (D) conflict between capitalists and workers
    (E) frontier experience in fostering democracy

4. Between 1890 and 1914, most immigrants to the United States came from

   (A) southern and eastern Europe
   (B) northern and western Europe
   (C) Latin America
   (D) Southeast Asia
   (E) Canada   Ⓐ Ⓑ Ⓒ Ⓓ Ⓔ

5. Which of the following is a correct statement about the United States at the close of the First World War?

   (A) It joined the League of Nations.
   (B) It emerged as the world's leading creditor nation.
   (C) It accorded diplomatic recognition to the Soviet Union.
   (D) It repealed the amendment to the Constitution that allowed Prohibition.
   (E) It received large reparations payments from Germany.

        Ⓐ Ⓑ Ⓒ Ⓓ Ⓔ

6. All of the following help to explain the presence of large numbers of expatriate American intellectuals in Europe during the 1920's EXCEPT the

   (A) repressive effects of Prohibition and the resurgence of conservatism in the United States
   (B) attraction of European cities, especially Paris, as centers of innovation and creativity
   (C) tradition among American writers of taking up temporary residence in Europe
   (D) claims of young American writers and critics that American culture was materialistic and hostile to the development of their art
   (E) European tradition of wealthy patrons supporting struggling American artists and writers

        Ⓐ Ⓑ Ⓒ Ⓓ Ⓔ

The Cash Register Chorus

Fitzpatrick in the *St. Louis Post-Dispatch*.

7. The political cartoonist who drew this picture probably believed that

(A) European nations were pleased with aid given them by the Coolidge administration

(B) governmental agencies were receiving too much financial support from the Coolidge administration

(C) American industrial and commercial leaders approved of the Coolidge administration's business policies

(D) consumers had benefited from the Federal Reserve Board's tight money policy from 1925 through 1928

(E) Congress was pleased by President Coolidge's accommodating stance toward pork barrel legislation

8. Which of the following is true of the forced relocation of Japanese Americans from the West Coast during the Second World War?

   (A) President Roosevelt claimed that military necessity justified the action.
   (B) The Supreme Court declared the action unconstitutional.
   (C) The relocation was implemented according to congressional provisions for the internment of dissidents.
   (D) The Japanese Americans received the same treatment as that accorded German Americans and Italian Americans.
   (E) Few of the Japanese Americans relocated were actually United States citizens.

   Ⓐ Ⓑ Ⓒ Ⓓ Ⓔ

9. Which of the following is correct about United States involvement in the Vietnam War?

   (A) It was justified by invoking the Open Door policy.
   (B) It was the exclusive responsibility of the Johnson and Nixon administrations.
   (C) It came about only after a formal declaration of war.
   (D) It was primarily anti-Soviet in purpose.
   (E) It grew out of policy assumptions and commitments dating from the end of the Second World War.

   Ⓐ Ⓑ Ⓒ Ⓓ Ⓔ

10. Which of the following generated the most anxiety about the possibility of nuclear war between the United States and the Soviet Union?

    (A) The Berlin Blockade
    (B) The Cuban missile crisis
    (C) The Pueblo incident
    (D) The Suez Crisis
    (E) The U-2 incident

11. Which of the following would have been most likely to vote for William Jennings Bryan in 1896?

(A) A Kansas farmer
(B) A Chicago industrial worker
(C) A Philadelphia homemaker
(D) A university professor of economics
(E) A New York Republican party member

Ⓐ Ⓑ Ⓒ Ⓓ Ⓔ

12. A number of changes took place in the intellectual life of college-educated Americans between about 1880 and 1930. Which of the following changes is LEAST characteristic of this group during this period?

(A) Expanded popularity of nonrational explanations for human behavior
(B) Rise of pluralistic and relativistic worldviews
(C) Accelerated professionalization of intellectual roles
(D) Growth in influence of religious fundamentalism
(E) Increased attention to the methods and outlook of the sciences

Ⓐ Ⓑ Ⓒ Ⓓ Ⓔ

Museum of the City of New York.

13. The photograph above is representative of the social reform photography of

(A) Jacob Riis
(B) Ansel Adams
(C) Alfred Stieglitz
(D) Dorothea Lange
(E) Margaret Bourke-White

Ⓐ Ⓑ Ⓒ Ⓓ Ⓔ

14. All of the following were among Woodrow Wilson's Fourteen Points EXCEPT

    (A) a general association of nations
    (B) freedom to navigate the high seas in peace and war
    (C) an independent Poland
    (D) a partitioned Germany
    (E) abolition of secret diplomacy ⒶⒷⒸⒹⒺ

15. "The productive methods and facilities of modern industry have been completely transformed. . . . Skilled artisans make up only a small proportion of the workers. Obviously the bargaining strength of employees, under these conditions, no longer rests in organizations of skilled artisans. It is dependent upon a national union representing all employees — whether skilled or unskilled, or whether working by brain or brawn — in each basic industry."

    The statement above best represents the views of

    (A) Emma Goldman
    (B) John L. Lewis
    (C) William Green
    (D) Bernard M. Baruch
    (E) Jane Addams ⒶⒷⒸⒹⒺ

16. Many Mexicans migrated to the United States during the First World War because

    (A) revolution in Mexico had caused social upheaval and dislocation
    (B) the United States offered special homestead rights to relatives of Mexican Americans serving in the armed forces
    (C) the war in Europe had disrupted the Mexican economy
    (D) American Progressives generally held liberal views on the issue of racial assimilation
    (E) the United States government recruited Mexican workers to accelerate the settlement of the Southwest ⒶⒷⒸⒹⒺ

The Only Way We Can Save Her

Carey Orr. *The Tribune* (Chicago), 1939.

17. This cartoon from the 1930's suggests that the cartoonist

(A) wished to see Europe destroyed
(B) believed that Japan was a greater threat to the United States than Germany was
(C) did not distinguish among the European belligerents in terms of war aims or forms of government
(D) believed that the United States must enter the war to make the world safe for democracy
(E) believed that Europe was doomed to communism

Ⓐ Ⓑ Ⓒ Ⓓ Ⓔ

18. American participation in the Second World War had which of the following major effects on the home front?

    (A) A movement of women into heavy industry
    (B) The breakdown of racial segregation in the South
    (C) The growth of isolationism in the Midwest
    (D) The introduction of a system of national health insurance
    (E) A decline in farm income

    Ⓐ Ⓑ Ⓒ Ⓓ Ⓔ

19. President Truman's decision to recall General MacArthur from his command of United Nations forces in Korea was primarily based on the principle of

    (A) containment of communism
    (B) limited rather than total warfare
    (C) isolationism rather than interventionism
    (D) civilian control of the military
    (E) self-determination for all free people

    Ⓐ Ⓑ Ⓒ Ⓓ Ⓔ

20. In which of the following cases did the Supreme Court decision substantially increase the congressional representation of urban areas with high concentrations of Black and Hispanic residents?

    (A) *Gitlow* v. *New York*
    (B) *Baker* v. *Carr*
    (C) *Dennis et al.* v. *United States*
    (D) *Miranda* v. *Arizona*
    (E) *Gideon* v. *Wainwright*

    Ⓐ Ⓑ Ⓒ Ⓓ Ⓔ

21. Which of the following constitutes a significant change in the treatment of American Indians during the last half of the nineteenth century?

    (A) The beginning of negotiations with individual tribes
    (B) The start of a removal policy
    (C) The abandonment of the reservation system
    (D) The admission of American Indians to United States citizenship
    (E) The division of the tribal lands among individual members

22. The anticombination laws passed by numerous states in the late 1880's were a response to which of the following organizational innovations?

    (A) The creation and growth of international cartels
    (B) The development of industry-wide trade associations
    (C) The joining of skilled and unskilled workers in industrial unions
    (D) The formation of agricultural marketing cooperatives
    (E) The use of stockholding trusts to create business oligopolies

    Ⓐ Ⓑ Ⓒ Ⓓ Ⓔ

Wadsworth Atheneum, Hartford.
The Ella Sumner and Mary Catlin Sumner Collection Fund.

23. The 1907 painting shown above is representative of the

(A) Impressionist painting of Mary Cassatt
(B) Hudson River school art of Asher B. Durand
(C) Surrealism of Giorgio de Chirico
(D) Abstract Expressionist work of Jackson Pollock
(E) Ashcan school art of John Sloan

Ⓐ Ⓑ Ⓒ Ⓓ Ⓔ

24. Reformers of the Progressive era proposed all of the following changes in city government and politics at the turn of the century EXCEPT

(A) a large city council elected by wards
(B) civil service
(C) home rule for cities
(D) city manager and commission governments
(E) nonpartisan elections

Ⓐ Ⓑ Ⓒ Ⓓ Ⓔ

25. In the period 1890-1915, all of the following were generally true about Black Americans EXCEPT

(A) Voting rights previously gained were denied through changes in state laws and constitutions.
(B) Back-to-Africa movements were widely popular among Black residents of cities.
(C) Black leaders disagreed on the principal strategy for attaining equal rights.
(D) Numerous physical attacks on Black individuals occurred in both the North and the South.
(E) Black people from the rural South migrated to both southern and northern cities.

26. Franklin D. Roosevelt was LEAST successful in securing congressional support for which of the following?

(A) Negotiation of tariff agreements by the executive department
(B) Reduction of the gold content of the dollar
(C) Removal of the restraints of the antitrust acts to permit voluntary trade associations
(D) The levying of processing taxes on agricultural products
(E) Reform of the judiciary to permit the enlargement of the Supreme Court

27. The main purpose of the Wagner Act (National Labor Relations Act) of 1935 was to

(A) end the sit-down strike in Flint, Michigan
(B) settle the struggle between the AFL and the CIO
(C) guarantee workers a minimum wage
(D) ensure workers' right to organize and bargain collectively
(E) exempt organized labor from the Sherman Antitrust Act

Ⓐ Ⓑ Ⓒ Ⓓ Ⓔ

28. Which of the following was the LEAST important consideration in the United States decision to drop the atomic bombs on Japan in August 1945?

(A) Dropping the bombs would give a new and powerful argument to the Japanese government to cease fighting.
(B) Dropping the bombs would presumably shorten the war and therefore save the lives of American soldiers that would be lost in an invasion of the Japanese homeland.
(C) Scientists wished to demonstrate to Congress that the $2 billion spent, after long debate, on the six-year Manhattan Project had not been wasted.
(D) Scientists could propose no acceptable technical demonstration of the atomic bomb likely to convince Japan that further fighting was futile.
(E) The President and the State Department hoped to end the war in the Far East without Soviet assistance.

Ⓐ Ⓑ Ⓒ Ⓓ Ⓔ

29. In the period 1945 to 1965, which of the following constituted the largest group of immigrants to the United States?

(A) Survivors of Second World War concentration camps
(B) Africans
(C) Southeast Asians and Chinese
(D) Foreign-born wives and dependents of military personnel
(E) Mexicans

Ⓐ Ⓑ Ⓒ Ⓓ Ⓔ

30. Reform activity during the Progressive era was similar to that of the 1960's in all of the following ways EXCEPT

    (A) Civil rights for Black Americans were supported by the federal government.
    (B) Reform activity was encouraged by strong and active Presidents.
    (C) Many reformers advocated changes in the area of women's rights.
    (D) Governmental reform initiatives were curtailed by war.
    (E) Reform occurred despite the absence of severe economic depression.

    Ⓐ Ⓑ Ⓒ Ⓓ Ⓔ

31. The Reconstruction Acts of 1867 provided for

    (A) temporary Union military supervision of the former Confederacy
    (B) federal monetary support for the resettlement of Black Americans in Africa
    (C) denial of property-holding and voting rights to Black Americans
    (D) implementation of anti-Black vagrancy laws in the South
    (E) lenient readmission of the formerly Confederate states to the Union

    Ⓐ Ⓑ Ⓒ Ⓓ Ⓔ

32. The second Sioux War (1875-1876), in which Custer was defeated at the Battle of Little Bighorn, was caused by all of the following EXCEPT

    (A) the extension of the route of the Northern Pacific Railroad
    (B) a concentrated effort on the part of the major Protestant denominations to convert the Sioux to Christianity
    (C) the gold rush in the Black Hills
    (D) corruption within the Department of the Interior
    (E) overland migration of settlers to the Pacific Northwest

    Ⓐ Ⓑ Ⓒ Ⓓ Ⓔ

33. "This, then, is held to be the duty of the man of wealth: to consider all surplus revenues which come to him simply as trust funds, which he is called upon to administer and strictly bound as a matter of duty to administer in the manner which, in his judgment, is best calculated to produce the most beneficial results for the community — the man of wealth thus becoming the mere agent and trustee for his poorer brethren."

   The sentiments expressed above are most characteristic of

   (A) transcendentalism
   (B) pragmatism
   (C) the Gospel of Wealth
   (D) the Social Gospel
   (E) social Darwinism

34. The so-called lost generation after the First World War was

   (A) represented by Ernest Hemingway in the figures of Jake Barnes and Lady Brett Ashley
   (B) depicted in Sylvia Plath's *The Bell Jar*
   (C) glorified by T. S. Eliot in "The Love Song of J. Alfred Prufrock"
   (D) portrayed as the principal subject of Sinclair Lewis' *Babbitt*
   (E) portrayed as the principal subject of Theodore Dreiser's *An American Tragedy*

   Ⓐ Ⓑ Ⓒ Ⓓ Ⓔ

35. "I believe that it must be the policy of the United States to support free peoples who are resisting attempted subjugation by armed minorities or by outside pressures. I believe that we must assist free peoples to work out their own destinies in their own way. I believe that our help should be primarily through economic and financial aid which is essential to economic stability and orderly political processes."

The statement above is taken from

(A) Woodrow Wilson's request for a declaration of war against Germany (1917)
(B) Herbert Hoover's statement on Japanese aggression in China (1931)
(C) Franklin D. Roosevelt's request for a declaration of war against Japan (1941)
(D) Harry S. Truman's request for funds to support Greece and Turkey against communism (1947)
(E) an address by Jeane Kirkpatrick to the United Nations (1983)

(A) (B) (C) (D) (E)

36. "The problem with hatred and violence is that they intensify the fears of the White majority, and leave them less ashamed of their prejudices toward Negroes. In the guilt and confusion confronting our society, violence only adds to chaos. It deepens the brutality of the oppressor and increases the bitterness of the oppressed. Violence is the antithesis of creativity and wholeness. It destroys community and makes brotherhood impossible."

During the 1960's all the following Black leaders would probably have supported the view expressed above EXCEPT

(A) Roy Wilkins
(B) Martin Luther King, Jr.
(C) James Farmer
(D) Stokely Carmichael
(E) Whitney M. Young, Jr.

(A) (B) (C) (D) (E)

37. Following the Second World War, President Truman was unable to expand significantly his predecessor's New Deal programs primarily because of

    (A) the continuation of the Great Depression
    (B) the need to maintain a large military force in Asia
    (C) budget expenditures required to rebuild Europe
    (D) controversy surrounding the Truman Doctrine
    (E) the domination of Congress by Republicans and conservative
        Democrats

    Ⓐ Ⓑ Ⓒ Ⓓ Ⓔ

38. Which of the following was the greatest source of tension between the United States and the Soviet Union during the Second World War?

    (A) The Soviet refusal to fight Japan
    (B) The delay on the part of the United States in opening a second front
        in Europe
    (C) Lend-Lease allocations
    (D) The United States refusal to share atomic secrets
    (E) The Soviet massacre of Polish officers at Katyn Forest

    Ⓐ Ⓑ Ⓒ Ⓓ Ⓔ

39. Franklin D. Roosevelt's farm policy was primarily designed to

    (A) reduce farm prices to make food cheaper for the consumer
    (B) increase production by opening new lands to farmers
    (C) reduce production in order to boost farm prices
    (D) use price and wage controls to stabilize farm prices
    (E) end federal controls over agriculture

    Ⓐ Ⓑ Ⓒ Ⓓ Ⓔ

40. In the twentieth century, United States Supreme Court decisions have done all of the following EXCEPT

    (A) end the experiment in Prohibition
    (B) ban official prayers in the public schools
    (C) protect a woman's right to an abortion
    (D) protect property rights
    (E) expand minority rights

    Ⓐ Ⓑ Ⓒ Ⓓ Ⓔ

Human Growth and Development

(Infancy, Childhood, Adolescence)

Description of the Examination

The Subject Examination in Human Growth and Development (Infancy, Childhood, Adolescence) covers material that is generally taught in a one-semester introductory course in child psychology, child development, or developmental psychology, with primary emphasis on infancy, early childhood, and middle childhood. An understanding of the major theories and research related to physical, cognitive, social, personality, and emotional development is required, as is the ability to apply this knowledge.

   The exam is 90 minutes long and includes approximately 90 multiple-choice questions to be answered in two separately timed 45-minute sections.

Knowledge and Skills Required

Each question on the exam requires the student to demonstrate one or more of the following abilities.

- Knowledge of basic facts and terminology

- Understanding of generally accepted concepts and principles

- Understanding of theories and recurrent developmental issues

- Applications of knowledge to particular problems or situations

The exam questions are drawn from the 13 major categories listed below. For each category, several key words and phrases identify topics with which candidates should be familiar. The approximate percent of the exam devoted to each category is also shown below.

Approximate Percent of Examination

10%   Theories of development

   Behavioral-learning

   Cognitive-developmental

   Psychoanalytic

➡ *Approximate Percent of Examination*

5% Research strategies and methodology
- Experimental
- Longitudinal
- Cross-sectional
- Correlational
- Case study

10% Biological development
- Prenatal influences
- Perinatal influences
- Physical growth and maturation
- Development of nervous system
- Motor development
- Heredity, genetics, genetic counseling
- Nutritional influences
- Sexual maturation
- Influences of drugs

7% Perceptual and sensorimotor development
- Vision
- Hearing
- Sensorimotor activities
- Critical periods
- Sensory deprivation

12% Cognitive development
- Piaget
- Information-processing (e.g., attention, memory)
- Concept formation
- Cognitive styles and creativity
- Play
- Environmental influences on cognitive development

       ➤   *Approximate Percent of Examination*

8%   Language development

         Vocalization and sounds

         Development of grammar

         Semantic development

         Language and thought

         Referential communication

         Environmental influences on language development

4%   Intelligence

         Concepts of intelligence

         Heredity and environment

         Developmental stability and change

10%   Social development

         Attachment

         Aggression

         Prosocial behavior

         Moral development

         Sex roles

         Peer relationships

8%   Family and society

         Parent-child relationships

         Cross-cultural and ethnic variations

         Social class influences

         Sibling and birth-order influences

         Influences of divorce, single-parent families

         Child abuse, parental neglect

         Mass media influences

➤ *Approximate Percent of Examination*

8% Personality and emotions
>   Temperament
>   Self-control
>   Achievement strivings
>   Locus of control
>   Development of emotions

8% Learning
>   Habituation
>   Classical conditioning
>   Operant conditioning
>   Observational learning and imitation
>   Discrimination and generalization

5% Schooling and intervention
>   Applications of developmental principles within the school
>   Preschool, day care
>   Intervention programs and services
>   Training in parenting skills

5% Atypical development
>   Giftedness
>   Consequences of hereditary diseases
>   Learning disabilities, handicapping conditions
>   Retardation
>   Hyperactivity
>   Asocial behavior, fears, phobias, obsessions
>   Antisocial behavior, delinquency
>   Autism, childhood psychosis

Sample Questions

The 25 sample questions that follow are similar to questions on the Human Growth and Development exam, but they do not appear on the actual exam. CLEP exams are designed so that average students completing a course in the subject can usually answer about half the questions correctly.

Before attempting to answer the sample questions, read all the information about the Human Growth and Development exam on the preceding pages. Additional suggestions for preparing for CLEP exams are provided in Chapter 4.

Try to answer correctly as many questions as possible. Then compare your answers with the correct answers, given in Appendix A.

Directions: Each of the questions or incomplete statements below is followed by five suggested answers or completions. Select the one that is best in each case.

1. The first negative emotion clearly exhibited during infancy is best described as

   (A) fear
   (B) anger
   (C) disgust
   (D) distress
   (E) jealousy   Ⓐ Ⓑ Ⓒ Ⓓ Ⓔ

2. Which of the following variables is LEAST likely to be related to the quality of language displayed by a three-year-old child?

   (A) The child's sex
   (B) The child's environment
   (C) The child's general intelligence
   (D) The child's birth order
   (E) The child's body build   Ⓐ Ⓑ Ⓒ Ⓓ Ⓔ

3. According to behavioral psychologists, which of the following treatments would be most likely to extinguish aggressive behavior in preschool children?

(A) Threatening to isolate them immediately after such behavior
(B) Ignoring them so that they do not receive the attention they are seeking
(C) Severely scolding them
(D) Discouraging them but not punishing them
(E) Reasoning with them and explaining that their behavior is wrong

Ⓐ Ⓑ Ⓒ Ⓓ Ⓔ

4. The length of time that it takes to toilet train a young child depends most on which of the following?

(A) Presence or absence of older siblings
(B) Severity of the training practices the parents use
(C) Verbal ability of the parents
(D) The child's feeding regimen in infancy
(E) Age at which the parents begin to train the child

Ⓐ Ⓑ Ⓒ Ⓓ Ⓔ

5. Which of the following conditions is most characteristic of autism?

(A) An obsessive attachment to the mother
(B) A lack of motor coordination
(C) Unresponsiveness to others
(D) Low intelligence
(E) Physical deformity

Ⓐ Ⓑ Ⓒ Ⓓ Ⓔ

6. Anxiety over performance can positively motivate academic achievement in children as long as the degree of anxiety is

(A) very high
(B) high
(C) moderate
(D) low
(E) very low

Ⓐ Ⓑ Ⓒ Ⓓ Ⓔ

7. According to Piaget, cognitive development begins with which of the following?

   (A) Preoperations
   (B) Concrete operations
   (C) Intuitive thought
   (D) Sensorimotor activities
   (E) Formal operations   Ⓐ Ⓑ Ⓒ Ⓓ Ⓔ

8. Social class differences in the amount of infant vocalization are primarily the result of social class differences in which of the following?

   (A) Maternal anxiety
   (B) Verbal stimulation
   (C) Paternal illness
   (D) Sibling rivalry
   (E) Marital discord   Ⓐ Ⓑ Ⓒ Ⓓ Ⓔ

9. Studies in which the same people are tested at different ages are called

   (A) longitudinal
   (B) cross-sectional
   (C) normative
   (D) naturalistic
   (E) experimental   Ⓐ Ⓑ Ⓒ Ⓓ Ⓔ

10. Which of the following is most central to the concept of "critical period"?

   (A) Growth spurts must occur at specific ages.
   (B) A certain chronological age must be reached before specific behaviors can occur.
   (C) A given function emerges automatically during a particular time period, regardless of learning experiences.
   (D) Particular experiences are crucial during a certain time period in development.
   (E) Children go through a negativistic stage as part of their cognitive development.

   Ⓐ Ⓑ Ⓒ Ⓓ Ⓔ

11. According to psychoanalytic theories of personality development, undue stress occurring at any given stage of development is most likely to lead to

   (A) dominance of the conflicts associated with that stage in later personality organization
   (B) an unstable personality unable to participate in normal social relations
   (C) Oedipal problems that may affect later relations with spouse or children
   (D) delinquent behavior during adolescence and excessively aggressive behavior later in life
   (E) atypical behavior with a high susceptibility to schizophrenia

   Ⓐ Ⓑ Ⓒ Ⓓ Ⓔ

12. If reinforcement is to be most effective in learning, it should be

   (A) provided as sparingly as possible
   (B) used on a regularly scheduled basis
   (C) used primarily with high achievers
   (D) delayed until the end of the learning period
   (E) provided soon after the desired behavior occurs   Ⓐ Ⓑ Ⓒ Ⓓ Ⓔ

13. Studies of identical twins are particularly useful for

   (A) controlling observer bias
   (B) eliminating perceptual bias
   (C) controlling for parental bias
   (D) equating environmental factors
   (E) controlling hereditary factors   Ⓐ Ⓑ Ⓒ Ⓓ Ⓔ

14. Which of the following statements regarding chronic malnutrition in pregnant women is true?

    (A) It does not affect the birth weight of the infant but can impair central nervous system functioning.
    (B) It is a minor problem because the unborn baby takes its needed nourishment before the mother's metabolic needs are met.
    (C) It is associated with lower birth weight, as well as possible permanent damage to the central nervous system.
    (D) The results of recent research have been inconclusive in showing that maternal malnutrition has any adverse effects on the fetus.
    (E) It is of concern only in the overpopulated countries of the world.

    Ⓐ Ⓑ Ⓒ Ⓓ Ⓔ

15. In Harlow's experiments, infant monkeys raised with only wire or cloth "mothers" were LEAST fearful in strange situations in the presence of

    (A) the "mother" who had provided food
    (B) the "mother" who had provided contact comfort
    (C) the "mother" who had provided primary drive reduction
    (D) other young monkeys
    (E) their natural mother

    Ⓐ Ⓑ Ⓒ Ⓓ Ⓔ

16. Which of the following characteristics of a stimulus pattern is LEAST likely to elicit attention or exploratory behavior in a child?

    (A) Novelty
    (B) Complexity
    (C) Contrast
    (D) Surprisingness
    (E) Redundancy

    Ⓐ Ⓑ Ⓒ Ⓓ Ⓔ

17. Which of the following procedures would best predict what the intelligence test scores of a group of two-year-old children will be at age twenty-one?

    (A) Using the children's scores on the Stanford-Binet Intelligence Scale
    (B) Using the children's scores on a test of motor development
    (C) Using the children's mothers' intelligence test scores
    (D) Using the children's scores on a measure of temperament
    (E) Predicting an adult IQ of 100 for every child

    Ⓐ Ⓑ Ⓒ Ⓓ Ⓔ

18. Sibling rivalry in a toddler is LEAST likely to be manifested in which of the following ways?

   (A) Whining or crying easily
   (B) Regressing to an earlier stage of development
   (C) Trying to get parental attention
   (D) Displaying hostility toward the new sibling
   (E) Acting with increased independence

   Ⓐ Ⓑ Ⓒ Ⓓ Ⓔ

19. A sudden loud noise made in the vicinity of a newborn infant is likely to elicit the

   (A) Babinski reflex
   (B) Moro reflex
   (C) head-turning reflex
   (D) palmar grasp reflex
   (E) stepping reflex

   Ⓐ Ⓑ Ⓒ Ⓓ Ⓔ

20. On which of the following types of problems would a four-year-old child and a seven-year-old child be expected to perform most similarly?

   (A) Conservation of number
   (B) Reversal shift
   (C) Transposition
   (D) Object constancy
   (E) Superordinate concepts

   Ⓐ Ⓑ Ⓒ Ⓓ Ⓔ

21. Red-green color blindness is best described as

   (A) a sex-linked recessive trait
   (B) a sex-linked dominant trait
   (C) an autosomal recessive trait
   (D) an autosomal dominant trait
   (E) a trait resulting from chromosomal breakage

   Ⓐ Ⓑ Ⓒ Ⓓ Ⓔ

22. The primary reason that the recall memory of an older child is generally better than that of a younger child is that the older child

    (A) has better perceptual abilities
    (B) can organize information better
    (C) engages in concrete thinking
    (D) does not have to categorize information
    (E) recognizes information more easily

    Ⓐ Ⓑ Ⓒ Ⓓ Ⓔ

23. Which of the following theorists did NOT develop a "stage" theory?

    (A) Freud
    (B) Piaget
    (C) Skinner
    (D) Kohlberg
    (E) Erikson

    Ⓐ Ⓑ Ⓒ Ⓓ Ⓔ

24. Studies of maternal deprivation suggest that which of the following is most crucial for normal behavioral development during the first year of life?

    (A) Breast feeding
    (B) Social stimulation
    (C) Extensive discipline by the mother
    (D) Engaging the infant in vigorous motor activity
    (E) The infant's becoming attached to one and only one adult

    Ⓐ Ⓑ Ⓒ Ⓓ Ⓕ

25. According to psychoanalytic theory, which of the following mechanisms (and the attitude accompanying it) would be most important for working out a healthy solution of a little boy's Oedipus complex?

    (A) Identification with the father ("I am like Daddy.")
    (B) Object-choice of the father ("I love Daddy best.")
    (C) Identification with the mother ("I am like Mommy.")
    (D) Object-choice of the mother ("I love Mommy best.")
    (E) Projection onto the mother ("Mommy loves me best.")

    Ⓐ Ⓑ Ⓒ Ⓓ Ⓔ

Study Resources

To prepare for the Human Growth and Development exam, you should study the contents of at least one textbook used in child development and child psychology courses at the college level. These textbooks can be found in most college bookstores. When selecting a textbook, check the table of contents against the "Knowledge and Skills Required" section on pages 281-284. Since they may vary somewhat in content, approach, and emphasis, you are advised to consult more than one textbook on the major topics. You may find it helpful to supplement your reading with books and articles listed in the bibliographies found in most developmental psychology textbooks. The Internet is another resource you should explore.

Parents and others who work with children may have gained some preparation for this test through experience. However, knowledge of the basic facts, theories, and principles of child psychology and development is necessary to provide background for taking the exam.

Additional suggestions for preparing for CLEP exams are given in Chapter 4.

Introduction to Educational Psychology

Description of the Examination

The Subject Examination entitled Introduction to Educational Psychology covers the material that is usually taught in a one-semester undergraduate course in this subject. Emphasis is placed on principles of learning and cognition; teaching methods and classroom management; child growth and development; and evaluation and assessment of learning.

The exam contains approximately 100 multiple-choice questions to be answered in two separately timed 45-minute sections.

Knowledge and Skills Required

Questions on the exam require candidates to demonstrate one or more of the following abilities.

- Knowledge and comprehension of basic facts, concepts, and principles

- Association of ideas with given theoretical positions

- Awareness of important influences on learning and instruction

- Familiarity with research and statistical concepts and procedures

- Ability to apply various concepts and theories to particular teaching situations and problems

The subject matter of the Introduction to Educational Psychology exam is drawn from the following topics.

Approximate Percent of Examination

5%   Educational Aims or Philosophies

       Socialization

       Preparation for responsible citizenship

       Preparation for careers

       Lifelong learning

       Moral/character development

➡ *Approximate Percent of Examination*

15% Cognitive Perspective

Attention and perception

Memory capacity

Organization of long-term memory

Chunking/encoding

Mental imagery

Metacognition

Problem-solving

Transfer

11% Behavioristic Perspective

Classical conditioning

Law of Effect

Operant conditioning

Applications of behaviorism

Behavioral modification programs

Schedules of reinforcement

Token economies

Cognitive learning theory

15% Development

Cognitive

Social

Moral

Language acquisition

Gender identity/sex roles

Adolescence

Mental health

School readiness

➡ *Approximate Percent of Examination*

10%   Motivation

Theories of motivation

Achievement motivation

Locus of control/attribution theory

Learned helplessness

Reinforcement contingencies

Intrinsic motivation

Anxiety/stress

17%   Individual Differences

Nature vs. nurture

Intelligence

Aptitude/achievement

Reading ability

Exceptionalities in learning (e.g., giftedness, physical disabilities, and behavior disorders)

Creativity

Cultural influences

12%   Testing

Test construction (e.g., classroom tests)

Test validity

Test reliability

Norm- and criterion-referenced tests

Scaled scores/standard deviation

Bias in testing

Classroom assessment (e.g., grading procedures and formative evaluation)

Use and misuse of assessment techniques

Assessment of instructional objectives

Descriptive statistics

Approximate Percent of Examination

10%   Pedagogy

        Psychology of content areas

        Instructional design and technique

        Classroom management

        Advance organizers

        Discovery and reception learning

        Cooperative learning

        Clarity/organization

        Teacher expectations/Pygmalion effect/wait time

        Bilingual/ESL instruction

5%   Research design and analysis

        Experiments

        Surveys

        Longitudinal research

        Qualitative research/case studies

        Research analysis and statistics

Sample Questions

The 25 sample questions that follow are similar to questions on the Introduction to Educational Psychology exam, but they do not actually appear on the exam. CLEP exams are designed so that average students completing a course in the subject can usually answer about half the questions correctly.

Before attempting to answer the sample questions, read all the information about the Introduction to Educational Psychology exam on the preceding pages. Additional suggestions for preparing for CLEP exams are provided in Chapter 4.

Try to answer correctly as many questions as possible. Then compare your answers with the correct answers, given in Appendix A.

Directions: Each of the questions or incomplete statements below is followed by five suggested answers or completions. Select the one that is best in each case.

1. Which of the following learning outcomes usually undergoes the largest loss within 24 hours of acquisition?

   (A) The learning of meaningful material
   (B) The learning of rote material
   (C) The formulation of concepts
   (D) The application of principles
   (E) The making of generalizations   (A) (B) (C) (D) (E)

2. When Robert's classmates no longer showed approval of his clowning, his clowning behavior occurred less frequently. The concept best exemplified by Robert's change in behavior is

   (A) extinction   (B) discrimination
      (C) generalization   (D) transfer
       (E) learning set   (A) (B) (C) (D) (E)

3. Which of the following procedures draws a subgroup from a larger population in such a way that each member of the defined population has an equal chance of being included?

   (A) Pattern similarity selection
   (B) Simple random sampling
   (C) Stratified sampling
   (D) Proportional selection
   (E) Quota sampling   (A) (B) (C) (D) (E)

4. In a fifth-grade class that is working on a set of arithmetic problems, which of the following behaviors would be most characteristic of the pupil who is a divergent thinker?

(A) Writing down the principle used to solve the problem as well as the solution itself

(B) Making answers far more exact than is necessary

(C) Working as fast as possible in order to be the first to finish the assignment

(D) Finding a variety of ways to solve each problem

(E) Providing the correct solution to the greatest number of problems

5. To measure students' understanding of a theorem in geometry, it is best for a teacher to have the students do which of the following?

(A) Write out the theorem.

(B) Recall the proof of the theorem.

(C) Demonstrate that they have memorized the theorem.

(D) Solve a problem that is given in the textbook.

(E) Solve a related problem that is not in the textbook.

6. A child who is frightened by a dog and develops a fear of other dogs is exhibiting which of the following principles of learning?

(A) Discrimination learning

(B) Negative transfer

(C) Behavior shaping

(D) Stimulus generalization

(E) Cognitive dissonance

7. In experimental studies of the motor development of identical twins, one twin is generally given practice at a particular skill at an earlier period of development and the other twin at a later period of development. The fact that it generally takes less practice for the later-trained twin to acquire the skill is evidence for the importance of

(A) heredity   (B) maturation   (C) learning
    (D) individual differences   (E) early experience

8. In a fifth-grade class studying the ancient Inca culture, all of the following questions are likely to stimulate pupils to think creatively EXCEPT

   (A) Why do you suppose the clothing of the Incas was so different from today's?
   (B) What weapons and tools did the Incas use for hunting?
   (C) What would be the reaction of an ancient Inca toward modern Peru?
   (D) If the Incas had defeated the Spanish, how might things be different in Peru today?
   (E) If you had lived in Peru during the time of the Incas, what are the things you would have liked and disliked?

   Ⓐ Ⓑ Ⓒ Ⓓ Ⓔ

9. The psychological frame of reference that deals extensively with the effects of unconscious motivation on behavior is

   (A) behaviorism   (B) neobehaviorism   (C) psychoanalysis
     (D) humanism   (E) Gestalt psychology

   Ⓐ Ⓑ Ⓒ Ⓓ Ⓔ

10. Of the following, learning is best defined as

    (A) development that occurs without external stimulation
    (B) the process of overcoming obstacles during instinctual behavior
    (C) effort that is persistent, selective, and purposeful
    (D) the modification of behavior through experience
    (E) the gathering of data to test hypotheses

    Ⓐ Ⓑ Ⓒ Ⓓ Ⓔ

11. According to Kohlberg's theory of moral development, a teacher in the primary grades should expect that

    (A) children will learn and understand universal ethical principles
    (B) children will demonstrate ethical principles in their behavior, especially with their peers
    (C) children's moral development will proceed through a sequence of three broad levels
    (D) attempts to teach lessons on moral development will be useless
    (E) children will teach ethical principles to younger siblings

    Ⓐ Ⓑ Ⓒ Ⓓ Ⓔ

12. A preschool child sees a teacher roll a ball of clay into a sausage-like shape. The teacher asks, "Is the amount of clay the same as before?" The child insists that the sausage shape consists of more clay than the ball did. According to Piaget, this mistake by the child occurs principally because of which of the following?

   (A) A poorly stated question by the teacher
   (B) Erroneous earlier learning by the child
   (C) The greater attractiveness of the sausage shape
   (D) Functional retardation of the child
   (E) A lack of understanding of the conservation principle

13. A fourth-grade teacher wants her pupils to learn to recognize oak trees. Which of the following strategies would best lead to that goal?

   (A) Telling the pupils to visit the park after school and observe several oak trees
   (B) Showing the pupils sketches of oaks and other trees and pointing out the distinguishing characteristics of oaks
   (C) Giving each pupil one or two acorns to plant and presenting a lesson on how oak trees grow
   (D) Decorating the classroom bulletin boards with pictures of trees
   (E) Showing pupils a film of the major trees of North America and then giving the pupils a quiz on oak trees

14. Compared with traditional classroom teaching, a principal advantage of programmed instruction is that it

   (A) is easier to organize and make available to students
   (B) requires less concentration by the student
   (C) maintains student interest at a higher level
   (D) allows large-scale individualization of instruction
   (E) increases interaction between students and teachers

15. To say that a test is reliable is to say that the

  (A) results will be approximately the same if the test is given again under similar conditions
  (B) test measures what it was designed to measure
  (C) predictive validity of the test is high
  (D) objectives measured by the test are important
  (E) test scores can be interpreted objectively by anyone simply by using the test manual

  Ⓐ Ⓑ Ⓒ Ⓓ Ⓔ

16. The concept of developmental tasks refers to the

  (A) development of mental abilities, as distinguished from physical abilities
  (B) ability of the child to develop certain conceptual arrangements
  (C) behavior of the child that results from hereditary determinants
  (D) behaviors of the child that are expected at various ages
  (E) physiological development of the child

  Ⓐ Ⓑ Ⓒ Ⓓ Ⓔ

17. Which of the following correlation coefficients has the highest predictive value?

  (A) 0.80
  (B) 0.60
  (C) 0.00
  (D) – 0.70
  (E) – 0.90

  Ⓐ Ⓑ Ⓒ Ⓓ Ⓔ

18. Which of the following statistics is most affected by extreme scores?

  (A) Mean
  (B) Median
  (C) Mode
  (D) Rank correlation
  (E) Interquartile range

  Ⓐ Ⓑ Ⓒ Ⓓ Ⓔ

19. As compared with boys who have a low need to achieve, boys who have a high need to achieve are more likely to have parents who provide

    (A) social training and consistent approval independent of the child's level of performance
    (B) independence training and interest in the child's level of performance
    (C) high levels of aspiration and continual criticism independent of the child's level of performance
    (D) independence training and lack of interest in the child's level of performance
    (E) low levels of aspiration and infrequent criticism independent of the child's level of performance

    Ⓐ Ⓑ Ⓒ Ⓓ Ⓔ

20. Which of the following perspectives on teaching would most likely support the idea that instruction should emphasize a positive relationship between teachers and students?

    (A) Behavioral   (B) Humanistic   (C) Cognitive
        (D) Correlational   (E) Maturational

    Ⓐ Ⓑ Ⓒ Ⓓ Ⓔ

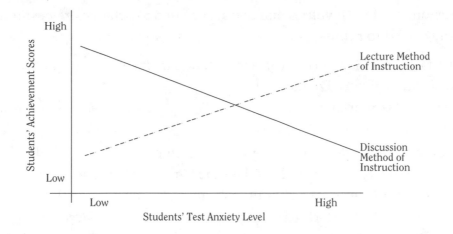

21. Which of the following statements best describes the relationships depicted in the graph above?

(A) Differences among students in test anxiety result in different achievement levels depending on instructional method received.

(B) Differences among students in test anxiety result in different achievement levels independent of instructional method received.

(C) The effect of two different instructional methods on students' achievement is positively correlated with students' test anxiety levels.

(D) The effect of two different instructional methods on students' achievement is negatively correlated with students' test anxiety levels.

(E) Students' achievement levels are independent of their test anxiety levels.

(A) (B) (C) (D) (F)

22. Laura, a fifteen-year-old, is capable of reasoning abstractly without the use of real objects to assist her. According to Piaget, Laura is in which of the following cognitive development stages?

(A) Concrete operations   (B) Tertiary circular reactions
  (C) Preoperations   (D) Formal operations   (E) Sensorimotor

(A) (B) (C) (D) (E)

23. Decisions about the values that are transmitted in schools are best related to the teacher's role as

    (A) instructional expert   (B) socialization agent
      (C) counselor   (D) motivator
        (E) classroom manager   Ⓐ Ⓑ Ⓒ Ⓓ Ⓔ

24. A teacher in a third-grade class presents each pupil with 20 small cardboard disks. Each pupil is asked to form separate small groups of disks, with a different number of disks in each group. Then the teacher asks that one disk be added to each group. When that is accomplished, pupils are to attempt to state a rule or generalization indicating what has happened to the number of disks in each group. This kind of learning is most accurately described as

    (A) rote   (B) directed   (C) discovery
      (D) deductive   (E) passive   Ⓐ Ⓑ Ⓒ Ⓓ Ⓔ

25. Using the principle of successive approximation involves which of the following?

    (A) Reinforcing responses that represent progress toward a desired response
    (B) Making a succession of trials designed to provide information about a problem
    (C) Acquiring a behavior change through imitation of models that demonstrate the behavior
    (D) Averaging repeated measures for adequate assessment of a variable
    (E) Testing possible solutions until success is obtained in problem solving

          Ⓐ Ⓑ Ⓒ Ⓓ Ⓔ

Study Resources

To prepare for the Introduction to Educational Psychology exam, you should study the contents of at least one textbook used in educational psychology courses at the college level. You can find these textbooks in most college bookstores. When selecting a textbook, check the table of contents against the "Knowledge and Skills Required" section on pages 293-296. Since they may vary somewhat in content, approach, and emphasis, you are advised to consult more than one textbook on the major topics.

You will find it helpful to supplement your reading with books listed in the bibliographies that can be found in most educational psychology textbooks. The Internet is another resource you could explore.

Additional suggestions for preparing for CLEP exams are provided in Chapter 4.

Principles of Macroeconomics

Description of the Examination

The Subject Examination in Principles of Macroeconomics covers material that is usually taught in a one-semester undergraduate course in the principles of macroeconomics. This aspect of economics deals with principles of economics that apply to a total economic system, particularly the general levels of output and income and interrelations among sectors of the economy. The test places particular emphasis on the determinants of aggregate demand and on the monetary and fiscal policies that are appropriate to achieve particular policy objectives. Within this context, candidates are expected to understand concepts such as the multiplier, the accelerator, and balance-of-payments equilibrium; terms such as inflation, deflationary gap, and depreciation; and institutional arrangements such as open-market operations, deficit spending, and flexible exchange rates.

The exam consists of approximately 80 multiple-choice questions to be answered in two separately timed 45-minute sections.

Knowledge and Skills Required

Questions on the Principles of Macroeconomics exam require candidates to demonstrate one or more of the following abilities.

- Understanding of important economic terms and concepts

- Interpretation and manipulation of economic graphs

- Interpretation and evaluation of economic data

- Application of simple economic models

The outline below indicates the material covered by the exam and the approximate percentage of questions in each category.

➡ *Approximate Percent of Examination*

8-12%	Basic economic concepts
	Scarcity: the nature of the economic system
	Opportunity costs and production possibilities curves
	Demand, supply, and price determination
10-18%	Measurement of economic performance
	Gross domestic and national products and national income concepts
	Inflation and price indices
	Unemployment
60-70%	National income and price determination
	Aggregate supply and demand: Keynesian and classical analysis (25-30%)
	Circular flow
	Components of aggregate supply and demand
	Multiplier
	Fiscal policy
	Long vs. short run
	Money and banking (15-20%)
	Definition of money and its creation
	Tools of central bank policy and monetary policy
	Fiscal and monetary policy combination (20-25%)
	Interaction of fiscal and monetary policy
	Debts and deficits
	Stabilization policies for aggregate demand and supply shocks
	Monetarist, supply-siders, and Keynesian controversies
10-15%	International economics and growth
	Comparative advantage, trade policy, international finance, and exchange rates
	Economic growth

Sample Questions

The 39 sample questions that follow are similar to questions on the Principles of Macroeconomics exam, but they do not appear on the actual exam. CLEP exams are designed so that average students completing a course in the subject can usually answer about half the questions correctly.

   Before attempting to answer the sample questions, read all the information about the Principles of Macroeconomics exam given above. Additional suggestions for preparing for CLEP exams are provided in Chapter 4.

   Try to answer correctly as many questions as possible. Then compare your answers with the correct answers, given in Appendix A.

Directions: Each of the questions or incomplete statements below is followed by five suggested answers or completions. Select the one that is best in each case.

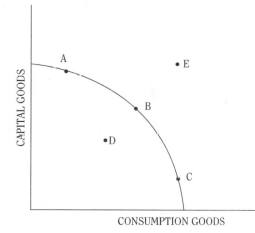

1. An economy that is fully employing all its productive resources but allocating less to investment than to consumption will be at which of the following positions on the production possibilities curve shown above?

   (A) A
   (B) B
   (C) C
   (D) D
   (E) E

   (A) (B) (C) (D) (E)

2. Assume that land in an agricultural economy can be used either for producing grain or for grazing cattle to produce beef. The opportunity cost of converting an acre from cattle grazing to grain production is the

(A) market value of the extra grain that is produced
(B) total amount of beef produced
(C) number of extra bushels of grain that are produced
(D) amount by which beef production decreases
(E) profits generated by the extra production of grain

Ⓐ Ⓑ Ⓒ Ⓓ Ⓔ

3. Which of the following is a possible cause of stagflation (simultaneous high unemployment and high inflation)?

(A) Increase in labor productivity
(B) Increase in price for raw materials
(C) The rapid growth and development of the computer industry
(D) A decline in labor union membership
(E) A low growth rate of the money supply

Ⓐ Ⓑ Ⓒ Ⓓ Ⓔ

4. Which of the following will occur as a result of an improvement in technology?

(A) The aggregate demand curve will shift to the right.
(B) The aggregate demand curve will shift to the left.
(C) The aggregate supply curve will shift to the right.
(D) The aggregate supply curve will shift to the left.
(E) The production possibilities curve will shift inward.

Ⓐ Ⓑ Ⓒ Ⓓ Ⓔ

5. Increases in real income per capita are made possible by

(A) improved productivity
(B) a high labor/capital ratio
(C) large trade surpluses
(D) stable interest rates
(E) high protective tariffs

Ⓐ Ⓑ Ⓒ Ⓓ Ⓔ

6. Which of the following is an example of "investment" as the term is used by economists?

(A) A schoolteacher purchases 10,000 shares of stock in an automobile company.
(B) Newlyweds purchase a previously owned home.
(C) One large automobile firm purchases another large automobile firm.
(D) A farmer purchases $10,000 worth of government securities.
(E) An apparel company purchases 15 new sewing machines.

Ⓐ Ⓑ Ⓒ Ⓓ Ⓔ

7. The United States government defines an individual as unemployed if the person

(A) does not hold a paying job
(B) has been recently fired
(C) works part-time but needs full-time work
(D) is without a job but is looking for work
(E) wants a job but is not searching because he or she thinks none is available

Ⓐ Ⓑ Ⓒ Ⓓ Ⓔ

8. If businesses are experiencing an unplanned increase in inventories, which of the following is most likely to be true?

(A) Aggregate demand is greater than output, and the level of spending will increase.
(B) Aggregate demand is less than output, and the level of spending will decrease.
(C) The economy is growing and will continue to grow until a new equilibrium level of spending is reached.
(D) Planned investment is greater than planned saving, and the level of spending will decrease.
(E) Planned investment is less than planned saving, and the level of spending will increase.

9. Which of the following workers is most likely to be classified as structurally unemployed?

(A) A high school teacher who is unemployed during the summer months
(B) A recent college graduate who is looking for her first job
(C) A teenager who is seeking part-time employment at a fast-food restaurant
(D) A worker who is unemployed because his skills are obsolete
(E) A woman who reenters the job market after her child begins elementary school

Ⓐ Ⓑ Ⓒ Ⓓ Ⓔ

10. According to the classical model, an increase in the money supply causes an increase in which of the following?

I. The price level
II. Nominal gross domestic product
III. Nominal wages

(A) I only
(B) II only
(C) III only
(D) II and III only
(E) I, II, and III

Ⓐ Ⓑ Ⓒ Ⓓ Ⓔ

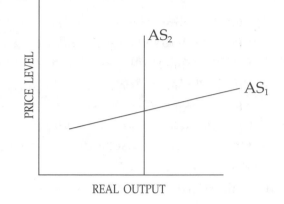

11. The diagram above shows two aggregate supply curves, AS_1 and AS_2. Which of the following statements most accurately characterizes the AS_1 curve relative to the AS_2 curve?

(A) AS_1 is Keynesian because it reflects greater wage and price flexibility.
(B) AS_1 is classical because it reflects greater wage and price flexibility.
(C) AS_1 is Keynesian because it reflects less wage and price flexibility.
(D) AS_1 is classical because it reflects less wage and price flexibility.
(E) AS_1 could be either classical or Keynesian because it reflects greater wage flexibility but less price flexibility.

Ⓐ Ⓑ Ⓒ Ⓓ Ⓔ

12. An increase in which of the following would cause the long-run aggregate supply curve to shift to the right?

(A) Corporate income tax rates
(B) Aggregate demand
(C) Potential output
(D) The average wage rate
(E) The price level

Ⓐ Ⓑ Ⓒ Ⓓ Ⓔ

13. According to the classical economists, which of the following is most sensitive to interest rates?

(A) Consumption
(B) Investment
(C) Government spending
(D) Transfer payments
(E) Intermediate goods

Ⓐ Ⓑ Ⓒ Ⓓ Ⓔ

14. In the circular flow diagram, which of the following is true?

(A) Businesses pay wages, rent, interest, and profits to households in return for use of factors of production.

(B) Businesses purchase goods and services from households in return for money payments.

(C) Households pay wages, rent, interest, and profits to businesses in return for use of factors of production.

(D) The relationship between households and businesses exists only in a traditional society.

(E) The relationship between households and businesses exists only in a command economy.

15. Which of the following would most likely lead to a decrease in aggregate demand, that is, shift the aggregate demand curve leftward?

(A) A decrease in taxes

(B) A decrease in interest rates

(C) An increase in household savings

(D) An increase in household consumption

(E) An increase in business firms' purchases of capital equipment from retained earnings

Ⓐ Ⓑ Ⓒ Ⓓ Ⓔ

16. According to the Keynesian model, equilibrium output of an economy may be less than the full-employment level of output because at full employment

(A) sufficient income may not be generated to keep workers above the subsistence level

(B) there might not be enough demand by firms and consumers to buy that output

(C) workers may not be willing to work the hours necessary to produce the output

(D) interest rates might not be high enough to provide the incentive to finance the production

(E) banks may not be willing to lend enough money to support the output

Ⓐ Ⓑ Ⓒ Ⓓ Ⓔ

17. If the Federal Reserve lowers the reserve requirement, which of the following is most likely to happen to interest rates and gross domestic product?

Interest Rates	Gross Domestic Product
(A) Increase	Decrease
(B) Increase	Increase
(C) Decrease	Decrease
(D) Decrease	Increase
(E) No change	No change

Ⓐ Ⓑ Ⓒ Ⓓ Ⓔ

18. If the marginal propensity to consume is 0.9, what is the maximum amount that the equilibrium gross domestic product could change if government expenditures increase by $1 billion?

(A) It could decrease by up to $9 billion.
(B) It could increase by up to $0.9 billion.
(C) It could increase by up to $1 billion.
(D) It could increase by up to $9 billion.
(E) It could increase by up to $10 billion.

Ⓐ Ⓑ Ⓒ Ⓓ Ⓔ

19. Expansionary fiscal policy will be most effective when

(A) the aggregate supply curve is horizontal
(B) the economy is at or above full-employment output
(C) transfer payments are decreased, while taxes remain unchanged
(D) wages and prices are very flexible
(E) the Federal Reserve simultaneously increases the reserve requirement

Ⓐ Ⓑ Ⓒ Ⓓ Ⓔ

20. Which of the following would increase the value of the multiplier?

(A) An increase in government expenditure
(B) An increase in exports
(C) A decrease in government unemployment benefits
(D) A decrease in the marginal propensity to consume
(E) A decrease in the marginal propensity to save

21. Assume that the reserve requirement is 25 percent. If banks have excess reserves of $10,000, which of the following is the maximum amount of additional money that can be created by the banking system through the lending process?

    (A) $2,500
    (B) $10,000
    (C) $40,000
    (D) $50,000
    (E) $250,000

    Ⓐ Ⓑ Ⓒ Ⓓ Ⓔ

22. The principal reason for requiring commercial banks to maintain reserve balances with the Federal Reserve is that these balances

    (A) provide the maximum amount of reserves a bank would ever need
    (B) give the Federal Reserve more control over the money-creating operations of banks
    (C) ensure that banks do not make excessive profits
    (D) assist the Treasury in refinancing government debt
    (E) enable the government to borrow cheaply from the Federal Reserve's discount window

    Ⓐ Ⓑ Ⓒ Ⓓ Ⓔ

23. The purchase of securities on the open market by the Federal Reserve will

    (A) increase the supply of money
    (B) increase the interest rate
    (C) increase the discount rate
    (D) decrease the number of Federal Reserve notes in circulation
    (E) decrease the reserve requirement

    Ⓐ Ⓑ Ⓒ Ⓓ Ⓔ

24. To counteract a recession, the Federal Reserve should

    (A) buy securities on the open market and raise the reserve requirement
    (B) buy securities on the open market and lower the reserve requirement
    (C) buy securities on the open market and raise the discount rate
    (D) sell securities on the open market and raise the discount rate
    (E) raise the reserve requirement and lower the discount rate

    Ⓐ Ⓑ Ⓒ Ⓓ Ⓔ

25. Total spending in the economy is most likely to increase by the largest amount if which of the following occur to government spending and taxes?

Government Spending	Taxes
(A) Decrease	Increase
(B) Decrease	No change
(C) Increase	Increase
(D) Increase	Decrease
(E) No change	Increase

Ⓐ Ⓑ Ⓒ Ⓓ Ⓔ

26. According to the Keynesian model, an increase in the money supply affects output more if

(A) investment is sensitive to interest rates

(B) money demand is sensitive to interest rates

(C) the unemployment rate is low

(D) consumption is sensitive to the Phillips curve

(E) government spending is sensitive to public opinion

Ⓐ Ⓑ Ⓒ Ⓓ Ⓔ

27. Supply-side economists argue that

(A) a cut in high tax rates results in an increased deficit and thus increases aggregate supply

(B) lower tax rates provide positive work incentives and thus shift the aggregate supply curve to the right

(C) the aggregate supply of goods can only be increased if the price level falls

(D) increased government spending should be used to stimulate the economy

(E) the government should regulate the supply of imports

28. Which of the following policies would most likely be recommended in an economy with an annual inflation rate of 3 percent and an unemployment rate of 11 percent?

(A) An increase in transfer payments and an increase in the reserve requirement

(B) An increase in defense spending and an increase in the discount rate

(C) An increase in income tax rates and a decrease in the reserve requirement

(D) A decrease in government spending and the open-market sale of government securities

(E) A decrease in the tax rate on corporate profits and a decrease in the discount rate

(A) (B) (C) (D) (E)

29. According to the monetarists, inflation is most often the result of

(A) high federal tax rates
(B) increased production of capital goods
(C) decreased production of capital goods
(D) an excessive growth of the money supply
(E) upward shifts in the consumption function

(A) (B) (C) (D) (E)

30. According to the Keynesian model, an expansionary fiscal policy would tend to cause which of the following changes in output and interest rates?

	Output	Interest Rates
(A)	Increase	Increase
(B)	Increase	Decrease
(C)	Decrease	Increase
(D)	Decrease	Decrease
(E)	No change	Decrease

(A) (B) (C) (D) (E)

31. Which of the following would result in the largest increase in aggregate demand?

(A) A $30 billion increase in military expenditure and a $30 billion open-market purchase of government securities

(B) A $30 billion increase in military expenditure and a $30 billion open-market sale of government securities

(C) A $30 billion tax cut and a $30 billion open-market sale of government securities

(D) A $30 billion tax increase and a $30 billion open-market purchase of government securities

(E) A $30 billion increase in social security payments and a $30 billion open-market sale of government securities

Ⓐ Ⓑ Ⓒ Ⓓ Ⓔ

32. Which of the following measures might be used to reduce a federal budget deficit?

   I. Raising taxes
   II. Reducing federal spending
   III. Lowering interest rates

(A) I only
(B) II only
(C) III only
(D) I and III only
(E) I, II, and III

Ⓐ Ⓑ Ⓒ Ⓓ Ⓔ

33. Which of the following would most likely be the immediate result if the United States increased tariffs on most foreign goods?

(A) The United States standard of living would be higher.
(B) More foreign goods would be purchased by Americans.
(C) Prices of domestic goods would increase.
(D) Large numbers of United States workers would be laid off.
(E) The value of the United States dollar would decrease against foreign currencies.

Ⓐ Ⓑ Ⓒ Ⓓ Ⓔ

34. Which of the following policies is most likely to encourage long-run economic growth in a country?

(A) An embargo on high-technology imports
(B) A decline in the number of immigrants to the country
(C) An increase in government transfer payments
(D) An increase in the per capita savings rate
(E) An increase in defense spending   Ⓐ Ⓑ Ⓒ Ⓓ Ⓔ

35. Which of the following would occur if the international value of the United States dollar decreased?

(A) United States exports would rise.
(B) More gold would flow into the United States.
(C) United States demand for foreign currencies would increase.
(D) The United States trade deficit would increase.
(E) Americans would pay less for foreign goods.   Ⓐ Ⓑ Ⓒ Ⓓ Ⓔ

36. If exchange rates are allowed to fluctuate freely and the United States demand for German marks increases, which of the following will most likely occur?

(A) Americans will have to pay more for goods made in Germany.
(B) Germans will find that American goods are getting more expensive.
(C) The United States balance-of-payments deficit will increase.
(D) The dollar price of marks will fall.
(E) The dollar price of German goods will fall.   Ⓐ Ⓑ Ⓒ Ⓓ Ⓔ

37. The replacement of some portion of the federal personal income tax with a general sales tax would most likely result in

(A) greater overall progressivity in the tax structure
(B) lesser overall progressivity in the tax structure
(C) stronger automatic stabilization through the business cycle
(D) increased consumption of liquor, cigarettes, and gasoline
(E) a smaller federal budget deficit

Ⓐ Ⓑ Ⓒ Ⓓ Ⓔ

38. A deficit in the United States trade balance can be described as

(A) an excess of the value of commodity imports over the value of commodity exports
(B) an excess of the value of commodity exports over the value of commodity imports
(C) an excess of payments to foreigners over receipts from foreigners
(D) an almost complete depletion of the gold stock
(E) the consequence of an undervalued dollar

Ⓐ Ⓑ Ⓒ Ⓓ Ⓔ

39. Problems faced by all economic systems include which of the following?

   I. How to allocate scarce resources among unlimited wants
   II. How to decentralize markets
   III. How to decide what to produce, how to produce, and for whom to produce
   IV. How to set government production quotas

(A) I only
(B) I and III only
(C) II and III only
(D) I, II, and III only
(E) I, II, III, and IV

Ⓐ Ⓑ Ⓒ Ⓓ Ⓔ

Study Resources

There are many introductory economics textbooks that vary greatly in difficulty. Most books are published in one-volume editions, which cover both microeconomics and macroeconomics; some are also published in two-volume editions, with one volume covering macroeconomics and the other microeconomics. A companion study guide/workbook is available for most textbooks. The study guides typically include brief reviews, definitions of key concepts, problem sets, and multiple-choice test questions with answers. Many publishers also make available computer-assisted learning packages. To prepare for the Principles of Macroeconomics and Microeconomics exams, you should study the contents of at least one college level introductory economics textbook. These textbooks can be found in most college bookstores. You would do well to consult two or three textbooks because they vary in content, approach, and emphasis. When selecting a textbook, check the table of contents against the "Knowledge and Skills Required" section on pages 307-308 and pages 323-324.

To broaden your knowledge of economic issues, you may read relevant articles published in the economics periodicals that are available in most college libraries — for example, *The Economist, The Margin,* and *The American Economic Review. The Wall Street Journal* and the *New York Times,* along with local papers, may also enhance your understanding of economic issues. The Internet is another resource you could explore.

Additional suggestions for preparing for CLEP exams are provided in Chapter 4.

Principles of Microeconomics

Description of the Examination

The Subject Examination in Principles of Microeconomics covers material that is usually taught in a one-semester undergraduate course in the principles of microeconomics. This aspect of economics deals with the principles of economics that apply to the behavior of groups, organizations, and individuals within the larger economic system. Questions on the exam require candidates to apply analytic techniques to hypothetical situations and to analyze and evaluate government policies on the basis of simple theoretical models. The exam emphasizes analytical capabilities rather than a factual understanding of United States institutions and policies.

The exam consists of approximately 80 multiple-choice questions to be answered in two separately timed 45-minute sections.

Knowledge and Skills Required

Questions on the Principles of Microeconomics exam require candidates to demonstrate one or more of the following abilities.

- Understanding of important economic terms and concepts

- Interpretation and manipulation of economic graphs

- Interpretation and evaluation of economic data

- Application of simple economic models

The outline below indicates the material covered by the exam and the approximate percent of questions in each category.

➡ *Approximate Percent of Examination*

8-12%   Basic economic concepts

               Scarcity: nature of economic systems

               Opportunity costs and production possibilities

               Comparative advantage

Approximate Percent of Examination

60-70% The nature and function of the product market

Supply and demand (15-20%)

Price and quantity demanded

Basic implementation of policy

Consumer demand (10-15%)

Consumer choice: utility and demand theory

Elasticity

Firm's production, costs, and revenue (10-15%)

Marginal product and diminishing returns

Total, average, and marginal costs and revenue

Long-run costs and economies of scale

Profit maximization: pricing, revenue, and output both in the long run and the short run and in the firm and the market (25-30%)

Perfect competition

Imperfect competition

Monopoly

Oligopoly and monopolistic competition

Efficiency and antitrust (4-6%)

10-15% Factor Market

Derived demand

Determination of wages and other factor prices

Distribution of income

4-6% Market failures and the role of government

Externalities

Public goods

Sample Questions

The 39 sample questions that follow are similar to questions on the Principles of Microeconomics exam, but they do not appear on the actual exam. CLEP exams are designed so that average students completing a course in the subject can usually answer about half the questions correctly.

Before attempting to answer the sample questions, read all the information about the Principles of Microeconomics exam given above. Additional suggestions for preparing for CLEP exams are provided in Chapter 4.

Try to answer correctly as many questions as possible. Then compare your answers with the correct answers, given in Appendix A.

Directions: Each of the questions or incomplete statements below is followed by five suggested answers or completions. Select the one that is best in each case.

Questions 1-2 are based on the following table.

PRODUCTION FUNCTION

(Figures in body of table represent amounts of output.)

Units of Labor	Units of Capital					
	1	2	3	4	5	6
1	141	200	245	282	316	346
2	200	282	346	400	448	490
3	245	346	423	490	548	600
4	282	400	490	564	632	692
5	316	448	548	632	705	775
6	346	490	—	692	775	846

1. Information given in the table can be used to illustrate the law of

   (A) diminishing returns
   (B) diminishing demand
   (C) diminishing utility
   (D) supply and demand
   (E) comparative advantage

   Ⓐ Ⓑ Ⓒ Ⓓ Ⓔ

2. If there are constant returns to scale throughout the production process, the amount of output that can be produced with 3 units of capital and 6 units of labor must be

(A) 490   (B) 548   (C) 600

  (D) 608   (E) 693   Ⓐ Ⓑ Ⓒ Ⓓ Ⓔ

3. Which of the following best states the thesis of the law of comparative advantage?

(A) Differences in relative costs of production are the key to determining patterns of trade.

(B) Differences in absolute costs of production determine which goods should be traded between nations.

(C) Tariffs and quotas are beneficial in increasing international competitiveness.

(D) Nations should not specialize in the production of goods and services.

(E) Two nations will not trade if one is more efficient than the other in the production of all goods.

                             Ⓐ Ⓑ Ⓒ Ⓓ Ⓔ

4. A retail firm planning to increase the price of a product it sells would hope that

(A) the good is an inferior good

(B) the price of complements would also go up

(C) the price of substitutes would go down

(D) demand for the product is perfectly elastic

(E) demand for the product is inelastic   Ⓐ Ⓑ Ⓒ Ⓓ Ⓔ

5. If it were possible to increase the output of military goods and simultaneously to increase the output of the private sector of an economy, which of the following statements about the economy and its current position relative to its production possibilities curve would be true?

(A) The economy is inefficient and inside the curve.

(B) The economy is inefficient and on the curve.

(C) The economy is efficient and on the curve.

(D) The economy is efficient and inside the curve.

(E) The economy is efficient and outside the curve.   Ⓐ Ⓑ Ⓒ Ⓓ Ⓔ

6. Which of the following would necessarily cause a fall in the price of a product?

(A) An increase in population and a decrease in the price of an input
(B) An increase in population and a decrease in the number of firms producing the product
(C) An increase in average income and an improvement in production technology
(D) A decrease in the price of a substitute product and an improvement in production technology
(E) A decrease in the price of a substitute product and an increase in the price of an input

Ⓐ Ⓑ Ⓒ Ⓓ Ⓔ

7. Agricultural price supports will most likely result in

(A) shortages of products if the price supports are above the equilibrium price
(B) shortages of products if the price supports are at equilibrium price
(C) surpluses of products if the price supports are above the equilibrium price
(D) surpluses of products if the price supports are below the equilibrium price
(E) a balance between quantity demanded and quantity supplied if the price floor is above the equilibrium price

Ⓐ Ⓑ Ⓒ Ⓓ Ⓔ

8. The market equilibrium price of home heating oil is $1.50 per gallon. If a price ceiling of $1.00 per gallon is imposed, which of the following will occur in the market for home heating oil?

I. Quantity supplied will increase.
II. Quantity demanded will increase.
III. Quantity supplied will decrease.
IV. Quantity demanded will decrease.

(A) II only
(B) I and II only
(C) I and IV only
(D) II and III only
(E) III and IV only

Ⓐ Ⓑ Ⓒ Ⓓ Ⓔ

9. Assume a consumer finds that her total expenditure on compact discs stays the same after the price of compact discs declines. Which of the following is true for this consumer over the price range?

(A) Compact discs are inferior goods.
(B) The consumer's demand for compact discs increased in response to the price change.
(C) The consumer's demand for compact discs is perfectly price elastic.
(D) The consumer's demand for compact discs is perfectly price inelastic.
(E) The consumer's demand for compact discs is unit price elastic.

Ⓐ Ⓑ Ⓒ Ⓓ Ⓔ

10. An improvement in production technology for a certain good leads to

(A) an increase in demand for the good
(B) an increase in the supply of the good
(C) an increase in the price of the good
(D) a shortage of the good
(E) a surplus of the good

Ⓐ Ⓑ Ⓒ Ⓓ Ⓔ

11. If the demand for a product is price elastic, which of the following is true?

(A) An increase in product price will have no effect on the firm's total revenue.
(B) An increase in product price will increase the firm's total revenue.
(C) A reduction in product price will increase the firm's total revenue.
(D) A reduction in product price will decrease the firm's rate of inventory turnover.
(E) A reduction in product price will decrease the total cost of goods sold.

Ⓐ Ⓑ Ⓒ Ⓓ Ⓔ

12. If an increase in the price of good X causes a drop in demand for good Y, good Y is

(A) an inferior good
(B) a luxury good
(C) a necessary good
(D) a substitute for good X
(E) a complement to good X

Ⓐ Ⓑ Ⓒ Ⓓ Ⓔ

13. The demand curve for cars is downward sloping because an increase in the price of cars leads to

   (A) the increased use of other modes of transportation
   (B) a fall in the expected future price of cars
   (C) a decrease in the number of cars available for purchase
   (D) a rise in the prices of gasoline and other oil-based products
   (E) a change in consumers' tastes in cars

   Ⓐ Ⓑ Ⓒ Ⓓ Ⓔ

14. Suppose that an effective minimum wage is imposed in a certain labor market above the equilibrium wage. If labor supply in that market subsequently increases, which of the following will occur?

   (A) Unemployment in that market will increase.
   (B) Quantity of labor supplied will decrease.
   (C) Quantity of labor demanded will increase.
   (D) Market demand will increase.
   (E) The market wage will increase.

   Ⓐ Ⓑ Ⓒ Ⓓ Ⓔ

15. Suppose that a family buys all its clothing from a discount store and treats these items as inferior goods. Under such circumstances, this family's consumption of discount store clothing will necessarily

   (A) increase when a family member wins the state lottery
   (B) increase when a family member gets a raise in pay at work
   (C) remain unchanged when its income rises or falls due to events
        beyond the family's control
   (D) decrease when a family member becomes unemployed
   (E) decrease when a family member experiences an increase in income

   Ⓐ Ⓑ Ⓒ Ⓓ Ⓔ

16. The primary distinction between the short run and the long run is that in the short run

(A) firms make profits, but in the long run no firm makes economic profits

(B) profits are maximized, but in the long run all costs are maximized

(C) some costs of production are fixed, but in the long run all costs are fixed

(D) some costs of production are fixed, but in the long run all costs are variable

(E) marginal costs are rising, but in the long run they are constant

Ⓐ Ⓑ Ⓒ Ⓓ Ⓔ

Questions 17-19 are based on the table below, which shows a firm's total cost for different levels of output.

Output	Total Cost
0	$24
1	33
2	41
3	48
4	54
5	61
6	69

17. Which of the following is the firm's marginal cost of producing the fourth unit of output?

(A) $54.00
(B) $13.50
(C) $ 7.50
(D) $ 6.00
(E) $ 1.50

Ⓐ Ⓑ Ⓒ Ⓓ Ⓔ

18. Which of the following is the firm's average total cost of producing 3 units of output?

(A) $48.00
(B) $16.00
(C) $14.00
(D) $13.50
(E) $ 7.00

Ⓐ Ⓑ Ⓒ Ⓓ Ⓔ

19. Which of the following is the firm's average fixed cost of producing 2 units of output?

(A) $24.00
(B) $20.50
(C) $12.00
(D) $ 8.00
(E) $ 7.50

Ⓐ Ⓑ Ⓒ Ⓓ Ⓔ

20. Marginal revenue is the change in revenue that results from a one-unit increase in the

(A) variable input
(B) variable input price
(C) output level
(D) output price
(E) fixed cost

Ⓐ Ⓑ Ⓒ Ⓓ Ⓔ

21. In the short run, if the product price of a perfectly competitive firm is less than the minimum average variable cost, the firm will

(A) raise its price
(B) increase its output
(C) decrease its output slightly but increase its profit margin
(D) lose more by continuing to produce than by shutting down
(E) lose less by continuing to produce than by shutting down

Ⓐ Ⓑ Ⓒ Ⓓ Ⓔ

22. Suppose that the license paid by each business to operate in a city increases from $400 per year to $500 per year. What effect will this increase have on a firm's short-run costs?

	Marginal Cost	Average Total Cost	Average Variable Cost
(A)	Increase	Increase	Increase
(B)	Increase	Increase	No effect
(C)	No effect	No effect	No effect
(D)	No effect	Increase	Increase
(E)	No effect	Increase	No effect

Ⓐ Ⓑ Ⓒ Ⓓ Ⓔ

23. Which of the following statements is true of perfectly competitive firms in long-run equilibrium?

(A) Firm revenues will decrease if production is increased.
(B) Total firm revenues are at a maximum.
(C) Average fixed cost equals marginal cost.
(D) Average total cost is at a minimum.
(E) Average variable cost is greater than marginal cost.

Ⓐ Ⓑ Ⓒ Ⓓ Ⓔ

24. If the chemical industry in an area has been dumping its toxic waste free of charge into a river, government action to ensure a more efficient use of resources would have which of the following effects on the industry's output and product price?

Output	Price
(A) Decrease	Decrease
(B) Decrease	Increase
(C) Increase	Decrease
(D) Increase	Increase
(E) Increase	No change

Ⓐ Ⓑ Ⓒ Ⓓ Ⓔ

25. Assume a perfectly competitive industry is in long-run equilibrium. A permanent increase in demand will eventually result in

(A) a decrease in demand because the price will increase and people will buy less of the output
(B) a decrease in supply because the rate of output and the associated cost will both increase
(C) an increase in price but no increase in output
(D) an increase in output
(E) a permanent shortage since the quantity demanded is now greater than the quantity supplied

Ⓐ Ⓑ Ⓒ Ⓓ Ⓔ

26. Economists are critical of monopoly principally because

    (A) monopolists gain too much political influence
    (B) monopolists are able to avoid paying their fair share of taxes
    (C) monopolists are unfair to poor people
    (D) monopoly leads to an inefficient use of scarce productive resources
    (E) monopolists cause international political tension by competing with
        one another overseas for supplies of raw materials

27. Which of the following statements has to be true in a perfectly
    competitive market?

    (A) A firm's marginal revenue equals price.
    (B) A firm's average total cost is above price in the long run.
    (C) A firm's average fixed cost rises in the short run.
    (D) A firm's average variable cost is higher than price in the long run.
    (E) Large firms have lower total costs than small firms.

    Ⓐ Ⓑ Ⓒ Ⓓ Ⓔ

28. A perfectly competitive firm produces in an industry whose product sells
    at a market price of $100. At the firm's current rate of production,
    marginal cost is rising and equal to $110. To maximize its profits, the firm
    should change its output and price in which of the following ways?

Output	Price
(A) Decrease	Increase
(B) Decrease	No change
(C) No change	Increase
(D) Increase	No change
(E) Increase	Decrease

    Ⓐ Ⓑ Ⓒ Ⓓ Ⓔ

29. The typical firm in a monopolistically competitive industry earns zero profit in long-run equilibrium because

(A) advertising costs make monopolistic competition a high-cost market structure rather than a low-cost market structure

(B) the firms in the industry do not operate at the minimum point on their long-run average cost curves

(C) there are no significant restrictions on entering or exiting from the industry

(D) the firms in the industry are unable to engage in product differentiation

(E) there are close substitutes for each firm's product

30. In the long run, compared with a perfectly competitive firm, a monopolistically competitive firm with the same costs will have

(A) a higher price and higher output
(B) a higher price and lower output
(C) a lower price and higher output
(D) a lower price and lower output
(E) the same price and lower output

31. Which of the following describes what will happen to market price and quantity if firms in a perfectly competitive market form a cartel and act as a profit-maximizing monopoly?

	Price	Quantity
(A)	Decrease	Decrease
(B)	Decrease	Increase
(C)	Increase	Increase
(D)	Increase	Decrease
(E)	Increase	No change

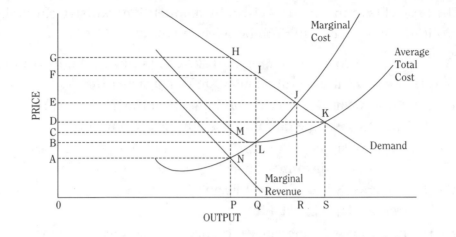

32. The diagram above depicts cost and revenue curves for a firm. What are the firm's profit-maximizing output and price?

	Output	Price
(A)	0S	0D
(B)	0R	0E
(C)	0Q	0F
(D)	0Q	0B
(E)	0P	0G

Ⓐ Ⓑ Ⓒ Ⓓ Ⓔ

33. Imperfectly competitive firms may be allocatively inefficient because they produce at a level of output such that

(A) average cost is at a minimum
(B) price equals marginal revenue
(C) marginal revenue is greater than marginal cost
(D) price equals marginal cost
(E) price is greater than marginal cost

Ⓐ Ⓑ Ⓒ Ⓓ Ⓔ

34. In a market economy, public goods such as community police protection are unlikely to be provided in sufficient quantity by the private sector because

    (A) private firms are less efficient at producing public goods than is the government

    (B) the use of public goods cannot be withheld from those who do not pay for them

    (C) consumers lack information about the benefits of public goods

    (D) consumers do not value public goods highly enough for firms to produce them profitably

    (E) public goods are inherently too important to be left to private firms to produce

Ⓐ Ⓑ Ⓒ Ⓓ Ⓔ

35. Assume that both input and product markets are competitive. If the product price rises, in the short run firms will increase production by increasing

    (A) the stock of fixed capital until marginal revenue equals the product price

    (B) the stock of fixed capital until the average product of capital equals the price of capital

    (C) labor input until the marginal revenue product of labor equals the wage rate

    (D) labor input until the marginal product of labor equals the wage rate

    (E) labor input until the ratio of product price to the marginal product of labor equals the wage rate

Ⓐ Ⓑ Ⓒ Ⓓ Ⓔ

36. In which of the following ways does the United States government currently intervene in the working of the market economy?

    I. It produces certain goods and services.
   II. It regulates the private sector in an effort to achieve a more efficient allocation of resources.
  III. It redistributes income through taxation and public expenditures.

(A) I only
(B) II only
(C) III only
(D) II and III only
(E) I, II, and III

Ⓐ Ⓑ Ⓒ Ⓓ Ⓔ

37. If hiring an additional worker would increase a firm's total cost by less than it would increase its total revenue, the firm should

(A) not hire the worker
(B) hire the worker
(C) hire the worker only if another worker leaves or is fired
(D) hire the worker only if the worker can raise the firm's productivity
(E) reduce the number of workers employed by the firm

Ⓐ Ⓑ Ⓒ Ⓓ Ⓔ

38. If a firm wants to produce a given amount of output at the lowest possible cost, it should use resources in such a manner that

(A) it uses relatively more of the less expensive resource
(B) it uses relatively more of the resource with the highest marginal product
(C) each resource has just reached the point of diminishing marginal returns
(D) the marginal products of each resource are equal
(E) the marginal products per dollar spent on each resource are equal

Ⓐ Ⓑ Ⓒ Ⓓ Ⓔ

39. If the firms in an industry pollute the environment and are not charged for the pollution, which of the following is true from the standpoint of the efficient use of resources?

   (A) Too much of the industry's product is produced, and the price of the product is too high.
   (B) Too much of the industry's product is produced, and the price of the product is too low.
   (C) Too little of the industry's product is produced, and the price of the product is too high.
   (D) Too little of the industry's product is produced, and the price of the product is too low.
   (E) The industry is a monopoly.

   Ⓐ Ⓑ Ⓒ Ⓓ Ⓔ

Study Resources

The study resources suggested for preparing for the Principles of Macroeconomics exam cover both microeconomics and macroeconomics and can be used in preparing for the Principles of Microeconomics exam.

Introductory Psychology

Description of the Examination

The Subject Examination in Introductory Psychology covers material that is usually taught in a one-semester undergraduate course in introductory psychology. It stresses basic facts, concepts, and generally accepted principles. Among the topics included on the exam are learning and cognition, behavior, personality, abnormal behavior, perception, motivation and emotion, and developmental and social psychology.

The exam is 90 minutes long and contains approximately 100 multiple-choice questions to be answered in two separately timed 45-minute sections.

Knowledge and Skills Required

Questions on the exam require candidates to demonstrate one or more of the following abilities.

- Knowledge of terminology, principles, and theory

- Comprehension, evaluation, and analysis of problem situations

- Application of knowledge to new situations

The Introductory Psychology exam requires knowledge of the following areas of psychology.

	Approximate Percent of Examination
8-9%	History, approaches, methods
	History of psychology
	Approaches: biological, behavioral, cognitive, humanistic, psychodynamic
	Research methods: experimental, clinical, correlational
	Ethics in research

Approximate Percent of Examination

8-9%   Biological bases of behavior
    Neuroanatomy
    Functional organization of the nervous system
    Endocrine system
    Physiological techniques
    Genetics

7-8%   Sensation and perception
    Receptor processes: vision, audition
    Sensory mechanisms: thresholds, adaptation
    Other senses: kinesthetic, olfactory, gustatory
    Perceptual development
    Perceptual processes
    Attention

5-6%   States of consciousness
    Sleep and dreaming
    Hypnosis and meditation
    Psychoactive drug effects

10-11%   Learning
    Biological bases
    Classical conditioning
    Operant conditioning
    Cognitive processes in learning

8-9%   Cognition
    Cognitive development
    Memory
    Language
    Thinking and problem solving
    Intelligence and creativity

➨ *Approximate Percent of Examination*

7-8%   Motivation and emotion

     Biological bases

     Theories of motivation

     Theories of emotion

     Hunger, thirst, sex, pain

     Social motivation

8-9%   Developmental psychology

     Theories of development

     Dimensions of development: physical, cognitive, social, moral

     Research methods: longitudinal, cross-sectional

     Heredity-environment issues

     Gender identity and sex roles

7-8%   Personality

     Personality theories and approaches

     Assessment techniques

     Research methods: idiographic, nomothetic

     Self-concept, self-esteem

     Growth and adjustment

8-9%   Abnormal psychology

     Theories of psychopathology

     Anxiety disorders

     Affective disorders

     Dissociative disorders

     Somatoform disorders

     Personality disorders

     Psychoses

Approximate Percent of Examination

7-8%   Treatment of psychological disorders
　　　　　　Insight therapies: psychodynamic/humanistic approaches
　　　　　　Behavioral therapies
　　　　　　Cognitive therapies
　　　　　　Biological therapies
　　　　　　Community and preventative approaches

7-8%   Social psychology
　　　　　　Group dynamics
　　　　　　Attribution processes
　　　　　　Interpersonal perception
　　　　　　Conformity, compliance, obedience
　　　　　　Attitudes and attitude change
　　　　　　Aggression/Antisocial behavior

3-4%   Statistics, tests, and measurement
　　　　　　Samples, populations, norms
　　　　　　Reliability and validity
　　　　　　Descriptive statistics
　　　　　　Inferential statistics
　　　　　　Types of tests
　　　　　　Theories of intelligence
　　　　　　Mental retardation

Sample Questions

The 35 questions that follow are similar to questions on the Introductory Psychology exam, but they do not appear on the actual exam. CLEP exams are designed so that average students completing a course in the subject can usually answer about half the questions correctly.

Before attempting to answer the sample questions, read all the information about the Introductory Psychology exam given above. Additional suggestions for preparing for CLEP exams are provided in Chapter 4.

Try to answer correctly as many questions as possible. Then compare your answers with the correct answers, given in Appendix A.

Directions: Each of the questions or incomplete statements below is followed by five suggested answers or completions. Select the one that is best in each case.

1. A psychologist tests the hypothesis that students from small families are more competitive in their concern about grades than are students from large families. In this study, which of the following are the independent and the dependent variables, respectively?

   (A) Course grades . . competitiveness
   (B) Course grades . . family size
   (C) Competitiveness . . family size
   (D) Competitiveness . . course grades
   (E) Family size . . competitiveness   Ⓐ Ⓑ Ⓒ Ⓓ Ⓔ

2. One theory of the effects of arousal holds that efficiency of behavior can be described as an inverted U-shaped function of increasing arousal. Which of the following accurately describes this relationship?

   (A) Greater arousal leads to better performance.
   (B) Greater arousal leads to poorer performance.
   (C) Low and high levels of arousal lead to poorest performance.
   (D) Overarousal leads to performance efficiency.
   (E) Underarousal leads to performance efficiency.   Ⓐ Ⓑ Ⓒ Ⓓ Ⓔ

3. The total number of chromosomes found in a human cell is

   (A) 16
   (B) 20
   (C) 46
   (D) 86
   (E) 102   Ⓐ Ⓑ Ⓒ Ⓓ Ⓔ

4. Shortly after learning to associate the word "dog" with certain four-legged furry animals, young children will frequently misidentify a cow or a horse as a dog. This phenomenon is best viewed as an example of

   (A) differentiation   (B) negative transfer
      (C) imprinting   (D) stimulus generalization
       (E) linear perspective   Ⓐ Ⓑ Ⓒ Ⓓ Ⓔ

5. In adults, total sensory deprivation for long periods of time produces

(A) a feeling of well-being similar to that achieved through meditation
(B) no change in emotions or cognition, provided the subject was
     mentally stable before the deprivation
(C) increased efficiency in the senses of sight, hearing, and touch
(D) profound apathy and a subjective sensation of powerlessness
(E) hallucinations and impaired efficiency in all areas of intellectual
     functioning

Ⓐ Ⓑ Ⓒ Ⓓ Ⓔ

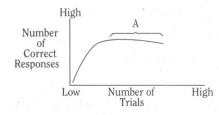

6. The portion of the performance curve above marked A represents

(A) extinction   (B) a plateau   (C) spontaneous recovery
    (D) a serial position effect   (E) response generalization

Ⓐ Ⓑ Ⓒ Ⓓ Ⓔ

7. In which of the following areas does psychological research show most
   clearly that girls develop earlier than boys?

(A) Independence from parents
(B) Athletic competence
(C) Intellectual achievement
(D) Physical growth spurt
(E) Self-actualization

Ⓐ Ⓑ Ⓒ Ⓓ Ⓔ

8. Research on the effectiveness of psychotherapy has indicated that

(A) psychotherapists differ among themselves as to the most appropriate method of intervention
(B) nondirective techniques are generally superior to directive ones
(C) the effectiveness of a method depends on the length of time a therapist was trained in the method
(D) psychoanalysis is the most effective technique for eliminating behavior disorders
(E) psychoanalysis is the most effective technique for curing anxiety disorders

Ⓐ Ⓑ Ⓒ Ⓓ Ⓔ

9. If on the last day of a psychology class, a student is asked to remember what was done in class each day during the term, she will likely be able to remember best the activities of the first and last class meetings. This situation is an example of

(A) retroactive inhibition   (B) positive transfer
   (C) the serial position effect   (D) interference
      (E) short-term memory

Ⓐ Ⓑ Ⓒ Ⓓ Ⓔ

10. When insulted by a friend, Sally's first impulse was to strike him. Instead, she yelled loudly and kicked a door several times. This means of reducing aggressive impulses exemplifies which of the following?

(A) Repression   (B) Abreaction   (C) Displacement
   (D) Cathexis   (E) Sublimation

Ⓐ Ⓑ Ⓒ Ⓓ Ⓔ

11. Which of the following parts of the brain is primarily responsible for relaying incoming sensory information to the cerebral cortex?

(A) Cerebellum   (B) Thalamus   (C) Medulla
   (D) Hypothalamus   (E) Reticular activating system

Ⓐ Ⓑ Ⓒ Ⓓ Ⓔ

12. A school psychologist informs a ninth-grade teacher that Jimmy "identifies" with his twelfth-grade brother. What the psychologist means is that Jimmy tends to

(A) feel inferior to his brother
(B) envy and to be jealous of his brother
(C) influence the way his brother views the world
(D) recognize similarities between his brother and himself
(E) accept his brother's values and to imitate his behavior

Ⓐ Ⓑ Ⓒ Ⓓ Ⓔ

13. According to Freud, the superego is the portion of the psyche which is

(A) socialized   (B) hedonistic   (C) narcissistic
(D) reality-oriented   (E) pleasure-oriented

Ⓐ Ⓑ Ⓒ Ⓓ Ⓔ

14. Brain waves during REM sleep generally appear as

(A) alternating high- and low-amplitude waves
(B) rapid low-amplitude waves
(C) unevenly paced medium-amplitude waves
(D) slow low-amplitude waves
(E) slow high-amplitude waves

Ⓐ Ⓑ Ⓒ Ⓓ Ⓔ

15. Which of the following statements does NOT accurately describe the retina?

(A) The rods are more dense in the fovea than in the periphery.
(B) The blind spot is closer to the fovea than to the edge of the retina.
(C) The image on the retina is upside down.
(D) It is located at the back of the eye.
(E) It contains two kinds of receptors: rods and cones.

Ⓐ Ⓑ Ⓒ Ⓓ Ⓔ

16. Which of the following is a true statement about the relationship between test validity and test reliability?

    (A) A test can be reliable without being valid.
    (B) A test that has high content validity will have high reliability.
    (C) A test that has low content validity will have low reliability.
    (D) The higher the test's validity, the lower its reliability will be.
    (E) The validity of a test always exceeds its reliability.

    Ⓐ Ⓑ Ⓒ Ⓓ Ⓔ

17. Proactive inhibition describes a process by which

    (A) people remember digits better than words
    (B) people remember images better than words
    (C) people remember elements in pairs
    (D) prior learning interferes with subsequent learning
    (E) subsequent learning interferes with prior learning

    Ⓐ Ⓑ Ⓒ Ⓓ Ⓔ

18. Checking the coin return every time one passes a pay telephone or a vending machine is a type of behavior probably being maintained by which of the following schedules of reinforcement?

    (A) Fixed interval only
    (B) Fixed ratio only
    (C) Variable ratio only
    (D) Variable interval and fixed ratio
    (E) Fixed interval and variable ratio

    Ⓐ Ⓑ Ⓒ Ⓓ Ⓔ

19. Which of the following is the most common form of psychological disorder?

    (A) Psychotic   (B) Somatoform   (C) Dissociative
    (D) Psychosexual   (E) Mood

    Ⓐ Ⓑ Ⓒ Ⓓ Ⓔ

20. In an approach-avoidance conflict, as the person nears the goal, the levels of attraction and aversion change in which of the following ways?

    (A) Both increase.
    (B) Both decrease.
    (C) Attraction increases and aversion decreases.
    (D) Attraction decreases and aversion increases.
    (E) Both are extinguished.   Ⓐ Ⓑ Ⓒ Ⓓ Ⓔ

21. Which of the following kinds of therapy attempts to correct irrational beliefs that lead to psychological distress?

    (A) Behavioral   (B) Cognitive   (C) Existential
      (D) Gestalt   (E) Psychoanalytic   Ⓐ Ⓑ Ⓒ Ⓓ Ⓔ

22. "Give me a dozen healthy infants, well-formed, and my own specified world to bring them up in and I'll guarantee to take any one at random and train him to become any type of specialist I might select . . ."

    This statement was made by

    (A) James   (B) Thorndike   (C) Watson
      (D) Wertheimer   (E) Woodworth   Ⓐ Ⓑ Ⓒ Ⓓ Ⓔ

23. Similarity, proximity, and familiarity are important determinants of

    (A) observational learning
    (B) friendship formation
    (C) sexual orientation
    (D) aggression
    (E) imprinting   Ⓐ Ⓑ Ⓒ Ⓓ Ⓔ

24. A diagnosis of schizophrenia typically includes which of the following symptoms?

    (A) Delusions   (B) Panic attacks   (C) Hypochondriasis
      (D) Multiple personality   (E) Psychosexual dysfunction
                                          Ⓐ Ⓑ Ⓒ Ⓓ Ⓔ

25. A young child breaks her cookie into a number of pieces and asserts that "now there is more to eat." In Piaget's analysis, the child's behavior is evidence of

   (A) formal logical operations
   (B) concrete logical operations
   (C) conservation
   (D) preoperational thought
   (E) sensorimotor analysis

   Ⓐ Ⓑ Ⓒ Ⓓ Ⓔ

26. Carl G. Jung is associated with which of the following concepts?

   (A) Inferiority complex
   (B) Need for achievement
   (C) Collective unconscious
   (D) Self-esteem
   (E) Self-actualization

   Ⓐ Ⓑ Ⓒ Ⓓ Ⓔ

27. Which of the following types of research design is most appropriate for establishing a cause-and-effect relation between two variables?

   (A) Between subjects   (B) Within subjects   (C) Quantitative
      (D) Experimental   (E) Naturalistic

   Ⓐ Ⓑ Ⓒ Ⓓ Ⓔ

28. A neuron is said to be "polarized" when

   (A) it is in the refractory period
   (B) it is in a resting state
   (C) it is about to undergo an action potential
   (D) the synaptic terminals release chemicals into the synaptic gap
   (E) chemicals outside the cell body cross the cell membrane

   Ⓐ Ⓑ Ⓒ Ⓓ Ⓔ

29. Making the amount of time a child can spend playing video games contingent on the amount of time the child spends practicing the piano is an illustration of

(A) Bentham's adaptive hedonism principle
(B) Locke's law of association
(C) aversive conditioning
(D) classical conditioning
(E) operant conditioning

Ⓐ Ⓑ Ⓒ Ⓓ Ⓔ

30. Which of the following has been identified as correlating most closely with heart disease?

(A) Anxiety   (B) Physical overexertion   (C) Guilt
   (D) Muscle tension   (E) Hostility

Ⓐ Ⓑ Ⓒ Ⓓ Ⓔ

31. The term "etiology" refers to the study of which of the following aspects of an illness?

(A) Origins and causes
(B) Characteristic symptoms
(C) Expected outcome following treatment
(D) Frequency of occurrence
(E) Level of contagiousness

Ⓐ Ⓑ Ⓒ Ⓓ Ⓔ

32. Erikson's and Freud's theories of personality development are most similar in that they both

(A) emphasize the libido
(B) focus on adult development
(C) discount the importance of culture
(D) are based on stages
(E) view behavior as a continuum

Ⓐ Ⓑ Ⓒ Ⓓ Ⓔ

33. Higher-level cognitive processes, such as decision-making, and lower-level perceptual processes, such as color discrimination, respectively, involve primarily

    (A) features analysis and top-down processing
    (B) perceptual set and expectancy
    (C) bottom-up processing and expectancy
    (D) bottom-up processing and top-down processing
    (E) top-down processing and bottom-up processing

    Ⓐ Ⓑ Ⓒ Ⓓ Ⓔ

34. Developmental psychologists would most likely prefer longitudinal research designs to cross-sectional research designs because longitudinal designs

    (A) usually yield results much more quickly
    (B) offer the advantage of between-subjects comparisons
    (C) are much less likely to be influenced by cultural changes that occur over time
    (D) utilize the subjects as their own experimental controls
    (E) are more valid

    Ⓐ Ⓑ Ⓒ Ⓓ Ⓔ

35. An individual undergoing psychotherapy shows improvement due only to that person's belief in the therapy and not because of the therapy itself. This result illustrates a

    (A) transference effect
    (B) placebo effect
    (C) cathectic effect
    (D) primary gain
    (E) conditioned response

    Ⓐ Ⓑ Ⓒ Ⓓ Ⓔ

Study Resources

To prepare for the Introductory Psychology exam, you should study the contents of at least one textbook used in introductory psychology courses at CLEP-user institutions. Visit your local college bookstore to determine which textbooks are used by the college for introductory psychology courses. When selecting a textbook, check the table of contents against the "Knowledge and Skills Required" section on pages 339-342. Since they may vary somewhat in content, approach, and emphasis, you are advised to consult more than one textbook on the major topics.

You will find it helpful to supplement your reading with books listed in the bibliographies found in most psychology textbooks. The Internet is another resource you should explore. Additional suggestions for preparing for CLEP exams are given in Chapter 4.

Introductory Sociology

Description of the Examination

The Subject Examination in Introductory Sociology covers material that is usually taught in a one-term introductory sociology course at most colleges and universities. Exam questions deal with social institutions; stratification; social patterns, processes, and changes; and the sociological perspective. The exam emphasizes basic facts and concepts as well as general theoretical approaches used by sociologists. Highly specialized knowledge of the subject and methodology of the discipline is not included.

The exam is composed of approximately 100 multiple-choice questions to be answered in two separately timed 45-minute sections.

Knowledge and Skills Required

Questions on the exam require candidates to demonstrate one or more of the following abilities.

- Identification of specific names, facts, and concepts from sociological literature

- Understanding of relationships between concepts, empirical generalizations, and theoretical propositions of sociology

- Understanding of the methods by which sociological relationships are established

- Application of concepts, propositions, and methods to hypothetical situations

- Interpretation of tables and charts

The subject matter of the Introductory Sociology exam is drawn from the following topics.

	Approximate Percent of Examination
20%	Institutions
	Family
	Economic
	Political
	Educational
	Religious
	Criminal justice
	Medicine
	Communications/Mass media
30%	Social stratification (process and structure)
	Social mobility
	Social class
	Power and social inequality
	Professions and occupations
	Race and ethnic relations
	Gender roles
	Aging in society
	Global inequality
15%	Social patterns
	Community
	Demography
	Human ecology
	Rural-urban patterns

| ➡ | *Approximate Percent of Examination* |

20%   Social processes
          Roles
          Groups
          Aggregates
          Deviance and social control
          Social change
          Collective behavior
          Socialization
          Culture

15%   The sociological perspective
          History of sociology
          Methods and measurement
          Sociological theory (classical; contemporary)

Sample Questions

The 20 sample questions that follow are similar to questions on the Introductory Sociology exam, but they do not actually appear on the exam. CLEP exams are designed so that average students completing a course in the subject can usually answer about half the questions correctly.

Before attempting to answer the sample questions, read all the information about the Introductory Sociology exam given above. Additional suggestions for preparing for CLEP exams are provided in Chapter 4.

Try to answer correctly as many questions as possible. Then compare your answers with the correct answers, given in Appendix A.

Directions: Each of the questions or incomplete statements below is followed by five suggested answers or completions. Select the one that is best in each case.

1. All of the following are examples of voluntary associations EXCEPT the

   (A) Republican party
   (B) League of Women Voters
   (C) Federal Bureau of Investigation
   (D) Veterans of Foreign Wars
   (E) Knights of Columbus

   Ⓐ Ⓑ Ⓒ Ⓓ Ⓔ

2. A sex ratio of 120 means that there are

(A) 120 more males in a population than females
(B) 120 more females in a population than males
(C) 120 males for every 100 females in a population
(D) 120 females for every 100 males in a population
(E) 12% more men than women in a population ⒶⒷⒸⒹⒺ

3. Industrialization is most likely to reduce the importance of which of the following functions of the family?

(A) Economic production
(B) Care of young children
(C) Fulfillment of sexual needs
(D) Socialization of the individual
(E) Social control ⒶⒷⒸⒹⒺ

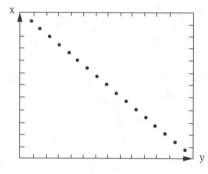

4. Which of the following best describes the relationship between x and y on the scattergram above?

(A) A perfect positive correlation
(B) A perfect negative correlation
(C) A perfect curvilinear correlation
(D) A low negative correlation
(E) A correlation of zero ⒶⒷⒸⒹⒺ

5. The process by which an individual learns how to live in his or her social surroundings is known as

(A) amalgamation   (B) association
   (C) collective behavior   (D) socialization
      (E) innovation

Ⓐ Ⓑ Ⓒ Ⓓ Ⓔ

6. Which of the following may properly be considered norms?

   I. Laws
   II. Folkways
   III. Mores

(A) I only   (B) III only   (C) I and II only
   (D) II and III only   (E) I, II, and III

Ⓐ Ⓑ Ⓒ Ⓓ Ⓔ

7. Which of the following theorists argued that class conflict was inevitable in a capitalistic society and would result in revolution?

(A) C. Wright Mills   (B) Karl Marx
   (C) Émile Durkheim   (D) Hannah Arendt
      (E) Karl Mannheim

Ⓐ Ⓑ Ⓒ Ⓓ Ⓔ

8. Which of the following relies most heavily on sampling methods?

(A) Small group experiment
(B) Case study
(C) Participant observation
(D) Survey
(E) Laboratory experiment

Ⓐ Ⓑ Ⓒ Ⓓ Ⓔ

9. Humans can be found in many physical environments on the Earth's surface, and the basis for this adaptation is

(A) instinct   (B) heredity   (C) culture
   (D) stratification   (E) ethnocentrism

Ⓐ Ⓑ Ⓒ Ⓓ Ⓔ

10. According to Émile Durkheim, a society that lacks clear-cut norms to govern aspirations and moral conduct is characterized by

(A) rationalism   (B altruism   (C) egoism
   (D) secularism   (E) anomie

Ⓐ Ⓑ Ⓒ Ⓓ Ⓔ

11. The process by which an immigrant or an ethnic minority is absorbed socially into a receiving society is called

(A) assimilation   (B) accommodation

(C) cooperation   (D) interaction

(E) equilibrium

12. Which of the following characteristics is unique to human societies?

(A) A normative order   (B) Territorial boundaries

(C) Sustained interaction   (D) A division of labor

(E) Group autonomy

Ⓐ Ⓑ Ⓒ Ⓓ Ⓔ

13. Demographic patterns have clearly demonstrated that more males than females are born in

(A) technologically developing countries only
(B) technologically developed countries only
(C) virtually every known human society
(D) highly urbanized developing countries only
(E) countries with high nutritional standards only   Ⓐ Ⓑ Ⓒ Ⓓ Ⓔ

14. Which of the following correctly lists Max Weber's three dimensions of social stratification?

(A) Class, politics, education
(B) Prestige, politics, occupation
(C) Residence, occupation, religion
(D) Status, class, party
(E) Status, religion, prestige   Ⓐ Ⓑ Ⓒ Ⓓ Ⓔ

15. In order for an occupation to be considered a profession by a sociologist, it must be an occupation that

(A) requires knowledge of a body of specialized information with a
    theoretical foundation
(B) has high public visibility in the community
(C) requires training from a specialized school rather than from a
    university
(D) serves government and industry as well as individuals
(E) is a full-time position paying a regular salary

358

16. In the study of social class, the sociologist would be LEAST likely to focus on problems of

    (A) power (B) social mobility (C) style of life
      (D) motivation (E) occupational status

    Ⓐ Ⓑ Ⓒ Ⓓ Ⓔ

17. An example of a folkway in American society is

    (A) joining a religious cult
    (B) eating a sandwich for lunch
    (C) not paying income taxes on time
    (D) stopping for a red light
    (E) being fined for jaywalking

    Ⓐ Ⓑ Ⓒ Ⓓ Ⓔ

18. Malthus' prediction that food production could not keep pace with the growth of population is based in part on which of the following propositions?

    (A) The law of large numbers
    (B) The law of diminishing returns
    (C) Economies of scale
    (D) The fallacy of composition
    (E) Constant costs

    Ⓐ Ⓑ Ⓒ Ⓓ Ⓔ

19. Personality formation and the learning of social roles take place

    (A) only in childhood
    (B) mainly in adolescence
    (C) mainly in early adulthood
    (D) through the productive years only
    (E) throughout the life cycle

    Ⓐ Ⓑ Ⓒ Ⓓ Ⓔ

20. According to the United States Bureau of the Census, the fastest growing household type in 1980 was the

    (A) traditional nuclear family (B) extended family
      (C) single person (D) couple without children
        (E) family with three or more children

    Ⓐ Ⓑ Ⓒ Ⓓ Ⓔ

Study Resources

Visit your local college bookstore to determine which textbooks are used by the college for introductory sociology courses. You should read two or three textbooks because authors tend to emphasize different areas. When selecting a textbook, check the table of contents against the "Knowledge and Skills Required" section on pages 353-355.

As you read, take notes that address the following issues, which are fundamental to most questions that appear on the test.

- What is society? What is culture? What is common to all societies, and what is characteristic of American society?

- What are other basic concepts in sociology that help to describe human nature, human interaction, and the collective behavior of groups, organizations, institutions, and societies?

- What methods do sociologists use to study, describe, analyze, and observe human behavior?

Additional suggestions for preparing for CLEP exams are provided in Chapter 4.

Western Civilization I: Ancient Near East to 1648

Description of the Examination

The Subject Examination in Western Civilization I: Ancient Near East to 1648 tests subject matter that is usually covered in the first semester of a two-semester course in Western Civilization. Questions deal with the civilizations of the Ancient Near East, Greece, and Rome; the Middle Ages; the Renaissance and Reformation; and early modern Europe. Candidates may be asked to choose the correct definition of a historical term, select the historical figure whose political viewpoint is described, identify the correct relationship between two historical factors, or detect the inaccurate pairing of an individual with a historical event. Groups of questions may require candidates to interpret, evaluate, or relate the contents of a passage, a map, a picture, or a cartoon to other information, or to analyze and utilize the data contained in a graph or table.

The exam is 90 minutes long and contains approximately 120 multiple-choice questions to be answered in two separately timed 45-minute sections.

Knowledge and Skills Required

Questions on the exam require candidates to demonstrate one or more of the following abilities.

- Understanding of important factual knowledge of developments in Western Civilization (about 25-35 percent of the exam)

- Ability to identify the causes and effects of major historical events (about 5-15 percent of the exam)

- Ability to analyze, interpret, and evaluate textual and graphic materials (about 20-30 percent of the exam)

- Ability to distinguish the relevant from the irrelevant (about 15-25 percent of the exam)

- Ability to reach conclusions on the basis of facts (about 10-20 percent of the exam)

The subject matter of the Western Civilization I exam is drawn from the following topics.

Approximate Percent of Examination

8-11% Ancient Near East

Political evolution

Religion, culture, and technical developments in Egypt, Mesopotamia, Palestine

15-17% Ancient Greece and Hellenistic Civilization

Political evolution to Periclean Athens

Periclean Athens to Peloponnesian Wars

Culture, religion, and thought of Ancient Greece

The Hellenistic political structure

The culture, religion, and thought of Hellenistic Greece

15-17% Ancient Rome

Political evolution of the Republic and of the Empire (economic and geographical context)

Roman thought and culture

Early Christianity

The Germanic invasions

The decline of Rome

23-27% Medieval History

Early medieval politics and culture through Charlemagne

Feudal and manorial institutions

The medieval Church

Medieval thought and culture

Rise of the towns and changing economic forms

Feudal monarchies

The decline of the Church

Approximate Percent of Examination

13-17%   Renaissance and Reformation

The Renaissance in Italy

The Renaissance outside Italy

The New Monarchies

Protestantism and Catholicism reformed and reorganized

10-15%   Early Modern Europe, 1560-1648

The opening of the Atlantic

The Commercial Revolution

Dynastic and religious conflicts

Thought and culture

Sample Questions

The 25 sample questions that follow are similar to questions on the Western Civilization I exam, but they do not actually appear on the exam. CLEP exams are designed so that average students completing a course in the subject can usually answer about half the questions correctly.

Before attempting to answer the sample questions, read all the information about the Western Civilization I exam on the preceding pages. Additional suggestions for preparing for CLEP exams are provided in Chapter 4.

Try to answer correctly as many questions as possible. Then compare your answers with the correct answers, given in Appendix A.

Directions: Each of the questions or incomplete statements below is followed by five suggested answers or completions. Select the one that is best in each case.

1. The earliest urban settlements arose in which of the following types of areas?

    (A) Coastal plains   (B) Inland deforested plains
        (C) Desert oases   (D) Fertile river valleys
            (E) Narrow valleys well protected by mountains   Ⓐ Ⓑ Ⓒ Ⓓ Ⓔ

2. "The great wealth of the palaces and the widespread prosperity of the land were due to the profits of trade, protected or exploited by naval vessels equipped with rams. The palaces and towns were unfortified, and peaceful scenes predominated in the frescoes, which revealed a love of dancing, boxing, and a sport in which boys and girls somersaulted over the backs of charging bulls."

The culture described above was that of the ancient

(A) Minoans (B) Hittites (C) Macedonians
  (D) Assyrians (E) Persians   Ⓐ Ⓑ Ⓒ Ⓓ Ⓔ

3. "These people maintained their skill as seafarers, traders, and artists. They planted Carthage and other colonies in the western Mediterranean. They developed a new script in which a separate sign stood not for a syllable, but for a consonant or vowel sound."

The people described above were the

(A) Phoenicians
(B) Hittites
(C) Assyrians
(D) Mycenaeans
(E) Philistines   Ⓐ Ⓑ Ⓒ Ⓓ Ⓔ

4. Pharaoh Akhenaton of Egypt (c. 1375-1358 B.C.) is best known today for

(A) building the largest pyramid in the Valley of the Kings
(B) conquering large expanses of territory outside of the Nile Valley
(C) developing a monotheistic religion
(D) uniting upper and lower Egypt under a single administrative system
(E) writing down the first code of Egyptian law

   Ⓐ Ⓑ Ⓒ Ⓓ Ⓔ

5. Among the ancient Hebrews, a prophet was

(A) a teacher who expounded the Scriptures
(B) a king with hereditary but limited powers
(C) a judge who administered traditional law
(D) a priest with exclusive rights to perform functions at the temple
(E) an individual who was inspired by God to speak to the people

   Ⓐ Ⓑ Ⓒ Ⓓ Ⓔ

6. The outstanding achievement of King Hammurabi of Mesopotamia was that he

   (A) issued a more comprehensive law code than had any known predecessor
   (B) conquered and established dominion over all of Egypt
   (C) built the hanging gardens of Babylon
   (D) established the first democratic government
   (E) successfully defended his kingdom against the Assyrians

   Ⓐ Ⓑ Ⓒ Ⓓ Ⓔ

7. Of the following, which helps explain why the Roman Republic gave way to dictatorship during the first century B.C.?

   (A) The government that was suitable for a small city-state failed to meet the needs of an empire.
   (B) A strong leader was needed because the upper classes feared a rebellion on the part of the slave population.
   (C) Outside pressures on boundaries could not be resisted by republican armies.
   (D) Rome's period of expansion was over.
   (E) The Roman senatorial class was declining in number.

   Ⓐ Ⓑ Ⓒ Ⓓ Ⓔ

8. All of the following were emphasized by the early Christian church EXCEPT a

   (A) ritual fellowship meal in memory of Christ
   (B) toleration of other religious sects
   (C) belief in the value of the souls of women and slaves as well as those of free men
   (D) belief in life after death for all believers in Christ
   (E) belief in the value of martyrdom, defined as dying for the faith

   Ⓐ Ⓑ Ⓒ Ⓓ Ⓔ

9. All of the following invaded the Roman Empire EXCEPT the

   (A) Vikings
   (B) Ostrogoths
   (C) Visigoths
   (D) Vandals
   (E) Huns

   Ⓐ Ⓑ Ⓒ Ⓓ Ⓔ

10. The craft guilds of the Middle Ages had as their primary purpose the

    (A) promotion of trade and the protection of merchants
    (B) control of town government
    (C) regulation of production and quality
    (D) guardianship of the social and financial affairs of their members
    (E) accumulation of capital and the lending of money

    Ⓐ Ⓑ Ⓒ Ⓓ Ⓔ

11. The orders of Franciscan and Dominican friars founded in the thirteenth century differed from earlier monastic orders principally in that the friars

    (A) took vows of poverty, chastity, and obedience
    (B) broke away from the control of the pope
    (C) introduced the ideas of Plato and other early Greek philosophers into their teaching
    (D) devoted themselves mainly to copying ancient manuscripts
    (E) traveled among the people instead of living in monasteries

    Ⓐ Ⓑ Ⓒ Ⓓ Ⓔ

12. All of the following factors played a part in bringing about the Hundred Years' War EXCEPT

    (A) The English king had lands in Gascony.
    (B) A French princess was the mother of an English king.
    (C) Flemish towns were dependent on England for raw wool.
    (D) The Holy Roman Emperor wanted to bring pressure on the Swiss cantons.
    (E) The Capetian dynasty had come to an end.   Ⓐ Ⓑ Ⓒ Ⓓ Ⓔ

13. Civil peace and personal security were enjoyed to a greater degree in Norman England than in continental Europe principally because the Norman kings

    (A) maintained a large standing army
    (B) claimed the direct allegiance of the mass of the peasantry
    (C) avoided conflicts with the Church
    (D) kept their vassals occupied with continental conflicts
    (E) developed a centralized and efficient type of feudalism

    (A) (B) (C) (D) (E)

14. Which of the following could have been made immediately available to the reading public in large quantities as soon as it was written?

    (A) *On Christian Liberty,* Martin Luther
    (B) *Travels,* Marco Polo
    (C) *The Divine Comedy,* Dante Alighieri
    (D) *Canterbury Tales,* Geoffrey Chaucer
    (E) English translation of the Bible, John Wycliffe

    (A) (B) (C) (D) (E)

15. A central feature of the Catholic Reformation was the

    (A) Roman Catholic church's inability to correct abuses
    (B) establishment of new religious orders such as the Jesuits
    (C) transfer of authority from Rome to the bishoprics
    (D) rejection of Baroque art
    (E) toleration of Protestants in Roman Catholic countries

    (A) (B) (C) (D) (E)

16. A sixteenth-century traveler would have been most likely to encounter the type of architecture shown above in which of the following European countries?

    (A) Spain
    (B) France
    (C) Germany
    (D) England
    (E) Sweden   Ⓐ Ⓑ Ⓒ Ⓓ Ⓔ

17. The major and most immediate social consequence of the rise of towns in the eleventh and twelfth centuries was

    (A) a lessening of the distinction among social classes
    (B) the concept of the prosperous caring for the indigent
    (C) the decline of royal authority
    (D) a new social class enriched by manufacturing and trade
    (E) the decline in the social status of the lesser clergy

                                  Ⓐ Ⓑ Ⓒ Ⓓ Ⓔ

18. In *The Prince*, Machiavelli asserted that

   (A) historical examples are useless for understanding political behavior
   (B) the intelligent prince should keep his state neutral in the event of war
   (C) people are not trustworthy and cannot be relied on in time of need
   (D) the prince should be guided by the ethical principles of Christianity
   (E) luck is of no consequence in the success or failure of princes

   Ⓐ Ⓑ Ⓒ Ⓓ Ⓔ

19. On which of the following issues did Luther and Calvin DISAGREE?

   (A) Toleration for minority viewpoints
   (B) Relationship of the church to civil authority
   (C) The authority of the Scriptures
   (D) The existence of the Trinity
   (E) The retention of the sacrament of baptism

   Ⓐ Ⓑ Ⓒ Ⓓ Ⓔ

20. Between 1629 and 1639, Charles I of England tried to obtain revenues by all of the following means EXCEPT

   (A) the levying of ship money
   (B) income from crown lands
   (C) forced loans
   (D) the sale of monopolies
   (E) grants from Parliament

   Ⓐ Ⓑ Ⓒ Ⓓ Ⓔ

21. All of the following are associated with the commercial revolution in early modern Europe EXCEPT

   (A) an increase in the number of entrepreneurial capitalists
   (B) the appearance of state-run trading companies
   (C) a large influx of precious metals into Europe
   (D) an expansion of the guild system
   (E) a "golden age" for the Netherlands

   Ⓐ Ⓑ Ⓒ Ⓓ Ⓔ

22. Castiglione's *Book of the Courtier* (1528) was intended as

   (A) a collection of entertaining travel stories
   (B) a guide to the military affairs of the Italian peninsula
   (C) a collection of meditations and spiritual reflections
   (D) a guide to refined behavior and etiquette
   (E) an allegory of courtly love

   Ⓐ Ⓑ Ⓒ Ⓓ Ⓔ

23. Which of the following resulted from the defeat of the Spanish Armada in 1588?

(A) Spanish domination of the Mediterranean was ended.
(B) The invasion of England was prevented.
(C) Dutch sympathies for the Spanish cause increased.
(D) War broke out between England and France.
(E) There was a series of uprisings in the Spanish colonies of Central and South America.

Ⓐ Ⓑ Ⓒ Ⓓ Ⓔ

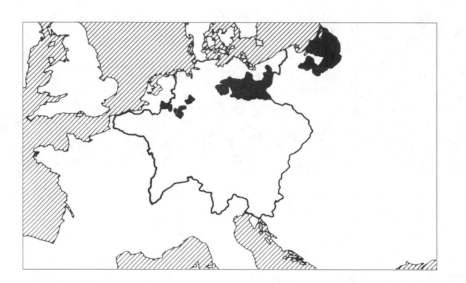

24. In the mid-seventeenth century, the area shaded black on the map above belonged to

(A) Russia
(B) Poland
(C) Sweden
(D) Austria
(E) Brandenburg-Prussia

Ⓐ Ⓑ Ⓒ Ⓓ Ⓔ

25. The theory concerning the solar system that was published by Copernicus in 1543 DENIED the popular belief that the

(A) Earth revolves around the Sun
(B) Earth revolves around the Moon
(C) Earth is the center of the universe
(D) Sun is the center of the universe
(E) stars revolve around the Sun

Ⓐ Ⓑ Ⓒ Ⓓ Ⓔ

Study Resources

To prepare for the Western Civilization I: Ancient Near East to 1648 and Western Civilization II: 1648 to the Present exams, you should study the appropriate chapters in at least one college textbook in this subject. Most textbooks cover the historical periods from the Ancient Near East to the Present and can, therefore, be used in preparing for either or both of the exams. Most Western Civilization textbooks cover approximately the same chronological span, but the material they emphasize differs. You can find these textbooks in most college bookstores. When selecting a textbook, check the table of contents against the "Knowledge and Skills Required" section on pages 361-363 and pages 373-376. Your local college bookstore is a good place to look for college level textbooks.

You will find it helpful to supplement your reading with books listed in the bibliographies found in most history textbooks. In addition, contemporary novels and plays, as well as works by Homer, Shakespeare, and Dickens, provide rich sources of information. Classic works of nonfiction are equally valuable; for example, Machiavelli's *The Prince*, Mill's *On Liberty*, and Paine's *The Rights of Man*. Books of documents are an excellent source for sampling primary materials; *A Documentary History of Modern Europe*, edited by T. G. Barnes and G. D. Feldman (Little, Brown), is one such collection. Actual works of art in museums can bring to life not only the reproductions found in books but history itself. Films such as *A Man for All Seasons* and *The Return of Martin Guerre* and television series such as "Civilisation," "I, Claudius," "Elizabeth R," and the "Ascent of Man" provide enjoyable reinforcement to what is learned through reading. The Internet is another resource you should explore.

Additional suggestions for preparing for CLEP exams appear in Chapter 4.

Western Civilization II: 1648 to the Present

Description of the Examination

The Subject Examination in Western Civilization II: 1648 to the Present covers material that is usually taught in the second semester of a two-semester course in Western Civilization. Questions cover European history from the seventeenth century through the post-Second World War period including political, economic, and cultural developments such as Scientific Thought, the Enlightenment, the French and Industrial Revolutions, Nationalism, Imperialism, the Russian Revolution, and the First and Second World Wars. Candidates may be asked to choose the correct definition of a historical term, select the historical figure whose political viewpoint is described, identify the correct relationship between two historical factors, or detect the inaccurate pairing of an individual with a historical event. Groups of questions may require candidates to interpret, evaluate, or relate the contents of a passage, a map, a picture, or a cartoon to other information or to analyze and use the data contained in a graph or table.

The exam is 90 minutes long and includes approximately 120 questions to be answered in two separately timed 45-minute sections.

Knowledge and Skills Required

Questions on the exam require candidates to demonstrate one or more of the following abilities.

- Understanding of important factual knowledge of developments in Western Civilization (about 25-35 percent of the exam)

- Ability to identify the causes and effects of major historical events (about 5-15 percent of the exam)

- Ability to analyze, interpret, and evaluate textual and graphic materials (about 20-30 percent of the exam)

- Ability to distinguish the relevant from the irrelevant (about 15-25 percent of the exam)

- Ability to reach conclusions on the basis of facts (about 10-20 percent of the exam)

The subject matter of the Western Civilization II exam is drawn from the following topics.

	Approximate Percent of Examination

7-9% Absolutism and Constitutionalism, 1648-1715

    The Dutch Republic

    The English Revolution

    The France of Louis XIV

    Formation of Austria and Prussia

    The "westernization" of Russia

4-6% Competition for empire and economic expansion

    Global economy of the eighteenth century

    Western Europe after Utrecht 1713-1740

    Economic and demographic change in the eighteenth century

5-7% The scientific view of the world

    Bacon, Descartes, and Newton

    New knowledge about the individual and society

    Political theory

7-9% Enlightenment and enlightened despotism

    The Philosophes

    Enlightened despotism

    Partitions of Poland

    The British Reform Movement

10-12% The French Revolution and Napoleonic Europe

    The Revolution of 1789

    The Revolution and Europe

    The Terror

    The Constitutional Republic

    The Consulate

    The French Empire

    The continental system

    The overthrow of Napoleon

7-9% The Industrial Revolution

    Causes of the Industrial Revolution

    Impact of industrialization on the working and middle classes

    The advent of the "isms"

6-8% Political developments, 1815-1848

    Conservative politics

    Liberalism

    Nationalism

    The Revolutions of 1830 and 1848

8-10% Politics and diplomacy in the Age of Nationalism, 1850-1914

    The Second French Empire, 1852-1870

    The unification of Italy

    The founding of the German Empire

    Austria-Hungary

    Russia

    The Third French Republic

    Socialism and labor unions

    Waning of classical liberalism

    European diplomacy, 1871-1900

➤ *Approximate Percent of Examination*

7-9%   Economy, culture, and imperialism, 1850-1914

     Demography

     World economy of the nineteenth century

     Technological developments

     Science, philosophy, and the arts

     Imperialism in Africa and Asia

     The Russo-Japanese War

     The Balkan Wars

10-12%   The First World War, the Russian Revolution, and postwar Europe, 1914-1924

     The causes of the First World War

     The economic and social impact of the war

     The Peace of Paris, 1919

     The Revolution of 1917

     The impact of the Russian Revolution on Europe

7-9%   Europe between the wars

     Stalin's five-year plans and purges

     International politics, 1919-1939

     The Great Depression

     Italy and Germany between the wars

8-10%   The Second World War and contemporary Europe

     The causes and course of the Second World War

     Postwar Europe

     Science, philosophy, the arts, and religion

     Contemporary social developments

Sample Questions

The 25 sample questions that follow are similar to questions on the Western Civilization II exam, but they do not actually appear on the exam. CLEP exams are designed so that average students completing a course in the subject can usually answer about half the questions correctly.

Before attempting to answer the sample questions, read all the information about the Western Civilization II exam on the preceding pages. Additional suggestions for preparing for CLEP exams are provided in Chapter 4.

Try to answer correctly as many questions as possible. Then compare your answers with the correct answers, given in Appendix A.

Directions: Each of the questions or incomplete statements below is followed by five suggested answers or completions. Select the one that is best in each case.

1. Colbert's economic policies ran into difficulties chiefly because of the

   (A) relative poverty of France
   (B) loss of France's colonial empire
   (C) wars of Louis XIV
   (D) abandonment of the salt tax
   (E) reckless spending by the nobility   Ⓐ Ⓑ Ⓒ Ⓓ Ⓔ

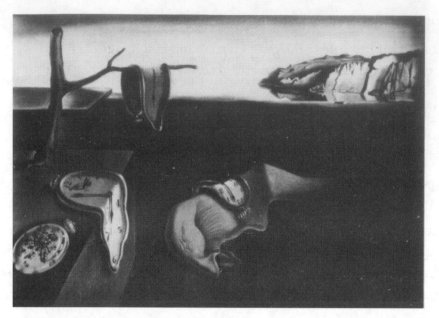

Collection, The Museum of Modern Art, New York.

2. Which of the following is a major theme depicted in the painting above?

   (A) A scientific view of the world
   (B) Enlightened rationalism
   (C) Romantic concern with nature
   (D) Realistic appraisal of industrial progress
   (E) The world of the unconscious mind   Ⓐ Ⓑ Ⓒ Ⓓ Ⓔ

3. Which of the following occurred as a result of the War of the Austrian Succession (1740-1748) and the Seven Years' War (1756-1763)?

   (A) Prussia emerged as an important economic and military power.
   (B) Sweden ceased to be a great power.
   (C) Russia extended its territory to the shores of the Baltic Sea.
   (D) Hapsburg claims to Polish territory were dropped.
   (E) France acquired the provinces of Alsace and Lorraine.

                                            Ⓐ Ⓑ Ⓒ Ⓓ Ⓔ

4. Which of the following statements best describes Romanticism?

   (A) A belief that the rules of art are eternal and unchanging
   (B) Interest in expressing general and universal truths rather than
       particular and concrete ones
   (C) Emphasis on logical reasoning and exact factual knowledge
   (D) Emphasis on a high degree of emotional subjectivity
   (E) A value system that rejects idealism

   Ⓐ Ⓑ Ⓒ Ⓓ Ⓔ

5. All of the following were related to the Eastern Question EXCEPT

   (A) Pan-Slavism
   (B) the Congress of Berlin of 1878
   (C) the Crimean War
   (D) the Kruger Telegram
   (E) the Treaty of San Stefano

   Ⓐ Ⓑ Ⓒ Ⓓ Ⓔ

6. The cartoon above refers to the

   (A) Napoleonic Wars
   (B) Crimean War
   (C) Boer War
   (D) Russo-Japanese War
   (E) First World War

   Ⓐ Ⓑ Ⓒ Ⓓ Ⓔ

7. All of the following were instrumental in the emergence of Italy as a modern nation-state EXCEPT

(A) Mazzini
(B) Napoleon III
(C) Cavour
(D) Francis II
(E) Garibaldi   Ⓐ Ⓑ Ⓒ Ⓓ Ⓔ

8. "Men being by nature all free, equal, and independent, no one can be put out of this estate and subjected to the political power of another without his own consent, which is done by agreeing with other men, to join and unite into a community for their comfortable, safe, and peaceable living in a secure enjoyment of their properties."

The quotation above is from a work by

(A) John Locke
(B) Karl Marx
(C) Edmund Burke
(D) Voltaire
(E) Adam Smith   Ⓐ Ⓑ Ⓒ Ⓓ Ⓔ

9. Which of the following characterizes the size of the population of Europe during the eighteenth century?

(A) It increased rapidly.
(B) It stayed about the same.
(C) It declined.
(D) It dropped drastically in Western Europe, but rose in Eastern Europe.
(E) It dropped drastically in Eastern Europe, but rose in Western Europe.

Ⓐ Ⓑ Ⓒ Ⓓ Ⓔ

10. The term "collective security" would most likely be discussed in which of the following studies?

(A) A book on the twentieth-century welfare state
(B) A monograph on Soviet agricultural policy during the 1920's
(C) A book on Bismarckian imperialism
(D) A treatise on Social Darwinism
(E) A work on European diplomacy during the 1930's

Ⓐ Ⓑ Ⓒ Ⓓ Ⓔ

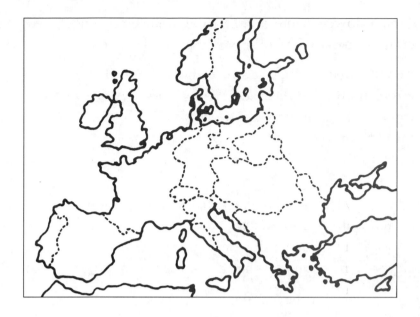

11. The map above shows national boundaries in which of the following years?

    (A) 1789
    (B) 1812
    (C) 1815
    (D) 1870
    (E) 1914

12. The British economist John Maynard Keynes did which of the following?

    (A) He urged governments to increase mass purchasing power in times of deflation.
    (B) He defended the principles of the Versailles Treaty.
    (C) He helped to establish the British Labour party.
    (D) He prophesied the inevitable economic decline of capitalism.
    (E) He originated the concept of marginal utility to replace the labor theory of value.

    Ⓐ Ⓑ Ⓒ Ⓓ Ⓔ

13. The vast increase in German military expenditures in the two decades preceding the First World War occurred primarily because Germany

   (A) had extended its imperialistic activities to the Far East
   (B) was planning to militarize the provinces of Alsace and Lorraine
   (C) was extending military aid to Russia
   (D) feared an attack from France
   (E) was rapidly expanding its navy   Ⓐ Ⓑ Ⓒ Ⓓ Ⓔ

14. In comparison to a preindustrial economy, the most distinctive feature of a modern economy is its

   (A) greater capacity to sustain growth over time
   (B) increased democratization of the workplace
   (C) lower wages for the literate middle class
   (D) lack of economic cycles
   (E) elimination of hunger and poverty   Ⓐ Ⓑ Ⓒ Ⓓ Ⓔ

15. The chief professed aim of Marxist socialists in the latter half of the nineteenth century was to

   (A) establish constitutional government
   (B) ensure equal rights for women
   (C) end government regulation of business
   (D) institute trial by jury in all criminal cases
   (E) abolish private ownership of the means of production

                                                      Ⓐ Ⓑ Ⓒ Ⓓ Ⓔ

16. "Each individual, bestowing more time and attention upon the means of preserving and increasing his portion of wealth than is or can be bestowed by government, is likely to take a more effectual course than what, in this instance and on his behalf, would be taken by government."

   The quotation above best illustrates which of the following?

   (A) Fascism
   (B) Mercantilism
   (C) Syndicalism
   (D) Classical liberalism
   (E) Utopian socialism   Ⓐ Ⓑ Ⓒ Ⓓ Ⓔ

17. The aim of the Soviet Union's First Five-Year Plan was to

(A) acquire foreign capital

(B) produce an abundance of consumer goods

(C) encourage agricultural production by subsidizing the kulaks

(D) build up heavy industry

(E) put industrial policy in the hands of the proletariat

Ⓐ Ⓑ Ⓒ Ⓓ Ⓔ

POPULATION DENSITY IN FRANCE PER SQUARE KILOMETER

1801   1846

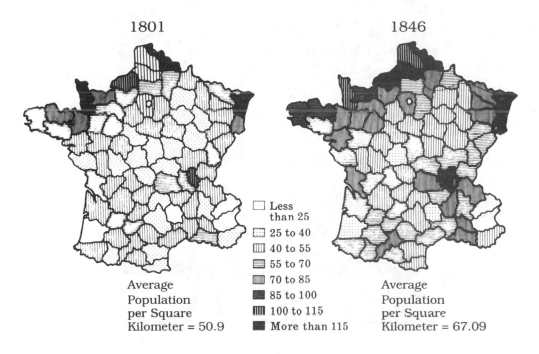

☐ Less than 25

▦ 25 to 40

▥ 40 to 55

▤ 55 to 70

▨ 70 to 85

◼ 85 to 100

▥ 100 to 115

◼ More than 115

Average Population per Square Kilometer = 50.9

Average Population per Square Kilometer = 67.09

18. The increase in population density between 1801 and 1846 shown above indicates that

(A) the growth of Paris absorbed any natural population increase

(B) there was a reversing trend in which industry moved to the center of France while agriculture moved to the north

(C) the population distribution in existence in 1801 was almost unchanged in 1846

(D) by 1846 southern France was declining in population

(E) by 1846 central France was declining in population

Ⓐ Ⓑ Ⓒ Ⓓ Ⓔ

19. The National Assembly in France (1789-1791) did all of the following EXCEPT

(A) issue assignats
(B) ban strikes
(C) pass the Civil Constitution of the Clergy
(D) abolish guilds
(E) abolish private property   Ⓐ Ⓑ Ⓒ Ⓓ Ⓔ

20. The cartoon above, published in 1955, suggested that

(A) the Soviet Union intended to seize and control the bone of contention
(B) France and Germany should cooperate with each other to meet the Soviet threat
(C) France and Germany were industrially and economically weak
(D) communism dominated Western Europe
(E) France, Germany, and the communist nations should seek to form a tripartite pact in Europe

     Ⓐ Ⓑ Ⓒ Ⓓ Ⓔ

21. Historical explanations for nineteenth-century European imperialism include all of the following EXCEPT a

    (A) need to discover new sources of raw materials
    (B) need to find new markets for manufactured goods
    (C) desire to establish world government
    (D) need to invest excess financial resources
    (E) desire to maintain the European balance of power

    Ⓐ Ⓑ Ⓒ Ⓓ Ⓔ

22. All of the following factors contributed to the rise of the National Socialist German Workers' party (Nazis) EXCEPT

    (A) the weakness of the Weimar Republic
    (B) dissatisfaction with the Versailles Treaty
    (C) the impact of the Great Depression
    (D) the support of German conservatives
    (E) the support of Socialist trade unions

    Ⓐ Ⓑ Ⓒ Ⓓ Ⓔ

23. "He used extreme methods and mass repressions at a time when the Revolution was already victorious, when the Soviet state was strengthened, when the exploiting classes were already liquidated and Socialist relations were rooted solidly in all phases of the national economy, when our party was politically consolidated and had strengthened itself both numerically and ideologically."

    In the quotation above, which of the following spoke and about whom?

    (A) Khrushchev about Stalin
    (B) Khrushchev about Trotsky
    (C) Stalin about Trotsky
    (D) Trotsky about Lenin
    (E) Brezhnev about Lenin

    Ⓐ Ⓑ Ⓒ Ⓓ Ⓔ

24. Albert Einstein's theory of relativity proposed

    (A) a new structure for the atom
    (B) a new conception of space and time
    (C) the fundamental concepts for developing the computer
    (D) the origin of the universe from the explosion of a single mass
    (E) the particulate nature of light

    Ⓐ Ⓑ Ⓒ Ⓓ Ⓔ

25. Which of the following is a central and essential component of the European welfare state?

(A) Nationalization of all major sectors of the economy
(B) Decentralization of the state
(C) State responsibility for assuring access to medical care for all citizens
(D) Elimination of large private fortunes through taxation
(E) Elimination of independent trade unions

Study Resources

The study resources for Western Civilization II: 1648 to the Present are the same as for Western Civilization I: Ancient Near East to 1648.

Calculus with Elementary Functions

Description of the Examination

The Calculus with Elementary Functions exam covers skills and concepts that are usually taught in a one-year college course in calculus with elementary functions. The major emphasis of the exam is divided equally between topics from differential and integral calculus. Properties of algebraic, trigonometric, exponential, and logarithmic functions as well as limits are also measured. The exam is primarily concerned with an intuitive understanding of calculus and experience with its methods and applications. Knowledge of preparatory mathematics, including algebra, plane and solid geometry, trigonometry, and analytic geometry, is assumed. Students are permitted, but not required, to use a scientific calculator (non-graphing, non-programmable) during the exam.

   The exam includes approximately 45 multiple-choice questions to be answered in two separately timed 45-minute sections.

Knowledge and Skills Required

The subject matter of the Calculus with Elementary Functions exam is drawn from the following topics.

Approximate Percent of Examination

10%   Elementary Functions (algebraic, trigonometric, exponential, and logarithmic)

- Properties of functions

   Definition, domain, and range

   Sum, product, quotient, and composition

   Absolute value, e.g., $|f(x)|$ and $f(|x|)$

   Inverse

   Odd and even

   Periodicity

   Graphs; symmetry and asymptotes

   Zeros of a function

- Limits

  Statement of properties, e.g., limit of a constant, sum, product, and quotient

  The number e such that $\lim\limits_{n\to\infty}\left(1+\dfrac{1}{n}\right)^n = e$ and $\lim\limits_{x\to 0}\dfrac{e^x - 1}{x} = 1$

  Limits that involve infinity, e.g., $\lim\limits_{x\to 0}\dfrac{1}{x^2}$ is nonexistent and $\lim\limits_{x\to\infty}\dfrac{\sin\ x}{x} = 0$

  Continuity

45%   Differential Calculus

- The derivative

  Definitions of the derivative; e.g.,

  $$f'(a) = \lim_{x\to a}\frac{f(x)-f(a)}{x-a}\ \text{and}$$
  $$f'(x) = \lim_{h\to 0}\frac{f(x+h)-f(x)}{h}$$

  Derivatives of elementary functions

  Derivatives of sum, product, quotient (including tan x and cot x)

  Derivative of a composite function (chain rule); e.g., sin (ax + b), ae^{kx}, ln (kx)

  Derivative of an implicitly defined function

  Derivative of the inverse of a function (including Arcsin x and Arctan x)

  Logarithmic differentiation

  Derivatives of higher order

  Statement (without proof) of the Mean Value Theorem; applications and graphical illustrations

  Relation between differentiability and continuity

  Use of L'Hôpital's rule (quotient and indeterminate forms)

- Applications of the derivative

    Slope of a curve; tangent and normal lines to a curve

    Curve sketching: increasing and decreasing functions; relative and absolute maximum and minimum points; concavity; points of inflection

    Extreme value problems

    Velocity and acceleration of a particle moving along a line

    Average and instantaneous rates of change

    Related rates of change

    Newton's method

45% Integral Calculus

- Antiderivatives
- Applications of antiderivatives

    Distance and velocity from acceleration with initial conditions

    Solutions of $y' = ky$ and applications to growth and decay

    Solutions of $f(y)\, dy = g(x)\, dx$ (variables separable)

- Techniques of integration

    Basic integration formulas

    Integration by substitution (use of identities, change of variable)

    Simple integration by parts, such as

    $\int x\, \cos x\ dx$ and $\int \ln x\ dx$

- The definite integral

    Concept of the definite integral as an area

    Approximations to the definite integral using rectangles or trapezoids

    Definition of the definite integral as the limit of a sum

    Properties of the definite integral

    The fundamental theorem —

$$\left(\frac{d}{dx}\int_a^x f(t)\, dt = f(x) \ \text{ and } \ \int_a^b f(x)\, dx = F(b) - F(a), \right.$$
$$\left. \text{where} \ F'(x) = f(x) \right)$$

- Applications of the integral

    Average value of a function on an interval

    Area between curves

    Volume of a solid of revolution

    (disc, washer, and shell methods) about the x- and
    y-axes or lines parallel to the axes

Sample Questions

The following 25 questions are provided to give an indication of the types of questions that appear on the Calculus with Elementary Functions exam. CLEP exams are designed so that average students completing a course in the subject can usually answer about half the questions correctly.

Before attempting to answer the sample questions, read all the information about the Calculus with Elementary Functions exam on the preceding pages. Additional suggestions for preparing for CLEP exams are provided in Chapter 4.

Try to answer correctly as many questions as possible. Then compare your answers with the correct answers, given in Appendix A.

Directions: Solve the following problems. Do not spend too much time on any one problem.

Notes: (1) In this exam, ln x denotes the natural logarithm of x (that is, logarithm to the base e).

(2) Unless otherwise specified, the domain of a function f is assumed to be the set of all real numbers x for which f(x) is a real number.

Be sure to examine the form of the answer choices for each multiple-choice question before you make use of a calculator because, in some cases, the form of the answer may not be readily obtainable on a calculator. For example, the answer choices may involve radicals or numbers such as π and e.

1. If the graph of $y = 2^{-x} - 1$ is reflected in the x-axis, then an equation of the reflection is y =

    (A) $2^x - 1$
    (B) $1 - 2^x$
    (C) $1 - 2^{-x}$
    (D) $\log_2 (x + 1)$
    (E) $\log_2 (1 - x)$

    Ⓐ Ⓑ Ⓒ Ⓓ Ⓔ

2. What is $\lim\limits_{h \to 0} \dfrac{\cos (\frac{\pi}{2} + h) - \cos \frac{\pi}{2}}{h}$?

    (A) $-\infty$
    (B) -1
    (C) 0
    (D) 1
    (E) $+\infty$

    Ⓐ Ⓑ Ⓒ Ⓓ Ⓔ

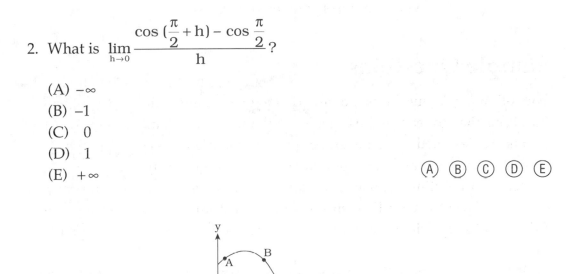

3. At which of the five points on the graph in the figure above are $\dfrac{dy}{dx}$ and $\dfrac{d^2y}{dx^2}$ both negative?

    (A) A
    (B) B
    (C) C
    (D) D
    (E) E

    Ⓐ Ⓑ Ⓒ Ⓓ Ⓔ

4. If $y = x + \sin(xy)$, then $\dfrac{dy}{dx} =$

(A) $1 + \cos(xy)$

(B) $1 + y\cos(xy)$

(C) $\dfrac{1}{1 - \cos(xy)}$

(D) $\dfrac{1}{1 - x\cos(xy)}$

(E) $\dfrac{1 + y\cos(xy)}{1 - x\cos(xy)}$

Ⓐ Ⓑ Ⓒ Ⓓ Ⓔ

5. Which of the following statements about the curve $y = x^4 - 2x^3$ is true?

(A) The curve has no relative extremum.
(B) The curve has one point of inflection and two relative extrema.
(C) The curve has two points of inflection and one relative extremum.
(D) The curve has two points of inflection and two relative extrema.
(E) The curve has two points of inflection and three relative extrema.

Ⓐ Ⓑ Ⓒ Ⓓ Ⓔ

6. If h is the inverse function of f and if $f(x) = \dfrac{1}{x}$, then $h(x) =$

(A) $\ln x$

(B) $-\dfrac{1}{x^2}$

(C) $-\dfrac{1}{x}$

(D) x

(E) $\dfrac{1}{x}$

Ⓐ Ⓑ Ⓒ Ⓓ Ⓔ

7. A smooth curve has the property that for all x the value of its slope at 2x is twice the value of its slope at x. The slope at 0 is

(A) not defined
(B) negative
(C) zero
(D) positive
(E) not determinable from the information given

Ⓐ Ⓑ Ⓒ Ⓓ Ⓔ

8. Let $f(x) = \dfrac{1}{k}\cos(kx)$. For what value of k does f have period 3 ?

(A) $\dfrac{2}{3}$

(B) $\dfrac{2\pi}{3}$

(C) $\dfrac{3\pi}{2}$

(D) 6

(E) 6π

Ⓐ Ⓑ Ⓒ Ⓓ Ⓔ

9. $\displaystyle\int (x-1)\sqrt{x}\,dx =$

(A) $\dfrac{3}{2}\sqrt{x} - \dfrac{1}{\sqrt{x}} + C$

(B) $\dfrac{2}{3}x^{\frac{3}{2}} + \dfrac{1}{2}x^{\frac{1}{2}} + C$

(C) $\dfrac{1}{2}x^2 - x + C$

(D) $\dfrac{2}{5}x^{\frac{5}{2}} - \dfrac{2}{3}x^{\frac{3}{2}} + C$

(E) $\dfrac{1}{2}x^2 + 2x^{\frac{3}{2}} - x + C$

Ⓐ Ⓑ Ⓒ Ⓓ Ⓔ

10. What is $\lim\limits_{x \to \infty} \dfrac{x^2 - 4}{2 + x - 4x^2}$?

    (A) -2

    (B) $-\dfrac{1}{4}$

    (C) $\dfrac{1}{2}$

    (D) 1

    (E) The limit does not exist.   Ⓐ Ⓑ Ⓒ Ⓓ Ⓔ

11. The area of the region in the first quadrant between the graph of $y = x\sqrt{4 - x^2}$ and the x-axis is

    (A) $\dfrac{2}{3}\sqrt{2}$

    (B) $\dfrac{8}{3}$

    (C) $2\sqrt{2}$

    (D) $2\sqrt{3}$

    (E) $\dfrac{16}{3}$ Ⓐ Ⓑ Ⓒ Ⓓ Ⓔ

12. For which of the following functions does the property $\dfrac{d^3y}{dx^3} = \dfrac{dy}{dx}$ hold?

    I. $y = e^x$
    II. $y = e^{-x}$
    III. $y = \sin x$

    (A) I only
    (B) II only
    (C) III only
    (D) I and II
    (E) II and III   Ⓐ Ⓑ Ⓒ Ⓓ Ⓔ

13. Let $a < c < b$ and let f be differentiable on $[a, b]$. Which of the following is NOT necessarily true?

(A) $\int_a^b f(x)dx = \int_a^c f(x)dx + \int_c^b f(x)dx$

(B) There exists d in $[a, b]$ such that $f'(d) = \dfrac{f(b)-f(a)}{b-a}$.

(C) $\int_a^b f(x)dx \geq 0$

(D) $\lim\limits_{x \to c} f(x) = f(c)$

(E) If k is a real number, then $\int_a^b kf(x)dx = k\int_a^b f(x)dx$.

Ⓐ Ⓑ Ⓒ Ⓓ Ⓔ

14. The function $f(x) = \ln(\sin x)$ is defined for all x in which of the following intervals?

(A) $0 < x < \pi$

(B) $0 \leq x \leq \pi$

(C) $\dfrac{3\pi}{2} < x < \dfrac{5\pi}{2}$

(D) $\dfrac{3\pi}{2} \leq x \leq \dfrac{5\pi}{2}$

(E) $\dfrac{3\pi}{2} < x < 2\pi$

Ⓐ Ⓑ Ⓒ Ⓓ Ⓔ

15. $\int_{-3}^{3} |x+2| dx =$

(A) 0

(B) 9

(C) 12

(D) 13

(E) 14

Ⓐ Ⓑ Ⓒ Ⓓ Ⓔ

16. The volume generated by revolving about the x-axis the region enclosed by the graphs of $y = 2x$ and $y = 2x^2$, for $0 \leq x \leq 1$, is

(A) $\pi \int_0^1 (2x - 2x^2)^2 \, dx$

(B) $\pi \int_0^1 (4x^2 - 4x^4) \, dx$

(C) $2\pi \int_0^1 x(2x - 2x^2) \, dx$

(D) $\pi \int_0^2 \left(\sqrt{\dfrac{y}{2}} - \dfrac{y}{2} \right)^2 \, dy$

(E) $\pi \int_0^2 \left(\dfrac{y}{2} - \dfrac{y^2}{2} \right) \, dy$

Ⓐ Ⓑ Ⓒ Ⓓ Ⓔ

17. Let f be defined as follows, where $a \neq 0$.

$$f(x) = \begin{cases} \dfrac{x^2 - a^2}{x - a}, & \text{for } x \neq a, \\ 0, & \text{for } x = a. \end{cases}$$

Which of the following are true about f ?

   I. $\lim\limits_{x \to a} f(x)$ exists.
  II. $f(a)$ exists.
  III. $f(x)$ is continuous at $x = a$.

(A) None
(B) I only
(C) II only
(D) I and II only
(E) I, II, and III

Ⓐ Ⓑ Ⓒ Ⓓ Ⓔ

18. Which of the following definite integrals is NOT equal to 0?

(A) $\displaystyle\int_{-\pi}^{\pi} \sin^3 x \, dx$

(B) $\displaystyle\int_{-\pi}^{\pi} x^2 \sin x \, dx$

(C) $\displaystyle\int_{0}^{\pi} \cos x \, dx$

(D) $\displaystyle\int_{-\pi}^{\pi} \cos^3 x \, dx$

(E) $\displaystyle\int_{-\pi}^{\pi} \cos^2 x \, dx$

Ⓐ Ⓑ Ⓒ Ⓓ Ⓔ

19. The acceleration at time t of a particle moving on the x-axis is $4\pi \cos t$. If the velocity is 0 at t = 0, what is the average velocity of the particle over the interval $0 \leq t \leq \pi$?

(A) 0

(B) $\dfrac{4}{\pi}$

(C) 4

(D) 8

(E) 8π

Ⓐ Ⓑ Ⓒ Ⓓ Ⓔ

20. $\displaystyle\int_{0}^{1} x e^{-x} dx =$

(A) $\dfrac{e-2}{e}$

(B) $\dfrac{2-e}{e}$

(C) $\dfrac{e+2}{e}$

(D) $\dfrac{e}{e-2}$

(E) $\dfrac{e}{2-e}$

Ⓐ Ⓑ Ⓒ Ⓓ Ⓔ

21. Let $f(x) = x^3 + x$. If h is the inverse function of f, then $h'(2) =$

(A) $\dfrac{1}{13}$

(B) $\dfrac{1}{4}$

(C) 1

(D) 4

(E) 13

Ⓐ Ⓑ Ⓒ Ⓓ Ⓔ

22. $\displaystyle\int \cos^2 x \sin x \, dx =$

(A) $-\dfrac{\cos^3 x}{3} + C$

(B) $-\dfrac{\cos^3 x \, \sin^2 x}{6} + C$

(C) $\dfrac{\sin^2 x}{2} + C$

(D) $\dfrac{\cos^3 x}{3} + C$

(E) $\dfrac{\cos^3 x \, \sin^2 x}{6} + C$

Ⓐ Ⓑ Ⓒ Ⓓ Ⓔ

23. If r is positive and increasing, for what value of r is the rate of increase of r^3 twelve times that of r ?

(A) $\sqrt[3]{4}$
(B) 2
(C) $\sqrt[3]{12}$
(D) $2\sqrt{3}$
(E) 6

Ⓐ Ⓑ Ⓒ Ⓓ Ⓔ

24. If f is continuous for all x, which of the following integrals necessarily have the same value?

I. $\displaystyle\int_a^b f(x)dx$

II. $\displaystyle\int_a^{b-a} f(x+a)dx$

III. $\displaystyle\int_{a+c}^{b+c} f(x+c)dx$

(A) I and II only
(B) I and III only
(C) II and III only
(D) I, II, and III
(E) No two necessarily have the same value.

Ⓐ Ⓑ Ⓒ Ⓓ Ⓔ

25. The normal to the curve represented by the equation $y = x^2 + 6x + 4$ at the point $(-2, -4)$ also intersects the curve at $x =$

(A) -6

(B) $-\dfrac{9}{2}$

(C) $-\dfrac{7}{2}$

(D) -3

(E) $-\dfrac{1}{2}$

Ⓐ Ⓑ Ⓒ Ⓓ Ⓔ

Study Resources

To prepare for the Calculus exam, a candidate is advised to study one or more introductory college level calculus textbooks, which can be found in most college bookstores. When selecting a textbook, check the table of contents against the "Knowledge and Skills Required" section on pages 387-390. In addition, the Barron's book provides helpful test preparation suggestions, and the Schaum Outline provides a condensed version of the important topics usually covered in a college calculus course. Both of these books contain many sample problems; many of those in the Barron's book are taken from old forms of Advanced Placement and CLEP exams.

College Algebra

Description of the Examination

The Subject Examination in College Algebra covers the material that is usually taught in a one-semester college course in algebra. About half the exam is made up of routine problems requiring basic algebraic skills; the remainder involves solving nonroutine problems in which candidates must demonstrate their understanding of concepts. The exam includes questions on basic algebraic operations; linear and quadratic equations, inequalities, and graphs; algebraic, exponential, and logarithmic functions; and miscellaneous other topics. It is assumed that the candidate is familiar with currently taught algebraic vocabulary, symbols, and notation. The exam places little emphasis on arithmetic calculations, and it does not contain any questions that require the use of a calculator. However, the use of a scientific calculator (non-graphing, non-programmable) is permitted during the exam.

The exam consists of approximately 70 multiple-choice questions to be answered in two separately timed 45-minute sections.

Knowledge and Skills Required

The subject matter covered by the College Algebra exam is distributed approximately as follows.

    ➡   *Approximate Percent of Examination*

25%   Algebraic operations
        Combining algebraic expressions
        Factoring
        Simplifying algebraic fractions
        Operating with powers and roots

20%   Equations, inequalities, and their graphs
        Linear equations and inequalities
        Quadratic equations and inequalities
        Systems of equations and inequalities

Approximate Percent of Examination

25% Algebraic, exponential, and logarithmic functions and their
       graphs
           Domain
           Range
           Composition
           Inverse of functions

30% Miscellaneous topics
           Theory of equations
           Sets
           Real numbers
           Complex numbers
           Sequences and series

Within the subject matter described above, questions on the exam require candidates to demonstrate the abilities given below in the approximate proportions indicated.

- Solving routine, straightforward problems (about 50 percent of the exam)

- Solving nonroutine problems requiring an understanding of concepts and the application of skills and concepts (about 50 percent of the exam)

Sample Questions

The 28 questions that follow are similar to questions on the College Algebra exam, but they do not appear on the actual exam. CLEP exams are designed so that average students completing a course in the subject can usually answer about half the questions correctly.

Before attempting to answer the sample questions, read all the information about the College Algebra exam on the preceding pages. Additional suggestions for preparing for CLEP exams are provided in Chapter 4.

Try to answer correctly as many questions as possible. Then compare your answers with the correct answers, given in Appendix A.

Directions: Solve the following problems. Do not spend too much time on any one problem.

Notes: (1) Unless otherwise specified, the domain of any function f is assumed to be the set of all real numbers x for which f(x) is a real number.

(2) i will be used to denote $\sqrt{-1}$.

(3) Figures that accompany the following problems are intended to provide information useful in solving the problems. They are drawn as accurately as possible EXCEPT when it is stated in a specific problem that its figure is not drawn to scale. All figures lie in a plane unless otherwise indicated.

1. If R = {1,2}, S = {2,3,4}, and T = {2,4}, then (R∪S)∩T is

(A) {2}
(B) {4}
(C) {2,4}
(D) {1,2,3,4}
(E) The empty set

Ⓐ Ⓑ Ⓒ Ⓓ Ⓔ

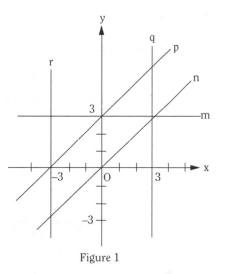

Figure 1

2. Which of the lines in Figure 1 is the graph of x = 3 ?

(A) m
(B) n
(C) p
(D) q
(E) r

Ⓐ Ⓑ Ⓒ Ⓓ Ⓔ

3. If $f(x) = 2x - 1$, then $f(3x) =$

   (A) $3x - 1$
   (B) $6x - 1$
   (C) $6x - 3$
   (D) $6x^2 - 1$
   (E) $6x^2 - 3x$ (A) (B) (C) (D) (E)

4. If $x + 2 = y$, what is the value of $|x - y| + |y - x|$?

   (A) -4
   (B) 0
   (C) 2
   (D) 4
   (E) It cannot be determined from the information given.

     (A) (B) (C) (D) (E)

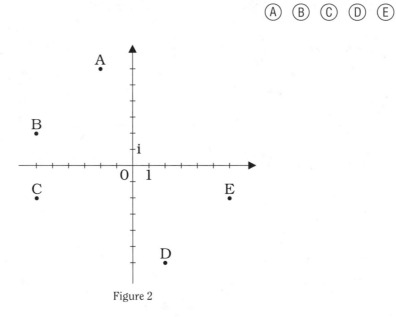

Figure 2

5. Which point in Figure 2 represents the complex number $6 - 2i$?

   (A) A   (B) B   (C) C   (D) D   (E) E   (A) (B) (C) (D) (E)

6. Where defined, $(x^a)^a =$

   (A) $x^{\frac{a}{2}}$
   (B) x^{a^2}
   (C) x^{a+2}
   (D) x^{2a}
   (E) $2x^a$ (A) (B) (C) (D) (E)

7. Which of the shaded regions below represents the graph of $\{(x,y) \mid x \geqq 2 \text{ and } y \leqq 0\}$?

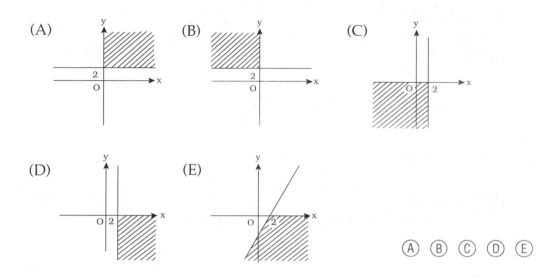

(A)   (B)   (C)   (D)   (E)

Ⓐ Ⓑ Ⓒ Ⓓ Ⓔ

8. Where defined, $\dfrac{x^3-1}{x-1} =$

(A) $x + 1$
(B) $x^2 + 1$
(C) $x^2 - x + 1$
(D) $x^2 - x - 1$
(E) $x^2 + x + 1$

Ⓐ Ⓑ Ⓒ Ⓓ Ⓔ

9. $\displaystyle\sum_{k=-1}^{3} k^2 =$

(A) 5   (B) 10   (C) 13   (D) 14   (E) 15

Ⓐ Ⓑ Ⓒ Ⓓ Ⓔ

10. Where defined, $\dfrac{x-\dfrac{4y^2}{9x}}{\dfrac{3x}{2}+y}=$

 (A) $\dfrac{9x(3x-2y)}{2y(3x+2y)}$

 (B) $\dfrac{2(3x+2y)^2}{9(3x-2y)}$

 (C) $\dfrac{3x+2y}{9}$

 (D) $\dfrac{2(3x-2y)}{9x}$

 (E) $\dfrac{(3x-2y)(3x+2y)^2}{18x}$

Ⓐ Ⓑ Ⓒ Ⓓ Ⓔ

11. For what real numbers x is $y=2^{-x}$ a negative number?

 (A) All real x
 (B) x > 0 only
 (C) x ≧ 0 only
 (D) x < 0 only
 (E) No real x

Ⓐ Ⓑ Ⓒ Ⓓ Ⓔ

12. If $\log_x 16 = 8$, then x =

 (A) $\dfrac{1}{2}$

 (B) $\dfrac{1}{\sqrt{2}}$

 (C) $\sqrt{2}$

 (D) 2

 (E) $2\sqrt{2}$

Ⓐ Ⓑ Ⓒ Ⓓ Ⓔ

13. The set of all real numbers that satisfy the inequality $|x-2| \leqq 5$ is

 (A) {x: −5 ≦ x ≦5}
 (B) {x: −3 ≦ x ≦ 7}
 (C) {x: −7 ≦ x ≦ 3}
 (D) {x: x < −5}
 (E) {x: x < −7 or x > 3}

Ⓐ Ⓑ Ⓒ Ⓓ Ⓔ

14. If $f(x) = 2x + 1$ and $g(x) = 3x - 1$, then $f(g(x)) =$

(A) $6x - 1$
(B) $6x + 2$
(C) $x - 2$
(D) $5x$
(E) $6x^2 + x - 1$

Ⓐ Ⓑ Ⓒ Ⓓ Ⓔ

15. If the remainder is 7 when $x^3 + kx^2 - 3x - 15$ is divided by $x - 2$, then $k =$

(A) 5
(B) 6
(C) 7
(D) 9
(E) 11

Ⓐ Ⓑ Ⓒ Ⓓ Ⓔ

16. The set of all values of b for which the equation $4x^2 + bx + 1 = 0$ has one or two real roots is defined by

(A) $b > 4$
(B) $b < 4$
(C) $b \geq 4$ or $b \leq -4$
(D) $b > 4$ or $b < -4$
(E) $b \geq 1$ or $b \leq -1$

Ⓐ Ⓑ Ⓒ Ⓓ Ⓔ

17. Given the two complex numbers $Z = p + qi$ and $\overline{Z} = p - qi$, where p and q are real numbers different from zero, which of the following statements involving Z and $\overline{Z}$ must be true?

(A) $Z = -\overline{Z}$
(B) $(\overline{Z})^2$ is a real number.
(C) $Z \cdot \overline{Z}$ is a real number.
(D) $(\overline{Z})^2 = Z^2$
(E) $Z^2 = -(\overline{Z})^2$

Ⓐ Ⓑ Ⓒ Ⓓ Ⓔ

18. $\dfrac{(n+1)!}{n!} - n =$

   (A) 0

   (B) 1

   (C) n

   (D) n + 1

   (E) n!

Ⓐ Ⓑ Ⓒ Ⓓ Ⓔ

19. In how many points do the graphs of $x^2 + y^2 = 9$ and $x^2 = 8y$ intersect?

   (A) One

   (B) Two

   (C) Three

   (D) Four

   (E) More than four

Ⓐ Ⓑ Ⓒ Ⓓ Ⓔ

20. $\dfrac{1+2i}{1-2i} =$

   (A) $\dfrac{4-3i}{-3}$

   (B) $\dfrac{-3+4i}{5}$

   (C) 1

   (D) $\dfrac{3-4i}{5}$

   (E) $\dfrac{4-3i}{3}$

Ⓐ Ⓑ Ⓒ Ⓓ Ⓔ

21. A colony of bacteria starts with 2 bacteria at noon. If the number of bacteria triples every 40 minutes, how many bacteria will be present at 4:00 p.m. on the same day?

   (A) 486   (B) 729   (C) 1,458   (D) 46,656   (E) 118,098

Ⓐ Ⓑ Ⓒ Ⓓ Ⓔ

$$\begin{cases} 2x + y - z = 3 \\ x + 3y - 2z = 7 \\ 3x - y + 4z = 11 \end{cases}$$

22. What is the value of z in the solution set of the system of equations above?

(A) $-\dfrac{11}{3}$

(B) $-\dfrac{3}{2}$

(C) 1

(D) 2

(E) 3   Ⓐ Ⓑ Ⓒ Ⓓ Ⓔ

23. Which quadrants of the plane contain points of the graph of $2x - y > 4$?

(A) First, second, and third only
(B) First, second, and fourth only
(C) First, third, and fourth only
(D) Second, third, and fourth only
(E) First, second, third, and fourth   Ⓐ Ⓑ Ⓒ Ⓓ Ⓔ

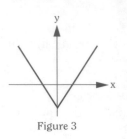

Figure 3

24. Figure 3 is the graph of $y = f(x)$. Which of the following is the graph of $y = |f(x)|$?

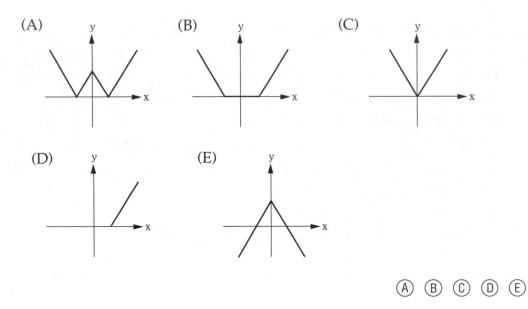

(A) (B) (C) (D) (E)

25. If x, $3x + 2$, and $8x + 3$ are the first three terms of an arithmetic progression, then $x =$

(A) –1

(B) $-\dfrac{1}{5}$

(C) 0

(D) $\dfrac{1}{3}$

(E) 3

(A) (B) (C) (D) (E)

26. What is the middle term in the expansion of $\left(x - \dfrac{1}{x}\right)^6$?

  (A) $20x^3$

  (B) $\dfrac{20}{x^3}$

  (C) $-15x^2$

  (D) -15

  (E) -20 Ⓐ Ⓑ Ⓒ Ⓓ Ⓔ

27. A driver decides to stop her car by tapping the brake pedal once every 5 seconds. After each tap of the brake pedal her speed is 3/4 of what it was before the tap. If the initial speed of the car is 60 miles per hour (88 feet per second), how many feet will the car travel from the first tap of the brake until the car comes to a stop?

  (A) 264   (B) 440   (C) 900   (D) 1,320   (E) 1,408

  Ⓐ Ⓑ Ⓒ Ⓓ Ⓔ

28. The set of <u>real</u> solutions of $\dfrac{2}{3-x} = \dfrac{1}{3} - \dfrac{1}{x}$ is

  (A) the empty set   (B) {3}   (C) {–3}

  (D) {3, –3}   (E) {3i, –3i}   Ⓐ Ⓑ Ⓒ Ⓓ Ⓔ

Study Resources

To prepare for the College Algebra exam, you should study the contents of at least one college level algebra textbook. These textbooks can be found in most college bookstores. You would do well to consult two or three textbooks because they vary in content, approach, and emphasis. When selecting a textbook, check the table of contents against the "Knowledge and Skills Required" section on pages 401-402.

Additional suggestions for preparing for CLEP exams are provided in Chapter 4.

Trigonometry

Description of the Examination

The Subject Examination in Trigonometry covers material that is usually taught in a one-semester college course in trigonometry with primary emphasis on analytical trigonometry. More than half the exam is made up of routine problems requiring basic trigonometric skills; the remainder involves solving nonroutine problems in which candidates must demonstrate their understanding of concepts. The exam includes questions on trigonometric functions and their relationships; evaluation of trigonometric functions of positive and negative angles; trigonometric equations and inequalities; graphs of trigonometric functions; trigonometry of the triangle; and miscellaneous other topics. It is assumed that the candidate is familiar with currently taught trigonometric vocabulary and notation and with both radian and degree measure. The exam places little emphasis on arithmetic calculations, and the use of calculators and other computing devices is not permitted during the exam.

The exam consists of approximately 80 multiple-choice questions to be answered in two separately timed 45-minute sections.

Knowledge and Skills Required

The following subject matter is included on the Trigonometry exam.

➨   *Approximate Percent of Examination*

30%   Trigonometric functions and their relationships

        Cofunction relationships

        Reciprocal relationships

        Pythagorean relationships such as $\sin^2\theta + \cos^2\theta = 1$

        Functions of two angles such as $\sin(\alpha+\beta)$

        Functions of double angles such as $\cos 2\theta$

        Functions of half angles such as $\sin \dfrac{\theta}{2}$

        Identities

Approximate Percent of Examination

20%   Evaluation of trigonometric functions of angles with terminal sides in the various quadrants or on the axes, including positive and negative angles greater than 360° (or 2π radians)

10%   Trigonometric equations and inequalities

10%   Graphs of trigonometric functions

10%   Trigonometry of the triangle including the law of sines and the law of cosines

20%   Miscellaneous

               Inverse functions (arc sin, arc cos, arc tan)

               Trigonometric form (polar form) of complex numbers including DeMoivre's theorem

Within the subject matter described above, questions on the exam require candidates to demonstrate the abilities given below in the approximate proportions indicated.

- Solving routine problems involving basic trigonometric skills (about 60 percent of the exam)

- Solving nonroutine problems requiring an understanding of concepts and the application of skills and concepts (about 40 percent of the exam)

Sample Questions

The 25 questions that follow are similar to questions on the Trigonometry exam, but they do not actually appear on the exam. CLEP exams are designed so that average students completing a course in the subject can usually answer about half the questions correctly.

Before attempting to answer the sample questions, read all the information about the Trigonometry exam on the preceding pages. Additional suggestions for preparing for CLEP exams are provided in Chapter 4.

Try to answer correctly as many questions as possible. Then compare your answers with the correct answers, given in Appendix A.

Directions: Solve the following problems. Do not spend too much time on any one problem.

Note: On this test the inverse function of a trigonometric function f(x) may be expressed as either $f^{-1}(x)$ or arc f(x).

1. $\cos 60° \sin 30° =$

   (A) $\dfrac{1}{4}$ (B) $\dfrac{1}{2}$ (C) $\dfrac{3}{4}$ (D) 1   (E) 2

   Ⓐ Ⓑ Ⓒ Ⓓ Ⓔ

2. If $0 < x < \pi$ and $\tan x = 1$, then $x =$

   (A) $\dfrac{\pi}{6}$ (B) $\dfrac{\pi}{4}$ (C) $\dfrac{\pi}{2}$ (D) $\dfrac{2\pi}{3}$ (E) $\dfrac{3\pi}{4}$

   Ⓐ Ⓑ Ⓒ Ⓓ Ⓔ

3. A circular gear turns 60 degrees per hour. Through how many radians does it turn in 12 hours?

   (A) $\dfrac{4}{\pi}$ (B) $\dfrac{36}{\pi}$ (C) 4π (D) 12π (E) 36π

   Ⓐ Ⓑ Ⓒ Ⓓ Ⓔ

4. If x is the measure of an acute angle such that $\tan x = \dfrac{k}{3}$, then

   $\sin x =$

   (A) $\dfrac{k}{3+k}$ (B) $\dfrac{3}{\sqrt{9-k^2}}$ (C) $\dfrac{k}{\sqrt{9-k^2}}$

   (D) $\dfrac{3}{\sqrt{9+k^2}}$ (E) $\dfrac{k}{\sqrt{9+k^2}}$

   Ⓐ Ⓑ Ⓒ Ⓓ Ⓔ

5. $\cos 240° =$

   (A) $- \sin 240°$
   (B) $- \cos 60°$
   (C) $\sin (-240°)$
   (D) $\sin 150°$
   (E) $\cos 60°$

   Ⓐ Ⓑ Ⓒ Ⓓ Ⓔ

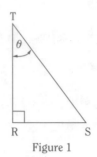

Figure 1

6. In right triangle RST in Figure 1, RS is 9 and $\tan\theta = \dfrac{3}{4}$.

   What is the area of $\triangle RST$?

   (A) 18   (B) 27   (C) 36   (D) 54   (E) 108

   Ⓐ Ⓑ Ⓒ Ⓓ Ⓔ

7. If θ is an angle in standard position such that the terminal ray of θ passes through the point (12, –5), then $\sin\theta =$

   (A) $-\dfrac{12}{13}$ (B) $-\dfrac{5}{13}$ (C) $-\dfrac{5}{17}$ (D) $\dfrac{5}{17}$ (E) $\dfrac{12}{13}$

   Ⓐ Ⓑ Ⓒ Ⓓ Ⓔ

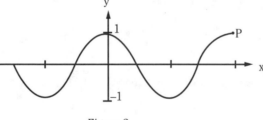

Figure 2

8. On the portion of the graph of $y = \cos\dfrac{2}{3}x$ in Figure 2, what is the x-coordinate of point P if the y-coordinate is 1 ?

   (A) $\dfrac{2\pi}{3}$ (B) 2π (C) 3π (D) 4π (E) 6π

   Ⓐ Ⓑ Ⓒ Ⓓ Ⓔ

9. If $\sin x = 2\cos x$, what is $\tan x$?

   (A) $\dfrac{1}{2}$ (B) $\dfrac{\sqrt{2}}{2}$ (C) $\sqrt{2}$ (D) 2

   (E) It cannot be determined from the information given.

   Ⓐ Ⓑ Ⓒ Ⓓ Ⓔ

10. If $\sin \theta = 0.8$, then $\cos 2\theta =$

   (A) -0.36 (B) -0.28 (C) -0.20
   (D) 0.20 (E) 0.36

   (A) (B) (C) (D) (E)

11. $\cos [\sin^{-1}(-\frac{1}{2})] =$

   (A) $-\frac{\pi}{6}$ (B) $\frac{\pi}{3}$ (C) $\frac{1}{2}$ (D) $\frac{\sqrt{3}}{2}$ (E) $2\sqrt{3}$

   (A) (B) (C) (D) (E)

12. Wherever defined, $\dfrac{\csc x}{\sec x} =$

   (A) $1 - \cos^2 x$ (B) $\cos x$ (C) $\cot x$
   (D) $\sin x$ (E) $\tan x$

   (A) (B) (C) (D) (E)

13. For $0 \leq x \leq 2\pi$, $\sin x > \cos x$ if and only if

   (A) $0 < x < \frac{\pi}{4}$ (B) $\frac{\pi}{6} < x < \frac{\pi}{2}$ (C) $0 < x \leq \frac{\pi}{2}$
   (D) $\frac{\pi}{4} \leq x < \frac{\pi}{2}$ (E) $\frac{\pi}{4} < x < \frac{5\pi}{4}$

   (A) (B) (C) (D) (E)

14. $(\cos \theta \tan \theta)^2 =$

   (A) 0 (B) 1 (C) $\cot^2 \theta$
   (D) $\sin^2 \theta$ (E) $\cos^2 \theta \csc^2 \theta$

   (A) (B) (C) (D) (E)

15. How many values of t are there between 0° and 360°, inclusive, for which $\cos t = 0$?

   (A) None   (B) One   (C) Two   (D) Three   (E) Four

   (A) (B) (C) (D) (E)

16. $\sin (\arctan 1) =$

   (A) 0 (B) $\frac{1}{2}$ (C) $\frac{\sqrt{2}}{2}$ (D) $\frac{\sqrt{3}}{2}$ (E) 1

   (A) (B) (C) (D) (E)

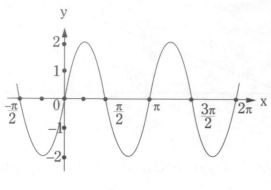

Figure 3

17. The graph shown in Figure 3 above is part of the graph of which of the following equations?

(A) $y = \sin \dfrac{x}{2} + 1$ (B) $y = \sin 2x$ (C) $y = 2 \sin \dfrac{x}{2}$

(D) $y = 2 \sin x$ (E) $y = 2 \sin 2x$

Ⓐ Ⓑ Ⓒ Ⓓ Ⓔ

18. If $0 < y < x < \dfrac{\pi}{2}$, which of the following are true?

  I. $\sin y < \sin x$
  II. $\cos y < \cos x$
  III. $\tan y < \tan x$

(A) None   (B) I and II only   (C) I and III only

(D) II and III only   (E) I, II, and III

Ⓐ Ⓑ Ⓒ Ⓓ Ⓔ

19. What is the solution set of $\cos^2 x + 2 \cos x = 0$, where

$-\dfrac{\pi}{2} \leqq x \leqq \dfrac{\pi}{2}$?

(A) $\{-\dfrac{\pi}{2}, \dfrac{\pi}{2}\}$ (B) $\{-\dfrac{\pi}{2}, \pi\}$ (C) $\{-\pi, \pi\}$

(D) $\{-\pi, 0, \pi\}$ (E) The empty set

Ⓐ Ⓑ Ⓒ Ⓓ Ⓔ

20. Where defined, $\dfrac{\sin x}{-1 + \sec x} + \dfrac{\sin x}{1 + \sec x} =$

(A) $-2 \cot x$ (B) $-2 \tan x$ (C) $2 \cot x$

(D) $2 \tan x$ (E) $\tan 2x$

Ⓐ Ⓑ Ⓒ Ⓓ Ⓔ

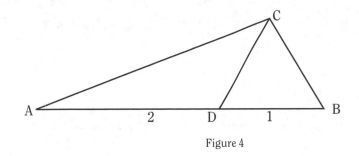

Figure 4

21. In Figure 4, if $\triangle BCD$ is equilateral, what is the length of side AC in $\triangle ABC$?

    (A) $\sqrt{5}$ (B) $\sqrt{7}$ (C) $2\sqrt{2}$ (D) 3
      (E) It cannot be determined from the information given.

    Ⓐ Ⓑ Ⓒ Ⓓ Ⓔ

22. What are all the real numbers x for which $\sin(-x) = \sin x$?

    (A) No number
    (B) Zero
    (C) All integral multiples of π
    (D) All integral multiples of $\frac{\pi}{2}$
    (E) All numbers

    Ⓐ Ⓑ Ⓒ Ⓓ Ⓔ

23. Using DeMoivre's theorem, $[4 (\cos \frac{\pi}{3} + i \sin \frac{\pi}{3})]^3$ can be expressed as

    (A) -64 (B) $-64i$ (C) $12 + 12i$
      (D) $12 - 12i$ (E) $-12 - 12i$

    Ⓐ Ⓑ Ⓒ Ⓓ Ⓔ

24. Which of the following represents part of the graph of $y = 3 \sin 2x$?

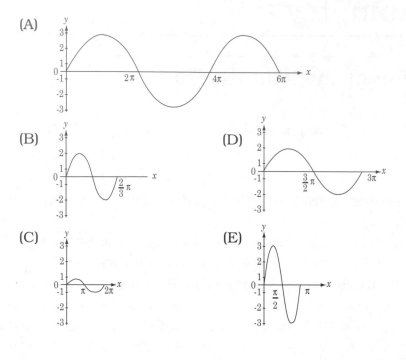

Ⓐ Ⓑ Ⓒ Ⓓ Ⓔ

25. If $0 \leqq \theta \leqq \dfrac{\pi}{2}$ and, where defined, $\dfrac{2 \tan \theta}{1 - \tan^2 \theta} = \cot \theta$, then $\theta =$

(A) $\dfrac{\pi}{2}$ (B) $\dfrac{\pi}{3}$ (C) $\dfrac{\pi}{4}$ (D) $\dfrac{\pi}{6}$ (E) 0

Ⓐ Ⓑ Ⓒ Ⓓ Ⓔ

Study Resources

To prepare for the Trigonometry exam, you should study the contents of at least one college level textbook, which you can find in most college bookstores. You would do well to consult several textbooks because the approaches to certain topics may vary. When selecting a textbook, check the table of contents against the "Knowledge and Skills Required" sections on pages 413-414.

Additional suggestions for preparing for CLEP exams are provided in Chapter 4.

College Algebra — Trigonometry

Description of the Examination

The Subject Examination in College Algebra-Trigonometry covers material that is usually taught in a one-semester course that includes both algebra and trigonometry. Such a course is usually taken by students who have studied algebra and geometry in high school, but who need additional study of precalculus mathematics before enrolling in calculus and other advanced courses at the college level.

The College Algebra-Trigonometry exam requires all the knowledge and skills required by the exams in College Algebra and in Trigonometry. The combined exam consists of two separately timed 45-minute sections, each containing approximately 40 multiple-choice questions. One section is devoted exclusively to College Algebra; the other to Trigonometry. The exam places little emphasis on arithmetic calculations, and the use of calculators is not permitted during the exam.

Separate scores are not reported for College Algebra and Trigonometry. Candidates wishing to earn credit for both of these courses by exam should take the separate exams in these subjects.

Sample Questions

Sample questions for this exam can be found in the two preceding sections.

Study Resources

The suggested study resources for both the College Algebra and the Trigonometry exams can also be used to prepare for the College Algebra-Trigonometry exam.

General Biology

Description of the Examination

The Subject Examination in General Biology covers material that is usually taught in a one-year biology course at the college level. The subject matter tested covers the broad field of the biological sciences, organized into three major areas: molecular and cellular biology, organismal biology, and population biology. The exam gives approximately equal weight to these three areas, and the questions relating to them are interspersed randomly throughout the exam.

The exam consists of approximately 120 multiple-choice questions to be answered in two separately timed 45-minute sections.

Knowledge and Skills Required

Questions on the exam require candidates to demonstrate one or more of the following abilities.

- Knowledge of facts, principles, and processes of biology

- Understanding of the means by which information is collected and how it is interpreted

- Understanding of how one hypothesizes from available information and how one draws conclusions and makes further predictions

- Understanding that science is a human endeavor with social consequences

The subject matter of the General Biology exam is drawn from the following topics.

Approximate Percent of Examination

33%   Molecular and Cellular Biology

Chemical composition of organisms

Simple chemical reactions and bonds

Properties of water

Chemical structure of carbohydrates, lipids, proteins, organic acids, nucleic acids

Cells

　　Structure and function of cell organelles

　　Properties of cell membranes

　　Comparison of prokaryotic and eukaryotic cells

Enzymes

　　Enzyme-substrate complex

　　Role of coenzymes

　　Inorganic cofactors

　　Prosthetic groups

Energy transformations

　　Glycolysis, respiration, anaerobic pathways

　　Photosynthesis

Cell division

　　Structure of chromosomes

　　Mitosis, meiosis, and cytokinesis in plants and animals

Chemical nature of the gene

　　Watson-Crick model of nucleic acids

　　DNA replication

　　Mutations

　　Control of protein synthesis: transcription, translation, post-transcriptional processing

　　Structural and regulatory genes

　　Transformation and transduction

The origin of life

　　Modern theories

　　Experimental evidence

34%   Organismal Biology

 Structure and function in plants with emphasis on angiosperms

  Root, stem, leaf, flower, seed, fruit

  Water and mineral absorption and transport

  Food translocation and storage

 Plant reproduction and development

  Alternation of generations in ferns, pines, and flowering plants

  Gamete formation and fertilization

  Growth and development: hormonal control

  Tropism and photoperiodicity

 Structure and function in animals with emphasis on vertebrates

  Major systems

  Homeostatic mechanisms

  Hormonal control in homeostasis and reproduction

 Animal reproduction and development

  Gamete formation, fertilization

  Cleavage, gastrulation, germ layer formation, differentiation of organ systems

  Experimental analysis of vertebrate development

  Extraembryonic membranes of vertebrates

  Formation and function of the mammalian placenta

  Blood circulation in the human embryo

 Principles of heredity

  History of early experiments in heredity

  Mendelian inheritance (dominance, segregation, independent assortment)

  Chromosomal basis of inheritance

  Linkage

  Sex-linked, sex-influenced, sex-limited inheritance

  Polygenic inheritance (height, skin color)

  Multiple alleles (human blood groups)

◄ *Approximate Percent of Examination*

33%   Population Biology

Principles of ecology

Energy flow and productivity in ecosystems

Biogeochemical cycles

Population growth and regulation (natality, mortality, competition, migration, density)

Community structure, growth, regulation (major biomes, succession and climax communities)

Habitat (biotic and abiotic factors)

Concept of niche

Principles of evolution

History of evolutionary concepts, Lamarckian and Darwinian theories

Modern concepts of natural selection (differential reproduction, mutation, Hardy-Weinberg equilibrium, speciation)

Adaptive radiation

Major features of plant and animal evolution

Concepts of homology and analogy

Convergence, extinction, balanced polymorphism, genetic drift

Classification of living organisms

Evolutionary history of humans

Principles of behavior

Stereotyped, learned social behavior

Societies (ants, bees, birds, primates)

Social biology

Problem of human population growth (age composition, birth and fertility rates, theory of demographic transition)

Human intervention in the natural world (management of resources, environmental pollution)

Implications of biomedical progress (control of human reproduction, genetic engineering)

Sample Questions

The 25 sample questions that follow are similar to questions on the General Biology exam, but they do not actually appear on the exam. CLEP exams are designed so that average students completing a course in the subject can usually answer about half the questions correctly.

Before attempting to answer the sample questions, read all the information about the General Biology exam given above. Additional suggestions for preparing for CLEP exams are provided in Chapter 4.

Try to answer correctly as many questions as possible. Then compare your answers with the correct answers, given in Appendix A.

Directions: Each of the questions or incomplete statements below is followed by five suggested answers or completions. Select the one that is best in each case.

1. In which of the following ways do social insects benefit most from having several types or castes within the species?

   (A) Each colony is able to include a large number of individuals.
   (B) The secretions or odors produced by the protective caste are an effective defense.
   (C) The division of the species into castes ensures the survival of the fittest.
   (D) Large numbers of the worker caste can migrate to start new colonies.
   (E) The specialized structure of each caste permits division of labor and greater efficiency.

2. The greatest diversity of structure and of methods of locomotion is exhibited in the individuals of

   (A) a class
   (B) a family
   (C) an order
   (D) a species
   (E) a phylum

   Ⓐ Ⓑ Ⓒ Ⓓ Ⓔ

3. Of the following, which is an example of a mutualistic relationship?

   (A) The protozoan *Trichonympha* digesting wood in the gut of termites
   (B) The sporozoan *Plasmodium* reproducing in human blood cells and
       liberating toxins into the human body
   (C) Two species of *Paramecium* deriving food from a common laboratory
       culture
   (D) Rabbits being eaten by foxes
   (E) Humans inadvertently providing food for cockroaches

   Ⓐ Ⓑ Ⓒ Ⓓ Ⓔ

4. Evidence that multicellular green plants may have evolved from green
   algae is supplied by the fact that in both

   (A) the gametophyte generation is dominant
   (B) the sporophyte generation is dominant
   (C) chlorophylls *a* and *b* are photosynthetic pigments
   (D) xylem vessels are pitted and spiraled
   (E) male gametes are nonflagellated

   Ⓐ Ⓑ Ⓒ Ⓓ Ⓔ

5. All of the following statements concerning the light-dependent phase of
   photosynthesis are true EXCEPT

   (A) An initial event is the excitation of electrons from chlorophyll by light
       energy.
   (B) The excited electrons are raised to a higher energy level.
   (C) If not captured in the reaction, the excited electrons drop back to their
       initial energy levels.
   (D) If captured in the reaction, some of the energy of the excited electrons
       is used to split carbon dioxide to carbon and oxygen.
   (E) The reaction occurs in grana.

   Ⓐ Ⓑ Ⓒ Ⓓ Ⓔ

6. Which of the following statements best explains the hypothesis that the development of sexual reproduction has resulted in acceleration of the rate of evolution?

   (A) Mutations are more likely to occur in spermatogenesis and oogenesis than in mitotically dividing cells.

   (B) Sexual reproduction results in more offspring than does asexual reproduction.

   (C) Those members of a species that are best adapted to their environment are most likely to be successful in sexual reproduction.

   (D) Mutations usually do not occur in the production of spores or in cells dividing by fission.

   (E) Sexual reproduction is more likely to result in genetic recombination than is asexual reproduction.

A frog gastrocnemius muscle gives a smooth tetanic contraction at any rate of stimulation above 20 per second. At threshold stimulus intensity, a response of some specific strength will be obtained. Increase of the stimulus intensity by 50 percent will increase the strength of response nearly 50 percent. If the intensity is again increased 50 percent, the response will increase only about another 25 percent. Further increase in the stimulus intensity produces no further increase in response.

7. The observations above are best explained by which of the following?

   (A) A muscle functions with an all-or-none mechanism.
   (B) Muscle-fiber sarcolemma is electrically resistant.
   (C) The fibers of a muscle do not all contract at the same rate.
   (D) The fibers of a muscle fatigue at varying rates.
   (E) The fibers of a muscle have varying thresholds for response.

8. In an amphibian gastrula, transplantation experiments that involve the dorsal lip of the blastopore indicate that this tissue

   (A) is destined to be ectoderm
   (B) does not differ from other tissues of the blastula in any significant manner
   (C) will cause a concentration of yolk in adjacent cells
   (D) has the power to initiate differentiation of the embryonic neural tube
   (E) is so sensitive that it will develop into any embryonic structure depending on its surroundings

   Ⓐ Ⓑ Ⓒ Ⓓ Ⓔ

9. Deposits of coal in Greenland and the Antarctic indicate that

   (A) these regions once contained numerous mollusks that deposited carbohydrates in their shells
   (B) the Earth's crust in these regions contains vast amounts of limestone
   (C) these regions were once thickly vegetated
   (D) there is a rich store of dissolved carbon dioxide in the seas surrounding these regions
   (E) a geologic uplift of coral rock and ocean bed has recently occurred in these regions

   Ⓐ Ⓑ Ⓒ Ⓓ Ⓔ

10. Thirst, loss of weight, and sugar in the urine result from the undersecretion of a hormone by which of the following?

    (A) Thyroid
    (B) Parathyroids
    (C) Islets of Langerhans
    (D) Adrenals
    (E) Thymus

    Ⓐ Ⓑ Ⓒ Ⓓ Ⓔ

11. Considering the role of mitochondria in cells, one would expect to find mitochondria most abundant in which of the following?

    (A) Mature red blood cells
    (B) Callous cells of the skin
    (C) Cells of the heart muscle
    (D) Epithelial cells of the cheek lining
    (E) Fat cells

    Ⓐ Ⓑ Ⓒ Ⓓ Ⓔ

12. All of the following statements about enzymes are true EXCEPT

(A) A single enzyme molecule can be used over and over again.
(B) Most enzymes are highly specific with regard to the reactions they catalyze.
(C) Some enzymes contain an essential nonprotein component.
(D) Enzymes can function only within living cells.
(E) Enzymes are destroyed by high temperatures.

Ⓐ Ⓑ Ⓒ Ⓓ Ⓔ

13. Which of the following factors figures most significantly in limiting the size to which an animal cell may grow?

(A) The ratio of cell surface to cell volume
(B) The abundance of mitochondria in the cytoplasm
(C) The chemical composition of the cell membrane
(D) The presence of an inelastic cell wall
(E) The relative number of nucleoli

Ⓐ Ⓑ Ⓒ Ⓓ Ⓔ

14. Which of the following best describes the effect on heart action of the stimulation of the parasympathetic nerve fibers of the vagus nerve?

(A) There is a decrease in the volume of blood pumped and an increase in the heartbeat rate.
(B) There is an increase in the volume of blood pumped without a decrease in the heartbeat rate.
(C) There is a prolonged acceleration in the heartbeat rate.
(D) There is a decrease in the heartbeat rate.
(E) There is an initial increase in the heartbeat rate, followed by a decrease.

Ⓐ Ⓑ Ⓒ Ⓓ Ⓔ

15. If poorly drained soils encourage the growth of bacteria that convert nitrate to nitrogen, the effect on higher plants will be to

(A) increase lipid production
(B) decrease protein production
(C) increase carbohydrate production
(D) produce unusually large fruits
(E) stimulate chlorophyll production

Ⓐ Ⓑ Ⓒ Ⓓ Ⓔ

16. A patient is placed on a restricted diet of water, pure cooked starch, olive oil, adequate minerals, and vitamins. If a urinalysis several weeks later reveals the presence of relatively normal amounts of urea, the urea probably came from the

(A) food eaten during the restricted diet
(B) withdrawal of reserve urea stored in the liver
(C) chemical combination of water, carbon dioxide, and free nitrogen
(D) deamination of cellular proteins
(E) urea synthesized by kidney tubule cells

Ⓐ Ⓑ Ⓒ Ⓓ Ⓔ

Directions: The following group of questions consists of five lettered headings followed by a list of numbered phrases. For each numbered phrase select the one heading that is most closely related to it. A heading may be used once, more than once, or not at all.

Questions 17-19

(A) Fertilization
(B) Meiosis
(C) Mitosis
(D) Pollination
(E) Nondisjunction

17. The process by which a zygote is formed

Ⓐ Ⓑ Ⓒ Ⓓ Ⓔ

18. The process by which somatic (body) cells divide

Ⓐ Ⓑ Ⓒ Ⓓ Ⓔ

19. The process by which monoploid (haploid) cells are formed from diploid cells

Ⓐ Ⓑ Ⓒ Ⓓ Ⓔ

Directions: Each group of questions below concerns an experimental situation. In each case, first study the description of the situation. Then choose the best answer to each question following it.

Questions 20-22

Expenditures of solar energy, calculated by C. Juday for Lake Mendota in southern Wisconsin, appear in the table below.

Reflected or otherwise lost 49.5%
Absorbed in evaporation of water 25.0%
Raising of temperatures in the lake 21.7%
Melting of ice in the spring 3.0%
Directly used by organisms 0.8%

The pyramid of biomass for this same lake is represented by the following diagram.

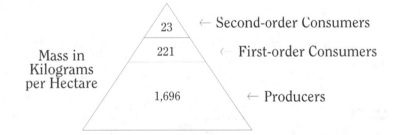

20. The most probable explanation for the relative masses of the first- and second-order consumers is that

   (A) each link in the food chain of an ecosystem has less available energy than the previous link has
   (B) only a small fraction of sunlight that reaches the Earth is transformed into chemical energy by photosynthesis
   (C) the total energy of the decomposers is greater than that of the rest of the organisms put together
   (D) seasonal fluctuations in weather limit the number of consumers
   (E) second-order consumers require more total energy than first-order consumers do

   Ⓐ Ⓑ Ⓒ Ⓓ Ⓔ

21. The energy incorporated into this ecosystem is most dependent on the

    (A) photoperiod
    (B) total amount of photosynthesis
    (C) predator-prey relationships
    (D) length of the food chains
    (E) total amount of respiration   Ⓐ Ⓑ Ⓒ Ⓓ Ⓔ

22. If the lake is assumed to be a typical ecosystem, the percent of radiant energy from the Sun that is trapped in photosynthesis is about

    (A) 100%
    (B)   10%
    (C)   1%
    (D)   0.1%
    (E)   0.01%   Ⓐ Ⓑ Ⓒ Ⓓ Ⓔ

Questions 23-25

Inheritance of certain characteristics of the fruit fly, *Drosophila*, is as indicated by the table below.

Characteristic	Dominant	Recessive
Body color	Gray	Black
Eye color	Red	White

A female fruit fly had a gray body and white eyes. After being mated with a male fruit fly, she laid 112 eggs that developed into the following kinds of offspring.

Number	Body	Eyes
28	Gray	Red
29	Gray	White
28	Black	Red
27	Black	White

23. With respect to body color, the male parent of the 112 offspring was most probably

(A) homozygous gray
(B) heterozygous gray
(C) homozygous black
(D) heterozygous black
(E) of a genotype that cannot be determined from the data given

24. Examination revealed that all of the 56 red-eyed offspring were females and all of the 56 white-eyed offspring were males. This observation indicates that

(A) red and white eye colors segregate independently of sex
(B) all of the red-eyed offspring inherited their eye color from their female parent
(C) all of the red-eyed offspring were homozygous
(D) the gene for eye color is linked to the gene for body color
(E) the gene for red or for white eye color is carried on the X-chromosome

25. In this experiment, the number of offspring that exhibit both recessive characters is

(A) 1
(B) 27
(C) 28
(D) 55
(E) 56

Study Resources

Most textbooks used in college-level introductory biology courses cover the topics in the outline given earlier, but their approaches to certain topics and the emphases given to them may differ. To prepare for the General Biology exam, a candidate is advised to study one or more college textbooks, which can be found in most college bookstores. When selecting a textbook, check the table of contents against the "Knowledge and Skills Required" section on pages 423-426. In addition, candidates would do well to consult pertinent articles from the monthly magazine *Scientific American,* available in most libraries. The Internet is another resource the candidate could explore.

General Chemistry

Description of the Examination

The Subject Examination in General Chemistry covers material usually taught in a one-year introductory course in general chemistry. Understanding of the structure and states of matter, reaction types, equations and stoichiometry, equilibrium, kinetics, thermodynamics, and descriptive and experimental chemistry is required, as is the ability to interpret and apply this material to new and unfamiliar problems.

Battery-operated, hand-held calculators may be used during the exam; however, all calculator memories must be cleared of programs and data, both before and after the exam. It may be helpful to use a calculator for some questions on the exam. A Periodic Table of the elements is included in the exam booklet.

The exam contains approximately 80 multiple-choice questions to be answered within two separately timed 45-minute periods.

Knowledge and Skills Required

Questions on the exam require candidates to demonstrate one or more of the following abilities.

- Recall: remember specific facts; demonstrate straightforward knowledge of information and familiarity with terminology

- Application: understand concepts and reformulate information into other equivalent terms; apply knowledge to unfamiliar and/or practical situations; solve mathematical problems

- Interpretation: infer and deduce from data available and integrate information to form conclusions; recognize unstated assumptions

The subject matter of the General Chemistry exam is drawn from the following topics.

→ *Approximate Percent of Examination*

20%   Structure of Matter

- Atomic theory and atomic structure

  Evidence for the atomic theory

  Atomic masses; determination by chemical and physical means

  Atomic number and mass number; isotopes

  Electron energy levels: atomic spectra, quantum numbers, atomic orbitals

  Periodic relationships including, for example, atomic radii, ionization energies, electron affinities, oxidation states

- Chemical bonding

  Binding forces

  Forces within species: covalent, ionic, metallic

  Intermolecular forces: hydrogen bonding, dipole-dipole, London dispersion forces

  Relationships to states, structure, and properties

  Polarity of bonds, electronegativities

  Molecular models

  Lewis structures

  Valence bond theory; hybridization of orbitals, resonance, sigma and pi bonds

  VSEPR

  Geometry of molecules, ions, and coordination complexes; dipole moments of molecules; relation of properties to structure

- Nuclear chemistry: nuclear equations, half-lives, and radioactivity; chemical applications

---

19%   States of Matter

- Gases

    Laws of ideal gases; equations of state for an ideal gas; partial pressures

    Kinetic-molecular theory

    Interpretation of ideal gas laws on the basis of this theory

    Avogadro's hypothesis and the mole concept

    Dependence of kinetic energy of molecules on temperature

    Deviations from ideal gas laws

- Liquids and solids

    Liquids and solids from the kinetic-molecular viewpoint

    Phase diagrams of one-component systems

    Changes of state, including critical points and triple points

    Structure of solids; lattice energies

- Solutions

    Types of solutions and factors affecting solubility

    Methods of expressing concentration

    Raoult's law and colligative properties (nonvolatile solutes); osmosis

    Non-ideal behavior (qualitative aspects)

38%   Reactions

- Reaction types (12%)

    Acid-base reactions; concepts of Arrhenius, Brönsted-Lowry, and Lewis; amphoterism; coordination complexes

    Precipitation reactions

    Oxidation-reduction reactions

    The role of the electron in oxidation-reduction

    Electrochemistry: electrolytic and voltaic cells; Faraday's laws; standard half-cell potentials; Nernst equation; prediction of the direction of redox reactions

- Equations and Stoichiometry (10%)

  The mole concept; Avogadro's number

  Ionic and molecular species present in chemical systems; net ionic equations

  Balancing of equations including those for redox reactions

  Mass and volume relations with emphasis on the mole concept, including empirical formulas and limiting reactants

- Equilibrium (7%)

  Concept of dynamic equilibrium, physical and chemical; Le Chatelier's principle; equilibrium constants

  Quantitative treatment

  Equilibrium constants for gaseous reactions in terms of both molar concentrations and partial pressure (K_c, K_p)

  Equilibrium constants for reactions in solutions

  Constants for acids and bases; pK; pH

  Solubility product constants and their application to precipitation and the dissolution of slightly soluble compounds

  Common ion effect; buffers; hydrolysis

- Kinetics (4%)

  Concept of rate of reaction

  Use of differential rate laws to determine order of reaction and rate constant from experimental data

  Effect of temperature change on rates

  Energy of activation; the role of catalysts

◄   *Approximate Percent of Examination*

- Thermodynamics (5%)

  State functions

  First law: heat of formation; heat of reaction; change in
  enthalpy; Hess's law; heats of vaporization and fusion

  Second law: free energy of formation; free energy of reaction;
  dependence of change in free energy on enthalpy and
  entropy changes

  Relationship of change in free energy to equilibrium
  constants and electrode potentials

14%   Descriptive Chemistry

- The accumulation of certain specific facts of chemistry is
  essential to enable students to comprehend the development
  of principles and concepts, to demonstrate applications
  of principle, to relate fact to theory and properties to
  structure, and to develop an understanding of systematic
  nomenclature, which facilitates communication. The
  following areas are normally included on the exam.

  Chemical reactivity and products of chemical reactions

  Chemistry of the main groups and transition elements,
  including typical examples of each

  Organic compounds as exemplary material in areas such
  as bonding, acid-base reactions, structure, solutions,
  intermolecular forces

9%   Experimental Chemistry

- Some questions are based on laboratory experiments widely
  performed in general chemistry and ask about the equipment
  used, observations made, calculations performed, and
  interpretation of the results. The questions are designed to
  provide a measure of students' understanding of the basic
  tools of chemistry and their applications to simple chemical
  systems.

Sample Questions

The 46 sample questions that follow are similar to questions on the General Chemistry exam, but they do not appear on the actual exam. CLEP exams are designed so that average students completing a course in the subject can usually answer about half the questions correctly. Because a Periodic Table is provided with the actual exam, you should refer to a Periodic Table as needed when working through the sample questions.

Before attempting to answer the sample questions, read all the information about the General Chemistry exam on the preceding pages. Additional suggestions for preparing for CLEP exams are provided in Chapter 4.

Try to answer correctly as many questions as possible. Then compare your answers with the correct answers, given in Appendix A.

Note: For all questions involving solutions and/or chemical equations, assume that the system is in pure water and at room temperature unless otherwise stated.

Part A

Directions: Each set of lettered choices below refers to the numbered questions or statements immediately following it. Select the one lettered choice that best answers each question or best fits each statement. A choice may be used once, more than once, or not at all in each set.

Questions 1-3

    (A) F
    (B) S
    (C) Mg
    (D) Ar
    (E) Mn

1. Forms monatomic ions with 2^- charge in solutions   Ⓐ Ⓑ Ⓒ Ⓓ Ⓔ

2. Forms a compound having the formula KXO_4 Ⓐ Ⓑ Ⓒ Ⓓ Ⓔ

3. Forms oxides that are common air pollutants and that yield acidic solutions in water
       Ⓐ Ⓑ Ⓒ Ⓓ Ⓔ

Questions 4-6

    (A) Hydrofluoric acid
    (B) Carbon dioxide
    (C) Aluminum hydroxide
    (D) Ammonia
    (E) Hydrogen peroxide

4. Is a good oxidizing agent   Ⓐ Ⓑ Ⓒ Ⓓ Ⓔ

5. Is used extensively for the production of fertilizers   Ⓐ Ⓑ Ⓒ Ⓓ Ⓔ

6. Has amphoteric properties   Ⓐ Ⓑ Ⓒ Ⓓ Ⓔ

Questions 7-8

    (A) A network solid with covalent bonding
    (B) A molecular solid with zero dipole moment
    (C) A molecular solid with hydrogen bonding
    (D) An ionic solid
    (E) A metallic solid

7. Solid ethyl alcohol, C_2H_5OH Ⓐ Ⓑ Ⓒ Ⓓ Ⓔ

8. Silicon dioxide, SiO_2 Ⓐ Ⓑ Ⓒ Ⓓ Ⓔ

Questions 9-11

    (A) CO_3^{2-}
    (B) MnO_4^-
    (C) NH_4^+
    (D) Ba^{2+}
    (E) Al^{3+}

Assume that you have an "unknown" consisting of an aqueous solution of a salt that contains one of the ions listed above. Which ion must be <u>absent</u> on the basis of each of the following observations of the "unknown"?

9. The solution is colorless.   Ⓐ Ⓑ Ⓒ Ⓓ Ⓔ

10. No odor can be detected when a sample of the solution is added drop by drop to a warm solution of sodium hydroxide.

Ⓐ Ⓑ Ⓒ Ⓓ Ⓔ

11. No precipitate is formed when a dilute solution of H_2SO_4 is added to a sample of the solution.

Ⓐ Ⓑ Ⓒ Ⓓ Ⓔ

Questions 12-13

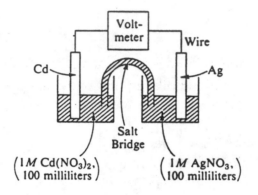

The spontaneous reaction that occurs when the cell above operates is

$$2\,Ag^+ + Cd(s) \rightarrow 2\,Ag(s) + Cd^{2+}$$

(A) Voltage increases.
(B) Voltages decreases but remains above zero.
(C) Voltage becomes zero and remains at zero.
(D) No change in voltage occurs.
(E) Direction of voltage change cannot be predicted without additional information.

Which of the above occurs for each of the following circumstances?

12. The silver electrode is made larger.

Ⓐ Ⓑ Ⓒ Ⓓ Ⓔ

13. The salt bridge is replaced by a platinum wire.

Ⓐ Ⓑ Ⓒ Ⓓ Ⓔ

Part B

Directions: Each of the questions or incomplete statements below is followed by five suggested answers or completions. Select the one that is best in each case.

14.

Hydrogen Halide	Normal Boiling Point, °C
HF	+19
HCl	–85
HBr	–67
HI	–35

The liquefied hydrogen halides have the normal boiling points given above. The relatively high boiling point of HF can be correctly explained by which of the following?

(A) HF gas is more ideal.
(B) HF is the strongest acid.
(C) HF molecules have a smaller dipole moment.
(D) HF is much less soluble in water.
(E) HF molecules tend to form hydrogen bonds. Ⓐ Ⓑ Ⓒ Ⓓ Ⓔ

$$1s^2\ 2s^2\ 2p^6\ 3s^2\ 3p^3$$

15. Atoms of an element, X, have the electronic configuration shown above. The compound most likely formed with magnesium, Mg, is

(A) MgX   (B) Mg_2X (C) MgX_2
  (D) Mg_2X_3 (E) Mg_3X_2 Ⓐ Ⓑ Ⓒ Ⓓ Ⓔ

16. The density of an unknown gas is 4.20 grams per liter at 3.00 atmospheres pressure and 127°C. What is the molecular mass of this gas? ($R = 0.0821$ liter-atm/mole-K)

   (A) 14.6
   (B) 46.0
   (C) 88.0
   (D) 94.1
   (E) 138   Ⓐ Ⓑ Ⓒ Ⓓ Ⓔ

Questions 17-18

$$H_3AsO_4 + 3\ I^- + 2\ H_3O^+ \rightarrow H_3AsO_3 + 3\ I_3^- + 3\ H_2O$$

The oxidation of iodide ions by arsenic acid in acidic aqueous solution occurs according to the stoichiometry shown above. The experimental rate law for the reaction is:

$$\text{Rate} = k[H_3AsO_4]\ [I^-]\ [H_3O^+]$$

17. What is the order of the reaction with respect to I^-?

    (A) 1   (B) 2   (C) 3   (D) 5   (E) 6   Ⓐ Ⓑ Ⓒ Ⓓ Ⓔ

18. According to the rate law for the reaction shown above, an increase in the concentration of hydronium ion has what effect on this reaction?

    (A) The rate of reaction increases.
    (B) The rate of reaction decreases.
    (C) The value of the equilibrium constant increases.
    (D) The value of the equilibrium constant decreases.
    (E) Neither the rate nor the value of the equilibrium constant is changed.

    Ⓐ Ⓑ Ⓒ Ⓓ Ⓔ

19. The critical temperature of a substance is the

    (A) temperature at which the vapor pressure of the liquid is equal to the external pressure
    (B) temperature at which the vapor pressure of the liquid is equal to 760 mm Hg
    (C) temperature at which the solid, liquid, and vapor phases are all in equilibrium
    (D) temperature at which liquid and vapor phases are in equilibrium at 1 atmosphere
    (E) lowest temperature above which a substance cannot be liquefied at any applied pressure

20. $Cu(s) + 2\,Ag^+ \rightarrow Cu^{2+} + 2\,Ag(s)$

If the equilibrium constant for the reaction above is 3.7×10^{15}, which of the following correctly describes the standard voltage, $E°$, and the standard free energy change, $\Delta G°$, for this reaction?

(A) $E°$ is positive and $\Delta G°$ is negative.
(B) $E°$ is negative and $\Delta G°$ is positive.
(C) $E°$ and $\Delta G°$ are both positive.
(D) $E°$ and $\Delta G°$ are both negative.
(E) $E°$ and $\Delta G°$ are both zero.

Ⓐ Ⓑ Ⓒ Ⓓ Ⓔ

21. When $^{214}_{84}Po$ decays, the emission consists consecutively of an α particle, then two β particles, and finally another α particle. The resulting stable nucleus is

(A) $^{206}_{83}Bi$ (B) $^{210}_{83}Bi$ (C) $^{206}_{82}Bi$
(D) $^{208}_{82}Pb$ (E) $^{210}_{81}Tl$

Ⓐ Ⓑ Ⓒ Ⓓ Ⓔ

22. The pH of 0.1-molar ammonia is approximately

(A) 1 (B) 4 (C) 7 (D) 11 (E) 14

Ⓐ Ⓑ Ⓒ Ⓓ Ⓔ

23. $\ldots CrO_2^- + \ldots OH^- \rightarrow \ldots CrO_4^{2-} + \ldots H_2O + \ldots e^-$

When the equation for the half-reaction above is balanced, what is the ratio of the coefficients $OH^- : CrO_2^-$?

(A) $1:1$ (B) $2:1$ (C) $3:1$
(D) $4:1$ (E) $5:1$

Ⓐ Ⓑ Ⓒ Ⓓ Ⓔ

24. $CuO(s) + H_2(g) \rightleftarrows Cu(s) + H_2O(g)$ $\Delta H = -2.0$ kilojoules

When the substances in the equation above are at equilibrium at pressure P and temperature T, the equilibrium can be shifted to favor the products by

(A) increasing the pressure by means of a moving piston at constant T
(B) increasing the pressure by adding an inert gas such as nitrogen
(C) decreasing the temperature
(D) allowing some gases to escape at constant P and T
(E) adding a catalyst

Ⓐ Ⓑ Ⓒ Ⓓ Ⓔ

25. The molality of the glucose in a 1.0-molar glucose solution can be obtained by using which of the following?

    (A) Volume of the solution
    (B) Temperature of the solution
    (C) Solubility of glucose in water
    (D) Degree of dissociation of glucose
    (E) Density of the solution   Ⓐ Ⓑ Ⓒ Ⓓ Ⓔ

26. The geometry of the SO_3 molecule is best described as

    (A) trigonal planar
    (B) trigonal pyramidal
    (C) square pyramidal
    (D) bent
    (E) tetrahedral   Ⓐ Ⓑ Ⓒ Ⓓ Ⓔ

27. Which of the following molecules has the shortest bond length?

    (A) N_2 (B) O_2 (C) Cl_2
    (D) Br_2 (E) I_2 Ⓐ Ⓑ Ⓒ Ⓓ Ⓔ

28. What number of moles of O_2 is needed to produce 14.2 grams of P_4O_{10} from P? (Molecular mass P_4O_{10} = 284)

    (A) 0.0500 mole
    (B) 0.0625 mole
    (C) 0.125 mole
    (D) 0.250 mole
    (E) 0.500 mole   Ⓐ Ⓑ Ⓒ Ⓓ Ⓔ

29. If 0.060 faraday is passed through an electrolytic cell containing a solution of In^{3+} ions, the maximum number of moles of In that could be deposited at the cathode is

    (A) 0.010 mole
    (B) 0.020 mole
    (C) 0.030 mole
    (D) 0.060 mole
    (E) 0.18 mole   Ⓐ Ⓑ Ⓒ Ⓓ Ⓔ

30. $CH_4(g) + 2\,O_2(g) \rightarrow CO_2(g) + 2\,H_2O(\ell)$ $\Delta H° = -889.1$ kJ

$$\Delta H_f° \; H_2O(\ell) = -285.8 \text{ kJ/mole}$$
$$\Delta H_f° \; CO_2(g) = -393.3 \text{ kJ/mole}$$

What is the standard heat of formation of methane, $\Delta H_f° \; CH_4(g)$, as calculated from the data above?

(A) -210.0 kJ/mole
(B) -107.5 kJ/mole
(C) -75.8 kJ/mole
(D) 75.8 kJ/mole
(E) 210.0 kJ/mole

Ⓐ Ⓑ Ⓒ Ⓓ Ⓔ

31. Each of the following can act as both a Brönsted acid and a Brönsted base EXCEPT

(A) HCO_3^- (B) $H_2PO_4^-$ (C) NH_4^+
(D) H_2O (E) HS^-

Ⓐ Ⓑ Ⓒ Ⓓ Ⓔ

32. Two flexible containers for gases are at the same temperature and pressure. One holds 0.50 gram of hydrogen and the other holds 8.0 grams of oxygen. Which of the following statements regarding these gas samples is FALSE?

(A) The volume of the hydrogen container is the same as the volume of the oxygen container.
(B) The number of molecules in the hydrogen container is the same as the number of molecules in the oxygen container.
(C) The density of the hydrogen sample is less than that of the oxygen sample.
(D) The average kinetic energy of the hydrogen molecules is the same as the average kinetic energy of the oxygen molecules.
(E) The average speed of the hydrogen molecules is the same as the average speed of the oxygen molecules.

Ⓐ Ⓑ Ⓒ Ⓓ Ⓔ

33. Pi (π) bonding occurs in each of the following species EXCEPT

(A) CO_2 (B) C_2H_4 (C) CN^-
(D) C_6H_6 (E) CH_4

Ⓐ Ⓑ Ⓒ Ⓓ Ⓔ

34. $3 \, Ag(s) + 4 \, HNO_3 \rightleftarrows 3 \, AgNO_3 + NO(g) + 2 \, H_2O$

    The reaction of silver metal and dilute nitric acid proceeds according to the equation above. If 0.10 mole of powdered silver is added to 10. milliliters of 6.0-molar nitric acid, the number of moles of NO gas that can be formed is

    (A) 0.015 mole
    (B) 0.020 mole
    (C) 0.030 mole
    (D) 0.045 mole
    (E) 0.090 mole   (A) (B) (C) (D) (E)

35. Which, if any, of the following species is in the greatest concentration in a 0.100-molar solution of H_2SO_4 in water?

    (A) H_2SO_4 molecules
    (B) H_3O^+ ions
    (C) HSO_4^- ions
    (D) SO_4^{2-} ions
    (E) All species are in equilibrium and therefore have the same
        concentrations.

                                          (A) (B) (C) (D) (E)

36. At 20.°C, the vapor pressure of toluene is 22 mm Hg and that of benzene is 75 mm Hg. An ideal solution, equimolar in toluene and benzene, is prepared. At 20.°C, what is the mole fraction of benzene in the vapor in equilibrium with this solution?

    (A) 0.23   (B) 0.29   (C) 0.50
      (D) 0.77   (E) 0.83   (A) (B) (C) (D) (E)

37. Which of the following aqueous solutions has the highest boiling point?

    (A) 0.10 M potassium sulfate, K_2SO_4
    (B) 0.10 M hydrochloric acid, HCl
    (C) 0.10 M ammonium nitrate, NH_4NO_3
    (D) 0.10 M magnesium sulfate, $MgSO_4$
    (E) 0.20 M sucrose, $C_{12}H_{22}O_{11}$ (A) (B) (C) (D) (E)

38. When 70. milliliters of 3.0-molar Na_2CO_3 is added to 30. milliliters of 1.0-molar $NaHCO_3$, the resulting concentration of Na^+ is

(A) 2.0 M (B) 2.4 M (C) 4.0 M

(D) 4.5 M (E) 7.0 M

Ⓐ Ⓑ Ⓒ Ⓓ Ⓔ

39. Which of the following species CANNOT function as an oxidizing agent?

(A) $Cr_2O_7^{2-}$ (B) MnO_4^- (C) NO_3^-

(D) S   (E) I^-

Ⓐ Ⓑ Ⓒ Ⓓ Ⓔ

40. A student wishes to prepare 2.00 liters of 0.100-molar KIO_3 (molecular mass 214). The proper procedure is to weigh out

(A) 42.8 grams of KIO_3 and add 2.00 kilograms of H_2O

(B) 42.8 grams of KIO_3 and add H_2O until the final homogeneous solution has a volume of 2.00 liters

(C) 21.4 grams of KIO_3 and add H_2O until the final homogeneous solution has a volume of 2.00 liters

(D) 42.8 grams of KIO_3 and add 2.00 liters of H_2O

(E) 21.4 grams of KIO_3 and add 2.00 liters of H_2O

Ⓐ Ⓑ Ⓒ Ⓓ Ⓔ

41. A 20.0-milliliter sample of 0.200-molar K_2CO_3 solution is added to 30.0 milliliters of 0.400-molar $Ba(NO_3)_2$ solution. Barium carbonate precipitates. The concentration of barium ion, Ba^{2+}, in solution after reaction is

(A) 0.150 M

(B) 0.160 M

(C) 0.200 M

(D) 0.240 M

(E) 0.267 M

Ⓐ Ⓑ Ⓒ Ⓓ Ⓔ

42. One of the outermost electrons in a strontium atom in the ground state can be described by which of the following sets of four quantum numbers?

(A) $5, 2, 0, \frac{1}{2}$

(B) $5, 1, 1, \frac{1}{2}$

(C) $5, 1, 0, \frac{1}{2}$

(D) $5, 0, 1, \frac{1}{2}$

(E) $5, 0, 0, \frac{1}{2}$ Ⓐ Ⓑ Ⓒ Ⓓ Ⓔ

43. Which of the following reactions does NOT proceed significantly to the right in aqueous solutions?

(A) $H_3O^+ + OH^- \rightarrow 2\ H_2O$
(B) $HCN + OH^- \rightarrow H_2O + CN^-$
(C) $Cu(H_2O)_4^{2+} + 4\ NH_3 \rightarrow Cu(NH_3)_4^{2+} + 4\ H_2O$
(D) $H_2SO_4 + H_2O \rightarrow H_3O^+ + HSO_4^-$
(E) $H_2O + HSO_4^- \rightarrow H_2SO_4 + OH^-$ Ⓐ Ⓑ Ⓒ Ⓓ Ⓔ

44. A compound is heated to produce a gas whose molecular mass is to be determined. The gas is collected by displacing water in a water-filled flask inverted in a trough of water. Which of the following is necessary to calculate the molecular mass of the gas, but does NOT need to be measured during the experiment?

(A) Mass of the compound used in the experiment
(B) Temperature of the water in the trough
(C) Vapor pressure of the water
(D) Barometric pressure
(E) Volume of water displaced from the flask   Ⓐ Ⓑ Ⓒ Ⓓ Ⓔ

45. A 27.0-gram sample of an unknown hydrocarbon was burned in excess oxygen to form 88.0 grams of carbon dioxide and 27.0 grams of water. What is a possible molecular formula of the hydrocarbon?

(A) CH_4 (B) C_2H_2 (C) C_4H_3
    (D) C_4H_6 (E) C_4H_{10} Ⓐ Ⓑ Ⓒ Ⓓ Ⓔ

46. If the acid dissociation constant, K_a, for an acid HA is 8×10^{-4} at 25°C, what percent of the acid is dissociated in a 0.50-molar solution of HA at 25°C?

(A) 0.08%   (B) 0.2%   (C) 1%
(D) 2%   (E) 4%

Ⓐ Ⓑ Ⓒ Ⓓ Ⓔ

Study Resources

Textbooks that are frequently used in first-year chemistry courses can help you to prepare for the General Chemistry exam. You can find college-level general chemistry textbooks at most college bookstores. When selecting a textbook, check the table of contents against the "Knowledge and Skills Required" section on pages 437-441.

Since textbooks vary in their approach and emphasis, you should consult more than one textbook.

Additional suggestions for preparing for CLEP exams appear in Chapter 4.

Information Systems and Computer Applications

Description of the Examination

The Information Systems and Computer Applications exam covers material that is usually taught in an introductory college-level business course. Questions on the exam are about equally divided between those testing knowledge of terminology and basic concepts and those asking students to apply that knowledge. Although the exam assumes a general familiarity with information systems and computer applications, it does not emphasize the details of hardware design, language-specific programming techniques, or specific application packages. There are occasional references to applications such as word processing, spreadsheets, and data management, but questions that involve these applications do not draw heavily on one's knowledge of a specific product. Rather, the focus is on concepts and techniques applicable to a variety of products and environments.

The exam contains approximately 100 multiple-choice questions to be answered in two separately timed 45-minute sections.

Knowledge and Skills Required

Questions on the exam require candidates to demonstrate the following abilities in the approximate proportions indicated. A single question may require both abilities.

- Knowledge of terminology and basic concepts (about 50 percent of the exam)

- Application of knowledge (about 50 percent of the exam)

The subject matter of the Information Systems and Computer Applications exam is drawn from the following topics.

	Approximate Percent of Examination
15%	Computer Hardware and Its Functions
	Processing, storage, and I/O devices
	Data concepts and representation

Approximate Percent of Examination

10%   Computer Software
> Systems software
> Programming languages
> Standards

15%   System Development Life Cycle
> System development life cycle methodologies
> Analysis/design tools and techniques

5%   Computer Programming
> Program life cycle (analysis, design, coding, testing)
> Program design tools
> Programming logic (sequence, selection, repetition, case)

10%   Data Management
> File organization (direct, sequential, indexed)
> Database concepts and models (hierarchical, network, relational)

10%   Telecommunications
> Equipment and its functions
> Networks

20%   Organizational and User Support Systems: Concepts and Applications
> Design support systems
> Artificial intelligence and expert systems
> Office systems (conferencing, voice mail, fax, electronic mail)
> End-user applications (word processing, spreadsheet, data management, graphics)

Approximate Percent of Examination

10% Information Processing Management

Types of information processing (batch, real-time, transaction)

Controls in information processing (I/O, security, backup, recovery)

Information processing careers

5% Social and Ethical Issues (economic, privacy, security, legal)

Sample Questions

The 25 sample questions given here are similar to questions on the Information Systems and Computer Applications exam, but they do not appear on the actual exam. CLEP exams are designed so that average students completing a course in the subject can usually answer about half the questions correctly.

Before attempting to answer the sample questions, read all the information about the Information Systems and Computer Applications exam on the preceding pages. Additional suggestions for preparing for CLEP exams are provided in Chapter 4.

Try to answer correctly as many questions as possible. Then compare your answers with the correct answers, given in Appendix A.

Directions: Each of the questions or incomplete statements below is followed by five suggested answers or completions. Select the one that is best in each case.

1. In most computer languages, the absence of parentheses implies that the order of mathematical operation from highest to lowest precedence is

   (A) exponentiation, addition and subtraction, multiplication and division
   (B) addition and subtraction, multiplication and division, exponentiation
   (C) multiplication and division, exponentiation, addition and subtraction
   (D) exponentiation, multiplication and division, addition and subtraction
   (E) exponentiation, multiplication, division, addition and subtraction

   Ⓐ Ⓑ Ⓒ Ⓓ Ⓔ

2. The ability of computerized systems to store and exchange information represents a potential threat to our right of

   (A) free speech   (B) assembly
      (C) equal access to information   (D) privacy
         (E) consumer protection

3. Should there be a power failure, the contents of RAM will be

   (A) automatically printed out
   (B) automatically saved on disk
   (C) displayed on the screen
   (D) lost
   (E) refreshed

4. In a spreadsheet formula, what type of cell address is fixed and does not change when the formula is copied?

   (A) Relative address   (B) Absolute address
      (C) Fixed address   (D) Static address
         (E) Constant address

Ⓐ Ⓑ Ⓒ Ⓓ Ⓔ

5. Which of the following specifies running two or more programs concurrently on the same computer sharing the computer's resources?

   (A) Booting   (B) Paging   (C) Multiprogramming
      (D) Multiprocessing   (E) Thrashing

Ⓐ Ⓑ Ⓒ Ⓓ Ⓔ

6. Which DBMS data model uses 2-dimensional tables to describe data structures?

   (A) Relational   (B) Hierarchical
      (C) Network   (D) Navigational
         (E) CODASYL

7. Data values A and B are stored in memory locations X and Y, respectively. Which of the following is true after execution of an instruction that moves A to Y?

   (A) B is erased.
   (B) Y contains A, and X contains B.
   (C) A is eliminated from location X.
   (D) The sum A + B is stored at location Y.
   (E) Y contains A + B, and X contains B.

   (A) (B) (C) (D) (E)

8. The following pseudocode depicts the logic in a section of a computer program.

   SET A TO 1
   SET B TO 3
   SET A TO A + B
   WHILE A < 20
       SET A TO (Λ*Λ)/2
   END WHILE

   The value of variable A following execution of the program segment is

   (A) 16   (B) 20   (C) 21   (D) 32   (E) 64

   (A) (B) (C) (D) (E)

9. Over which type of transmission line do data travel in both directions simultaneously?

   (A) Simplex   (B) Half-duplex   (C) Full-duplex
      (D) Double-duplex   (E) Parallel-duplex

   (A) (B) (C) (D) (E)

10. Which of the following would NOT be used as an input device for a computer system?

    (A) Optical scanner   (B) Tape drive   (C) Hard disk
       (D) Floppy disk   (E) Microfilm reader

    (A) (B) (C) (D) (E)

11. In many computers, input/output (I/O) devices are connected to primary storage by devices that enable I/O operations to overlap with CPU operations. These devices are called

    (A) buffers   (B) channels   (C) selectors
       (D) cables   (E) busses   Ⓐ Ⓑ Ⓒ Ⓓ Ⓔ

12. If A = 4, B = 2, C = 6, and D = 2, then the execution of the statement

    X = A*B + C/D

    would set X to

    (A) 7   (B) 8   (C) 11   (D) 16   (E) 10   Ⓐ Ⓑ Ⓒ Ⓓ Ⓔ

13. Which of the statements concerning real-time processing is generally FALSE?

    (A) A real-time system requires online processing methods.
    (B) A real-time system requires sequential file access.
    (C) A real-time system requires online files.
    (D) A real-time processing operation is one in which all transactions are processed soon after they occur.
    (E) Real-time processing requires direct access storage.

                                                     Ⓐ Ⓑ Ⓒ Ⓓ Ⓔ

14. One responsibility that is NOT traditionally given to a beginning programmer is

    (A) coding   (B) debugging   (C) program testing
       (D) documentation   (E) systems design
                                                     Ⓐ Ⓑ Ⓒ Ⓓ Ⓔ

15. The person responsible for establishing a data dictionary that standardizes data item definitions is usually the

    (A) systems analyst
    (B) applications programmer
    (C) data definition analyst
    (D) database administrator
    (E) librarian   Ⓐ Ⓑ Ⓒ Ⓓ Ⓔ

16. Pseudocode is frequently a useful aid in all of the following activities EXCEPT

(A) writing the program
(B) running the program
(C) debugging the program
(D) explaining the program to others who are not programmers
(E) making changes in the program after it is completed and checked out

Ⓐ Ⓑ Ⓒ Ⓓ Ⓔ

17. In which phase of the system development life cycle is the user LEAST involved?

(A) Analysis   (B) Design   (C) Development
   (D) Implementation   (E) Maintenance

Ⓐ Ⓑ Ⓒ Ⓓ Ⓔ

18. The use of a computer with a modem in the office allows for data communications to take place in which of the following forms?

  I. Electronic mail
 II. Computer conferencing
III. Voicemail

(A) I only   (B) II only   (C) III only
   (D) I and II only   (E) I, II, and III

Ⓐ Ⓑ Ⓒ Ⓓ Ⓔ

19. The major difference between direct access storage devices and magnetic tape is that records on direct access devices

(A) are recorded serially
(B) can be of fixed or variable length
(C) can be blocked or unblocked
(D) can be accessed directly or sequentially
(E) are more easily verified

Ⓐ Ⓑ Ⓒ Ⓓ Ⓔ

20. When applied to the development of computer systems, the term "ergonomics" means

   (A) designing computer systems to maximize the cost-benefit ratio
   (B) applying human factors principles to maximize the efficiency of the human-machine interface
   (C) following the systems development life cycle
   (D) fostering development team interaction through the use of computer-aided software engineering tools
   (E) optimizing the throughput rate by adjusting the operating system interrupts

(A) (B) (C) (D) (E)

Study Resources

If you plan to obtain credit at a particular institution, check the textbooks that are currently being used in the relevant course; the exam is likely to be reasonably consistent with introductory information processing textbooks at most institutions. If you plan to prepare for the exam and have no specific institution in mind, visit a college bookstore and select a textbook from each of the two categories listed below.

- textbooks that deal with general computer concepts and applications software.

- textbooks that focus on information processing.

   When selecting a textbook, you should check also the table of contents against the "Knowledge and Skills Required" section on pages 455-457. The Internet is another resource you could explore.

   Additional suggestions for preparing for CLEP exams appear in Chapter 4.

Principles of Management

Description of the Examination

The Subject Examination in Principles of Management covers the material that is usually taught in an introductory course in the essentials of management and organization. The fact that such courses are offered by different types of institutions and in a number of fields other than business has been taken into account in the preparation of this exam. The exam requires a knowledge of human resources and operational and functional aspects of management, but primary emphasis is placed on functional aspects of management.

The exam is 90 minutes long and includes approximately 100 multiple-choice questions to be answered in two separately timed 45-minute sections.

Knowledge and Skills Required

Questions on the exam require candidates to demonstrate one or more of the following abilities.

- Specific factual knowledge, recall, and general understanding of purposes, functions, and techniques of management (about 10 percent of the exam)

- Understanding of and ability to associate the meaning of specific terminology with important management ideas, processes, techniques, concepts, and elements (about 40 percent of the exam)

- Understanding of theory and significant underlying assumptions, concepts, and limitations of management data, including a comprehension of the rationale of procedures, methods, and analyses (about 40 percent of the exam)

- Application of knowledge, general concepts, and principles to specific problems (about 10 percent of the exam)

The subject matter of the Principles of Management exam is drawn from the following topics.

➡ *Approximate Percent of Examination*

20% **Organization and Human Resources**

Personnel administration

Collective bargaining

Human relations and motivation

Training and development

Performance appraisal

Organizational development

Effective communication

Legal concerns

Work force diversity

15% **Operational Aspects of Management**

Operations planning and control

Work scheduling

Quality management (e.g., TQM)

Information processing and management

Strategic planning and analysis

Productivity

➥ *Approximate Percent of Examination*

50%   Functional Aspects of Management
          Planning
          Organizing
          Directing
          Controlling
          Authority
          Decision making
          Organization charts
          Leadership
          Organizational structure
          Budgeting
          Communication
          Problem solving
          Group dynamics
          Conflict resolution
          Effective communication
          Change
          Organizational theory

15%   Miscellaneous Aspects of Management
          Historical aspects
          Social responsibilities of business
          Systems
          International management and competition
          Environment
          Ethics
          Government regulation
          Management theory and theorists

Sample Questions

The 24 sample questions that follow are similar to questions on the Principles of Management exam, but they do not appear on the actual exam. CLEP exams are designed so that average students completing a course in the subject can usually answer about half the questions correctly.

Before attempting to answer the sample questions, read all the information about the Principles of Management exam on the preceding pages. Additional suggestions for preparing for CLEP exams are provided in Chapter 4.

Try to answer correctly as many questions as possible. Then compare your answers with the correct answers, given in Appendix A.

Directions: Each of the questions or incomplete statements below is followed by five suggested answers or completions. Select the one that is best in each case.

1. Which of the following words is NOT logically related to the others?

    (A) Planning (B) Directing (C) Producing
      (D) Controlling (E) Organizing

2. Program Evaluation and Review Technique (PERT) is a system for

    (A) developing the organization chart for a company
    (B) scheduling and finding the critical path for production
    (C) evaluating the performance of workers
    (D) reviewing the overall financial condition of the company
    (E) programming a computer

3. Which of the following is a correct statement about controlling as a management function?

    (A) It can be performed independently of planning.
    (B) It is performed only by the controller of an organization.
    (C) It is more prevalent in business than in government.
    (D) It assumes a certain approach to motivating employees.
    (E) To work effectively, it must be closely related to planning.

4. Decentralization tends to be encouraged by which of the following business trends?

   I. Product diversification
  II. Use of electronic computers
 III. Geographical expansion of operations

(A) I only   (B) II only   (C) III only
   (D) I and III only   (E) II and III only

Ⓐ Ⓑ Ⓒ Ⓓ Ⓔ

5. Which of the following can be best determined by consulting an organization chart?

(A) The size of the company
(B) The relationships of people
(C) The nature of work performed
(D) The relationship of positions
(E) The quality of management of the firm

Ⓐ Ⓑ Ⓒ Ⓓ Ⓔ

6. Which of the following best illustrates informal organization?

(A) Line authority, such as that of the field marshal and battalion commander in the military
(B) Staff authority, such as that of personnel or cost control in manufacturing
(C) Functional authority, such as corporate supervision of the legal aspect of pension plans in branch plants
(D) The acceptance of authority by subordinates
(E) Groupings based on such things as technical ability, seniority, and personal influence

Ⓐ Ⓑ Ⓒ Ⓓ Ⓔ

7. The number of subordinates who directly report to a superior refers to the manager's

(A) span of control   (B) organizational role
  (C) organizational structure   (D) chain of command
   (E) general staff

Ⓐ Ⓑ Ⓒ Ⓓ Ⓔ

8. The choice of organizational structure to be used in a business should be

   (A) made by mutual agreement among all the people affected
   (B) based on consideration of the type of organizational structures used
        by competitors
   (C) subject to definite and fixed rules
   (D) based on the objectives of each individual business
   (E) made by organization specialists rather than managers

   (A) (B) (C) (D) (E)

9. The concept of hierarchy of needs attempts to explain which of the
   following?

   (A) Functional supervision   (B) Unity of command
      (C) Line-staff conflict   (D) Heuristic programming
         (E) Personal motivation

   (A) (B) (C) (D) (E)

10. Frederick Taylor is considered a pioneer in the school of management
    referred to as the

    (A) management-process school
    (B) empirical school
    (C) scientific-management school
    (D) behaviorist school
    (E) social-system school

    (A) (B) (C) (D) (E)

11. Preparation of which of the following is the most logical first step in
    developing an annual operating plan?

    (A) A sales forecast by product
    (B) A production schedule by product
    (C) A flow-of-funds statement by product
    (D) A plant and equipment requirement forecast
    (E) A pro forma income statement and balance sheet

    (A) (B) (C) (D) (E)

12. A large span of control throughout an organization invariably results in

    (A) low morale
    (B) high morale
    (C) an excess work load for each manager
    (D) a flat (horizontal) organizational structure
    (E) a tall (vertical) organizational structure   Ⓐ Ⓑ Ⓒ Ⓓ Ⓔ

13. Which of the following is an example of a line position in a manufacturing organization?

    (A) The sales manager concerned with selling a product in a given territory
    (B) The head of research and development concerned with new products
    (C) The controller concerned with establishing budgets
    (D) The personnel manager concerned with employing workers
    (E) The quality control manager concerned with maintaining quality standards in a production plant

    Ⓐ Ⓑ Ⓒ Ⓓ Ⓔ

14. Which of the following is a conflict-resolution practice that seeks to satisfy both parties to a conflict?

    (A) Avoidance
    (B) Stipulation
    (C) Competition
    (D) Collaboration
    (E) Appeal to authority   Ⓐ Ⓑ Ⓒ Ⓓ Ⓔ

15. Which of the following goals is most likely to produce the desired results?

    (A) "Do your best."
    (B) "Outproduce your competitor by 5%."
    (C) "Introduce new products to the market at an unprecedented rate."
    (D) "Increase sales volume by 10% while maintaining current rate of expenditures."
    (E) "Reduce defects due to poor work habits."   Ⓐ Ⓑ Ⓒ Ⓓ Ⓔ

16. The practice in large companies of establishing autonomous divisions whose heads are entirely responsible for what happens is referred to as

(A) management by exception
(B) decentralization of authority
(C) delegation of authority
(D) integration
(E) informal organization

Ⓐ Ⓑ Ⓒ Ⓓ Ⓔ

17. Which of the following control techniques is most likely to emphasize the importance of time?

(A) Break-even charts
(B) Physical standards
(C) Quality circles
(D) Variable budgeting
(E) PERT (program evaluation and review technique)

Ⓐ Ⓑ Ⓒ Ⓓ Ⓔ

18. In profit-decentralized companies, which of the following responsibilities of division managers should be subject to the LEAST restriction by top managers?

(A) approval of advertising and product promotion programs
(B) approval of the selection of key division executives
(C) approval of major capital expenditures
(D) establishment of procedures in functional areas
(E) setting of long-range objectives and annual goals

19. Isabel Myers, Katherine Briggs, and Carl Jung have developed different models to help individuals understand

(A) different approaches to decision making
(B) personal aptitude for international careers
(C) the relevance of cultural background
(D) the stages of human relationships
(E) the limitations of measures of the intelligence quotient

20. In a labor negotiation, if a third party has the power to determine a solution to a labor dispute between two parties, the negotiation is known as

   (A) a grievance
   (B) an arbitration
   (C) a conciliation
   (D) a mediation
   (E) a concession   (A) (B) (C) (D) (E)

21. A type of control device for assessing the progress of planned activities and the expenditure of resources allocated to their accomplishments is referred to as

   (A) a strategic plan
   (B) an organizational chart
   (C) a tactical plan
   (D) a budget
   (E) a proposal   (A) (B) (C) (D) (E)

22. Which of the following do managerial/leadership grids, team-building, and sensitivity training have in common?

   (A) They are crucial to operations management.
   (B) They are tools for organizational development.
   (C) They were developed by Peter Drucker.
   (D) They are necessary to the budgeting process.
   (E) They are the key elements of positive-reinforcement programs.

23. According to Maslow, the need to feel genuinely respected by peers, both in and out of the work environment, is included in which of the following need classifications?

   (A) Physiological
   (B) Safety
   (C) Stability
   (D) Esteem
   (E) Self-actualization   (A) (B) (C) (D) (E)

24. Which of the following management activities is most typically described as a controlling function?

(A) Goal setting
(B) Purchasing
(C) Coordinating
(D) Budgeting
(E) Recruiting

Ⓐ Ⓑ Ⓒ Ⓓ Ⓔ

Study Resources

To prepare for the Principles of Management exam, you should study the contents of at least one textbook used in introductory management courses at the college level. You can find textbooks used for college-level introductory management courses in college many bookstores. When selecting a textbook, check the table of contents against the "Knowledge and Skills Required" section on pages 463-465. Since they may vary somewhat in content, approach, and emphasis, you may wish to consult more than one textbook on the major topics. The Internet is another resource you could explore.

Principles of Accounting

Description of the Examination

The Subject Examination in Principles of Accounting covers the information and skills taught in two semesters (or the equivalent) of college-level accounting. The emphasis of the exam is on financial and managerial accounting. Colleges may award credit for a one- or two-semester course in financial accounting including some managerial accounting topics, or for one semester of financial accounting and one semester of managerial accounting.

Battery-operated, hand-held calculators may be used during the exam, but all calculator memories must be cleared of both programs and data, and no peripheral devices such as magnetic cards or tapes are permitted. Although the exam was designed to be taken without a calculator, candidates may find one helpful for some of the questions.

The exam is 90 minutes long and includes approximately 78 multiple-choice questions to be answered in two separately timed 45-minute sections.

Knowledge and Skills Required

Questions on the exam require candidates to demonstrate one or more of the following abilities.

- Familiarity with accounting concepts and terminology

- Preparation, use, and analysis of accounting data and financial reports issued for both internal and external purposes

- Application of accounting techniques to simple problem situations involving computations

- Understanding of the rationale for generally accepted accounting principles and procedures

The subject matter of the Principles of Accounting exam is drawn from the following topics.

	Approximate Percent of Examination
60-70%	Financial accounting (concerned with providing financial statements and reports of interest to company managers as well as bankers, investors, and other outsiders who must make a financial assessment of a company)

- Generally accepted accounting principles
- Rules of double-entry accounting
- The accounting cycle
- Presentation of and relationships between general-purpose financial statements
- Valuation of accounts and notes receivable
- Valuation of inventories
- Initial costs of plant assets
- Depreciation
- Liabilities
- Investments
- Capital
- Cash and stock dividends
- Treasury stock
- Purchase and sale of merchandise
- Revenue and cost apportionments
- Cash control
- Division of profits and losses in partnership accounting
- Cash flow analysis

30-40%	Managerial accounting (concerned with the use of accounting data for internal purposes to help management in planning and controlling functions of the company)

- The manufacturing environment
- Analysis of departmental operations
- Process and job-order cost systems

Approximate Percent of Examination

     Standard costs and variances

     Direct costing and absorption costing

     Cost-volume profit (break-even) analysis

     Use of differential (relevant) cost

     Budgeting

     Performance evaluation

     Financial statement analysis

Sample Questions

The following 25 questions are similar to questions on the Principles of Accounting exam, but they do not appear on the actual exam. CLEP exams are designed so that average students completing a course in the subject can usually answer about half the questions correctly.

Before attempting to answer the sample questions, read all the information about the Principles of Accounting exam on the preceding pages. Additional suggestions for preparing for CLEP exams are provided in Chapter 4.

Try to answer correctly as many questions as possible. Then compare your answers with the correct answers given in Appendix A.

Directions: Each of the questions or incomplete statements below is followed by five suggested answers or completions. Select the one that is best in each case.

1. The owner's equity in a business may derive from which of the following sources?

   I.   Excess of revenue over expenses
   II. Investments by the owner
  III. Accounts payable

  (A) I only
  (B) II only
  (C) III only
  (D) I and II only
  (E) I, II, and III   Ⓐ Ⓑ Ⓒ Ⓓ Ⓔ

2. Entries made on the books at the end of a period to take care of changes occurring in accounts are called

(A) fiscal entries
(B) closing entries
(C) reversing entries
(D) correcting entries
(E) adjusting entries
    Ⓐ Ⓑ Ⓒ Ⓓ Ⓔ

3. In accounting, net income should be defined as an increase in

(A) assets
(B) cash
(C) merchandise
(D) sales
(E) capital
    Ⓐ Ⓑ Ⓒ Ⓓ Ⓔ

4. Treasury stock may be correctly defined as

(A) a corporation's own stock that has been issued and then reacquired
(B) new issues of a corporation's stock before they are sold on the open market
(C) stock issued by the United States Office of the Treasury
(D) any stock that a corporation acquires and holds for more than 90 days
(E) any stock held by a corporation that receives dividends in excess of 5% of initial cost of the stock
    Ⓐ Ⓑ Ⓒ Ⓓ Ⓔ

5. The Accumulated Depreciation account should be shown in the financial statements as

(A) an operating expense
(B) an extraordinary loss
(C) a liability
(D) stockholders' equity
(E) a contra (deduction) to an asset account
    Ⓐ Ⓑ Ⓒ Ⓓ Ⓔ

6. If fixed expenses are $26,000 and variable expenses are 75 percent of sales, the net income that would result from $500,000 in sales is

(A) $ 75,000
(B) $ 99,000
(C) $200,000
(D) $375,000
(E) $401,000

Ⓐ Ⓑ Ⓒ Ⓓ Ⓔ

7. Cost of goods sold is determined by which of the following?

(A) Beginning inventory plus net purchases minus ending inventory
(B) Beginning inventory plus purchases plus purchase returns minus ending inventory
(C) Beginning inventory minus net purchases plus ending inventory
(D) Purchases minus transportation-in plus beginning inventory minus ending inventory
(E) Net sales minus ending inventory

Ⓐ Ⓑ Ⓒ Ⓓ Ⓔ

8. Company X produces chairs of a single type; it has a plant capacity of 50,000 chairs per year and total fixed expenses of $100,000 per year. Variable costs per chair are $2 and the current selling price is $5 per chair. At the beginning of 19x1, the company purchases a specialized machine that costs $10,000, lasts one year, and reduces variable costs to $1.50 per chair. If the company produces and sells at 90 percent of capacity, what is the net income for 19x1?

(A) $ 8,750
(B) $23,000
(C) $47,500
(D) $50,000
(E) $83,000

Ⓐ Ⓑ Ⓒ Ⓓ Ⓔ

9. The accounting concept that emphasizes the existence of a business firm separate and apart from its owners is ordinarily termed the

(Λ) business separation concept
(B) consistency concept
(C) going-concern concept
(D) business materiality concept
(E) business entity concept

Ⓐ Ⓑ Ⓒ Ⓓ Ⓔ

10. Green Corporation with assets of $5,000,000 and liabilities of $2,000,000 has 6,000 shares of capital stock outstanding (par value $300). What is the book value per share?

(A) $200
(B) $300
(C) $500
(D) $833
(E) None of the above

Ⓐ Ⓑ Ⓒ Ⓓ Ⓔ

11. All the following T-accounts contain the correct sides that would be used for increasing and decreasing an account EXCEPT

(A) $$\frac{\text{Revenue}}{\text{Decrease} \mid \text{Increase}}$$ (B) $$\frac{\text{Assets}}{\text{Increase} \mid \text{Decrease}}$$

(C) $$\frac{\text{Expenses}}{\text{Increase} \mid \text{Decrease}}$$ (D) $$\frac{\text{Owner's Equity}}{\text{Increase} \mid \text{Decrease}}$$

(E) $$\frac{\text{Liabilities}}{\text{Decrease} \mid \text{Increase}}$$

Ⓐ Ⓑ Ⓒ Ⓓ Ⓔ

12. At the end of the fiscal year, a company estimates that $4,300 of Accounts Receivable will be uncollectible. If, prior to adjustment, the company's Allowance for Bad Debts account has a credit balance of $1,600, what is the appropriate adjusting entry?

	DEBIT	CREDIT	AMOUNT
(A)	Allowance for Bad Debts	Bad Debts Expense	$4,300
(B)	Allowance for Bad Debts	Accounts Receivable	$4,300
(C)	Accounts Receivable	Allowance for Bad Debts	$1,600
(D)	Bad Debts Expense	Allowance for Bad Debts	$2,700
(E)	Bad Debts Expense	Accounts Receivable	$2,700

Ⓐ Ⓑ Ⓒ Ⓓ Ⓔ

13. A fast-moving widget stamping machine was purchased for cash. The list price was $4,000 with an applicable trade discount of 20 percent and a cash discount allowable of 2/10, n/30. Payment was made within the discount period. Freight costs of $100, F.O.B. origin, were paid. In order to install the machine properly, a platform was built and wiring installed for a total cost of $200. The trial run costs were $300 for labor and $50 for materials. The cost of the machine would be recorded as

   (A) $3,626
   (B) $3,628
   (C) $3,786
   (D) $3,828
   (E) $4,178   Ⓐ Ⓑ Ⓒ Ⓓ Ⓔ

14. All of the following expenditures should be charged to an asset account rather than to an expense account of the current period EXCEPT the cost of

   (A) overhauling a delivery truck, which extends its useful life by two years
   (B) purchasing a new component for a machine, which serves to increase the productive capacity of the machine
   (C) constructing a parking lot for a leased building
   (D) installing a new equipment item
   (E) replacing worn-out tires on a delivery truck
   　　　　　　　　　　　　　　　　　　　　Ⓐ Ⓑ Ⓒ Ⓓ Ⓔ

15. In a period of rising prices, which of the following inventory methods results in the highest cost of goods sold?

   (A) FIFO
   (B) LIFO
   (C) Average cost
   (D) Periodic inventory
   (E) Perpetual inventory   Ⓐ Ⓑ Ⓒ Ⓓ Ⓔ

16. A company forecasts that during the next year it will be able to sell 80,000 units of its special product at a competitive selling price of $10 per unit. The company has the capacity to produce 120,000 units per year. Its total fixed costs are $528,000. Its variable costs are estimated at $3 per unit. The company has the opportunity to sell 10,000 additional units during the same year at a special contract price of $50,000. This special contract will not affect the regular sales volume or price. Acceptance of the contract will cause the year's net income to

   (A) increase by $20,000
   (B) increase by $26,000
   (C) increase by $50,000
   (D) decrease by $50,000
   (E) decrease by $24,000   Ⓐ Ⓑ Ⓒ Ⓓ Ⓔ

17. Which of the following standard cost variances provides information about the extent to which the manufacturing plant of a company was used at normal capacity?

   (A) Materials quantity (usage) variance
   (B) Labor efficiency (time) variance
   (C) Labor rate variance
   (D) Overhead spending (controllable) variance
   (E) Overhead volume variance   Ⓐ Ⓑ Ⓒ Ⓓ Ⓔ

18. Equity investors are most interested in which aspect(s) of a company?
   I. Book value
   II. Profitability
   III. Cash flow

   (A) I only
   (B) II only
   (C) III only
   (D) I and II only
   (E) II and III only   Ⓐ Ⓑ Ⓒ Ⓓ Ⓔ

19. X Corporation declares and issues a 5 percent stock dividend on common stock, payable in common stock, shortly after the close of the year. All of the following statements about the nature and effect of the dividend are true EXCEPT

    (A) The total stockholders' equity in the corporation is not changed.
    (B) The dividend does not constitute income to the stockholders.
    (C) The book value per share of common stock is not changed.
    (D) The amount of retained earnings is reduced.
    (E) The amount of total assets is not changed.

    Ⓐ Ⓑ Ⓒ Ⓓ Ⓔ

20. The financial statement that includes classifications for operating, financing, and investing activities of a business entity for a period of time is called the

    (A) Income Statement
    (B) Statement of Retained Earnings
    (C) Balance Sheet
    (D) Statement of Changes in Owners' Equity
    (E) Statement of Cash Flows

    Ⓐ Ⓑ Ⓒ Ⓓ Ⓔ

21. A feature of the process cost system that is NOT a feature of the job order cost system is

    (A) computation of the equivalent units of production
    (B) compilation of the costs of each batch or job produced
    (C) use of the Raw Materials Inventory account
    (D) preparation of a Cost of Goods Manufactured Statement for each accounting period
    (E) application of manufacturing overhead on a predetermined basis

    Ⓐ Ⓑ Ⓒ Ⓓ Ⓔ

22. Net purchases for the year amounted to $80,000. The merchandise inventory at the beginning of the year was $19,000. On sales of $120,000, a 30 percent gross profit on the selling price was realized. The inventory at the end of the year was

(A) $13,000
(B) $15,000
(C) $17,000
(D) $25,000
(E) $63,000

Ⓐ Ⓑ Ⓒ Ⓓ Ⓔ

23. The balance sheet of Harold Company shows current assets of $200,000 and current liabilities of $100,000. The company uses cash to acquire merchandise inventory. As a result of this transaction, which of the following is true of working capital and the current ratio?

(A) Both are unchanged.
(B) Working capital is unchanged; the current ratio increases.
(C) Both decrease.
(D) Working capital decreases; the current ratio increases.
(E) Working capital decreases; the current ratio is unchanged.

Ⓐ Ⓑ Ⓒ Ⓓ Ⓔ

24. "In determining net income from business operations, the costs involved in generating revenue should be charged against that revenue."

The statement above best describes which of the following?

(A) The cost principle
(B) The going-concern principle
(C) The profit principle
(D) The matching principle
(E) The business entity principle

 Ⓐ Ⓑ Ⓒ Ⓓ Ⓔ

25. A long-term investment in stock classified as an available-for-sale security requires an end of the year adjustment that impacts on which of the following?

    (A) current assets
    (B) stockholders' equity
    (C) net income
    (D) cash flow
    (E) intangible assets

    Ⓐ Ⓑ Ⓒ Ⓓ Ⓔ

Study Resources

To prepare for the Principles of Accounting exam you should study the contents of at least one textbook designed for a full-year undergraduate course in principles of accounting. You can find textbooks used for college level accounting courses in many college bookstores. While most textbooks cover both financial and managerial accounting topics, their approach and emphasis varies. You may therefore wish to consult more than one textbook on the more important topics. When selecting a textbook, check the table of contents against the Knowledge and Skills Required section on pages 473-475.

Additional suggestions for preparing for CLEP exams are given in Chapter 4.

Introductory Business Law

Description of the Examination

The Subject Examination in Introductory Business Law covers subject matter usually taught in an introductory one-semester college course in this subject. The exam places major emphasis on understanding the functions of contracts in American business law, but also includes questions on the history and sources of American law; legal systems and procedures; agency and employment; sales; and other topics.

   The exam is 90 minutes long and includes approximately 100 multiple-choice questions to be answered in two separately timed 45-minute sections.

Knowledge and Skills Required

Questions on the exam require candidates to demonstrate one or more of the following abilities.

- Knowledge of basic facts and terms (about 30-35 percent of the exam)

- Understanding of concepts and principles (about 30-35 percent of the exam)

- Ability to apply knowledge to specific case problems (about 30-35 percent of the exam)

The subject matter of the Introductory Business Law exam is drawn from the following topics.

	Approximate Percent of Examination
11%	History and sources of American law
12%	American legal systems and procedures

→ *Approximate Percent of Examination*

60%   Contracts

Meaning of terms

Formation of contracts

Consideration

Joint obligations

Contracts for the benefit of third parties

Assignment/Delegation

Statute of frauds

Scope and meaning of contracts

Breach of contract

Bar to remedies for breach of contract

Discharge of contracts

Illegal contracts

3%   Agency and employment

4%   Sales

10%   Miscellaneous

Torts

Property

Product liability

Commercial paper

Consumer protection

Sample Questions

The 24 sample questions that follow are similar to questions on the Introductory Business Law exam, but they do not appear on the actual exam. CLEP exams are designed so that average students completing a course in the subject can usually answer about half the questions correctly.

Before attempting to answer the sample questions, read all the information about the Introductory Business Law exam on the preceding pages. Additional suggestions for preparing for CLEP exams are provided in Chapter 4.

Try to answer correctly as many questions as possible. Then compare your answers with the correct answers, given in Appendix A.

Directions: Each of the questions or incomplete statements below is followed by five suggested answers or completions. Select the one that is best in each case.

1. The authority of a court to hear and decide cases is known as

    (A) jurisdiction   (B) habeas corpus
       (C) demurrer   (D) quo warranto
          (E) stare decisis

    Ⓐ Ⓑ Ⓒ Ⓓ Ⓔ

2. Law that is formed by a group of individuals, acting as representatives for other individuals, is best termed

    (A) criminal law   (B) civil law
       (C) legislative law   (D) adjective law
          (E) tort law

    Ⓐ Ⓑ Ⓒ Ⓓ Ⓔ

3. A contract will be unenforceable if

    (A) one party to the contract feels he or she has been taken advantage of
    (B) a statute declares such a contract illegal
    (C) performance becomes difficult
    (D) public authorities voice disapproval of the contract
    (E) the parties involved believe the contract to be illegal

    Ⓐ Ⓑ Ⓒ Ⓓ Ⓔ

4. Angela promises to work for Barbara during the month of July, and Barbara promises to pay Angela $600 for her services. In this situation, what kind of contract has been made?

    (A) Unilateral   (B) Executed   (C) Quasi
       (D) Bilateral   (E) Bilingual

    Ⓐ Ⓑ Ⓒ Ⓓ Ⓔ

5. Which of the following is an essential element of fraud?

    (A) Injury to a business interest
    (B) Misrepresentation of a material fact
    (C) Destruction of property
    (D) Knowledge of the consequences
    (E) Mistake about the identity of the subject matter

    Ⓐ Ⓑ Ⓒ Ⓓ Ⓔ

6. Clyde received the following letter from Joe: "I will sell you the books you examined yesterday for $10 each or $100 for the entire set." Clyde, not sure he would get much use from the books, told his brother, Michael, about the offer. Michael tendered Joe $100 for the books, but Joe refused to sell the books to Michael.

If Michael sued Joe, the court would probably hold that Michael

(A) can accept the offer because he is Clyde's brother
(B) can accept the offer if he will do so within a reasonable period of time
(C) cannot accept the offer until Clyde's rejection is communicated to Joe
(D) cannot accept the offer because it was not made to him
(E) cannot accept the offer unless he does so in writing

Ⓐ Ⓑ Ⓒ Ⓓ Ⓔ

7. All of the following have the right to enforce a contract EXCEPT

(A) a third-party creditor beneficiary
(B) an assignee
(C) a third-party donee beneficiary
(D) a transferee
(E) a third-party incidental beneficiary

8. A method of discharging a contract that returns each party to his or her original position is

(A) an assignment
(B) an accord
(C) a revocation
(D) a rescission
(E) a novation

Ⓐ Ⓑ Ⓒ Ⓓ Ⓔ

9. A contract clause that requires both parties to act simultaneously is called a

(A) condition subsequent
(B) condition concurrent
(C) condition precedent
(D) negative condition
(E) restrictive condition

Ⓐ Ⓑ Ⓒ Ⓓ Ⓔ

10. Benson, a seventeen-year-old college freshman, was adequately supplied with clothes by his father. Smith, a clothing merchant, learned that Benson was spending money freely and solicited clothing orders from him. Benson bought $750 worth of ready-made clothing from Smith on credit. Benson failed to pay Smith.

    If Smith sued Benson, the court would probably hold that

    (A) Benson is liable for the $750 because by accepting and wearing the clothes he ratified the contract
    (B) Benson is not liable for the reasonable value of the clothing because Smith solicited the sales
    (C) Benson can disaffirm the contract, return the clothing, and escape liability
    (D) Benson is liable for the $750 because under these circumstances the clothing was a necessity
    (E) Benson's father is liable to Smith for the $750

    Ⓐ Ⓑ Ⓒ Ⓓ Ⓔ

11. The enforcement of a contract may be barred, according to operation of law, by

    (A) a merger
    (B) a consolidation
    (C) a material breach
    (D) the statute of limitations
    (E) a novation

    Ⓐ Ⓑ Ⓒ Ⓓ Ⓔ

12. A purchase from each of the following would be considered a purchase in the ordinary course of trade or business EXCEPT a purchase from a

    (A) pawnshop
    (B) department store
    (C) supermarket
    (D) discount department store
    (E) used car lot

    Ⓐ Ⓑ Ⓒ Ⓓ Ⓔ

13. Which of the following promises would be enforceable by the majority of courts?

(A) Avery finds Bond's dog and returns it to Bond. Later Bond promises to pay Avery a reward.

(B) Husband, in consideration of the love and affection given him by Wife, promises to pay her $1,000.

(C) Avery is extremely ill and placed in a hospital. Avery's neighbor, Bond, mows Avery's yard while Avery is recuperating. Later Avery promises to pay Bond the reasonable value of his services.

(D) Avery owes Bond $100, which debt is discharged in bankruptcy. Later Avery writes Bond a letter promising to pay Bond the $100.

(E) Daughter mows the family yard. In absence of an express agreement, Daughter can claim an implied promise on Father's part to pay for her services.

Ⓐ Ⓑ Ⓒ Ⓓ Ⓔ

14. Base Electric Company has entered an agreement to buy its actual requirements of brass wiring for six months from the Valdez Metal Wire Company, and Valdez Metal Wire Company has agreed to sell all the brass wiring Base Electric Company will require for six months. The agreement between the two companies is

(A) valid and enforceable
(B) unenforceable because of lack of consideration
(C) unenforceable because it is too indefinite
(D) lacking in mutuality of obligations
(E) illusory

Ⓐ Ⓑ Ⓒ Ⓓ Ⓔ

15. Ordinarily an employer is liable for which of the following acts committed by an employee for the benefit of the employer and in the scope of the employment?

I. Torts
II. Contracts
III. Misrepresentations

(A) I only
(B) II only
(C) III only
(D) II and III only
(E) I, II, and III

Ⓐ Ⓑ Ⓒ Ⓓ Ⓔ

16. Abbott was orphaned at the age of five. For the next fifteen years his material needs were met by his uncle, Barton. On his thirtieth birthday, Abbott wrote Barton and promised to pay him $100 per month as long as Barton lived. Abbott never made any payments. Barton died ten months later.

    If Barton's estate sued Abbott for the amount of the promised payments, the court would probably hold that Barton's estate is

    (A) not entitled to recover because past consideration will not support Abbott's promise
    (B) not entitled to recover because of the statute of limitations
    (C) not entitled to recover unless it can be shown that Barton's relatives were in desperate need
    (D) entitled to recover on the promise
    (E) entitled to recover because of Barton's previous aid to Abbott

    Ⓐ Ⓑ Ⓒ Ⓓ Ⓔ

17. An agreement among creditors that each will accept a certain percentage of his or her claim as full satisfaction is called

    (A) accord and satisfaction   (B) creditor agreement
       (C) composition of creditors   (D) liquidation
          (E) bankruptcy

    Ⓐ Ⓑ Ⓒ Ⓓ Ⓔ

18. Which of the following decisions could NOT be made by an appellate court?

    (A) Ordering a case to be tried in the appellate court
    (B) Affirming a decision of a lower court
    (C) Instructing a lower court to enter a judgment in accordance with the appellate court's opinion
    (D) Remanding a case for a new trial
    (E) Reversing the decision of a lower court

    Ⓐ Ⓑ Ⓒ Ⓓ Ⓔ

19. Upon delivery of nonconforming goods, a buyer may do which of the following?

    I. Reject all the goods.
    II. Accept all the goods.
    III. Accept those units which conform and reject the rest.

    (A) I only   (B) III only   (C) I and II only
      (D) II and III only   (E) I, II, and III

Ⓐ Ⓑ Ⓒ Ⓓ Ⓔ

20. All of the following are usual functions performed by judges of trial courts having general jurisdiction EXCEPT

    (A) issuing writs of habeas corpus
    (B) conducting pretrial conferences in civil cases
    (C) determining questions of fact in equity cases
    (D) guiding the jury on questions of law in criminal and civil cases
    (E) imposing pretrial settlements on parties who cannot agree

Ⓐ Ⓑ Ⓒ Ⓓ Ⓔ

21. Which of the following will apply if the parties to a contract knew or should have known that a word has a customary usage in their particular trade or community?

    (A) No contract will result if the parties cannot voluntarily agree on the definition of the word.
    (B) Parol evidence may not be used to define the meaning of the word.
    (C) Parol evidence may be used to define the meaning of the word.
    (D) Courts will not impose a definition that is contrary to the meaning supported by one party.
    (E) A mistaken assumption regarding the definition by one of the parties will result in a voidable contract.

Ⓐ Ⓑ Ⓒ Ⓓ Ⓔ

22. Webster insured her residence with Old Home Insurance Company. Assuming that the policy contained no provision with respect to assignment, which of the following statements is correct?

(A) Webster may assign the policy to any person having capacity to contract.

(B) If Webster suffers an insured loss, she may assign the amount due under the policy to anyone.

(C) If Webster sells her residence, she must assign the policy to the purchaser.

(D) If Webster suffers an insured loss, she may assign the amount due under the policy only to a party furnishing material or labor for repair of the residence.

(E) Webster may assign the policy to any person having capacity to contract who agrees to pay the premium.

Ⓐ Ⓑ Ⓒ Ⓓ Ⓔ

23. Recovery in quasi contract is based on a judgment that determines the presence of

(A) unjust enrichment
(B) an express contract
(C) an implied in fact contract
(D) a violation of the statute of frauds
(E) mutual mistake

Ⓐ Ⓑ Ⓒ Ⓓ Ⓔ

24. A modern-day body of law that can be traced to the early law merchant is

(A) the administrative system
(B) the Uniform Commercial Code
(C) constitutional law
(D) civil law
(E) the court of equity

Ⓐ Ⓑ Ⓒ Ⓓ Ⓔ

Study Resources

To prepare for the Introductory Business Law exam, you should study the contents of at least one textbook used in business law courses at the college level, focusing on the topics listed in the "Knowledge and Skills Required" section on pages 485-486 and omitting topics that are not included in the section. Most textbooks contain many cases and case problems in addition to text material on theory and principles. Most also contain the complete text of the Uniform Commercial Code and a glossary of law terms. Although most textbooks cover the topics listed in the "Knowledge and Skills Required" section, they may vary somewhat in content, approach, and emphasis. You may therefore wish to consult more than one textbook on the major topics. You can find textbooks used in college level business law courses in many college bookstores. The Internet is another resource you should explore.

Additional suggestions for preparing for CLEP exams are given in Chapter 4.

Principles of Marketing

Description of the Examination

The Principles of Marketing exam covers the material that is commonly taught in a one-semester introductory course in marketing. Such a course is usually known as Basic Marketing, Introduction to Marketing, Fundamentals of Marketing, Marketing, or Marketing Principles. The exam covers the role of marketing in society and within a firm; understanding consumer and organizational markets; marketing strategy planning; the marketing mix; marketing institutions; and other selected topics such as international marketing, ethics, marketing research, services, and not-for-profit marketing. The candidate is also expected to have a basic knowledge of the economic/demographic, social/cultural, political/legal, and technological trends that are important to marketing.

The exam is 90 minutes long and includes approximately 100 multiple-choice questions to be answered in two separately timed 45-minute sections.

Knowledge and Skills Required

Questions on the exam require candidates to demonstrate one or more of the following abilities.

- Knowledge of basic terms used in marketing today

- Understanding, analysis, interpretation, and application of concepts and principles

- Ability to apply knowledge, concepts, and principles to specific situations or problems

- Ability to demonstrate basic computational skills as they relate to marketing

The subject matter of the Principles of Marketing exam is drawn from the following topics.

	Approximate Percent of Examination
5 - 8%	The role of marketing in society, including the historical development of marketing in the United States, marketing in different economic systems, and basic marketing functions
7 - 11%	The role of marketing within a firm, the marketing concept, planning and organization, and the marketing environment (e.g., the political/legal, social/cultural, economic/demographic, and technological environments)
15 - 20%	Consumer and industrial markets, including their demographic and behavioral dimensions, measuring and forecasting demand, and marketing segmentation, targeting, and positioning
40 - 50%	The marketing mix, including product planning and management, pricing policies and methods, channels of distribution, advertising and sales promotion, and sales management
8 - 10%	Marketing institutions, including aspects of the structure of wholesale and retail markets and the role of intermediaries
11 - 14%	Other topics such as international marketing, marketing of services, marketing information and research, ethics, and not-for-profit marketing

Sample Questions

The 32 sample questions that follow are similar to questions on the Principles of Marketing exam, but they do not actually appear on the exam. CLEP exams are designed so that average students completing a course in the subject can usually answer about half the questions correctly.

Before attempting to answer the sample questions, read all the information about the Principles of Marketing exam on the preceding pages. Additional suggestions for preparing for CLEP exams are provided in Chapter 4.

Try to answer correctly as many questions as possible. Then compare your answers with the correct answers, given in Appendix A.

Directions: Each of the questions or incomplete statements below is followed by five suggested answers or completions. Select the one that is best in each case.

1. Which of the following has the greatest influence on the amount of aggregate marketing demand?

   (A) Product supply
   (B) Current level of taxes
   (C) Purchasing power
   (D) Availability of raw materials
   (E) Production cost

   Ⓐ Ⓑ Ⓒ Ⓓ Ⓔ

2. A manufacturer of car batteries, who has been selling through an automotive parts wholesaler to garages and service stations, decides to sell directly to retailers. Which of the following will necessarily occur?

   (A) Elimination of the wholesaler's profit will result in a lower price to the ultimate consumer.
   (B) Elimination of the wholesaler's marketing functions will increase efficiency.
   (C) The total cost of distribution will be reduced because of the elimination of the wholesaler.
   (D) The marketing functions performed by the wholesaler will be eliminated.
   (E) The wholesaler's marketing functions will be shifted to or shared by the manufacturer and the retailer.

   Ⓐ Ⓑ Ⓒ Ⓓ Ⓔ

3. Which of the following strategies for entering the international market would involve the highest risk?

   (A) Joint ventures   (B) Exporting
       (C) Licensing   (D) Direct investment
           (E) Franchising

   Ⓐ Ⓑ Ⓒ Ⓓ Ⓔ

4. For a United States manufacturer of major consumer appliances, the most important leading indicator for forecasting sales is

   (A) automobile sales
   (B) furniture sales
   (C) educational level of consumers
   (D) housing starts
   (E) number of business failures   Ⓐ Ⓑ Ⓒ Ⓓ Ⓔ

5. Which of the following is an example of a societal marketing approach?

   (A) Revamping the sales force training program
   (B) Making constant product improvements
   (C) Recalling voluntarily a product that is rumored to be defective
   (D) Implementing a marketing information system
   (E) Increasing efficiency by improving production facilities

                                            Ⓐ Ⓑ Ⓒ Ⓓ Ⓔ

6. In contrast to a selling orientation, a marketing orientation to business management seeks to

   (A) increase market share by emphasizing promotion
   (B) increase sales volume by lowering price
   (C) lower the cost of distribution by direct marketing
   (D) satisfy the needs of targeted consumers at a profit
   (E) market products that make efficient use of the firm's resources

                                            Ⓐ Ⓑ Ⓒ Ⓓ Ⓔ

7. All of the following are characteristics of services EXCEPT

   (A) intangibility   (B) inconsistency   (C) inseparability
      (D) perishability   (E) inflexibility

                                            Ⓐ Ⓑ Ⓒ Ⓓ Ⓔ

8. A fertilizer manufacturer who traditionally markets to farmers through farm supply dealers and cooperatives decides to sell current products to home gardeners through lawn and garden shops. This decision is an example of

   (A) market penetration   (B) market development
      (C) product development   (D) diversification
         (E) vertical integration   Ⓐ Ⓑ Ⓒ Ⓓ Ⓔ

9. A manufacturer who refuses to sell to dealers its popular line of office copiers unless the dealers also agree to stock the manufacturer's line of paper products would most likely be in violation of which of the following?

   (A) Robinson–Patman Act
   (B) Clayton Act
   (C) Magnusson–Moss Act
   (D) Miller–Tydings Act
   (E) Interstate Commerce Act

   (A) (B) (C) (D) (E)

10. Prior to ultimate consumption, the last member in an indirect distribution channel is the

    (A) retailer   (B) wholesaler   (C) manufacturer
    (D) factor   (E) freight forwarder

    (A) (B) (C) (D) (E)

11. In which of the following situations is the number of buying influences most likely to be greatest?

    (A) A university buys large quantities of paper for computer printers on a regular basis.
    (B) A computer manufacturer is building a new headquarters and is trying to choose a line of office furniture.
    (C) A consumer decides to buy a different brand of potato chips because they are on sale.
    (D) A retail chain is searching for a vendor of lower priced cleaning supplies.
    (E) A purchasing manager has been asked to locate a second source of supply for corrugated shipping cartons.

    (A) (B) (C) (D) (E)

12. If a small firm with many competitors is able to segment the market successfully and develop a unique marketing mix for each target market, the firm will most likely face which of the following kinds of competition?

    (A) Static oligopoly   (B) Oligopoly   (C) Monopoly
    (D) Monopolistic competition   (E) Pure competition

    (A) (B) (C) (D) (E)

13. What price should a retailer charge for an item that costs the retailer $12 if the retailer wants a 25 percent markup on the selling price?

(A) $ 9
(B) $15
(C) $16
(D) $22
(E) It cannot be determined without knowledge of the retailer's
     fixed costs.

(A) (B) (C) (D) (E)

14. Because of demographic shifts in the United States over the last thirty years, marketing strategy planners must take into account the

(A) increase in the number of farm families
(B) increased number of working women
(C) increasing rate of population growth in the "snow belt" states
(D) decline in the number of consumers who are over age 55
(E) decreasing total population

(A) (B) (C) (D) (E)

15. Roy Smith sells sets of encyclopedias door-to-door to families in low-income neighborhoods. Although the encyclopedias are priced above $300, they can be purchased for weekly installments of only $3. Roy's favorite sales pitch is "Would you deny your child a chance to become President of the United States someday just to save $3 per week?" Roy's selling approach appears to be an example of

(A) deceptive advertising
(B) questionable ethics
(C) trade promotion
(D) bait-and-switch pricing
(E) customer-oriented selling

(A) (B) (C) (D) (E)

16. Cooperative advertising is usually undertaken by manufacturers in order to

(A) secure the help of the retailer in promoting a given product
(B) divide responsibilities between the retailers and wholesalers within a channel of distribution
(C) satisfy legal requirements
(D) create a favorable image of a particular industry in the minds of consumers
(E) provide a subsidy for smaller retailers that enables them to match the prices set by chain stores

Ⓐ Ⓑ Ⓒ Ⓓ Ⓔ

17. Which of the following is usually the major DISADVANTAGE of keeping the level of a retail store's inventory low?

(A) Inventory turnover will be slow.
(B) Insurance costs per item will multiply dramatically.
(C) Buyer resistance will increase.
(D) Markups will be low.
(E) Items customers want may frequently be out of stock.

Ⓐ Ⓑ Ⓒ Ⓓ Ⓔ

18. A marketer usually offers a noncumulative quantity discount in order to

(A) reward customers for repeat purchases
(B) reduce advertising expenses
(C) encourage users to purchase in large quantities
(D) encourage buyers to submit payment promptly
(E) ensure the prompt movement of goods through the channel of distribution

Ⓐ Ⓑ Ⓒ Ⓓ Ⓔ

19. A toy manufacturing firm sold its product through a toy wholesaler, who in turn sold to appropriate retailers. The manufacturer's price is $20 to the wholesaler, whose markup is usually 20 percent on the selling price to the retailer. If the retailer's markup on the selling price to the customer is 50 percent, what is the price to the customer?

   (A) $24.00
   (B) $30.00
   (C) $36.00
   (D) $37.50
   (E) $50.00   Ⓐ Ⓑ Ⓒ Ⓓ Ⓔ

20. Missionary salespersons are most likely to do which of the following?

   (A) Sell cosmetics directly to consumers in their own homes
   (B) Explain how air conditioners can be used in cold climates
   (C) Describe drugs and other medical supplies to physicians
   (D) Secure government approval to sell heavy machinery to a foreign
        government
   (E) Take orders for custom-tailored garments or other specially produced
        items

                      Ⓐ Ⓑ Ⓒ Ⓓ Ⓔ

21. The demand for industrial goods is sometimes called "derived" because it depends on

   (A) economic conditions
   (B) demand for consumer goods
   (C) governmental activity
   (D) availability of labor and materials
   (E) the desire to make a profit   Ⓐ Ⓑ Ⓒ Ⓓ Ⓔ

22. Behavioral research generally indicates that consumers' attitudes

   (A) do not usually change very easily or quickly
   (B) are usually very easy to change through promotion
   (C) cannot ever be changed
   (D) can only be developed through actual experience with products
   (E) are very accurate predictors of actual purchasing behavior

                      Ⓐ Ⓑ Ⓒ Ⓓ Ⓔ

23. A channel of distribution refers to the

    (A) routing of goods through distribution centers
    (B) sequence of marketing intermediaries from producer to consumer
    (C) methods of transporting goods from producer to consumer
    (D) marketing intermediaries who perform a variety of functions
    (E) traditional handlers of a product line

    Ⓐ Ⓑ Ⓒ Ⓓ Ⓔ

24. A major advantage of distributing products by truck is

    (A) speed relative to rail or air
    (B) low probability of loss or damage to cargo
    (C) accessibility to pick-up and delivery locations
    (D) low cost relative to rail or water
    (E) ability to handle a wider variety of products than other means

    Ⓐ Ⓑ Ⓒ Ⓓ Ⓔ

25. If a firm is using penetration pricing for its new product, the firm is most likely trying to achieve which of the following pricing objectives?

    (A) Product quality leadership
    (B) Market-share maximization
    (C) High gross margin
    (D) Status quo
    (E) Geographic flexibility

    Ⓐ Ⓑ Ⓒ Ⓓ Ⓔ

26. The basic marketing functions include all of the following EXCEPT

    (A) transporting and storing
    (B) producing and consuming
    (C) buying and selling
    (D) standardization and grading
    (E) financing and risk-taking

    Ⓐ Ⓑ Ⓒ Ⓓ Ⓔ

27. The marketer of which of the following products would be most likely to use a promotional mix with a heavy emphasis on personal selling?

    (A) Life insurance   (B) Pencils   (C) Transistor radios
       (D) Bread   (E) Crackers

    Ⓐ Ⓑ Ⓒ Ⓓ Ⓔ

28. When manufacturers attempt to determine differences among buyers that may affect marketing to those buyers, the manufacturers are practicing a policy of

(A) product diversification
(B) product differentiation
(C) product–line maximization
(D) market segmentation
(E) market expansion

Ⓐ Ⓑ Ⓒ Ⓓ Ⓔ

29. Marketing strategy planning consists of

(A) supervising the activities of the firm's sales force
(B) determining the most efficient way to manufacture products
(C) selecting a target market and developing the marketing mix
(D) redefining the firm's mission and setting its goals
(E) monitoring how customers are responding to the firm's marketing mix

Ⓐ Ⓑ Ⓒ Ⓓ Ⓔ

30. During the early 1990's, in which of the following countries did exports account for the lowest percentage of the country's gross national product?

(A) The United States
(B) The United Kingdom
(C) Saudi Arabia
(D) Japan
(E) The Netherlands

Ⓐ Ⓑ Ⓒ Ⓓ Ⓔ

31. A brand that has achieved brand insistence and is considered a specialty good by the target market suggests which of the following distribution objectives?

(A) Widespread distribution near probable points of use
(B) Limited or exclusive distribution
(C) Intensive distribution
(D) Enough exposure to facilitate price comparison
(E) Widespread distribution at low cost

Ⓐ Ⓑ Ⓒ Ⓓ Ⓔ

32. Market segmentation that is concerned with people over 65 years of age is called

   (A) geographic   (B) socioeconomic   (C) demographic
      (D) psychographic   (E) behavioral

Ⓐ Ⓑ Ⓒ Ⓓ Ⓔ

Study Resources

To prepare for the Principles of Marketing exam, you should study the contents of at least one textbook that covers the basic principles of marketing. When selecting a textbook, check the table of contents against the "Knowledge and Skills Required" section on pages 495-496. Since such textbooks vary in content, approach, and emphasis, you are advised to consult more than one textbook on the major topics. Please note that textbooks are updated frequently; it is important to use the latest editions of the textbooks you choose. Most textbooks now have study guides, computer applications, and case studies to accompany them. These learning aids could prove useful in the understanding and application of marketing concepts and principles. You can find textbooks used for college level marketing courses in most college bookstores.

You can broaden your understanding of marketing principles and their applications by keeping abreast of current developments in the field from articles in newspapers and news magazines as well as in business publications such as *The Wall Street Journal, Business Week, Harvard Business Review, Fortune, Ad Week,* and *Advertising Age.* Journals found in most college libraries that will help you expand your knowledge of marketing principles include *Journal of Marketing, Marketing Today, Journal of the Academy of Marketing Sciences, American Demographics,* and *Marketing Week.* Books of readings, such as *Annual Editions – Marketing,* also are sources of current thinking. The Internet is another resource you could explore.

Additional suggestions for preparing for CLEP exams are given in Chapter 4.

Appendices

Appendix A
Answers to Sample Questions

English Composition

1. D	26. A
2. D	27. B
3. A	28. D
4. E	29. A
5. D	30. B
6. C	31. D
7. B	32. C
8. A	33. B
9. E	34. E
10. C	35. D
11. C	36. C
12. B	37. B
13. B	38. E
14. A	39. D
15. C	40. A
16. D	41. C
17. A	42. D
18. B	43. A
19. D	44. C
20. B	45. B
21. C	46. E
22. B	47. A
23. D	48. E
24. C	49. C
25. E	

Humanities

1. D	
2. E	
3. C	
4. E	
5. A	
6. A	
7. C	
8. E	
9. A	
10. E	
11. D	
12. B	
13. A	
14. D	
15. B	
16. A	
17. E	
18. E	
19. A	
20. D	
21. C	
22. D	
23. B	
24. B	
25. A	

College Mathematics

1. B	
2. B	
3. C	
4. D	
5. B	
6. C	
7. C	
8. B	
9. C	
10. A	
11. C	
12. D	
13. B	
14. B	
15. B	
16. C	
17. A	
18. D	
19. B	
20. D	

Natural Sciences

1. D	
2. E	
3. E	
4. B	
5. D	
6. C	
7. A	
8. D	
9. C	
10. C	
11. D	
12. A	
13. C	
14. C	
15. E	
16. B	
17. C	
18. A	
19. D	
20. A	
21. A	
22. B	
23. B	
24. C	
25. A	

Social Sciences and History

1. E	26. C
2. E	27. A
3. A	28. D
4. B	29. B
5. D	30. D
6. C	31. B
7. A	32. A
8. E	33. D
9. A	34. A
10. B	35. B
11. C	36. B
12. D	37. D
13. D	38. C
14. D	39. E
15. C	40. C
16. D	
17. B	
18. C	
19. C	
20. D	
21. A	
22. C	
23. E	
24. C	
25. E	

American Literature

1. B	
2. A	
3. B	
4. D	
5. A	
6. D	
7. E	
8. B	
9. B	
10. E	
11. D	
12. C	
13. A	
14. C	
15. E	
16. E	
17. B	
18. C	
19. D	
20. A	
21. B	
22. A	
23. B	

Analyzing and Interpreting Literature

1. C	26. B
2. C	27. A
3. B	28. B
4. E	29. C
5. C	30. D
6. E	31. A
7. A	32. E
8. C	33. C
9. A	34. D
10. D	35. C
11. B	36. B
12. C	37. C
13. B	38. A
14. E	
15. E	
16. A	
17. A	
18. C	
19. B	
20. A	
21. A	
22. E	
23. D	
24. C	
25. E	

English Literature

1. C	
2. C	
3. D	
4. D	
5. A	
6. C	
7. A	
8. E	
9. A	
10. C	
11. A	
12. D	
13. B	
14. E	
15. E	
16. A	
17. C	
18. C	
19. C	
20. B	
21. D	
22. B	
23. E	
24. A	
25. A	
26. B	

Freshman College Composition

1. D	26. B		
2. D	27. D		
3. C	28. A		
4. E	29. A		
5. D	30. B		
6. C	31. E		
7. B	32. E		
8. B	33. C		
9. A	34. D		
10. D	35. A		
11. B	36. B		
12. B	37. B		
13. A	38. E		
14. C	39. A		
15. D	40. E		
16. D	41. C		
17. C	42. A		
18. B	43. C		
19. B	44. C		
20. C	45. A		
21. B	46. D		
22. D	47. A		
23. C	48. E		
24. E	49. B		
25. A	50. E		

College French — Levels 1 and 2

1. A	26. C
2. C	27. A
3. B	28. B
4. D	29. C
5. A	30. C
6. A	31. D
7. B	32. A
8. A	33. D
9. B	34. C
10. A	35. B
11. C	
12. B	
13. D	
14. D	
15. B	
16. D	
17. C	
18. C	
19. C	
20. A	
21. D	
22. A	
23. B	
24. A	
25. D	

College Level German Language

1. C	26. C
2. C	27. D
3. B	28. B
4. A	29. D
5. D	30. C
6. C	31. A
7. C	32. A
8. D	33. A
9. C	34. D
10. C	35. B
11. B	36. A
12. B	37. C
13. C	38. D
14. D	
15. D	
16. C	
17. A	
18. B	
19. C	
20. A	
21. D	
22. B	
23. A	
24. D	
25. B	

College Level Spanish Language

1. B	26. B
2. C	27. B
3. D	28. D
4. C	29. B
5. C	30. C
6. A	31. D
7. C	32. C
8. A	33. B
9. A	34. C
10. D	35. A
11. B	
12. D	
13. B	
14. B	
15. D	
16. D	
17. B	
18. A	
19. D	
20. A	
21. B	
22. A	
23. A	
24. C	
25. A	

American Government

1. C	26. C
2. B	27. E
3. B	28. C
4. D	29. C
5. B	30. D
6. B	31. A
7. A	32. B
8. C	33. B
9. C	34. A
10. C	35. A
11. B	36. D
12. E	37. E
13. D	38. C
14. C	39. A
15. C	40. D
16. E	
17. E	
18. A	
19. A	
20. C	
21. A	
22. C	
23. D	
24. A	
25. B	

American History I: Early Colonizations to 1877

1. B	26. E
2. B	27. D
3. A	28. D
4. E	29. D
5. B	30. E
6. B	31. E
7. A	32. A
8. E	33. C
9. D	34. C
10. D	35. D
11. E	36. B
12. E	37. B
13. D	38. A
14. B	39. B
15. B	40. C
16. C	
17. C	
18. B	
19. C	
20. E	
21. A	
22. D	
23. C	
24. D	
25. A	

History of the United States II: 1865 to the Present

1. C	26. E
2. A	27. D
3. E	28. C
4. A	29. E
5. B	30. A
6. E	31. A
7. C	32. B
8. A	33. C
9. E	34. A
10. B	35. D
11. A	36. D
12. D	37. E
13. A	38. B
14. D	39. C
15. B	40. A
16. A	
17. C	
18. A	
19. D	
20. B	
21. E	
22. E	
23. E	
24. A	
25. B	

Human Growth and Development

1. D
2. E
3. B
4. E
5. C
6. C
7. D
8. B
9. A
10. D
11. A
12. E
13. E
14. C
15. B
16. E
17. C
18. E
19. B
20. D
21. A
22. B
23. C
24. B
25. A

Introduction to Educational Psychology

1. B
2. A
3. B
4. D
5. E
6. D
7. B
8. B
9. C
10. D
11. C
12. E
13. B
14. D
15. A
16. D
17. E
18. A
19. B
20. B
21. A
22. D
23. B
24. C
25. A

Principles of Macroeconomics

1. C
2. D
3. B
4. C
5. A
6. E
7. D
8. B
9. D
10. E
11. C
12. C
13. B
14. A
15. C
16. B
17. D
18. E
19. A
20. E
21. C
22. B
23. A
24. B
25. D

26. A
27. B
28. E
29. D
30. A
31. A
32. E
33. C
34. D
35. A
36. A
37. B
38. A
39. B

Principles of Microeconomics

1. A
2. C
3. A
4. E
5. A
6. D
7. C
8. D
9. E
10. B
11. C
12. E
13. A
14. A
15. E
16. D
17. D
18. B
19. C
20. C
21. D
22. E
23. D
24. B
25. D

26. D
27. A
28. B
29. C
30. B
31. D
32. E
33. E
34. B
35. C
36. E
37. B
38. E
39. B

Introductory Psychology

1. E
2. C
3. C
4. D
5. E
6. B
7. D
8. A
9. C
10. C
11. B
12. E
13. A
14. B
15. A
16. A
17. D
18. C
19. E
20. A
21. B
22. C
23. B
24. A
25. D

26. C
27. D
28. B
29. E
30. E
31. A
32. D
33. E
34. D
35. B

Introductory Sociology

1. C
2. C
3. A
4. B
5. D
6. E
7. B
8. D
9. C
10. E
11. A
12. A
13. C
14. D
15. A
16. D
17. B
18. B
19. E
20. C

Western Civilization I: Ancient Near East to 1648

1. D
2. A
3. A
4. C
5. E
6. A
7. A
8. B
9. A
10. C
11. E
12. D
13. E
14. A
15. B
16. A
17. D
18. C
19. B
20. E
21. D
22. D
23. B
24. E
25. C

Western Civilization II: 1648 to the Present

1. C
2. E
3. A
4. D
5. D
6. E
7. D
8. A
9. A
10. E
11. B
12. A
13. E
14. A
15. E
16. D
17. D
18. C
19. E
20. B
21. C
22. E
23. A
24. B
25. C

Calculus with Elementary Functions

1. C
2. B
3. B
4. E
5. C
6. E
7. C
8. B
9. D
10. B
11. B
12. D
13. C
14. A
15. D
16. B
17. D
18. E
19. D
20. A
21. B
22. A
23. B
24. A
25. B

College Algebra

1.	C	26.	E
2.	D	27.	D
3.	B	28.	A
4.	D		
5.	E		
6.	B		
7.	D		
8.	E		
9.	E		
10.	D		
11.	E		
12.	C		
13.	B		
14.	A		
15.	A		
16.	C		
17.	C		
18.	B		
19.	B		
20.	B		
21.	C		
22.	E		
23.	C		
24.	A		
25.	D		

Trigonometry

1.	A
2.	B
3.	C
4.	E
5.	B
6.	D
7.	B
8.	C
9.	D
10.	B
11.	D
12.	C
13.	E
14.	D
15.	C
16.	C
17.	E
18.	C
19.	A
20.	C
21.	B
22.	C
23.	A
24.	E
25.	D

General Biology

1.	E
2.	E
3.	A
4.	C
5.	D
6.	E
7.	E
8.	C
9.	C
10.	C
11.	C
12.	D
13.	A
14.	D
15.	B
16.	D
17.	A
18.	C
19.	B
20.	A
21.	B
22.	C
23.	C
24.	E
25.	B

General Chemistry

1.	B	26.	A
2.	E	27.	A
3.	B	28.	D
4.	E	29.	B
5.	D	30.	C
6.	C	31.	C
7.	C	32.	E
8.	A	33.	E
9.	B	34.	A
10.	C	35.	B
11.	D	36.	D
12.	D	37.	A
13.	C	38.	D
14.	E	39.	E
15.	E	40.	B
16.	B	41.	B
17.	A	42.	E
18.	A	43.	E
19.	E	44.	C
20.	A	45.	D
21.	C	46.	E
22.	D		
23.	D		
24.	C		
25.	E		

Information Systems and Computer Applications

1.	D
2.	D
3.	D
4.	B
5.	C
6.	A
7.	A
8.	D
9.	C
10.	E
11.	B
12.	C
13.	B
14.	E
15.	D
16.	B
17.	C
18.	D
19.	D
20.	B

Principles of Management

1.	C
2.	B
3.	E
4.	D
5.	D
6.	E
7.	A
8.	D
9.	E
10.	C
11.	A
12.	D
13.	A
14.	D
15.	D
16.	B
17.	E
18.	D
19.	A
20.	B
21.	D
22.	B
23.	D
24.	C

Principles of Accounting

1.	D
2.	E
3.	E
4.	A
5.	E
6.	B
7.	A
8.	C
9.	E
10.	C
11.	D
12.	D
13.	C
14.	E
15.	B
16.	A
17.	E
18.	E
19.	C
20.	E
21.	A
22.	B
23.	A
24.	D
25.	B

Introductory Business Law

1.	A
2.	C
3.	B
4.	D
5.	B
6.	D
7.	E
8.	D
9.	B
10.	C
11.	D
12.	A
13.	D
14.	A
15.	E
16.	A
17.	C
18.	A
19.	E
20.	E
21.	C
22.	B
23.	A
24.	B

Principles of Marketing

1.	C	26.	B
2.	E	27.	A
3.	D	28.	D
4.	D	29.	C
5.	C	30.	A
6.	D	31.	B
7.	E	32.	C
8.	B		
9.	B		
10.	A		
11.	B		
12.	D		
13.	C		
14.	B		
15.	B		
16.	A		
17.	E		
18.	C		
19.	E		
20.	C		
21.	B		
22.	A		
23.	B		
24.	C		
25.	B		

Appendix B
Sample Answer Sheet

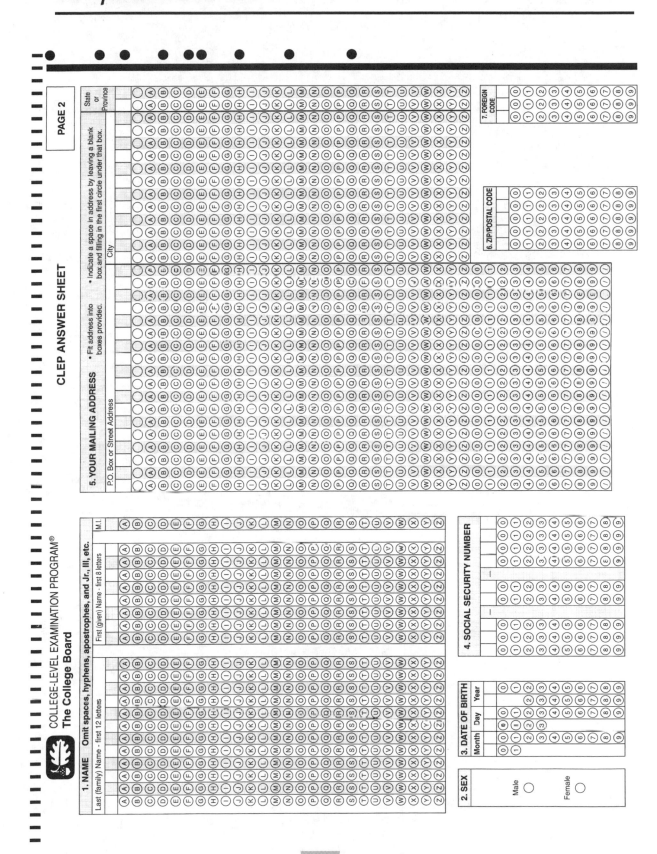

ANSWER SHEET

PAGE 3

Be sure each mark is dark and completely fills the intended circle. If you erase, do so completely. Mark your answers to both Section 1 and Section 2 on this page. If there are more circles than test questions, leave the extra circles blank.

(Answer grid: questions 1–150, each with circles A B C D E)

8. CURRENT EDUCATION LEVEL

1. High School
2. High School Graduate
3. College Freshman
4. College Sophomore
5. College Junior
6. College Senior
7. College Graduate

9. ETHNIC GROUP
How would you describe yourself?

1. Native American/American Indian
2. Black or African American
3. Mexican American or Chicano
4. Asian, Asian American, or Pacific Islander
5. Puerto Rican
6. Latin American, South American, Central American, or other Hispanic
7. White
8. Other

10. Do you understand English at least as well as any other language?

○ Yes   ○ No

11. Mark here if you have a disability.

○

12. How did you find out about CLEP?

○ College Counselor
○ Admissions Office
○ Friend/Word-of-mouth
○ Employer
○ Other

13. TEST CENTER CODE

14. SCORE REPORT RECIPIENT

If you do not have the code number, write 9999 in the boxes, fill in the appropriate circles, and print the institution's name and address.

CODE   Institution

NAME

STREET

CITY

STATE

ZIP CODE

16. DANTES FUNDED CIVILIAN USE ONLY

15. FEES PAID

Examination Fee   ○

Total Paid $

17. Are you taking the optional essay portion of this examination?

○ Yes   ○ No

18. Examination Name (Print)

Form Designation (Print)

19. TEST DATE

Month Day Year

20. TEST CODE

21. TEST BOOK

SERIAL NUMBER

22. SIGNATURE AND DATE

I accept the conditions set forth with the CLEP registration information concerning the administration of the tests and reporting of scores.

Today's Date

Appendix C
List of Participating Colleges and Universities

Following is a list by city and state of institutions that grant credit for satisfactory scores on one or more CLEP exams. This list was current at the time of publication. Each college is assigned a four-digit code number by CLEP, which appears to the left of the college's name. Use this number when you are designating a college to receive your exam scores to speed the process.

For a free copy of CLEP Colleges, which contains an up-to-date list of test centers and their address, write to or call: CLEP, P.O. Box 6601, Princeton, NJ 08541-6601; (609) 771-7865.

ALABAMA

Alexander City
1037 Central Alabama Community College

Andalusia
1429 Lurleen B Wallace State Junior College

Anniston
3334 Harry M. Ayers State Technical College

Athens
1024 Athens State College

Auburn University
1005 Auburn University

Bay Minette
1939 James H Faulkner State Community College

Bessemer
3231 Bessemer State Technical College

Birmingham
7089 Andrew Jackson University
1064 Birmingham – Southern College
1352 Jefferson State Community College
1933 Lawson State Community College
1302 Samford University
1723 Southeastern Bible College
1856 University of Alabama in Birmingham

Boaz
1721 Snead State Community College

Decatur
1356 Calhoun Community College

Dothan
1824 Troy State University
1264 Wallace College – Dothan

Enterprise
1213 Enterprise State Junior College

Fayette
1038 Bevill State Community College

Florence
1735 University of North Alabama

Gadsden
1262 Gadsden State Community College

Hanceville
3685 Wallace State College

Huntsville
1586 Oakwood College
1854 University of Alabama – Huntsville

Jacksonville
1736 Jacksonville State University

Jasper
7965 Uab Walker College

Livingston
1737 University West Alabama

Marion
1349 Judson College

Mobile
1517 S D. Bishop State Junior College
1733 Spring Hill College
1515 University Mobile
1880 University South Alabama

Montevallo
1004 University of Montevallo

Montgomery
1006 Alabama State University
1036 Auburn University at Montgomery
1034 Faulkner University
1303 Huntingdon College
1798 Troy State University – Montgomery

Muscle Shoals
7650 Northwest – Shoals Community College

Normal
1003 Alabama A & M University

Phil Campbell
1577 Northwest Alabama Community College

Phoenix City
7189 Chattahoochee Valley Community College
7849 Troy State University

Rainsville
1576 North East Alabama State Community College

Selma
3146 Wallace State Community College

Troy
1738 Troy State University

Tuscaloosa
3330 Shelton State Community College – Fredd Campus
3338 Shelton State Community College
1830 University of Alabama

Tuskegee
1813 Tuskegee University

Wadley
1728 Southern Union State College

ALASKA

Anchorage
4201 Alaska Pacific University
4896 University of Alaska – Anchorage
7866 Wayland Baptist University

Barrow
469 Arctic Sivunmun Ilisagvik

Bethel
4370 University of Alaska – Fairbanks Kuskokwim

Dillingham
7949 Bristol Bay Campus – University of Alaska

Fairbanks
4866 University of Alaska Fairbanks
7656 University of Alaska Fairbanks

Juneau
4897 University of Alaska Juneau – Southeast

Ketchikan
4379 University Alaska Southeast – Ketchikan

Kodiak
4372 University of Alaska – Kodiak College

Nome
4545 University Alaska – Northwest Campus

Sitka
4742 Sheldon Jackson College
4754 University of Alaska – Southeast Sitka

Soldotna
4373 University of Alaska – Kenai Peninsula

Unalaska
7884 University Alaska – Aleutian Program

Valdez
4636 Prince William Sound Community College

ARIZONA

Coolidge
4122 Central Arizona College

Douglas
4097 Cochise College

Flagstaff
4006 Northern Arizona University

Glendale
7057 American Graduate School of International Management
4003 American Graduate School of International Management
4338 Glendale Community College

Holbrook
325 Northland Pioneer College

Kingman
4495 Mohave County Community College

Mesa
4513 Mesa Community College

Phoenix
4223 Arizona College of the Bible
4518 Gateway Community College
4331 Grand Canyon University
4594 Ottawa University
4606 Phoenix College
4904 Rio Salado Community College
0997 Rio Salado Community College
4734 South Mountain Community College
4911 University Phoenix
1316 Western International University

Prescott
4305 Embry – Riddle Aeronautical University – Arizona
4996 Yavapai College

Scottsdale
4755 Scottsdale Community College
7563 Southwest College Naturpath Med

Tempe
4007 Arizona State University

Thatcher
4297 Eastern Arizona College

Tsaile
4550 Navajo Community College

Tucson
4622 Pima Community College – Downtown
4832 University of Arizona
4913 University of Phoenix – Tucson

Yuma
4013 Arizona Western College

ARKANSAS

Arkadelphia
6272 Henderson State University
6549 Ouachita Baptist University

Batesville
6009 Arkansas College

Beebe
6026 Arkansas State University – Beebe

Bentonville
7686 Northwest Arkansas Community College

Blytheville
6447 Mississippi County Community College

Camden
6704 Southern Arkansas University Technical

Clarksville
6111 University of the Ozarks

Conway
6273 Hendrix College
6012 University of Central Arkansas

De Queen
7141 Cossatot Technical College

El Dorado
6697 South Arkansas Community College

Fayetteville
6866 University Arkansas Fayetteville

Forrest City
6207 East Arkansas Community College

Fort Smith
6220 Westark Community College

Harrison
6517 North Arkansas Community College

Helena
6583 Phillips County Community College

Hot Springs
6243 Garland County Community College

Little Rock
6753 Arkansas Baptist College
6578 Philander Smith College
6368 University of Arkansas – Little Rock

Magnolia
6661 Southern Arkansas University

Malvern
6539 Ouachita Technical College

Mena
7746 Rich Mountain Community College

Monticello
6007 University of Arkansas – Monticello

North Little Rock
6649 Shorter College

Paragould
6131 Crowley's Ridge College

Pine Bluff
6004 University Arkansas – Pine Bluff

Russellville
6010 Arkansas Technical University

Searcy
6267 Harding University

Siloam Springs
6321 John Brown University

State University
6011 Arkansas State University

Walnut Ridge
6658 Williams Baptist College

CALIFORNIA

Angwin
4600 Pacific Union College

Arcata
4345 Humboldt State University

Atherton
4483 Menlo College

Azusa
4596 Azusa Pacific University

Bakersfield
4015 Bakersfield College
4110 California State University – Bakersfield

Barstow
4020 Barstow Community College

Belmont
4063 College Notre Dame

Berkeley
4008 Armstrong University

Burbank
4955 Woodbury University

Calexico
4743 San Diego State University

Camarillo
4673 Saint John's Seminary/College

Carlsbad
7072 Army & Navy Academy

Carson
4098 California State University – Dominguez Hills

Chico
4048 California State University Chico

Chula Vista
4726 Southwestern College

Claremont
4693 Scripps College

Coalinga
4056 West Hills Community College

Costa Mesa
4701 Southern California College

Diamond Bar
7939 University Phoenix – Diamond Bar

El Cajon
4150 Christian Heritage College

Emeryville
7264 Educational Testing Service

Fountain Valley
4822 University Phoenix – South California

Fresno
4123 California Christian College
4312 California State University – Fresno
4311 Fresno City College
4616 Fresno Pacific College
7675 Oak Brook College Law & Gov Policy
4748 San Joaquin College of Law

Fullerton
4589 California State University – Fullerton
4614 Pacific Christian College
7969 Western State University – College of Law

Gardena
7848 University Phoenix – Gardena

Gilroy
4678 Gavilan College

Glendale
7409 Glendale University College of Law

Glendora
4051 Citrus College

Hayward
4011 California State University Hayward

Inglewood
7957 University West Los Angeles – Paralegal

Irvine
4069 Concordia University
7638 National University

Kentfield
4061 College Marin

La Mesa
4254 Coleman College

La Mirada
4017 Biola University

La Verne
4381 University La Verne
7897 University La Verne – Vandenberg

Lancaster
4005 Antelope Valley College

Loma Linda
4062 Loma Linda University

Long Beach
4389 California State University – Long Beach
7134 California State University – Long Beach
7176 California State University – Long Beach

Los Altos Hills
4315 Foothill College

Los Angeles
4399 California State University – Los Angeles
7165 Committee of Bar Examiners of California
4391 Los Angeles City College
4493 Mount Saint Mary's College – Chalon
4966 West Coast University – Main Campus

Malibu
4326 Pepperdine University/Seaver

Marina Del Ray
7071 Antioch University – Los Angeles
4210 Antioch University – Los Angeles

Marysville
4994 Yuba Community College

McClellan
7289 Embry – Riddle Aeron University – California

Merced
4500 Merced College

Mission Viejo
4747 Saddleback College

Monterey
4507 Monterey Institute International Study
4490 Monterey Peninsula College

Moraga
4675 Saint Mary's College

Mountain View
7706 Peninsula University College of Law

Napa
4530 Napa Valley College

National City
7181 California College for Health & Science

Northridge
4707 California State University – Northridge

Oakland
4059 Holy Names College
4485 Mills College
4620 Patten College
4750 Samuel Merritt College of Nursing

Oceanside
4582 Mira Costa College

Ontario
7918 University Phoenix – Ontario

Orange
4139 Chapman College
4047 Chapman University

Orinda
4365 John F. Kennedy University

Oroville
4226 Butte Community College

Oxnard
4591 Oxnard College

Palm Desert
4085 College of the Desert

Pasadena
4612 Pacific Oaks College

Pleasanton
4917 University Phoenix – North California

Point Mugu
4812 University La Verne

Pomona
4082 California State Polytechnic University – Pomona

Porterville
4608 Porterville College

Quincy
4318 Feather River College

Rancho Cucamonga
4046 Chaffey College

Rancho Palos Verde
4515 Marymount College

Redding
4698 Simpson College

Redlands
4368 Johnston Center University Redlands
4848 University Redlands – Whitehead

Redwood City
4109 Canada College

Ridgecrest
4027 Cerro Coso Community College

Riverside
4094 California Baptist College
4380 La Sierra University
4839 University of California Riverside

Rohnert Park
4723 Sonoma State University

Sacramento
4004 American River College
7142 California State Board Accountancy
4671 California State University –
    Sacramento
7178 California State University –
    Sacramento
4121 Cosumnes River College
4320 Golden Gate University
4556 National University
4670 Sacramento City College
7653 University Phoenix – Sacramento

Salinas
4340 Hartnell College

San Bernardino
4099 California State University –
    San Bernardino

San Diego
4735 Mesa College
4557 National University
4559 National University
4558 National University – Inglewood
7641 National University – Vista
4605 Point Loma Nazarene College
4681 San Diego City College
4728 San Diego Miramar College
4682 San Diego State University
7874 Union Institute
4039 U.S. International University – San
    Diego
7876 University Phoenix – San Diego
4849 University of San Diego

San Francisco
4052 City College of San Francisco
4329 Golden Gate University
4555 New College of California
4036 San Francisco Art Institute
4765 San Francisco College of Mortuary
    Science
4744 San Francisco Conservatory of
    Music
4684 San Francisco State University
7986 University Phoenix – On Line
7923 University Phoenix – San Francisco
4850 University San Francisco

San Jacinto
4501 Mount San Jacinto College

San Jose
4273 Evergreen Valley College
4386 Lincoln Law School of San Jose
4613 Palmer College of Chiropractic –
    West
4756 San Jose Christian College
4687 San Jose State University
4914 University Phoenix – San Jose

San Marcos
4602 Palomar College

San Rafael
4284 Dominican College of San Rafael

Santa Ana
4689 Rancho Santiago College
4703 William Howard Taft University

Santa Barbara
7586 Antioch University Santa Barbara
4228 Brooks Institute of Photography
4950 Westmont College

Santa Clara
7587 Mission College

Santa Clarita
4117 College of the Canyons
4411 Masters College

Santa Cruz
4021 Bethany Bible College

Santa Maria
4002 Allan Hancock College

Santa Rosa
4275 Empire College School of Law

Saratoga
4958 West Valley College

Stockton
4346 Humphreys College
4706 San Joaquin Delta College
4065 University of the Pacific

Suisun
4930 Solano Community College

Sunnyvale
4057 Cogswell Polytechnic College

Thousand Oaks
4088 California Lutheran University

Turlock
4713 California State University –
    Stanislas

Vallejo
4035 California Maritime Academy

Van Nuys
7881 University Phoenix – Van Nuys

Ventura
7983 Ventura College of Law

Victorville
4932 Victor Valley College

Walnut
4194 Mount San Antonio College

Whittier
4663 Rio Hondo College

Wilmington
4395 Los Angeles Harbor College

Woodland Hills
4398 Pierce College

Yucaipa
4126 Crafton Hills College

COLORADO

Alamosa
4001 Adams State College

Aspen
4102 Colorado Mountain College

Aurora
4132 Columbia College

Boulder
3342 Naropa Institute
4841 University of Colorado – Boulder

Breckenridge
4124 Colorado Mountain College

Carbondale
4107 Colorado Mountain College

Colorado Springs
4022 Beth – El College of Nursing
4133 Colorado Technical University
4291 Pikes Peak Community College
4666 Regis University
4874 University of Colorado – Colorado
    Springs

Craig
7218 Colorado Northwestern Community
    College

Denver
4137 Community College Denver
4505 Metropolitan State College
4656 Regis University
4877 University Colorado – Health Science

4875 University Colorado – Denver
4842 University Denver

Durango
4310 Fort Lewis College

Eagle
7137 Colorado Mountain College

Englewood
4918 University Phoenix – Colorado

Fort Collins
4075 Colorado State University

Fort Morgan
4516 Morgan Community College

Glenwood Springs
4112 Colorado Mountain College
4120 Colorado Mountain College

Grand Junction
7114 Colorado Christian University
4484 Mesa State College

Greeley
4204 Aims Community College
4074 University Northern Colorado

Gunnison
4946 Western State College

La Junta
4588 Otero Junior College

Lakewood
4659 Colorado Christian University
4130 Red Rocks Community College

Lamar
4382 Lamar Community College

Leadville
4113 Colorado Mountain College

Littleton
4014 Arapahoe Community College

Pueblo
4634 Pueblo Community College
4611 University Southern Colorado

Rangely
4665 Colorado Northwestern Community
    College

Rifle
7145 Colorado Mountain College

Steamboat Springs
4140 Colorado Mountain College – Alpine

Sterling
4537 Northeastern Junior College

Trinidad
4821 Trinidad State Junior College

Vail
7140 Colorado Mountain College

Westminster
4119 Front Range Community College

CONNECTICUT

Bridgeport
3446 Housatonic Community-Technical
    College
3789 Saint Vincents College
3914 University of Bridgeport

Cromwell
3439 Holy Apostles College

Danbury
3350 Western Connecticut State University

Danielson
3716 Quinebaug Vall Community-
    Technical College

Enfield
3656 Asnuntuck Community-Technical
    College

Fairfield
3093 Bridgeport Engineering Institute
3390 Fairfield University
3780 Sacred Heart University

Farmington
3897 Tunxis Community-Technical
    College

Hamden
3699 Paier College of Art
3712 Quinnipiac College

Hartford
3421 Capitol Community Technical
    College
3539 Morse School of Business
3431 University of Hartford

Manchester
3544 Manchester Community-Technical
    College

Middletown
3551 Middlesex Community-Technical
    College
3556 Wilcox College of Nursing

New Britain
3898 Central Connecticut State
    University

New Haven
3001 Albertus Magnus College
3792 Gateway Community Technical
    College
3662 Southern Connecticut State
    University

New London
3528 Mitchell College
7944 University New Haven – Southeast
    Connecticut

Newington
3292 Charter Oak State College

North Haven
3425 Gateway Community Technical
    College

Norwalk
3470 Katherine Gibbs School
3677 Norwalk Community Technical
    College

Norwich
3558 Three Rivers Community-Technical
    College

Waterbury
3550 Naugatuck Vall Community
    Technical College
3698 Teikyo – Post University

West Hartford
3754 Saint Joseph College
3436 University Hartford
3299 University Hartford – Basic Study

West Haven
3663 University New Haven

Willimantic
3966 Eastern Connecticut State
    University

Winsted
3652 Northwestern County Community
    College

DELAWARE

Dover
5201 Delaware Technical & Community College
5326 Kent Christian College
5894 Wesley College

Georgetown
5169 Delaware Technical Community College – Southern
5431 Macqueen Gibbs Willis

New Castle
5925 Wilmington College

Newark
5204 Delaware Technical & Community College

Wilmington
5154 Delaware Technical & Community College
5255 Goldey – Beacon College
5081 Widener University – University College of Delaware

DISTRICT OF COLUMBIA

Washington
5007 American University
5240 Gallaudet University
5246 George Washington University
5422 Mount Vernon College
5632 Strayer College
7836 Strayer College – Takoma Park
5796 Trinity College
5929 University District of Columbia

FLORIDA

Avon Park
5666 South Florida Community College

Babson Park
5893 Webber College

Boca Raton
5229 Florida Atlantic University
5437 Lynn University

Bradenton
5427 Manatee Junior College

Brandon
7434 Hillsborough Community College

Clearwater
5142 Clearwater Christian College

Cocoa
5073 Brevard Community College

Coral Gables
5815 University of Miami

Dade City
5562 Pasco – Hernando Community College East

Daytona Beach
5061 Bethune-Cookman College
5159 Daytona Beach Community College

Deland
5630 Stetson University

Eglin
7858 Saint Leo College

Fort Lauderdale
5074 Broward Community College
5171 Fort Lauderdale College
5514 Nova Southeastern University

Fort Myers
5191 Edison Community College
7333 International College

Fort Pierce
5322 Indian River Community College

Fort Walton Beach
5791 Troy State University

Gainesville
5653 Santa Fe Community College
7829 Saint Leo College at Santa Fe Community College
5812 University of Florida

Graceville
5386 Florida Baptist Theological College

Haines City
5388 Landmark Baptist College

Hobe Sound
5306 Hobe Sound Bible College

Jacksonville
5182 Edward Waters College
5232 Florida Community College – Jacksonville
5331 Jacksonville University
5343 Jones College
5490 University North Florida

Key West
5236 Florida Keys Community College
7859 Saint Leo College

Lake City
5377 Lake City Community College

Lake Wales
5883 Warner Southern College

Lake Worth
5531 Palm Beach Community College

Lakeland
5218 Florida Southern College
5621 Southeastern College

Leesburg
5376 Lake-Sumter Community College

Macdill
7861 Saint Leo College

Madison
5503 North Florida Community College

Marianna
5106 Chipola Junior College

Melbourne
5080 Florida Institute Technology

Miami
5217 Florida Memorial College
5327 International Fine Arts College
5465 Miami – Dade Community College – Medical Center
5160 Miami – Dade Community College – North
5458 Miami – Dade Community College – South
5457 Miami – Dade Community College – Wolfson
5650 Saint John Vianney College Seminary
5076 Saint Thomas University
5463 Trinity International University

Miami Shores
5053 Barry University

Miramare
5202 Florida Bible College

Naples
7334 International College

New Port Richey
5559 Pasco-Hernado Community College

Niceville
5526 Okaloosa-Walton Community College

Ocala
5127 Central Florida Community College
7865 Saint Leo College

Orlando
7338 Florida Hospital College of Health & Science
5679 Southern College
5233 University of Central Florida
5869 Valencia Community College West Campus

Palatka
5641 Saint John's River Community College
7821 Saint Leo College

Panama City
5271 Gulf Coast Community College

Pensacola
5535 Pensacola Junior College
5833 University of West Florida

Saint Augustine
5235 Flagler College

Saint Leo
5638 Saint Leo College
7607 Saint Leo College

Saint Petersburg
5223 Eckerd College
7313 Florida Institute Trad Chinese Medical
7460 International Credentialing Association Incorporated

Sanford
5662 Seminole Community College

Sarasota
5573 Ringling School of Art & Design

Tallahassee
5215 Florida A & M University
5219 Florida State University
5794 Tallahassee Community College

Tampa
5304 Hillsborough Community College
7669 National-Louis University
5828 University South Florida
5819 University of Tampa

Temple Terrace
5216 Florida College

Titusville
5046 Brevard Community College

West Palm Beach
5553 Palm Beach Atlantic College

Winter Haven
5548 Polk Community College

Winter Park
5572 Rollins College

GEORGIA

Albany
5004 Albany State College
5026 Darton College

Americus
5250 Georgia Southwestern College

Athens
5813 University of Georgia

Atlanta
5429 Art Institute of Atlanta
5725 Atlanta Metropolitan College
5110 Clark Atlanta University
5187 Emory University
5247 Georgia Baptist College of Nursing
5251 Georgia State University
5417 Morris Brown College
7676 National-Louis University
7736 Office of Bar Admissions
5521 Oglethorpe University
5628 Spelman College

Augusta
5336 Augusta College
5406 Medical College of Georgia
5530 Paine College

Bainbridge
5062 Bainbridge College

Barnesville
5256 Gordon College

Brunswick
5078 Brunswick College

Carrollton
5900 West Georgia College

Clarkston
5165 DeKalb College
7248 DeKalb Technical Institute

Cleveland
5798 Truett Mcconnell College

Cochran
5411 Middle Georgia College

Columbus
5123 Columbus College

Cuthbert
5009 Andrew College

Dahlonega
5497 North Georgia College

Dalton
5167 Dalton College

Demorest
5537 Piedmont College

Douglas
5619 South Georgia College

East Point
5029 Atlanta Christian College

Fort Benning
5797 Troy State University

Fort McPherson
7879 Saint Leo College

Fort Stewart
7901 Saint Leo College

Fort Valley
5220 Fort Valley State College

Franklin Springs
5184 Emmanuel College

Gainesville
5066 Brena University College
5273 Gainesville College

Kennesaw
5359 Kennesaw State College

LaGrange
5362 LaGrange College

Lookout Mountain
6124 Covenant College

Macon
5439 Macon College
5409 Mercer University
5895 Wesleyan College

Marietta
7006 Life College
5626 Southern College of Technology

Milledgeville
5252 Georgia College
5249 Georgia Military College

Morrow
5145 Clayton State College

Mount Berry
5059 Berry College

Mount Vernon
5068 Brewton-Parker College

Rome
5237 Floyd College

Savannah
5012 Armstrong State College
7903 Saint Leo College
5609 Savannah State College
5157 South College

Statesboro
5253 Georgia Southern University

Thomasville
5072 Thomas College

Tifton
5001 Abraham Baldwin Agriculture
     College

Toccoa Falls
5799 Toccoa Falls College

Valdosta
5855 Valdosta State University

Waleska
5568 Reinhardt College

Waycross
5889 Waycross College

Young Harris
5990 Young Harris College

HAWAII

Hilo
4869 University of Hawaii – Hilo

Honolulu
4324 Cannons Business College
4105 Chaminade University – Honolulu
4352 Hawaii Pacific University
4362 International College
4377 Kapiolani Community College
4867 University of Hawaii-Manoa
7891 University Phoenix – Hawaii

Pearl City
4959 West Oahu University College –
     University of Hawaii

IDAHO

Boise
4018 Boise State University

Caldwell
4060 Albertson College of Idaho

Coeur D'Alene
4539 North Idaho College

Lewiston
4385 Lewis-Clark State College

Moscow
4843 University of Idaho

Nampa
4544 Northwest Nazarene College

Pocatello
4355 Idaho State University

Rexburg
4657 Ricks College

Twin Falls
4114 College of Southern Idaho

ILLINOIS

Arlington Heights
7053 Arlington Heights Memorial Library

Aurora
1027 Aurora University

Belleville
1057 Belleville Area College

Bloomington
1320 Illinois Wesleyan University

Canton
1154 Spoon River College

Carbondale
1726 Southern Illinois University
     Carbondale

Carlinville
1065 Blackburn College

Carterville
1357 John A. Logan College

Contralia
1108 Kaskaskia College

Champaign
1619 Parkland College

Charleston
1199 Eastern Illinois University

Chicago
7153 Chicago National College of
     Naprapathy
1118 Chicago State University
7146 City Colleges of Chicago
1165 De Paul University
1317 Illinois College of Optometry
1486 Moody Bible Institute
1556 North Park College
1090 Northeastern Illinois University
1578 Northwestern University
1670 Robert Morris College
1666 Roosevelt University
3262 Rush University
1713 School of the Art Institute
0697 Saint Augustine College
1708 Saint Xavier University
1851 University Illinois Chicago

Chicago Heights
1077 Prairie State College

Cicero
1489 Morton College

Crystal Lake
1525 McHenry County College

Danville
1160 Danville Area Community College

De Kalb
1559 Northern Illinois University

Decatur
1470 Millikin University
1976 Richland Community College

Deerfield
1810 Trinity International University

Des Plaines
1573 Oakton Community College

Dixon
1780 Sauk Valley Community College

East Peoria
1312 Illinois Central College

East Saint Louis
1749 State Community College

Edwardsville
1759 Southern Illinois University

Elgin
1203 Elgin Community College
1351 Judson College

Elmhurst
1204 Elmhurst College

Elsah
1630 Principia College

Eureka
1206 Eureka College

Evanston
265 Educational Testing Services
1366 Kendall College
1551 National-Louis University

Fairfield
7318 Frontier Community College

Forest Park
7749 Riveredge Hospital

Freeport
1233 Highland Community College –
     Illinois

Galesburg
1982 Carl Sandburg College
1372 Knox College

Glen Ellyn
1083 College of Dupage

Godfrey
1430 Lewis & Clark Community College

Grayslake
1983 College of Lake County

Greenville
1256 Greenville College

Harrisburg
1777 Southeastern Illinois College

Ina
1673 Rend Lake College

Jacksonville
1315 Illinois College
1435 MacMurray College

Joliet
1130 College of Saint Francis
1346 Joliet Junior College

Kankakee
1380 Kankakee Community College
1596 Olivet Nazarene University

Lake Forest
1052 Barat College
1392 Lake Forest College

Lebanon
1456 McKendree College

Lisle
1707 Illinois Benedictine College

Lombard
1567 National College Chiropractic

Macomb
1900 Western Illinois University

Malta
1385 Kishwaukee College

Mattoon
1424 Lake Land College

Moline
1483 Black Hawk College
4426 Trinity College of Nursing

Monmouth
1484 Monmouth College

Mount Carmel
1936 Wabash Valley College

Naperville
1555 North Central College

Normal
1319 Illinois State University

Oglesby
1397 Illinois Valley Community College

Olney
1305 Illinois Eastern Community College

Palatine
1932 William Rainey Harper College

Palos Heights
1820 Trinity Christian College

Palos Hills
1524 Moraine Valley Community College

Peoria
1070 Bradley University
3329 Midstate College

Quincy
1374 John Wood Community College
1645 Quincy University

River Forest
1140 Concordia University
1667 Rosary College

River Grove
1821 Triton College

Rockford
1674 Rock Valley College
1665 Rockford College

Romeoville
1404 Lewis University

South Holland
1806 South Suburban College

Springfield
1428 Lincoln Land Community College
1734 Springfield College Illinois
1787 University Illinois Springfield

Sugar Grove
1938 Waubonsee Community College

Ullin
1683 Shawnee Community College

University Park
1263 Governors State University

Urbana
1836 University of Illinois Champlain/
     Urbana

Wheaton
3259 Illinois Institute of Technology
7672 National-Louis University
1905 Wheaton College

Wilmette
1438 Mallinckrodt College

INDIANA

Anderson
1016 Anderson University

Angola
1811 Tri-State University

Bloomington
1324 Indiana University
7483 Ivy Technical State College – Bloomington

Columbus
1286 Ivy Technical State College – Columbus

Donaldson
1015 Ancilla College

Evansville
1277 Ivy Technical State College – Evansville
1208 University Evansville
1335 University Southern Indiana

Fort Harrison
7937 Vincennes University Extension

Fort Wayne
1323 Indiana Institute Technicalnology
1336 Indiana University – Purdue University
1278 Ivy Technical State College – Fort Wayne
1693 Saint Francis College
1227 Taylor University

Franklin
1228 Franklin College of Indiana

Gary
1338 Indiana University Northwest
1281 Ivy Technical State College – Gary

Goshen
1251 Goshen College

Hammond
1638 Purdue University – Calumet Camps

Huntington
1304 Huntington College

Indianapolis
1073 Butler University
1325 Indiana University – Purdue University
1311 Ivy Technical State College – Indianapolis
1442 Marian College
1321 University Indianapolis

Kokomo
1337 Indiana University at Kokomo
1329 Ivy Technical State College – Kokomo

Lafayette
1282 Ivy Technical State College – Lafayette

Marion
1446 Indiana Wesleyan University

Mishawaka
1079 Bethel College

Muncie
1051 Ball State University
1279 Ivy Technical State College – Muncie

New Albany
7408 Graceland University
1314 Indiana University – Southeast

North Manchester
1440 Manchester College

Notre Dame
1309 Holy Cross College
1702 Saint Mary's College

Oakland City
1585 Oakland City University

Rensselaer
1697 Saint Joseph's College

Richmond
1194 Indiana University – East
1283 Ivy Technical State College – Richmond

Saint Mary Woods
1704 Saint Mary of the Woods College

Saint Meinrad
1705 Saint Meinrad College

Sellersburg
1273 Ivy Technical State College – Sellersburg

South Bend
1339 Indiana University
1280 Ivy Technical State College – South Bend

Terre Haute
1322 Indiana State University
1284 Ivy Technical State College – Terre Haute

Upland
1802 Taylor University

Valparaiso
1873 Valparaiso Technical Institute
1874 Valparaiso University

Vincennes
1877 Vincennes University

West Lafayette
1631 Purdue University – West Lafayette

Westville
1640 Purdue University – North Central

Whiting
1776 Calumet College of Saint Joseph

Winona Lake
1252 Grace College

IOWA

Ames
6306 Iowa State University

Ankeny
6177 Des Moines Area Community College – Ankeny
6214 Faith Baptist Bible College

Bettendorf
6712 Scott Community College – Eastern Iowa

Calmar
6751 Northeast Iowa Community College

Cedar Falls
6307 University of Northern Iowa

Cedar Rapids
6101 Coe College
6027 Kirkwood Community College
6417 Mount Mercy College

Clarina
6098 Iowa Western Community College – Clarinda

Clinton
6100 Clinton Community College
6418 Mount Saint Clare College

Council Bluff
6302 Iowa Western Community College

Creston
6122 Southwestern Community College

Davenport
6617 Saint Ambrose University
6397 Teikyo Marycrest University

Decorah
6375 Luther College

Des Moines
6168 Drake University
6251 Grand View College

Dubuque
6099 Clarke College
1215 Emmaus Bible College
6370 Loras College
6869 University Dubuque

Eagle Grove
6185 Iowa Central Community College – Eagle Grove

Epworth
6174 Divine Word College

Estherville
6195 Iowa Lakes Community College Emmets
6196 Iowa Lakes Community College – Esther

Fairfield
4497 Maharishi University of Management

Fayette
6885 Upper Iowa University

Forest City
6925 Waldorf College

Fort Dodge
6217 Iowa Central Community College – Fort Dodge

Indianola
6650 Simpson College

Iowa City
6681 University of Iowa

Iowa Falls
6193 Ellsworth Community College – Iowa Valley

Keokuk
6340 Southeastern Community College – South

Lamoni
6249 Graceland College

Le Mars
6936 Westmar University

Marshalltown
6394 Marshalltown Community College

Mason City
6400 North Iowa Area Community College

Mount Pleasant
6308 Iowa Wesleyan College

Mount Vernon
6119 Cornell College

Muscatine
6422 Muscatine Community College – Eastern Iowa

Orange City
6490 Northwestern College

Oskaloosa
6943 William Penn College

Ottumwa
6299 Indian Hills Community College
6083 Indian Hills Community College – Centerville

Pella
6087 Central College

Peosta
6754 Northeast Iowa Community College

Sheldon
6504 Northwest Iowa Technical College

Sioux Center
6171 Dordt College

Sioux City
6046 Briar Cliff College
6415 Morningside College
6723 Saint Luke's College of Nursing & Health
6950 Western Iowa Technical Community College

Storm Lake
6047 Buena Vista University

Waterloo
6288 Hawkeye Community College

Waverly
6926 Wartburg College

Webster City
6932 Iowa Central Community College Webster College

West Burlington
6048 Southeastern Community College North

KANSAS

Arkansas City
6008 Cowley County Community College

Atchison
6056 Benedictine College

Chanute
6093 Neosho County Community College

Coffeyville
6102 Coffeyville Community College

Colby
6129 Colby Community College

Concordia
6137 Cloud County Community College

Dodge City
6166 Dodge City Community College

El Dorado
6191 Butler County Community College

Emporia
6335 Emporia State University
6103 Way College of Emporia

Fort Scott
6219 Fort Scott Community College

Garden City
6246 Garden City Community College

Great Bend
6060 Barton County Community College

Haviland
6228 Barclay College

Hays
6218 Fort Hays State University

6274 Hesston College

Highland
6276 Highland Community College

Hillsboro
6815 Tabor College

Hutchinson
6281 Hutchinson Community College

Independence
6304 Independence Community College

Iola
6305 Allen County Community College

Kansas City
6167 Donnelly College
6333 Kansas City Kansas Community College

Lawrence
6871 University of Kansas

Leavenworth
6630 Saint Mary College

Liberal
6714 Seward County Community College

Lindsborg
6034 Bethany College

Manhattan
6334 Kansas State University
6392 Manhattan Christian College

McPherson
6088 Central College
6404 McPherson College

North Newton
6037 Bethel College

Olathe
6437 Mid-America Nazarene College

Ottawa
6547 Ottawa University

Overland Park
6031 Baker University
6325 Johnson County Community College
6548 Ottawa University

Parsons
6576 Labette Community College

Pittsburg
6336 Pittsburg State University

Pratt
6581 Pratt Community College

Salina
6337 Kansas Wesleyan

Sterling
6684 Sterling College

Topeka
6928 Washburn University

Wichita
6224 Friends University
6615 Kansas Newman College
6884 Wichita State University

Winfield
6670 Southwestern College

KENTUCKY

Ashland
1023 Ashland Community College

Barbourville
1825 Union College

Berea
1060 Berea College

Bowling Green
1901 Western Kentucky University

Campbellsville
1097 Campbellsville College

Columbia
1409 Lindsey Wilson College

Crestview Hills
1876 Thomas More College

Danville
1109 Centre College

Elizabethtown
1211 Elizabethtown Community College

Frankfort
1368 Kentucky State University

Georgetown
1249 Georgetown College

Grayson
1377 Kentucky Christian College

Hazard
1275 Hazard Community College

Henderson
1307 Henderson Community College

Highland Height
1574 Northern Kentucky University

Jackson
1402 Lees College

Lexington
1474 Lexington Community College
1837 University of Kentucky

London
1741 Sue Bennett College

Louisville
1056 Bellarmine College
1328 Jefferson Community College
1552 Spalding University
3250 Sullivan College
1838 University of Louisville

Midway
1467 Midway College

Morehead
1487 Morehead State University

Murray
1494 Murray State University

Owensboro
1071 Brescia College
1369 Kentucky Wesleyan College

Pikeville
1625 Pikeville College

Pippa Passes
1098 Alice Lloyd College

Richmond
1200 Eastern Kentucky University

Saint Catharine
1690 Saint Catharine College

Somerset
1779 Somerset Community College

Williamsburg
1145 Cumberland College

Wilmore
1019 Asbury College
1020 Asbury Theological Seminary

LOUISIANA

Alexandria
1632 Louisiana State University – Alexandria

Baton Rouge
6373 Louisiana State University – Baton Rouge
6663 Southern University A & M College

Bossier City
6073 Bossier Parish Community College

Eunice
6386 Louisiana State University – Eunice

Hammond
6656 Southeastern Louisiana University

Lafayette
6672 University Southwestern Louisiana

Lake Charles
6403 McNeese State University

Monroe
6482 Northeast Louisiana University

Natchitoches
6492 Northwestern State University Louisiana

New Orleans
6176 Delgado Community College
6164 Dillard University
6353 Louisiana State University Nursing
6374 Loyola University – New Orleans
6472 New Orleans Baptist
6002 Our Lady of Holy Cross College
6711 Southern University – New Orleans
6379 University New Orleans
6975 Xavier University of Louisiana

Pineville
6371 Louisiana College

Ruston
6372 Louisiana Technical University

Saint Benedict
6689 Saint Joseph's Seminary

Shreveport
6082 Centenary College of Louisiana
6355 Louisiana State University
6719 Southern University at Shreveport – Bossier

Thibodaux
6221 Nicholls State University

MAINE

Augusta
3929 University of Maine – Augusta

Bangor
3074 Bangor Theological Seminary
3114 Beal College
3372 Eastern Maine Technical College
3440 Husson College

Biddeford
3751 University New England

Caribou
7439 Husson College

Castine
3505 Maine Maritime Academy

Farmington
3506 University of Maine at Farmington

Fort Kent
3393 University of Maine at Fort Kent

Lewiston
3302 Central Maine Medical Center

Machias
3956 University Maine – Machias

Orono
3916 University of Maine at Orono

Portland
3700 Casco Bay College
3441 Husson College South
3701 Maine College of Art
3691 University Southern Maine
3960 Westbrook College

Presque Isle
3631 Northern Maine Technical College
3008 University of Maine Presque Isle

South Portland
3535 Southern Maine Technical College

Standish
3764 Saint Joseph's College

Unity
3925 Unity College

Waterville
3903 Thomas College

Windham
3755 Saint Joseph's College

MARYLAND

Arnold
5019 Anne Arundel Community College

Baltimore
5051 Baltimore City Community College
5114 College Notre Dame – Maryland
5122 Coppin State College
5176 Dundalk Community College
5192 Essex Community College
5332 Johns Hopkins University
5370 Loyola College
5416 Morgan State University
5602 Saint Mary's Seminary & University
5657 Sojourner – Douglass College
5810 University of Baltimore
7915 University of Maryland
7916 University of Maryland – Baltimore
5835 University of Maryland – Balitmore County

Bel Air
5746 Eastern Christian College
5303 Harford Community College

Bowie
5401 Bowie State University

Catonsville
5137 Catonsville Community College

College Park
5814 University of Maryland
5804 University Maryland – University College
0988 University of Maryland – Munich

Columbia
5308 Howard Community College
7841 Traditional Acupuncture Institute

Cumberland
5028 Allegany Community College

Emmitsburg
5421 Mount Saint Mary's College

Frederick
5230 Frederick Community College
5296 Hood College

Frostburg
5402 Frostburg State University

Germantown
5393 Montgomery College
5414 Montgomery College

Hagerstown
5738 Antietam Bible College
5290 Hagerstown Junior College

La Plata
5144 Charles County Community College

Lanham
5884 Washington Bible College

Largo
5545 Prince Georges Community College

Laurel
5101 Capitol College

McHenry
5279 Garrett Community College

North East
5091 Cecil Community College

Princess Anne
5400 University Maryland – Eastern Shore

Rockville
5440 Montgomery College Rockville
7661 Potomoc College

Saint Mary's City
5601 Saint Mary's College of Maryland

Salisbury
5403 Salisbury State University

Stevenson
5856 Villa Julie College

Takoma Park
5890 Columbia Union College

Towson
5404 Towson State University

Westminister
5898 Western Maryland College

Wye Mills
5143 Chesapeake College

MASSACHUSETTS

Amherst
3769 University Massachusetts – Stockbridge School Agriculture
3917 University of Massachusetts Amherst

Beverly
3369 Endicott College

Boston
3107 Berklee College of Music
3084 Boston Conservatory
3087 Boston University
3123 Bunker Hill Community College
3367 Emerson College
3368 Emmanuel College
3391 Fisher College
3394 Franklin Institute of Boston
3473 Katharine Gibbs School
3516 Massachsetts College of Art
3659 New England Conservatory of Music

Bradford
3091 Bradford College

Bridgewater
3517 Bridgewater State College

Brighton
3773 Saint Elizabeth Hospital Boston
3295 Saint John's Seminary College

Brockton
3549 Massasoit Community College

Brookline
3435 Hebrew College
3449 Helena College/Holy Cross
3639 Newbury College – Brookline

Buzzards Bay
3515 Massachusetts College of Art

Cambridge
7177 Cambridge College
7435 Harvard University – Extension School
3483 Lesley College
7576 Lesley College
7577 Lesley College
7581 Lesley College – Outreach

Chestnut Hill
3689 Pine Manor College

Chicopee
3283 College of Our Lady of the Elms

Dudley
3666 Nichols College

Fitchburg
3518 Fitchburg State College

Framingham
3519 Framingham State College
3397 Framingham Union School of Nursing

Franklin
3352 Dean College

Gardner
3545 Mount Wachusett Community College

Greenfield
3420 Greenfield Community College

Haverhill
3674 Northern Essex Community College

Holyoke
3437 Holyoke Community College

Longmeadow
3078 Bay Path College

Lowell
3554 Middlesex Community College
3911 University of Massachusetts – Lowell

Lynn
3651 North Shore Community College

Marlboro
3637 New England Tel Learning Center

Medford
3488 Lawrence Memorial Hospital

Milton
3285 Curry College

Newton
3013 Aquinas College at Newton
3530 Mount Ida College

Newton Center
3650 Newton Institute of Art & Science – Mount Ida

North Adams
3521 North Adams State College

North Andover
3525 Merrimack College

North Dartmouth
3786 University of Massachusetts at Dartmouth

North Easton
3770 Stonehill College

Paxton
3005 Anna Maria College

Pittsfield
3102 Berkshire Community College

Quincy
3365 Eastern Nazarene College
3713 Quincy College

Salem
3522 Salem State College

South Lancaster
3010 Atlantic Union College

Springfield
3002 American International College
3787 Baystate Med Center School of Nursing
3763 Springfield College
3791 Springfield Technical Community College
3962 Western New England College

Waltham
3096 Bentley College

Wellesly Hills
3294 Mass Bay Community College

Wenham
3417 Gordon College

West Barnstable
3289 Cape Cod Community College

Westfield
3523 Westfield State College

Weston
3723 Regis College

Woburn
3974 Western New England College

Worcester
3009 Assumption College
3079 Becker Junior College – Worcester
3714 Quinsigamond Community College
3524 Worcester State College

MICHIGAN

Adrian
1001 Adrian College

Albion
1007 Albion College

Allendale
1258 Grand Valley State College

Alma
1010 Alma College

Alpena
1011 Alpena Community College

Ann Arbor
1094 Concordia College
1839 University of Michigan
1935 Washtenaw Community College

Auburn Hills
1606 Oakland Community College – Auburn Hills

Battle Creek
1375 Kellogg Community College

Benton Harbor
1137 Lake Michigan College

Berrien Springs
1030 Andrews University

Big Rapids
1222 Ferris State University

Bloomfield Hill
1607 Oakland Community College

Centreville
1261 Glen Oaks Community College

Dearborn
1181 Detroit College of Business
1293 Henry Ford Community College

Detroit
1035 Center For Creative Studies
1425 Lewis Business College
1452 Marygrove College
1686 Sacred Heart Major Seminary
1460 University of Detroit – Mercy
1937 Wayne County Community College
1898 Wayne State University

Dowagiac
1783 Southwestern Michigan College

East Lansing
1465 Michigan State University

Escanaba
1049 Bay De Noc Community College

Farmington Hills
1167 William Tyndale College

Flint
1853 University Michigan Flint

Gaylord
7775 Spring Arbor College

Grand Rapids
1018 Aquinas College
1095 Calvin College
1253 Cornerstone College
1183 Davenport College of Business
1265 Grace Bible College
1254 Grand Rapids Community College
1376 Kendall College of Art & Design
1672 Reformed Bible College

Hancock
1743 Suomi College

Hillsdale
1295 Hillsdale College

Holland
1301 Hope College

Houghton
1464 Michigan Technical University

Howell
1209 Cleary College – Livingston

Ironwood
1250 Gogebic Community College

Jackson
1340 Jackson Community College

Kalamazoo
3254 Bronson Methodist Hospital
1378 Kalamazoo Valley Community College
1902 Western Michigan University

Lansing
1414 Lansing Community College

Livonia
1437 Madonna University
1764 Schoolcraft College

Marquette
1560 Northern Michigan University

Midland
1568 Northwood Universtiy

Monroe
1514 Monroe County Community College

Mount Pleasant
1106 Central Michigan University

Muskegon
1527 Baker College of Muskegon
1495 Muskegon Community College

Olivet
1595 Olivet College

Orchard Lake
1753 Saint Mary's College

Petoskey
1569 North Central Michigan College

Port Huron
1628 Saint Clair County Community College

Rochester
1516 Michigan Christian College

Roscommon
1382 Kirtland Community College

Royal Oak
1497 Oakland University

Sault Ste. Marie
1421 Lake Superior State University

Scottville
1941 West Shore Community College

Sidney
1522 Montcalm Community College

Southfield
1399 Lawrence Technical University

Spring Arbor
1732 Spring Arbor College

University Center
1816 Delta College
1766 Saginaw Valley State University

Warren
1722 Macomb Community College

Ypsilanti
1123 Cleary College – Washtenaw
1201 Eastern Michigan University

MINNESOTA

Alexandria
7062 Alexandria Technical College

Austin
6017 Austin Community College

Bemidji
6676 Bemidji State University

Bloomington
6501 Normandale Community College

Brainerd
6045 Central Lakes College

Brooklyn Park
6498 North Hennepin Community College

Collegeville
6624 Saint John's University – College Saint Benedict

Crookston
6893 University of Minnesota – Crookston

Duluth
6107 College of State Scholastics
7913 University Minnesota – Duluth
6873 University of Minnesota – Duluth

Fergus Falls
6227 Fergus Falls Community College

Grand Rapids
6309 Itasca Community College

Hibbing
6275 Hibbing Community College

International Falls
6613 Rainy River Community College

Inver Grove Heights
6314 Inver Hills Community College

Mankato
6035 Bethany Lutheran College
6677 Mankato State University

Marshall
6703 Southwest State University

Minneapolis
6014 Augsburg College
6434 Minneapolis Community College
6505 North Central Bible College
7828 Saint Mary's University
6874 University of Minnesota

Moorhead
6113 Concordia College
6678 Moorhead State University

Morris
6890 University of Minnesota Morris

Rochester
6412 Minnesota Bible College
6610 Rochester Community College

Saint Bonifacius
6639 Crown College

Saint Cloud
6679 Saint Cloud State University
7824 Saint Cloud Technical College

Saint Paul
6038 Bethel College
6687 College Associated Arts
6114 Concordia College – Saint Paul
6265 Hamline University
6445 Metropolitan State University
6489 Northwestern College
6105 The College of Saint Catherine
7680 University Saint Thomas

Thief River Falls
6500 Northland Community & Technical College

White Bear Lake
6388 Lakewood Community College

Willmar
6949 Willmar Community College

Winona
6632 Saint Mary's University of Minnesota
6680 Winona State University

Worthington
6945 Worthington Community College

MISSISSIPPI

Blue Mountain
1066 Blue Mountain College

Booneville
1557 Northeast Mississippi Community College

Cleveland
1163 Delta State University

Clinton
1477 Mississippi College

Columbus
1481 Mississippi University – Women

Ellisville
1347 Jones County Junior College

Florence
1923 Wesley College

Fulton
1326 Itawamba Community College

Gautier
1354 Mississippi Gulf Coast Community College

Goodman
1299 Holmes Community College

Gulfport
1353 Mississippi Gulf Coast Community College

Hattiesburg
1479 University of Southern Mississippi
1907 William Carey College

Holly Springs
1669 Rust College

Itta Bena
1482 Mississippi Valley State University

Jackson
1055 Belhaven College
1341 Jackson State University
1471 Millsaps College
1884 University of Mississippi Medical Center

Lorman
1008 Alcorn State University

Mathiston
1924 Wood College

Mayhew
7254 East Mississippi Community College

Meridian
1461 Meridian Community College
3336 Mississippi State University – Meridian

Mississippi State
1480 Mississippi State University

Moorhead
1742 Mississippi Delta Community College

Perkinston
1623 Mississippi Gulf Coast Community College

Raymond
1296 Hinds Community College

Scooba
1197 East Mississippi Community College

Senatobia
1562 Northwest Mississippi Community College

Summit
1729 Southwest Mississippi Community College

Tougaloo
1807 Tougaloo College

University
1840 University of Mississippi

Wesson
1142 Copiah-Lincoln Community College

West Point
1450 Mary Holmes College

MISSOURI

Bolivar
6664 Southwest Baptist University

Boonville
6338 Kemper Military School College

Canton
6123 Culver-Stockton College

Cape Girardeau
7808 Southeast Missouri Hospital
6655 Southeast Missouri State University/College

Columbia
6095 Columbia College
6683 Stephens College
6875 University of Missouri – Columbia

Conception
6112 Conception Seminary College

Fayette
6089 Central Methodist College

Florissant
6728 Saint Louis Christian College

Fort Leonard Wood
7247 Drury College

Fulton
6937 Westminster College
6944 William Woods University

Hannibal
6266 Hannibal – La Grange College

Hillsboro
6320 Jefferson College

Independence
7230 Columbia College – Independence
6910 Vatterott College

Jefferson City
7231 Columbia College
6366 Lincoln University

Joplin
6322 Missouri Southern State College

Kansas City
6109 Avila College
6331 Calvary Bible College
7209 Cleveland Chiropractic
6330 Kansas City Art Institute
6436 Maple Woods Community College
6324 Penn Valley Community College
6872 University Missouri – Kansas City

Kirksville
6483 Truman State University

Kirkwood
6430 Saint Louis Community College – Meramec

Lees Summit
6359 Longview Community College

Lexington
6934 Wentworth Military Academy & Junior College

Liberty
6941 William Jewell College

Marshall
6413 Missouri Valley College

Maryville
6488 Northwest Missouri State University

Moberly
6414 Moberly Area Community College

Neosho
6138 Crowder College

Park Hills
6323 Mineral Area College

Parkville
6574 Park College

Point Lookout
6713 The School of the Ozarks

Poplar Bluff
6836 Three Rivers Community College

Rolla
6876 University of Missouri – Rolla

Saint Charles
6367 Lindenwood College

Saint Joseph
6625 Missouri Western State College

Saint Louis
793 Barnes College
7232 Columbia College – Saint Louis
6216 Fontbonne College
7309 Fontbonne College – Options
6269 Harris Stowe State College
6329 Jewish Hospital College
6399 Maryville University
6439 Missouri Baptist College
6461 National-Louis University
6626 Saint Louis College of Pharmacy
6225 Saint Louis Community College – Flor Valley
6226 Saint Louis Community College
6629 Saint Louis University
6889 University of Missouri Saint Louis
7889 University of Missouri Saint Louis
6933 Webster University

Sedalia
6709 State Fair Community College

Springfield
6085 Central Bible College
7558 Cox College of Nursing
6169 Drury College
6198 Evangel College
6665 Southwest Missouri State University – Springfield

Tarkio
6816 Tarkio College

Trenton
6830 North Central Missouri College

Union
6200 East Central College

Warrensburg
6090 Central Missouri State University

MONTANA

Billings
4298 Montana State University – Billings
4660 Rocky Mountain College

Bozeman
4488 Montana State University

Butte
4487 Montana College of Mineral Science Technology

Dillon
4945 Western Montana College

Glendive
4280 Dawson Community College

Great Falls
7691 Montana State University – North Great Falls
4058 University Great Falls

Havre
4538 Montana State University – Northern

Helena
4041 Carroll College

Miles City
4081 Miles Community College

Missoula
4489 University of Montana

NEBRASKA

Bellevue
6053 Bellevue College

Blair
6157 Dana College

Chadron
6466 Chadron State College

Columbus
6584 Central Community College – Platte

Crete
6165 Doane College

Fremont
6406 Midland Lutheran College

Hastings
6270 Hastings College

Kearny
6467 University Nebraska at Kearny

Lincoln
7748 Doane College Lincoln
6470 Nebraska Wesleyan University
6865 Union College
6877 University of Nebraska – Lincoln

McCook
6401 McCook Community College

Norfolk
6473 Northeast Community College

North Platte
6497 Mid-Plains Community College
6433 Mid-Plains Community College

Omaha
6049 Clarkson College
6106 College of State Mary
6121 Creighton University
6248 Grace University
7632 Metropolitan Community College – Fort Omaha Campus
7640 Metropolitan Community College – Fort Omaha Campus
5755 Metropolitan Community College
7671 Nebraska Methodist College
9366 Omaha College Health Careers
6420 University of Nebraska at Omaha
6896 University of Nebraska Medical Center

Peru
6468 Peru State College

Scottsbluff
6648 Western Nebraska Community College

Seward
6116 Concordia College

Wayne
6469 Wayne State College

York
6984 York College

NEVADA

Carson City
4972 Western Nevada Community College – South

Elko
4293 Great Basin College

Incline Village
4757 Sierra Nevada College – Lake Tahoe

Las Vegas
4861 University Nevada – Las Vegas
7626 University Phoenix – Las Vegas

North Las Vegas
4136 Community College Southern Nevada

Reno
4960 Truckee Meadows Community College
4844 University Nevada – Reno

NEW HAMPSHIRE

Berlin
7899 College For Lifelong Learning
3646 New Hampshire Technical College – Berlin

Chester
3977 White Pines College

Claremont
3684 New Hampshire Technical College

Concord
3814 College For Lifelong Learning
3389 Franklin Pierce College
3647 New Hampshire Technical Institute

Dover
3553 Mcintosh College

Durham
3918 University of New Hampshire

Hanover
3351 Dartmouth College

Henniker
3657 New England College

Keene
3376 Franklin Pierce College
3472 Keene State College

Lebanon
7741 College For Lifelong Learning

Manchester
3649 New Hampshire College
3660 New Hampshire Technical College/ Manchester
3670 Notre Dame College
3748 Saint Anselm College
2094 University New Hampshire – Manchester

Nashua
7206 College For Lifelong Learning
3648 Daniel Webster College
3388 Franklin Pierce College
3643 New Hampshire Technical College – Nashua
3728 Rivier College

New London
3281 Colby – Sawyer College

Plymouth
3690 Plymouth State College

Portsmouth
3363 Franklin Pierce College

Rindge
3395 Franklin Pierce College

Salem
3377 Franklin Pierce College

Stratham
3661 New Hampshire Technical College – Stratham

Windham
3310 Castle College

NEW JERSEY

Blackwood
2121 Camden County College

Bloomfield
2044 Bloomfield College

Caldwell
2072 Caldwell College

Camden
2742 Rutgers – the State University of New Jersey

Carneys Point
2868 Salem Community College

Cranford
2921 Union County College – Cranford

Edison
2441 Middlesex County College

Elizabeth
3150 Union County College – Elizabeth

Glassboro
2515 Rowan College of New Jersey

Hackensack
2232 Edward Williams College

Hackettstown
2080 Centenary College

Jersey City
2291 Hudson County Community College
2516 Jersey City State College
2806 Saint Peters College

Lakewood
2274 Georgian Court College

Lawrenceville
2758 Rider University

Lincroft
2181 Brookdale Community College

Lodi
2321 Felician College

Madison
2193 Drew University
2262 Fairleigh Dickinson University – Madison

Mahwah
2884 Ramapo College of New Jersey

Mays Landing
2024 Atlantic Community College

Montclair
2348 Katherine Gibbs School
2427 Mountainside Hospital School of Nursing

Morristown
2090 College of Saint Elizabeth

New Brunswick
2192 Douglass College
2384 Livingston College
2765 Rutgers State University – Rutgers College
2736 Rutgers University School of Arts
2170 Rutgers University – Cook College
2777 University College – Rutgers University

Newark
2237 Essex County College
2513 New Jersey Institute of Technical
2753 Rutgers University – Newark
2512 Rutgers University – Newark
2789 Rutgers – College of Nursing

Newton
2711 Sussex County Community College

Paramus
2032 Bergen Community College

Pemberton
2180 Burlington County College

Perth Amboy
2686 Raritan Bay Medical Center – Nursing

Piscataway
2838 Rutgers University – College of Engineering
2839 Rutgers University – College of Pharmacy

Pomona
2889 Richard Stockton College of New Jersey

Princeton
7272 Educational Testing Service
2974 Westminster Choir College

Randolph
2124 County College of Morris

Sewell
2281 Gloucester County College

Somerville
2867 Raritan Valley Community College

South Orange
2811 Seton Hall University

Teaneck
2263 Fairleigh Dickinson University – Teaneck

Toms River
2630 Ocean County College

Trenton
2444 Mercer County Community College
2442 Mercer Medical Center
2858 Saint Francis Medical Center
2748 Thomas A. Edison College
2519 Trenton State College

Union
2517 Kean College of New Jersey

Upper Montclair
2520 Montclair State University

Vineland
2118 Cumberland County College

Washington
2722 Warren County Community College

Wayne
2518 William Paterson College

West Long Branch
2416 Monmouth University

West Patterson
2061 Berkeley College of Business

NEW MEXICO

Albuquerque
4220 Albuquerque Technical Vocational Institute
4924 University Phoenix – New Mexico
4845 University of New Mexico

Carlsbad
4547 New Mexico State University – Carlsbad

Clovis
4921 Clovis Community College

Espanola
4560 Northern New Mexico Community College

Farmington
4732 San Juan College

Gallup
4895 University of New Mexico Gallup

Grants
4552 New Mexico State University – Grants

Hobbs
4116 College of the Southwest
4553 New Mexico Junior College

Las Cruces
4531 New Mexico State University

Las Vegas
4532 New Mexico Highlands University

Portales
4299 Eastern New Mexico University Portale

Roswell
4662 Eastern New Mexico University
4534 New Mexico Military Institute

Santa Fe
4676 College of Santa Fe
4816 Santa Fe Community College

Silver City
4535 Western New Mexico University

White Sands Military Reserve
7973 US Army – White Sands Military Reserve

NEW YORK

Albany
2013 Albany College Pharmacy
2091 College of Saint Rose
2434 Maria College of Albany
2472 Memorial Hospital School of Nursing
7737 New York State Dept of Education
7703 New York State Dept of Education
2899 Regents College
2343 Sage Junior College
2532 University at Albany

Alfred
2005 Alfred University
2522 State University of New York – Alfred State College

Amherst
2762 Daemen College

Auburn
2010 Cayuga Community College

Aurora
2971 Wells College

Batavia
2272 Genesee Community College

Binghamton
2535 Binghamton University
2048 Broome Community College

Brentwood
2604 C.W. Post Center Long Island University – Suffolk
2849 Suffolk County Community College – West

Brockport
2537 State University College of New York at Brockport

Bronx
2259 Fordham University – Ignatius College
2312 Herbert H. Lehman Community College
2463 Monroe College

Bronxville
2096 Concordia College

Brooklyn
2358 Kingsboro Community College
2369 Long Island University – Brooklyn Center
2796 Saint Francis College
2802 Saint Joseph's College
2534 State University of New York Health Science Center – Brooklyn

Brookville
2070 Long Island University – C.W. Post

Buffalo
2073 Canisius College
2197 D'Youville College
2213 Erie Community College – City
2422 Medaille College
2925 State University of New York at Buffalo
2533 State University of New York at Buffalo
2856 Trocaire College
2962 Villa Maria College Buffalo

Canandaigua
2134 Finger Lakes Community College

Canton
2805 Saint Lawrence University
2523 State University of New York College Technical – Canton

Cazenovia
2078 Cazenovia College

Cobleskill
2524 State University of New York College Agriculture & Technical

Corning
2106 Corning Community College

Cortland
2538 State University of New York – Cortland

Delhi
2525 State University of New York – College of Technical – Delhi

Dix Hills
3142 Five Towns College

Dobbs Ferry
2409 Mercy College

Dryden
2904 Tompkins Cortland Community College

Elmira
2016 Arnot – Ogden Medical Center
2226 Elmira College

Farmingdale
2526 State University of New York College Technical – Farmingdale

Flushing
2001 College of Aeronautics
2750 State University of New York Queens College

Fredonia
2539 State University of New York – Fredonia

Garden City
2563 Nassa University Community College

Geneseo
2540 State University of New York – Geneseo

Geneva
2294 Hobart College

Hamburg
2334 Hilbert College

Hamilton
2086 Colgate University

Hempstead
2295 Hofstra University

Herkimer
2316 Herkimer County Community College

Houghton
2299 Houghton College

Hudson
2138 Columbia – Greene Community College

Ithaca
2528 Cornell University
2325 Ithaca College

Jamaica
2799 Saint John's University
2992 York College

Jamestown
2335 Jamestown Community College – Jamestown

Johnstown
2254 Fulton Montgomery Community College

Keuka Park
2350 Keuka College

Long Island
2011 Dowling College

Long Island City
2246 LaGuardia Community College/City University of New York

Loudonville
2814 Siena College

Melville
4169 Katherine Gibbs School – Huntington

Middletown
7683 New School For Social Research
2625 Orange County Community College

Morrisville
2527 State University of New York at Morrisvlle

Mount Vernon
2455 Dorothea Hopfer School of Nursng

New Paltz
2541 State University of New York – New Paltz

New Rochelle
7207 College of New Rochelle
2089 College of New Rochelle
2324 Iona College

New York
2034 Baruch College
2901 Boricua College
2063 Borough of Manhattan Community College
2147 City University of New York
2115 City University of New York – John Jay College Crime & Justice
2751 City University of New York – Queensborough Community College
2112 College of Insurance
7724 Edna M. Clark School of Nursing
2302 Helene Fuld School of Nursing
2301 Hunter College
2380 Lab Institute of Merchandsing
2405 Marymount Manhattan College
2521 New School For Social Research
2562 New York University
7664 New York School of Interior Design
2635 Pace University – New York
2835 School of Visual Arts
2902 Touro College
2990 Yeshiva University

Niagara University
2558 Niagara University

Nyack
2560 Nyack College
7660 Nyack College – Adult Program

Ogdensburg
2436 Mater Dei College
2965 Wadhams Hall Seminary

Old Westbury
2561 New York Institute Technology – Main
2209 State University of New York – Empire State College Long Island
2866 State University of New York – Old Westbury

Olean
2329 Jamestown Community College – Cattaraugus

Oneonta
2288 Hartwick College
2542 State University of New York – Oneonta

Orangeburg
2190 Dominican College of Blauvelt

Orchard Park
2211 Erie Community College – South

Oswego
2543 State University of New York – Oswego

Patchogue
2841 Saint Joseph's College – Patchogue

Paul Smith's
2640 Paul Smith's College

Plattsburgh
2135 Clinton Community College
2544 State University of New York – Plattsburgh

Pleasantville
2685 Pace University

Potsdam
2084 Clarkson University
2545 State University of New York – Potsdam

Poughkeepsie
2198 Dutchess Community College
2400 Marist College
2956 Vassar College

Purchase
2878 Purchase College, State University of New York

Queensbury
2017 Adirondack Community College

Riverdale
2088 College of Mount State Vincent

Riverhead
2846 Suffolk County Community College – East

Rochester
2733 Empire State College
2429 Monroe Community College
2759 Roberts Wesleyan College
2770 Rochester Business Institute
2760 Rochester Institute of Technology
2798 Saint John Fisher College

Rome
2508 New School For Social Research

Saint Bonaventure
2793 Saint Bonaventure University

Sanborn
2568 Niagara County Community College

Saranac Lake
2571 North Country Community College

Saratoga Springs
2815 Skidmore College
2214 State University of New York – Empire State College

Schenectady
2879 Schenectady County Community College

Selden
2827 Suffolk County Community College

Southampton
2248 Friends World Program at Long Island University
2853 Long Island University Southampton

Sparkill
2807 Saint Thomas Aquinas College

Staten Island
2778 College of Staten Island
2845 Saint John's University Staten Island
2966 Wagner College

Stone Ridge
2938 Ulster County Community College

Suffern
2767 Rockland Community College

Syracuse
2530 College of Envi Science & Forestry
7201 Columbia College
2109 Crouse Irving Memorial Hospital
2366 Le Moyne College
2627 Onondaga Community College

2825 Saint Joseph's Hospital & Health Center
2547 State University of New York – Health Science Center – Syracuse
2823 Syracuse University
2840 Syracuse University – Project Advance

Tarrytown
2406 Marymount College

Troy
2300 Hudson Valley Community College
2764 Russell Sage College
2771 Sage Evening College

Utica
2414 Mohawk Valley Community College
2847 Saint Elizabeth School of Nursing
2896 State University of New York – Institute Technical Utica/Rome
2932 Utica College of Syracuse University

Valhalla
2972 Westchester Community College

Watertown
2345 Jefferson Community College

White Plains
2064 Berkeley College

Williamsville
2228 Erie Community College – North

Yonkers
2894 Saint John's Riverside Hospital

NORTH CAROLINA

Ahoskie
5564 Roanoke – Chowan Community College

Asheboro
5585 Randolph Community College

Asheville
5033 Asheville – Buncombe Technical Community College
5708 Cecils College
5013 University North Carolina Asheville

Banner Elk
5364 Lees-McRae College

Belmont
5055 Belmont Abbey College

Boiling Springs
5242 Gardner – Webb University

Boone
5010 Appalachian State University

Brevard
5067 Brevard College

Buies Creek
5100 Campbell University

Chapel Hill
5816 University of North Carolina Chapel Hill

Charlotte
5102 Central Piedmont Community College
5231 East Coast Bible College
5333 Johnson C. Smith University
5560 Queens College
5105 University North Carolina – Charlotte

Clinton
5661 Sampson Community College

Cullowhee
5897 Western Carolina University

Dobson
5656 Surry Community College

Dublin
5044 Bladen Community College

Durham
5495 North Carolina Central University
5915 Watts School of Nursing

Elizabeth City
5133 College of the Albemarle
5629 Elizabeth City State University
5597 Roanoke Bible College

Elon College
5183 Elon College

Fayetteville
5212 Fayetteville State University
5208 Fayetteville Technical Community College
5426 Methodist College

Fort Bragg
7219 Campbell University – Fort Bragg

Goldsboro
5926 Wayne Community College

Greensboro
5058 Bennett College
5260 Greensboro College
5261 Guilford College
5003 North Carolina Agricultural & Technical State University
5913 University North Carolina – Greensboro

Greenville
5180 East Carolina University
5556 Pitt Community College

Hamlet
5588 Richmond Community College

Henderson
5876 Vance-Granville Community College

Hickory
5365 Lenoir Rhyne College

High Point
5293 High Point University
5348 John Wesley College

Hudson
5146 Caldwell Communiyt College

Jacksonville
5134 Coastal Carolina Community College

Jamestown
5275 Guilford Technical Community College

Kenansville
5350 James Sprunt Community College

Kinston
5378 Lenoir Community College

Laurinburg
5214 Saint Andrews Presbyterian College

Lexington
5170 Davidson County Community College

Louisburg
5369 Louisburg College

Lumberton
5594 Robeson Community College

Marion
5454 McDowell Technical Community College

Mars Hill
5395 Mars Hill College

Misenheimer
5536 Pfeiffer College

Montreat
5423 Montreat College

Morehead City
5092 Carteret Community College

Morganton
5922 Western Piedmont Community College

Mount Olive
5435 Mount Olive College

Murfreesboro
5107 Chowan College

New Bern
5148 Craven Community College
7634 Mount Olive College – New Bern

Pembroke
5534 Pembroke State University

Pinehurst
5649 Sandhills Community College

Raleigh
5410 Meredith College
7561 North Carolina Wesleyan College
7562 North Carolina Wesleyan College
5928 Wake Technical Community College

Rocky Mount
5491 Nash Community College
5501 North Carolina Wesleyan College

Salisbury
5103 Catawba College
5367 Livingstone College
5589 Rowan – Cabarrus Community College

Sanford
5147 Central Carolina Community College

Shelby
5088 Cleveland Community College

Smithfield
5351 Johnston Community College

Spindale
5319 Isothermal Community College

Spruce Pine
5459 Mayland Community College

Statesville
5412 Mitchell Community College

Sylva
5667 Southwestern Community College

Tarboro
5199 Edgecombe Community College

Washington
5086 Beaufort County Community College

Wentworth
5582 Rockingham Community College

Wilkesboro
5921 Wilkes Community College

Williamston
5445 Martin Community College

Wilmington
5907 University of North Carolina Wilmington

Wilson
5016 Barton College
5930 Wilson Technicalnial Community College

Wingate
5908 Wingate University

Winston-Salem
5512 North Carolina School of Arts
5555 Piedmont Bible College
5607 Salem College
5909 Winston-Salem State University

NORTH DAKOTA

Bismarck
6041 Bismarck State College
6428 University of Mary

Devils Lake
6163 University North Dakota – Lake Region
6183 University North Dakota – Lake Region

Dickinson
6477 Dickinson State University

Ellendale
356 Trinity Bible College

Fargo
6474 North Dakota State University

Grand Forks
6878 University of North Dakota

Jamestown
6318 Jamestown College

Mayville
6478 Mayville State University

Minot
6479 Minot State University

Valley City
6480 Valley City State University

Wahpeton
6476 North Dakota State College Science

Williston
6905 University of North Dakota – Williston

OHIO

Ada
1591 Ohio Northern Univiversity

Akron
1829 University of Akron

Alliance
1492 Mount Union College

Ashland
1021 Ashland University

Athens
1593 Ohio University

Berea
1050 Baldwin – Wallace College

Bluffton
1067 Bluffton College

Bowling Green
1069 Bowling Green State University

Burton
1387 Kent State University – Geauga Campus

Canton
1439 Malone College
1688 Stark Technical College

Cedarville
1151 Cedarville College

Cincinnati
1091 Cincinnati Bible College & Seminary
1129 College of Mount State Joseph
7850 Temple Baptist College
1833 University of Cincinnati
1965 Xavier University

Circleville
1088 Circleville Bible College

Cleveland
1152 Cleveland Institute of Art
1221 Cleveland State University
1159 Cuyahoga Community College – Metro
1178 David N. Myers College
1219 Fairview Hospital School of Nursing
1342 John Carroll University
1566 Notre Dame College

Columbus
1099 Capital University
1148 Columbus State Community College
1229 Franklin University
7627 Mount Vernon Nazarene College – Excell
1131 Ohio Dominican College
1592 Ohio State University
1348 Pontifical College Josephinum

Dayton
1528 Miami – Jacobs College
1720 Sinclair Community College
1834 University of Dayton
1179 Wright State University

Defiance
1162 Defiance College

Elyria
1417 Lorain County Community College

Findlay
1223 University of Findlay

Granville
1164 Denison University

Hamilton
1526 Miami University – Hamilton

Hillsboro
1752 Southern State Community College

Hiram
1297 Hiram College

Huron
1045 Bowling Green State University – Fireland

Kettering
1386 Kettering College of Medical Arts

Lancaster
1610 Ohio University Lancaster

Mansfield
7693 North Central Technical College

Marietta
1444 Marietta College
7963 Washington State Community College

Mentor
1422 Lakeland Community College

Middletown
1509 Miami University

Mount Vernon
1531 Mount Vernon Nazarene College

New Concord
1496 Muskingum College

North Canton
1926 Walsh University

Orrville
1892 University Akron – Wayne College

Oxford
1463 Miami University

Painesville
1391 Lake Erie College

Parma
1985 Cuyahoga Community College – Western

Pepper Pike
1848 Ursuline College

Piqua
1191 Edison State Community College

Portsmouth
1790 Shawnee State University

Rio Grande
1663 University of Rio Grande

Saint Clairsville
1072 Belmont Technical College

Saint Martin
1143 Chatfield College

Salem
7529 Kent State University – Salem

Springfield
1922 Wittenberg University

Steubenville
1133 Franciscan University Steubenville
1333 Jefferson Community College

Sylvania
1427 Lourdes College

Tiffin
1292 Heidelberg College

Toledo
1175 Davis Junior College of Business
1845 University of Toledo

Urbana
1847 Urbana University

Warrensville
1978 Cuyahoga Community College – Eastern

Westerville
1597 Otterbein College

Wilberforce
1107 Central State University
1906 Wilberforce University

Wilmington
1909 Wilmington College

Wpafb
7637 Park College – Resident Center

Yellow Springs
1017 Antioch College – Ohio
1652 McGregor School of Antioch University

Youngstown
1975 Youngstown State University

Zanesville
1535 Muskingum Area Technical College

OKLAHOMA

Ada
6186 East Central University

Altus
6020 Western Oklahoma State College

Alva
6493 Northwestern Oklahoma State University

Bartlesville
6135 Bartlesville Wesleyan College

Bethany
6036 Southern Nazarene University
6555 Southwestern College of Christian Ministry

Chickasha
6544 University of Science & Arts of Oklahoma

Claremore
6545 Rogers State College

Durant
6657 Southeastern Oklahoma State University

Edmond
6091 University Central Oklahoma

El Reno
6192 Redlands Community College

Enid
6579 Phillips University

Goodwell
6571 Panhandle State University

Langston
6361 Langston University

Lawton
6080 Cameron University

Miami
6484 Northeastern Oklahoma A & M College

Midwest City
6559 Rose State College

Muskogee
6030 Bacone College

Norman
6879 University of Oklahoma

Oklahoma City
6257 Mid-America Bible College
6086 Oklahoma Christian
6640 Oklahoma City Community College
6543 Oklahoma City University
6556 Oklahoma State University

Poteau
6586 Carl Albert State College

Sayre
6646 Southwestern Oklahoma State University – Sayre

Seminole
6717 Seminole Junior College

Shawnee
6541 Oklahoma Baptist University
6621 Saint Gregory's College

Stillwater
6546 Oklahoma State University

Tahlequah
6485 Northeastern State University – Tahlequah

Tishomingo
6421 Murray State College

Tonkawa
6486 Northern Oklahoma College

Tulsa
6552 Oral Roberts University
6839 Tulsa Junior College
7989 University Center at Tulsa

Warner
6117 Connors State College

Weatherford
6673 Southwestern Oklahoma State University

Wilburton
6189 Eastern Oklahoma State College

OREGON

Albany
4413 Linn – Benton Community College

Ashland
4702 Southern Oregon State College

Astoria
4089 Clatsop Community College

Coos Bay
4729 Southwestern Oregon Community College

Corvallis
4586 Oregon State University

Eugene
4407 Lane Community College
4543 Northwest Christian College
4846 University of Oregon

Forest Grove
4601 Pacific University

Grants Pass
4653 Rogue Community College

Gresham
4508 Mount Hood Community College

Klamath Falls
4587 Oregon Institute of Technology

La Grande
4300 Eastern Oregon State College

Marylhurst
4480 Marylhurst College

McMinnville
4387 Linfield College

Monmouth
4585 Western Oregon State College

Newberg
4325 George Fox College

Ontario
4825 Treasure Valley Community College

Oregon City
4111 Clackamas Community College

Pendleton
4025 Blue Mountain Community College

Portland
4093 Cascade College
4079 Concordia University
4496 Multnomah School of Bible
4900 Oregon Health Sciences University
4610 Portland State University
4847 University of Portland
4595 Warner Pacific College

Roseburg
4862 Umqua Community College

Saint Benedict
4491 Mount Angel Seminary

Salem
4745 Chemeketa Community College
4956 Western Baptist College

PENNSYLVANIA

Allentown
2079 Cedar Crest College
2424 Muhlenberg College

Annville
2364 Lebanon Valley College

Aston
2628 Neumann College

Beaver Falls
2273 Geneva College

Bethlehem
2418 Moravian College
2573 Northampton County Area Community College

Bloomsburg
2646 Bloomsburg University

Bluebell
2445 Montgomery County Community College

Bradford
2935 University Pittsburgh – Bradford

Bryn Athyn
2002 Academy of the New Church College

Bryn Mawr
2287 Harcum College

Butler
2069 Butler County Community College

California
2647 California University of Pennsylvania

Center Valley
2021 Allentown College of Saint Francis

Chambersburg
2979 Wilson College

Chester
2642 Widener University

Clarion
2649 Clarion University of Pennsylvania

Clarks Summit
2036 Baptist Bible College of Pennsylvania

Collegeville
2931 Ursinus College

Coraopolis
2769 Robert Morris College

Cresson
2420 Mount Aloysius College

Dallas
2087 College Misericordia

Doylestown
2510 Delaware Valley College of Science & Agriculture

East Stroudsburg
2650 East Stroudsburg University

Edinboro
2651 Edinboro University of Pennsylvania

Elizabethtown
2225 Elizabethtown College
2243 Elizabethtown College – Continuing Education

Erie
2270 Gannon University
2410 Mercyhurst College

Glenside
2039 Beaver College

Grantham
2411 Messiah College

Greensburg
2812 Seton Hill College
2936 University of Pittsburgh – Greensburg

Greenville
2910 Thiel College

Grove City
2277 Grove City College

Gwynedd Valley
2278 Gwynedd-Mercy College

Harrisburg
2309 Harrisburg Area Community College
2918 University Center Harrisburg

Immaculata
2320 Immaculata College

Indiana
2652 Indiana University of Penna

Jenkintown
2260 Manor Junior College

Johnstown
2934 University of Pittsburgh

Kutztown
2653 Kutztown University of Pennsylvania

La Plume
2351 Keystone College

Lancaster
2261 Franklin and Marshall College
2388 Lancaster Bible College
2374 Lancaster Institute for Health Education

Langhorne
2661 Philadelphia College of Bible

Latrobe
2808 Saint Vincent College

Lewisburg
2050 Bucknell University

Lock Haven
2654 Lock Haven University of Pennsylvania

Loretto
2797 Saint Francis College

Mansfield
2655 Mansfield University of Pennsylvania

McKeesport
2707 Penn State University – McKeesport

Meadville
2006 Allegheny College

Media
2125 Delaware County Community College

Melrose Park
2280 Gratz College

Middletown
2708 Penn State University – Middletown

Millersville
2656 Millersville University

Monaca
2126 Beaver County Community College

Monroeville
2122 Community College Allegheny County – Boyce

Monto Alto
2710 Penn State University – Monto Alto

Nanticoke
2382 Luzerne County Community College

New Castle
2577 Erie Business Center South

New Wilmington
2975 Westminster College

Newtown
2066 Bucks County Community College

Oil City
7200 Clarion University of Pennsylvania – Venango

Overbrook
2794 Saint Charles Borromeo Seminary

Philadelphia
2682 Community College of Philadelphia
2100 Curtis Institute of Music
2194 Drexel University
2306 Hahnemann University
2297 Holy Family College
2363 La Salle University Evening Division
2458 Methodist Hospital
2674 Peirce College
2663 Philadelphia College of Pharmacy & Science
2666 Philadelphia College of Textiles & Science
2801 Saint Joseph's University
2906 Temple University Main Campus
2903 Thomas Jefferson University College of Health
2664 University of the Arts

Phoenixville
2579 Valley Forge Christian College

Pittsburgh
2029 Art Institute Pittsburgh
2421 Carlow College
2081 Chatham College
2156 Community College Allegheny County – Pittsbrugh
2196 Duquesne University
3823 ICM School of Business
2379 La Roche College
2676 Point Park College
2927 University Pittsburgh
2940 University Pittsburgh – General Studies

Radnor
2071 Cabrini College

Reading
2004 Albright College
2431 Alvernia College
2743 Reading Area Community College

Rosemont
2763 Rosemont College

Saint Davids
2220 Eastern College

Schnecksville
2381 Lehigh Carbon Community College

Scranton
2373 Lackawanna Junior College
2407 Marywood College
2929 University of Scranton

Selinsgrove
2820 Susquehanna University

Shippensburg
2657 Shippensburg University

Slippery Rock
2658 Slippery Rock University of Pennsylvania

Titusville
2937 University of Pittsburgh Titusville

Uniontown
2691 Penn State University – Fayette

University Park
2660 Penn State University – University Park

Villanova
2959 Villanova University

Washington
2967 Washington Jefferson College

Wayne
2955 Valley Forge Military College

Waynesburg
2969 Waynesburg College

West Chester
2129 Chester County Hospital
2659 West Chester University

West Mifflin
2123 Community College Allegheny County – South

Wilkes-Barre
2353 King's College
2977 Wilkes University

Williamsport
2372 Lycoming College
2989 Pennsylvania College of Technology

Willow Grove
2019 Abington Memorial Hospital School of Nursing

York
2991 York College of Pennsylvania

Youngwood
2968 Westmoreland County Community College

RHODE ISLAND

Kingston
3919 University of Rhode Island

Lincoln
3738 Community College of Rhode Island

Newport
3759 Salve Regina University

Providence
3094 Brown University
3465 Johnson and Wales University
3476 Katharine Gibbs School
3724 Rhode Island College
3729 Roger Williams University
3923 University Rhode Island – Providence

Smithfield
3095 Bryant College

SOUTH CAROLINA

Aiken
5037 Aiken Technical College
5840 University of South Carolina – Aiken

Anderson
5008 Anderson College

Beaufort
5047 Technical College of the Low Country
5845 University South Carolina – Beaufort

Central
5896 Southern Wesleyan University

Charleston
5079 Charleston Southern University
5113 College of Charleston
5407 Medical University of South Carolina
5108 The Citadel
5049 Trident Technical College – Main Campus

Cheraw
5095 Chesterfield-Marlboro Technical College

Clemson
5111 Clemson University

Columbia
5056 Benedict College
5166 Columbia Bible College
5116 Columbia Bible College
5117 Columbia College
5584 Midlands Technical College
5818 University of South Carolina – Columbia

Conway
5837 Coastal Carolina University
5305 Horry-Georgetown Technical College

Denmark
5744 Denmark Technical College
5863 Voorhees College

Due West
5188 Erskine College

Florence
5207 Florence Darlington Technical College
5442 Francis Marion University

Fort Jackson
7133 Coker College

Gaffney
5366 Limestone College

Greenville
5065 Bob Jones University
5278 Greenville Technical College

Greenwood
5363 Lander University
5550 Piedmont Technical College

Hartsville
5112 Coker College

Kingstree
5892 Williamsburg Technical College

Lancaster
5849 University of South Carolina – Lancaster

Newberry
5493 Newberry College

North Charleston
5551 Trident Technical College – Palmer

Orangeburg
5109 Claflin College

5527 Orangeburg – Calhoun Technical College
5663 Southern Methodist College

Pendleton
5789 Tri-County Technical College

Rock Hill
5910 Winthrop University
5989 York Technical College

Shaw
7779 Saint Leo College

Spartanburg
5627 Spartanburg Methodist College
5850 University of South Carolina – Spartanburg
5912 Wofford College

Sumter
5665 Central Carolina Technical College

Tigerville
5498 North Greenville Junior College

Union
5846 University of South Carolina – Union

SOUTH DAKOTA

Aberdeen
6487 Northern State University
6582 Presentation College

Brookings
6663 South Dakota State University

Huron
6279 Huron University

Kyle
6553 Oglala Lakota College

Madison
6247 Dakota State University

Mitchell
6155 Dakota Wesleyan University

Rapid City
6652 Ivanhoe International Center
6464 National College

Sioux Falls
6015 Augustana College
6149 Kilian Community College
6651 University of Sioux Falls

Spearfish
6042 Black Hills State University

Vermillion
6881 University South Dakota

Yankton
6416 Mount Marty College

TENNESSEE

Athens
1805 Tennessee Wesleyan College

Bristol
1371 King College

Brunswick
7045 American Technical Institute

Chattanooga
1084 Chattanooga State Technical Community College
7166 Covenant College Quest Program
1818 Tennessee Temple University
1831 University of Tennessee – Chattanooga

APPENDIX C

Clarksville
1028 Austin Peay State University

Cleveland
1981 Cleveland State Community College
1401 Lee College

Collegedale
1727 Southern College of Seventh Day Adventists

Cookeville
1804 Tennessee Technical University

Dayton
1908 Bryan College

Dyersburg
1187 Dyersburg State Community College

Gallatin
1881 Volunteer State Community College

Greeneville
1812 Tusculum College

Harriman
1656 Roane State Community College

Harrogate
1408 Lincoln Memorial University

Henderson
1230 Freed-Hardeman College

Jackson
1359 Jackson State Community College
1394 Lambuth University
1395 Lane College
1826 Union University

Jefferson City
1102 Carson – Newman College

Johnson City
1198 East Tennessee State University

Knoxville
1345 Johnson Bible College
1795 Pellissippi State Technical Community College
1843 University of Tennessee – Knoxville

Madisonville
1298 Hiwassee College

Martin
1844 University of Tennessee – Martin

Maryville
1454 Maryville College

McKenzie
1063 Bethel College

Memphis
1121 Christian Brothers University
1403 Lemoyne – Owen College
1511 Memphis College of Art
1746 Shelby State Community College
7928 Union University – BMH Campus
7924 Union University – BMH Campus
1459 University Memphis

Milligan College
1469 Milligan College

Morristown
1893 Walters State Community College

Murfreesboro
1466 Middle Tennessee State University

Nashville
1042 Aquinas College
1058 Belmont University
1161 David Lipscomb University
3261 Draughons Junior College
1232 Free Will Baptist Bible College
1648 Nashville State Technical Institute
1803 Tennessee State University
1809 Trevecca Nazarene College

Pulaski
1449 Martin Methodist College

Tullahoma
1543 Motlow State Community College

TEXAS

Abilene
6001 Abilene Christian University
6268 Hardin-Simmons University
6402 McMurray University

Alpine
6685 Sul Ross State University – Alpine

Alvin
6005 Alvin Community College

Amarillo
6006 Amarillo College
7875 Texas State Technical Institute – Amarillo

Arlington
6039 Arlington Baptist College
6013 University Texas – Arlington

Athens
6271 Trinity Valley Community College

Austin
6759 Austin Community College
6127 Concordia University at Austin
6280 Huston – Tillotson College
6619 Saint Edwards University
6882 University of Texas at Austin

Baytown
6363 Lee College

Beaumont
6360 Lamar University

Beeville
6055 Bee County College

Belton
6396 University of Mary Hardin – Baylor

Big Sandy
6261 Ambassador University

Big Spring
6277 Howard College

Borger
6222 Frank Phillips College

Brenham
6043 Blinn College

Brownsville
6825 University of Texas at Brownsville

Brownwood
6278 Howard Payne University

Canyon
6938 West Texas A & M University

Carthage
6572 Panola College

Cedar Hill
6499 Northwood University

Cisco
6096 Cisco Junior College

Clarendon
6097 Clarendon College

Cleburne
6285 Hill College

College Station
6003 Texas A & M University

Commerce
6188 East Texas State University

Corpus Christi
6160 Del Mar College
6849 Texas A & M University – Corpus Christi

Corsicana
6465 Navarro College

Dallas
7092 Bill Priest Institute of Economic Development
6159 Dallas Baptist University
6199 El Centro College
6438 Mountain View College
5861 Parker College of Chiropractic
6607 Richland College
6660 Southern Methodist University
6686 University of Texas Southwestern Medical Center

Denison
6254 Grayson County College

Denton
6481 University of North Texas

Edinburg
6570 University of Texas – Pan American

El Paso
6203 El Paso Community College
6829 University of Texas at El Paso

Farmers Branch
6070 Brookhaven College

Fort Worth
6845 Tarrant County Junior College – Northwest
6834 Tarrant County Junior College – South
6820 Texas Christian University
6828 Texas Wesleyan University

Gainesville
6245 North Central Texas College

Galveston
6255 Galveston College
6835 Texas A & M University at Galveston

Garland
6140 Amber University

Georgetown
6674 Southwestern University

Harlingen
6843 Texas State Technical College

Hawkins
6319 Jarvis Christian College

Houston
6282 Houston Baptist University
6296 Houston Community College
6609 Rice University
6729 San Jacinto College North
6922 University Houston – Downtown
6870 University Houston – University Park
6880 University Saint Thomas
6906 University Texas Health and Science – Houston

Huntsville
6643 Sam Houston State University

Hurst
6837 Tarrant County Junior College – Northeast

Ingleside
7777 Saint Leo College – Naval Station

Irving
6519 North Lake College
6868 University of Dallas

Jacksonville
6317 Jacksonville College
6369 Lon Morris College

Keene
6671 Southwestern Adventist College

Kilgore
6341 Kilgore College

Killeen
6130 Central Texas College
6756 University of Central Texas

Kingsville
6822 Texas A & M University – Kingsville

Lake Jackson
6054 Brazosport College

Lancaster
6148 Cedar Valley College

Laredo
6362 Laredo Community College
6838 Texas A & M International University

Levelland
6695 South Plains College

Longview
6344 Kilgore College – Longview Center
6365 LeTournea University
7557 LeTournea University

Lubbock
6378 Lubbock Christian University
6827 Texas Technical University

Lufkin
6025 Angelina College

Marshall
6187 East Texas Baptist University

Mesquite
6201 Eastfield College

Midland
6459 Midland College

Mount Pleasant
6531 Northeast Texas Community College

Odessa
6540 Odessa College

Paris
6573 Paris Junior College

Pasadena
6694 San Jacinto College – Central

Plainview
6930 Wayland Baptist University

Plano
1951 Collin County Community College

Prairie View
6580 Prairie View A & M University

Ranger
6608 Ranger Junior College

Richardson
6897 University of Texas at Dallas

San Angelo
6644 Angelo State University

San Antonio
6303 Incarnate Word College
6550 Our Lady of the Lake University
3730 Palo Alto College

530

6645 San Antonio College
6637 Saint Mary's University
6642 Saint Philips' College
6908 University of Texas Health & Science Center
6919 University of Texas San Antonio

San Marcos
6667 Southwest Texas State University

Seguin
6823 Texas Lutheran College

Sherman
6016 Austin College

Snyder
6951 Western Texas College

Stephenville
6817 Tarleton State University

Temple
6818 Temple Junior College

Texarkana
6819 Texarkana College

Texas City
6133 College of the Mainland

Tyler
6833 Tyler Junior College

Uvalde
7862 Rio Grande College – Sul Ross State University
6666 Southwest Texas Junior College

Vernon
6913 Vernon Regional Junior College

Victoria
6917 University of Houston Victoria
6915 Victoria College

Waco
6032 Baylor University
6429 Mclennan Community College
6577 Paul Quinn College
6328 Texas State Technical College

Waxahachie
6669 Southwestern Asemblies of God University

Weatherford
6931 Weatherford College

Webster
7078 Baywood Hospital

Wharton
6939 Wharton County Junior College

Wichita Falls
6408 Midwestern State University

UTAH

Blanding
7212 College Eastern Utah – San Juan

Cedar City
4092 Southern Utah State College

Ephraim
4727 Snow College

Logan
4857 Utah State University

Ogden
4751 Stevens Henager College – Ogden
4941 Weber State University

Orem
4870 Utah Valley State College

Price
4040 College of Eastern Utah

Provo
4019 Brigham Young University

Saint George
4283 Dixie College

Salt Lake City
4264 Hawthorne University

Salt Lake City
4412 Latter Day Saints Business College
4864 Salt Lake Community College
4920 University Phoenix – Utah
4853 University of Utah
4948 Westminster College of Salt Lake City

Vernal
7654 Utah State University – Utah Basin

VERMONT

Burlington
3291 Champlain College
3900 Trinity College
3920 University of Vermont

Castleton
3765 Castleton State College

Colchester
3757 Saint Michaels College

Johnson
3766 Johnson State College

Lyndonville
3767 Lyndon State College

Marlboro
3509 Marlboro College

Montpelier
3939 Norwich University

Northfield
3669 Norwich University

Old Bennington
3796 Southern Vermont College

Plainfield
3416 Goddard College

Poultney
3418 Green Mountain College

Randolph Center
3941 Vermont Technical College

Rutland
3297 College of Saint Joseph

Waterbury
3286 Community College of Vermont

VIRGINIA

Abingdon
5927 Virginia Highlands Community College

Alberta
5660 Southside Virginia Community College

Alexandria
5510 Northern Virginia Community College
7830 Strayer College

Annandale
5515 Northern Virginia Community College

Arlington
5405 Marymount University
7831 Strayer College – Arlington

Ashburn
7833 Strayer College – Loudown

Ashland
5566 Randolph – Macon College

Big Stone Gap
5451 Mountain Empire Community

Blacksburg
5859 Virginia Polytechnic Institute

Bluefield
5063 Bluefield College

Bristol
5857 Virginia Intermont College

Buena Vista
5625 Southern Virginia College

Charlottesville
5561 Piedmont Virginia Community College

Chester
5342 John Tyler Community College

Clifton Forge
5139 Dabney S. Lancaster Community College

Danville
5017 Averett College
5163 Danville Community College

Fairfax
5827 George Mason University

Farmville
5368 Longwood College

Ferrum
5213 Ferrum College

Fort Eustis
7735 Saint Leo College

Fort Lee
7993 Saint Leo College

Franklin
5557 Paul D. Camp Community College

Fredericksburg
5398 Mary Washington College
7032 Strayer College – Fredericksburg

Glenns
5590 Rappahannock Community College

Hampton
5292 Hampton University
5793 Thomas Nelson Community College

Harrisonburg
5181 Eastern Mennonite University
5392 James Madison University

Keysville
5669 Southside Virginia Community College

Langley
7840 Saint Leo College

Lawrenceville
5604 Saint Paul's College

Lynchburg
5141 Central Virginia Community College
5385 Liberty University
5372 Lynchburg College
5567 Randolph – Macon Woman's College

Manassas
5774 Northern Virginia Community College
7834 Strayer College – Manassas

Manassas Park
7023 American Military University

Martinsville
5549 Patrick Henry Community College

McLean
7674 National – Louis University

Melfa
5844 Eastern Shore Community College

Middletown
5381 Lord Fairfax Community College

Newport News
5128 Christopher Newport University

Norfolk
5864 Norfolk State University
5126 Old Dominion University
7826 Saint Leo College
5867 Virginia Wesleyan College

Petersburg
5574 Richard Bland College
5860 Virginia State University

Portsmouth
5226 Tidewater Community College Portsmouth

Radford
5565 Radford University

Richlands
5659 Southwest Virginia Community College

Richmond
5676 J. Sargeant Reynolds Community College
5569 University of Richmond
5570 Virginia Commonwealth University

Roanoke
5868 Virginia Western Community College

Salem
5571 Roanoke College

Staunton
5397 Mary Baldwin College

University of Richmond
5341 University of Richmond

Vienna
7048 Averett College

Winchester
5613 Shenandoah University

Woodbridge
5517 Northern Virginia Community College – Woodbrige
7835 Strayer College – Potomac Mills

WASHINGTON

Aberdeen
4332 Grays Harbor College

Auburn
4337 Green River Community College

Bellevue
4029 Bellevue Community Colllege
4033 City University

Bellingham
4974 Whatcom Community College

Bremerton
4583 Olympic College

Centralia
4045 Centralia College

Cheney
4301 Eastern Washington University

College Place
4940 Walla Walla College

Edmonds
4618 Puget Sound Christian College

Issaquah
4408 Lutheran Bible Institute

Kirkland
4447 Henry Cogswell College
7568 Lake Washington Technical College
4541 Northwest College

Lacey
4674 Saint Martin's College

Longview
4402 Lower Columbia College

Moses Lake
4024 Big Bend Community College

Mount Vernon
4699 Skagit Valley College

Olympia
4578 South Puget Sound Community College
4292 The Evergreen State College

Pasco
4077 Columbia Basin College

Port Angeles
4615 Peninsula College

Pullman
4705 Washington State University

Renton
4042 City University
7744 Renton Technical College

Richland
4369 Joint Center for Graduate Studies

Seattle
7585 Antioch University – Seattle
7069 Antioch University – Seattle
4801 Cornish College of the Arts
4741 Seattle Central Community College
4694 Seattle Pacific University
4695 Seattle University
4759 South Seattle Community College

Spokane
4330 Gonzaga University
4953 Whitworth College

Tacoma
7096 Bates Technical College
4597 Pacific Lutheran University
4103 Pierce College
4067 University of Puget Sound

Toppenish
4344 Heritage College

Walla Walla
4963 Walla Walla Community College

Wenatchee
4942 Wenatchee Valley College

Yakima
4993 Yakima Valley Community College

WEST VIRGINIA

Athens
5120 Concord College

Beckley
5054 College West Virginia

Bethany
5060 Bethany College

Bluefield
5064 Bluefield State College

Buckhannon
5905 West Virginia Wesleyan College

Charleston
5419 University Charleston

Elkins
5151 Davis and Elkins College

Fairmont
5211 Fairmont State College

Glenville
5254 Glenville State College

Huntington
5396 Marshall University

Institute
5903 West Virginia State College

Keyser
5539 Potomac State College

Logan
5446 Southern West Virginia Community College – Logan

Montgomery
5902 West Virginia Institute Technical

Morgantown
5904 West Virginia University

Parkersburg
5519 Ohio Valley College
5932 West Virginia University – Parkersburg

Philippi
5005 Alderson – Broaddus College

Salem
5608 Salem – Teikyo University

Shepherdstown
5615 Shepherd College

West Liberty
5901 West Liberty State College

Wheeling
5942 West Virginia Northern Community College
5906 Wheeling Jesuit College

Williamson
5447 Southern West Virginia Community College – Williamson

WISCONSIN

Ashland
1561 Northland College

Baraboo
1996 University of Wisconsin Baraboo/ Sauk County

Beloit
1059 Beloit College

Cleveland
7574 Lakeshore Technical College

Depere
1706 Saint Norbert College

Eau Claire
1913 University Wisconsin – Eau Claire

Fond Du Lac
1443 Marian College – Fond Du Lac
1433 Moraine Park Technical College – Beaver Dam
1499 Moraine Park Technical College – Fond Du Lac
4174 Moraine Park Technical College – West Bend

Green Bay
1046 Bellin College of Nursing
4190 Northeast Wisconsin Technical College
1859 University Wisconsin Green Bay

Janesville
1043 Blackhawk Technical College
1998 University of Wisconsin – Rock County

Kenosha
1103 Carthage College
1243 Gateway Technical College
1860 University of Wisconsin Parkside

La Crosse
1914 University of Wisconsin Louisiana Crosse
1878 Viterbo College

Ladysmith
1512 Mount Senario College

Madison
1202 Edgewood College
1536 Madison Area Technical College
1846 University Wisconsin Madison
7910 Upper Iowa University – Madison Center

Manitowoc
1300 Silver Lake College

Marinette
1891 University of Wisconsin – Marinette

Marshfield
1997 Universty of Wisconsin Center

Menomonie
1740 University of Wisconsin Stout

Mequon
1139 Concordia University – Wisconsin

Middleton
7167 Concordia University

Milwaukee
1012 Alverno College
1100 Cardinal Stritch College
1448 Marquette University
1519 Medical College Wisconsin – Nursing
1475 Milwaukee Area Technical College
1476 Milwaukee School Engineering
1490 Mount Mary College
3617 Stratton College
1473 University Wisconsin – Milwaukee
1513 Wisconsin Lutheran College

Oshkosh
1916 University of Wisconsin – Oshkosh

Platteville
1917 University Wisconsin – Platteville

Racine
1255 Gateway Technical College

Rhinelander
1549 Nicolet College – Technical Institute

Ripon
1664 Ripon College

River Falls
1918 University of Wisconsin – River Falls

Sheboygan
1393 Lakeland College

Stevens Point
1919 University of Wisconsin – Stevens Point

Superior
1920 University of Wisconsin – Superior

Watertown
1945 Madison Area Technical College – Watertown

Waukesha
1101 Carroll College
1999 University of Wisconsin – Center Waukesha

Wausau
1995 University of Wisconsin Center – Marathon

West Bend
1993 University of Wisconsin Washington County

Whitewater
1921 University of Wisconsin – Whitewater

WYOMING

Casper
4043 Casper College

Cheyenne
4415 Laramie County Community College

Gillette
4680 Sheridan College – Gillette

Laramie
4855 University of Wyoming

Powell
4542 Northwest College

Rawlins
7956 Carbon County Higher Education Center

Riverton
4115 Central Wyoming College

Rock Springs
4957 Western Wyoming Community College

Sheridan
4536 Sheridan College

Torrington
4700 Eastern Wyoming College

APO

Apo/AP
761 University Maryland – Asian Division

Apo/AA
909 Panama Canal College

Apo/AE
7372 City Colleges of Chicago

Apo/AE
7417 University of Maryland

Apo/AE
113 University of Maryland

Bethlehem Via
7101 Bethlehem University

INTERNATIONAL

BERMUDA

Devonshire 4 – 04
792 Bermuda College

GUAM

Magilao
959 University Guam

PUERTO RICO

Carolina
883 College University Del Este

San Juan
842 ETS Puerto Rico
873 Interamerican University Puerto Rico

VIRGIN ISLANDS

Saint Thomas
879 University Virgin Islands

Appendix D
What Your CLEP Score Means

Your score report shows the total scaled score for each exam you took. For the General Examinations, total scaled scores fall between 200 and 800, and for the Subject Examinations, between 20 and 80. For most Subject Examinations, you will also find a percentile rank on your score report. Percentile ranks indicate the percentage of exam-takers who scored at or below a given score.

For every CLEP exam, the number of right answers is counted and a fraction of the number of wrong answers is subtracted from that total. If your exam had questions with five answers, one-fourth of the number of wrong answers is subtracted. If your exam questions offered four choices, one-third of your wrong answers is subtracted. The resulting figure, a formula score, is converted to a CLEP scaled score. This scaled score provides an unchanging measure of performance regardless of which version of a particular exam you take or when you take it.

Exam scores are kept on file for 20 years. During this period, score reports may be sent to any institution, but only at the request of the candidate. A "Transcript Request Form" and instructions are included with each score report.

CLEP exams are developed and evaluated independently and are not linked to each other except by the Program's common purpose, format, and method of reporting results. For this reason, direct comparisons should not be made from one CLEP exam to another. Nor are CLEP scores comparable to SAT scores or scores of other tests that use similar scales.

To see whether you attained a score sufficient to receive college credit, compare your score to the one shown in Table 1. The scores that appear in this table are the credit-granting scores recommended by the American Council on Education (ACE). *Each college, however, reserves the right to set its own credit-granting policy, which may differ from that of ACE.* If you haven't already done so, contact your college as soon as possible to find out the score it requires to grant credit, the number of credit hours granted, and the course(s) that can be bypassed with a satisfactory score.

Tables 2 and 3 show, by subject, the percentile ranks for selected scores, as well as the mean scaled score and the standard deviation.

If you have a question about an exam item, your score report, or any other aspect of a CLEP exam that your exam center cannot answer, write to: CLEP, P.O. Box 6600, Princeton, NJ 08541-6600.

Visit us at our website!
http://www.collegeboard.org

Table 1

Recommended Credit-Granting Score and Number of Semester Hours of Credit

Examination	ACE* Recommended Credit Granting Scores C	No. of Semester Hours
General		
English Composition	420-500	6
Mathematics	420-500	6
Humanities	420-500	6
Natural Sciences	420-500	6
Social Sciences and History	420-500	6
Composition and Literature		
American Literature	46	6
Analyzing and Interpreting Literature	47	6
English Literature	46	6
Freshman College Composition	44	6
Foreign Languages		
College French (Levels 1 and 2)		
Level 1 (two semesters)	39	6
Level 2 (four semesters)	45	12
College Level German Language (Levels 1 and 2)		
Level 1 (two semesters)	36	6
Level 2 (four semesters)	42	12
College Level Spanish Language (Levels 1 and 2)		
Level 1 (two semesters)	45	6
Level 2 (four semesters)	50	12
Social Sciences and History		
American Government	47	3
History of the United States I: Early Colonizations to 1877	47	3
History of the United States II: 1865 to the Present	46	3
Human Growth and Development	45	3
Introduction to Educational Psychology	47	3
Principles of Macroeconomics	44	3
Principles of Microeconomics	41	3
Introductory Psychology	47	3
Introductory Sociology	47	3
Western Civilization I: Ancient Near East to 1648	46	3
Western Civilization II: 1648 to the Present	47	3
Science and Mathematics		
Calculus with Elementary Functions	41	6
College Algebra	46	3
College Algebra-Trigonometry	45	3
General Biology	46	6
General Chemistry	47	6
Trigonometry	50	3
Business		
Information Systems and Computer Applications	52	3
Principles of Management	46	3
Principles of Accounting	45	6
Introductory Business Law	51	3
Principles of Marketing	50	3

* The American Council on Education, founded in 1918, is the major voice in American higher education and serves as the focus for discussion and decision-making on higher education issues of national importance. As such, it strives to ensure quality education on the nation's campuses. Within ACE, the Center for Adult Learning and Educational Credentials is the pioneer in evaluating extrainstitutional learning, assisting postsecondary education institutions in establishing policies and procedures for awarding credit based on ACE evaluations.

The American Council on Education recommends that the minimum score for awarding credit be the mean test score of students who earn a grade of C in the corresponding course.

Table 2

Percentile Ranks for the General Examinations (Total Scores)

Examination	Date	No. of Students	Selected Scaled Scores													Mean	Standard Deviation
			800	750	700	650	600	550	500	450	400	350	300	250	200		
English Composition	1993	1,748	99	99	99	99	99	97	86	67	40	16	2	1	1	420	70
Humanities	1978	757	99	99	99	98	93	85	70	49	27	9	1	1	1	460	85
College Mathematics	1994	1,189	99	99	99	96	92	87	75	55	27	5	1	1	1	460	85
Natural Sciences	1995	883	99	99	98	95	88	79	67	51	32	13	4	1	1	460	103
Social Sciences and History	1994	894	99	99	99	99	97	89	72	48	21	6	1	1	1	430	82

NOTE 1: The American Council on Education recommends that institutions set their minimum for receiving credit within the scaled score range of 420-500 when institutional data are not available.

NOTE 2: The standard deviation is a measure of the spread of scores above and below the mean.

Table 3
Percentile Ranks for the Subject Examinations (Total Scores)

Examination	Date	No. of Students	Selected Scaled Scores*												Mean	Standard Deviation
			80	75	70	65	60	55	50	45	40	35	30	25	20		
Composition and Literature																	
American Literature	1971	659	99	99	98	93	83	70	51	33	18	6	1	1	1	50	10
Analyzing and Interpreting																	
Literature	1996	911	99	99	98	93	83	69	49	33	17	7	2	1	1	50	10
English Literature	1970-71	1,023	99	99	98	91	82	69	53	34	17	6	1	1	1	50	10
Freshman College Composition	1993	1,112	99	99	99	92	82	68	50	33	18	7	1	1	1	50	10
Foreign Languages																	
College French																	
(Levels 1 and 2)																	
Level 1 (two semesters)	1990	2,293	99	99	99	97	95	90	82	65	42	19	5	1	1	50	10
Level 2 (four semesters)	1990	655	99	99	98	92	83	69	51	31	15	6	1	1	1	50	10
College Level German																	
Language (Levels 1 and 2)																	
Level 1 (two semesters)	1994	748	99	99	99	99	97	92	84	74	57	32	7	1	1	41	9
Level 2 (four semesters)	1994	726	99	99	98	95	87	78	66	50	30	11	2	1	1	50	11
College Level Spanish																	
Language (Levels 1 and 2)																	
Level 1 (two semesters)	1995	1,639	99	98	97	95	90	82	68	47*	19	2	1	1	1	47	9
Level 2 (four semesters)	1995	936	99	95	87	78	66	52	36	20	6	1	1	1	1	52	9
Social Sciences and History																	
American Government	1985	2,743	99	99	98	94	85	66	49	31	17	8	2	1	1	50	10
History of the United States I:																	
Early Colonizations to 1877	1996	1,432	99	99	96	91	84	71	54	36	18	3	1	1	1	50	10
History of the United States II:																	
1865 to the Present	1995	747	99	98	96	92	84	73	56	33	16	4	1	1	1	50	10
Human Growth and																	
Development	1977	1,009	99	99	99	94	82	67	47	31	18	9	2	1	1	50	10
Introduction to																	
Educational Psychology	1990	1,957	99	99	98	93	83	69	52	32	17	7	2	1	1	50	10
Principles of Macroeconomics	1993	1,084	99	99	98	96	90	83	71	53	33	12	2	1	1	50	10
Principles of Microeconomics	1993	1,104	99	99	99	98	93	87	75	60	42	24	8	2	1	50	10
Introductory Psychology	1992	1,798	99	99	96	91	84	71	54	36	16	4	1	1	1	50	10
Introductory Sociology	1974	3,235	99	99	99	94	83	67	49	31	17	8	3	1	1	50	10
Western Civilization I:																	
Ancient Near East to 1648	1980	793	99	99	98	92	83	70	51	34	18	6	1	1	1	50	10
Western Civilization II:																	
1648 to the Present	1980	703	99	98	94	90	84	74	59	38	14	1	1	1	1	50	10
Science and Mathematics																	
Calculus with																	
Elementary Functions	1994	1,489	99	99	99	97	93	85	76	60	40	21	6	1	1	44	10
College Algebra	1993	1,042	99	99	99	95	86	75	61	43	27	12	3	1	1	50	10
College Algebra-Trigonometry	1979	1,116	99	99	98	91	80	65	49	33	21	12	6	1	1	50	11
General Biology	1977	2,207	99	99	97	92	82	69	52	36	18	4	1	1	1	50	10
General Chemistry	1978	3,016	99	99	97	92	84	69	52	33	17	6	1	1	1	50	10
Trigonometry	1979	1,517	99	99	94	85	71	53	36	22	10	4	1	1	1	54	10
Business																	
Information Systems and																	
Computer Applications	1990	1,990	99	99	96	91	83	70	55	35	17	3	1	1	1	50	10
Principles of Management	1993	1,207	99	99	99	95	85	72	54	35	20	11	6	2	1	50	10
Principles of Accounting	1995	1,102	99	99	97	92	83	71	52	33	17	5	2	1	1	50	10
Introductory Business Law	1970	1,116	99	99	98	92	78	62	47	29	16	6	2	1	1	50	10
Principles of Marketing	1992	1,248	99	99	99	93	83	68	47	32	18	7	2	1	1	50	10

*For example, a Level I scaled score of 45 on the College Level Spanish Language exam would give you a percentile rank of 47. That means you performed the same as or better than 47% of the students in the sample.